GOVERNING CORPORATE KNOWLEDGE COMMONS

Human interactions, in any group or social setting, rely on and generate shared knowledge and social understandings. These shared intellectual resources are just as important to the efficient operation of markets and organizations as are their shared legal and material infrastructures. *Governing Corporate Knowledge Commons* focuses on the formal and informal arrangements that govern the creation and community management of intellectual resources within and across organizational boundaries. It demonstrates how the Governing Knowledge Commons (GKC) framework can be fruitfully combined with existing theoretical work on firms and corporate governance found in economics, management, and sociology. The volume also proposes a new set of case studies, ranging from old industrial enterprises to modern venture capital, investor alliances, and decentralized autonomous organizations. Chapters explore the benefits of participatory approaches to the management of genomic or financial data, online gaming communities, and organic waste. This title is also available as open access on Cambridge Core.

David Gindis works at the intersections of corporate law, law and economics, institutional theory, and the history of economic thought. He is a cofounder of the World Interdisciplinary Network for Institutional Research (WINIR) and an Associate Professor at the University of Warwick School of Law (UK).

CAMBRIDGE STUDIES ON GOVERNING KNOWLEDGE COMMONS

The mission of the series is to provide an authoritative space for high quality scholarship on the governance of knowledge commons. Following the path pioneered by Elinor Ostrom, recipient of the Nobel Prize in Economics for her work on institutional analysis of commons regimes in the natural environment, and the editors' work in *Governing Knowledge Commons*, this series uses a similar framework to systematically study knowledge commons in various sectors. Readers seeking more information on knowledge commons and this series can visit http://knowledge-commons.net, a repository for scholarship produced by an international, interdisciplinary group of knowledge commons researchers.

Series Editors

Katherine J. Strandburg

Brett M. Frischmann

Michael J. Madison

Other Books in the Series

David Gindis, *Governing Corporate Knowledge Commons*

Anjanette Raymond, Scott J. Shackelford, Jessica Steinberg and Michael Mattioli, *The Environmental Knowledge Commons*

Madelyn Rose Sanfilippo and Melissa G. Ocepek, *Governing Misinformation in Everyday Knowledge Commons*

Brett M. Frischmann, Michael J. Madison and Madelyn Rose Sanfilippo, *Governing Smart Cities as Knowledge Commons*

Erwin Dekker and Pavel Kuchar, *Governing Markets as Knowledge Commons*

Madelyn Rose Sanfilippo, Brett M. Frischmann and Katherine J. Strandburg, *Governing Privacy in Knowledge Commons*

Katherine J. Strandburg, Brett M. Frischmann and Michael J. Madison, *Governing Medical Knowledge Commons*

Governing Corporate Knowledge Commons

Edited by

DAVID GINDIS

University of Warwick

CAMBRIDGE
UNIVERSITY PRESS

Shaftesbury Road, Cambridge CB2 8EA, United Kingdom

One Liberty Plaza, 20th Floor, New York, NY 10006, USA

477 Williamstown Road, Port Melbourne, VIC 3207, Australia

314–321, 3rd Floor, Plot 3, Splendor Forum, Jasola District Centre, New Delhi – 110025, India

Cambridge University Press is part of Cambridge University Press & Assessment, a department of the University of Cambridge.

We share the University's mission to contribute to society through the pursuit of education, learning and research at the highest international levels of excellence.

www.cambridge.org
Information on this title: www.cambridge.org/9781009431903

DOI: 10.1017/9781009431859

When citing this work, please include a reference to the DOI 10.1017/9781009431859

First published 2026

Cover image: BluIz60 / iStock / Getty Images Plus.

A catalogue record for this publication is available from the British Library

A Cataloging-in-Publication data record for this book is available from the Library of Congress

ISBN 978-1-009-43190-3 Hardback
ISBN 978-1-009-43186-6 Paperback

Contents

Figures

Tables

Contributors

Tanweer Ali is an Assistant Professor in the Faculty of Business Administration at the Prague University of Economics and Business (Czechia).

Amy J. Cohen is the Robert J. Reinstein Chair in Law at Temple University Beasley School of Law (USA) and Honorary Professor at the UNSW Sydney Faculty of Law and Justice (Australia).

Daniel H. Cole is the Robert H. McKinney Emeritus Professor of Law and Professor Emeritus of Public and Environmental Affairs at Indiana University Bloomington (USA).

Sinclair Davidson is a Professor of Institutional Economics at RMIT University (Australia).

Simon Deakin is a Professor of Law at the University of Cambridge (UK).

Joshua Getzler is a Professor of Law and Legal History and a Fellow in Law at St Hugh's College at the University of Oxford (UK) and Conjoint Professor at the UNSW Sydney Faculty of Law and Justice (Australia).

David Gindis is an Associate Professor at the University of Warwick School of Law (UK).

Benjamin Gregg is a Professor of Government at the University of Texas at Austin (USA).

Erkan Gürpinar is an Associate Professor in the Department of Economics at the Social Sciences University of Ankara (Turkey).

Stephen Healy is an Associate Professor of Geography and Urban Studies at Western Sydney University (Australia).

Marek Hudik is an Associate Professor of Economics at the Prague University of Economics and Business (Czechia).

Martin Komrska is Chief Economist at UniCredit Bank and an Adjunct Lecturer of Economics at the Prague University of Economics and Business (Czechia).

Michael J. Madison is a Professor of Law at the University of Pittsburgh (USA).

Abby Mellick Lopes is a Professor of Design Studies at the University of Technology Sydney (Australia).

Amelia Miazad is Acting Professor of Law at the University of California at Davis (USA).

Ilia Murtazashvili is a Professor of Public Policy at the University of Pittsburgh (USA).

Andi Rezda Rezal is an MA candidate in International Affairs, with a specialism in International Organizations and Global Public Policy, at Carleton University's Norman Paterson School of International Affairs (Canada).

Alberto R. Salazar is an Associate Professor in the Department of Law and Legal Studies at Carleton University (Canada).

Hanna Sitchenko is a Research Fellow at the University of Cambridge Judge Business School (UK).

Deike Schulz is a Professor of Organisations and Social Media at NHL-Stenden University of Applied Sciences (Netherlands).

Jeroen Veldman is a Professor of Corporate Governance at Nyenrode Business University (Netherlands).

Acknowledgments

This volume began some years ago as a discussion with Pavel Kuchař about how to extend Bloomington School ideas to business firms and other corporate entities. Simon Deakin had suggested in the context of the corporate governance debate that it was useful to think of the corporation as a commons, and we were drawn to this proposal and wanted to take it forward. We first spelled out a rather tentative position at the World Interdisciplinary Network for Institutional Research (WINIR) Workshop on Polycentricity, Markets, and Firms, which I organized online in December 2021. Given Pavel's work on *Governing Markets as Knowledge Commons* – a volume edited with Erwin Dekker that was published in this series roughly at the same time – the conversation naturally shifted toward what the Governing Knowledge Commons (GKC) framework had to offer. Shortly after, Pavel approached Brett Frischmann, Mike Madison, and Kathy Strandburg with the idea of putting together a GKC volume on corporations and received an enthusiastic response.

We solicited some contributions and selected the remainder through an open call. A workshop with many of the volume's current contributors was held at King's College London in February 2024, thanks to funding from the Centre for the Study of Governance and Society that Pavel arranged. I subsequently organized Governing Corporate Knowledge Commons sessions in June and September 2024, respectively, at the Workshop on the Ostrom Workshop in Bloomington, Indiana, and the WINIR Conference on Institutional Resilience and Recovery at the University of Pittsburgh. Special thanks go to Brett Frischmann for his thoughtful comments and encouragement in Pittsburgh, not to mention the invitation to present the volume at the GKC Convergence Conference held at the University of Villanova in May 2025.

Given his key role in the process, Pavel's retreat from the project for personal and professional reasons in March 2025, just as outstanding chapters were arriving and the session at the Villanova conference was in the works, was a huge loss. Although, as a result, I am now listed as the volume's sole editor, this is very much the fruition of a joint project, which owes much to Pavel's intellectual contributions and dedication. I therefore extend my gratitude to the editors of the Cambridge Studies on Governing Knowledge Commons for supporting this project on Pavel's behalf as well.

Of course, if this volume breaks new ground, it is thanks to the rich and diverse perspectives its excellent contributors have on the topic of corporate knowledge commons. Their engagement with feedback is greatly appreciated. Finally, I would like to thank the three reviewers of the book proposal for their helpful comments, and, of course, Matt Gallaway and Jadyn Fauconier-Herry at Cambridge University Press for their invaluable help along the way.

1

Introduction

Varieties of Corporate Knowledge Commons

David Gindis

Knowledge commons, as the homepage of the Workshop on Governing Knowledge Commons website informs us,[1] involve the governance of shared knowledge, information, and data resources in some community or collective setting. This idea extends quite naturally to the corporation – arguably one of the most ubiquitous collective settings for human interactions. Corporations are found everywhere, in all nooks and crannies of the economy and at all levels of society. Most of us spend much of our lives working for and interacting with corporations, including profit-seeking firms, cooperatives, nonprofits, charities, universities, hospitals, trade unions, churches and other religious institutions, political parties, government agencies, international organizations, and so on. Whatever their legal and organizational form, and whatever their purpose, corporations are examples of institutions for collective action, to borrow Elinor Ostrom's (1990) expression, that rest on some form of collaborative knowledge production and exchange.

Thriving corporations address, in one way or another, the collective action problems that inevitably arise in this process. They are organized, managed, or governed in ways that build on and expand the shared knowledge that feeds into and supports their success. Their ultimate success will depend on other things, including conditions in the external environment that are beyond their control, but a corporation that lacks mechanisms enabling its members to produce, pool, and share knowledge effectively, that is unable to ensure that the right decision-maker has access to the right information at the right time, is unlikely to succeed, even under favorable external conditions (Nonaka 1991; Grant 1996; Nonaka and Teece 2001; Amin and Cohendet 2004; Foss and Michailova 2009; Nooteboom 2009). Knowledge management is a strategic issue for any private or public corporation (Myers 1996; Choo and Bontis 2002; McNabb 2006; Bratianu 2022), and indeed for industries, regions, and nations (OECD 2000; Viale and Etzkowitz 2010; Lundvall et al. 2016).

[1] https://knowledge-commons.net.

Studies of corporate knowledge commons reveal in some detail what this entails by focusing attention on the rules and practices underpinning the community or collective governance of pooled knowledge, information, and data resources within the corporation, broadly understood as "distinguishable and bounded collectively managed enterprise" (Madison et al. 2010, 371). But they are not limited to those found within individual corporations, and in fact also focus on the knowledge commons different types of corporations contribute to, draw on, participate in, and govern alongside other sorts of private and public actors. In such instances where the collectively managed enterprise transcends corporate boundaries, attention shifts to epistemic communities and communities of practice in broader polycentric settings, examined at different levels of analysis. There is a wide array of corporate knowledge commons to study.

The inspiration for the volume is Simon Deakin's (2012) proposal to think of the corporation as a shared resource that is collectively held and managed for the benefit of multiple interests. A small but fascinating literature extended this insight to mutuals, cooperatives, and benefit corporations (Adams and Deakin 2017; Healy 2018; Hiller and Shackelford 2018; Tortia 2018), while an independent literature applied a similar line of Ostromian thinking to inter alia cities, land trusts, civil society organizations, and certain kinds of platforms (Forster and Iaione 2016; Bezdek 2021; DeMattee and Sziney 2021; Ridley-Duff and Bull 2021). All these studies note the importance of shared knowledge, but none deploy the Governing Knowledge Commons (GKC) framework (Ostrom and Hess 2007; Frischmann et al. 2014; Sanfilippo et al. 2018; Madison et al. 2019).[2] As it happens, one of the earliest contributions to the genre discussed the university (Madison et al. 2009) – historically one of the oldest types of corporation. There is thus a sense in which this volume comes back in full circle.

What this volume attempts to do is to steer the discussion toward a unifying framework. Like the Institutional Analysis and Development (IAD) framework (Ostrom 2005, 2011), the GKC framework is an organizing device that helps researchers from multiple disciplines identify the analytically important structural features that are found across diverse action situations where knowledge governance takes place. It asks that researchers characterize the knowledge resources of interest and identify the actors who create, access, or use them in specific interaction situations, given the set of formal and informal rules defining their roles and resources in the relevant communities. Attention is drawn to the social dilemmas stemming from the nature of the resources, the rules governing access to them, the actors' potentially conflicting objectives, and the tensions between individual and collective aims, among other things. The availability of dispute-resolution mechanisms is accordingly important for the sustainability of knowledge commons.

[2] This is also the case in other applications of Ostromian institutionalism to corporations (Gindis and Micheler 2024) or corporate business networks (Megyesi and Mike 2016).

The chapters that follow engage with some or all of these topics. Several chapters apply the GKC framework directly to their object of analysis, while others highlight alternative ways of thinking about knowledge commons, or combine the framework with other approaches from institutional economics or organizational sociology. Some chapters describe past examples of successful knowledge management in traditional corporations, while others analyze commons-style arrangements in new blockchain-based organizations, or call for such arrangements in the governance of various classes of data. Some are purely conceptual, while others are based on interviews or engage in action research. Whatever the chosen stance, what unites all the chapters is that they engage with the idea that corporations and ecosystems comprising corporate actors cohere around shared knowledge, values, and other kinds of intellectual or cognitive resources, the sustainable production and reproduction of which depends on specific practices and rule configurations.

In Chapter 2 ("Toward a Knowledge Commons Perspective on the Corporate Form"), David Gindis and Daniel H. Cole argue that if we want to take the corporation-as-commons idea forward, we must specify what we mean by "corporation" in this context. We also need to determine who shares the corporation and identify the rules and practices that enable its provision, production, and reproduction. Drawing on insights from the theory of the firm, Gindis and Cole focus on the firm's "corporate mask," a special kind of institutional resource provided by the legal system that enables the firm's members to operate as a singular actor in the legal and commercial spheres. They show how this helps address collective action problems, reduces transaction costs, and unlocks an important source of economies of scale and scope. But the corporate mask, they argue, is not merely a legal construct – the social recognition of the firm as a corporate actor, a reliable business partner, a reputable producer of goods or services, and so on, matter a great deal as well. The corporate mask, they conclude, is a legal and epistemic focal point shared by insiders and third parties with whom the firm contracts and more generally interacts in a network of adjacent action situations.

Corporations act as entities addressing the world with a single face and voice, with the law resorting to metaphors such as "person" and "body" to present the group as an entity distinct from its members, Joshua Getzler observes in Chapter 3 ("What Do Corporations Do?"). Four historic models of group action, which hybridize across time, provide an added functional analysis: the "cathedral" built by self-regulating guilds and societies, the "factory" resting on division of labor and hierarchical organization, the "bazaar" of adjoining enterprises providing some level of market integration between traders, and the "commune" resting on personalized bonds and common purposes. All four types are affected by coordination problems. While a group can be said to attain corporate status when it functions as a univocal entity owning its actions, Getzler argues, in order to act effectively, the corporation must develop techniques to gather and process information attained by its agents, much of which will be predictions of the conduct of other agents. The corporation effectively exists to cultivate and embody common knowledge. Preceding the conceptual analysis is a case study of the historically important and now-troubled aircraft manufacturer, Boeing.

A complementary study of how processes of knowledge production, transmission, and utilization give rise to various collective action problems and how firms address these problems is proposed by Marek Hudik and Martin Komrska in Chapter 4 ("Managing Knowledge in Baťa Enterprises"). Drawing on stakeholder theory in management studies, Hudik and Komrska distinguish three governance models – the hub-and-spoke model, the lead role governance model, and the shared governance model – each offering different solutions to these challenges. A case study of the famous Czech footwear firm Baťa Enterprises in the early twentieth century demonstrates the practical application of the lead role governance model, which grants employees high autonomy while maintaining management's central role in strategic decisions. Through profit-sharing schemes, decentralized workshops, and internal education, Baťa effectively aligned individual incentives with the firm's goals, mitigating collective action problems and fostering innovation. By analyzing Baťa's success, Hudik and Komrska advance our understanding of knowledge governance in firms and underscore the connections with Ostrom's design principles for the sustainable governance of knowledge resources.

The mechanisms that erode the sustainable governance of intrafirm knowledge are studied by Erkan Gürpinar in Chapter 5 ("Institutional Complementarities in the Governance of Corporate Knowledge Commons"). The chapter investigates the microlevel interdependence between technological advancements and intellectual property rights (IPR), integrating research on institutional complementarities into the GKC framework. The latter recognizes the importance of informal rules and community characteristics in knowledge governance, while the former reveals inefficiencies arising from the interdependent nature of knowledge ownership and creation. The combined framework reveals the interplay between the characteristics of knowledge as a shared resource and the formal and informal rules governing its production. Gürpinar shows how, in a world where IPRs are increasingly used to govern knowledge assets, the interdependence dynamics between IPR and technology can exclude knowledge workers from accessing and using the knowledge they produce, leading to the gradual deterioration of their skills and expertise. This vicious cycle further erodes the institutional diversity of corporate knowledge governance in favor of IPR-based governance mechanisms.

Part of the reason why IPRs are increasingly used to govern knowledge assets is because shareholders and investors demand it. Managers comply with these demands because they share the prevailing belief that shareholders own corporations. Tanweer Ali considers the misalignment between this attribute of the broader societal environment and academic legal opinion in Chapter 6 ("Who Owns a Corporation? Common-Sense Commons and Corporate Governance"). Though legally incorrect, the widespread representation of shareholders as corporate owners is rooted in common sense, and as such is used to close down discussions about the position of other stakeholders. Ali discusses the power and persuasiveness of the commonsensical position through the lens of discourse analysis, aided by concepts drawn from pragma-linguistics and sociology. He shows how common sense can be shaped by primary definers in strategic action fields to promote ideological ends, and suggests that to understand how the field of corporate control is structured and how it has evolved, what is needed is a deeper investigation into how common sense is produced, shaped, and curated over time.

Though framed in different terms, this question is addressed by Jeroen Veldman in Chapter 7 ("Corporate Governance and Knowledge Commons"). The GKC framework, Veldman points out, draws attention to the content, quality, and consequences of the production, the institutionalized (community) governance, and the sharing of knowledge. In the domain of corporate governance, the key knowledge in question concerns the rules, mechanisms, and infrastructures that enable corporations to be governed. But how do actors understand what is going on and what is at stake in the field of corporate governance? Like Ali, Veldman draws on the sociological theory of strategic action fields to provide an account of how different imaginaries of corporate status, architecture, governance, and purpose are actively created and promoted by different kinds of disciplinary specialists, standard setters, and practitioners. The chapter shows how the knowledge claims made by these epistemic communities up the 1960s and from the 1970s onward underpin two competing social norms of corporate governance, expressed in different configurations of position, boundary, choice, aggregation, information, payoff, and scope rules.

Bright line rules favoring the interests of capital holders over those of producers and communities dominate the orthodox legal account of venture capital (VC), which stresses the importance of US-style transactional flexibility in managing investment risks. At first sight, as Simon Deakin and Hanna Sitchenko observe in Chapter 8 ("Venture Capital as a Commons"), VC seems far removed from any notion of a commons, if that is taken to mean a shared resource constituted by emergent rules of conduct based on interactions between multiple stakeholders. However, Deakin and Sitchenko argue that VC ecosystems have many commons-like aspects, involving risk-sharing, information pooling, and the braiding of formal and informal rules. The public benefits of VC depend on the positive externalities generated by knowledge spillovers, which cannot be fully captured by private ordering. Looking at these features through Masahiko Aoki's theory of the firm as embedded cognition, and drawing on interviews with mostly Europe-based VC funds, entrepreneurs, and legal advisers, Deakin and Sitchenko show that the governance of VC should be concerned with maximizing the net social return from innovation, taking into account the multiple interests involved in knowledge creation and preservation.

Amelia Miazad indicates why investor alliances formed to manage decision-useful financially material climate risk data can also be likened to knowledge commons in Chapter 9 ("Investor Alliances as Knowledge Commons"). Given that climate-related information is fragmented and complex, Investor Climate Alliances (ICAs) have emerged as institutional responses, providing the infrastructure to produce, share, and interpret climate risk data across heterogeneous communities. Miazad examines ICAs as collective governance systems, that is, as institutions that coordinate knowledge production through formal rules, informal norms, and shared practices. ICAs, she argues, demonstrate that complex knowledge resources can be generated collaboratively. This underscores the frictions, Miazad concludes, between collaborative knowledge governance and corporate law's traditional paradigms, which constrain investor collaboration.

The challenges involved in the management of complex financial data are further explored by Alberto R. Salazar and Andi Rezda Rezal in Chapter 10 ("Data Commons, Data Oligopolies, and Consumer Financial Data Trusts"), the premise of which is that financial companies are increasingly leveraging financial technology to monopolize financial data, ostensibly to maximize profit for their clients and enhance their power in society. Salazar and Rezal worry that this trend exposes the serious limitations of individual consent models of data protection and undermines the nature of financial data as a shared resource by excluding data contributors from its governance. They posit that consumer associations, acting as data trusts, can play a crucial role in overseeing financial data-opolies while fostering the development of the community governance of data. Beyond addressing privacy harms, these associations can promote the attainment of important social goods, including the prevention of predatory and discriminatory lending and the expansion of access to financial capital. By leveraging and shaping formal and informal rules-in-use that may facilitate these efforts, consumer data trusts can ultimately enhance the legitimacy of financial data commons. A discussion of BlackRock's Aladdin platform and a European consumer association's lawsuit against Meta illustrates the argument.

The focus on new technologies continues in Chapter 11 ("Decentralised Autonomous Organisations as Commons"), in which Sinclair Davidson examines Decentralised Autonomous Organizations (DAOs) as emergent forms of software or knowledge commons. Davidson argues that DAOs, characterized by their reliance on blockchain-enabled smart contracts and elimination of hierarchical management, represent a novel form of collective decision-making and governance. Davidson distinguishes on-chain from off-chain governance models and in both cases considers the place of the DAO within the GKC framework. The analysis evaluates the effectiveness of the two governance models in ensuring decentralization and addressing internal conflicts, with a particular emphasis placed on the unique conflict resolution mechanisms available to DAOs (such as "forking" and "rage-quitting"). For Davidson, an important insight is that the rules-in-use in on-chain governance and off-chain governance are likely to be very different. The chapter also examines the robustness of DAOs in light of Ostrom's design principles.

DAOs, which rely primarily on socio-technical infrastructures supplied by blockchain technology and consist substantially of combinations of shared computer code and shared data, are also the focus of Michael J. Madison and Ilia Murtazashvili's Chapter 12 ("The Decentralized Autonomous Corporation as Knowledge Commons"). Madison and Murtazashvili characterize the basic model of the DAO using the tools provided by the GKC framework, contrasting the GKC perspective with long-standing views of the corporate form as a nexus of contracts, as an instance of hierarchy and decision theory, and as a complex system. The exercise reveals that the GKC framework focuses attention on elements of governance that often are not salient in conventional accounts. This is especially true, Madison and Murtazashvili argue, of the important question of how governance responds to and generates social dilemmas associated specifically with practices of sharing knowledge, information, and data.

In Chapter 13 ("The Human Genome as Knowledge Commons: Governance through Mutual-Benefit Participatory Democracy"), Benjamin Gregg points out that the non-rivalrous and non-excludable characteristics of human genetic information make it well suited to commons-based governance as a complement to state- and market-led models. Using the case of deCODE Genetics in Iceland, he shows the practical viability of such an approach, underscoring the importance of public cooperation, ethical safeguards, and consent. Yet the model faces a central dilemma: the need for broad data sharing to advance research versus the individual participant's right to privacy. Gregg reframes this tension by conceptualizing privacy not as the negation of sharing but as one of its dimensions. He then resolves the dilemma by proposing a participatory, procedurally legitimate system in which stakeholders (including data contributors, researchers, and clinicians) collectively determine rules of access, use, and privacy through democratic deliberation. By establishing a self-governing genomic commons based on democratic principles and community values, Gregg concludes, this framework offers a promising path to realize the genome's potential for public health while safeguarding individual rights.

Community values are central in Deike Schulz's case study of the video game influencer industry in Chapter 14 ("Commoning through Interactions: Governing Offline and Online Communities in the German Video Game Influencer Industry"). The study of INSTINCT3, a Germany-based video game influencer management agency, investigates how its employees (influencers) and external stakeholders (followers) operate as polycentric communities in two interconnected action arenas: an offline arena of intraorganizational interactions between employees, and an online arena in which influencer channels mediate interactions between influencers and followers. Schulz examines the transfer of organizational values between offline and online communities, relying on in-depth interviews to identify the resources, community attributes, and rules-in-use that are essential in developing a value-driven and responsible employee communityship. She also investigates how organizationally relevant rules-in-use are transferred by influencers through communicative practices in their online communities to their followers, and looks at how INSTINCT3 governs the two action arenas as part of a dynamic and multilayered process.

The need for participants to communicate and understand others' valuations in order to coordinate collective action and create common value is a central theme developed by Stephen Healy, Amy J. Cohen, and Abby Mellick Lopes in Chapter 15 ("Supply Chain Commons: Organic Waste, Climate Change, and Regenerative Farming in Peri-Urban Sydney"), which concludes the volume. Healy, Cohen, and Mellick Lopes recast the supply chain as a commons via an extended description of the shared social, intellectual, and regulatory resources currently producing an experiment in a circular economy for organic waste in Sydney. Organic waste, once composted, finds its way into high value-added crops like heirloom garlic, which are then sold back to consumers in Sydney. By foregrounding the practices of social learning and information sharing that is making this "circularity" possible, Healy, Cohen, and Mellick Lopes show how creating a material commons often depends on creating a knowledge commons to make it cohere. It also crucially depends on creating commoner-subjects who will do the work of caring for both.

REFERENCES

Adams, Zoe, and Simon Deakin. 2017. "Enterprise Form, Participation and Performance in Mutuals and Co-operatives." In *The Oxford Handbook of Mutual, Co-operative, and Co-owned Business*, eds. Jonathan Michie, Joseph R. Blasi, and Carlo Borzaga, 227–245. New York: Oxford University Press.

Amin, Ash, and Patrick Cohendet. 2004. *Architectures of Knowledge: Firms, Capabilities, and Communities*. New York: Oxford University Press.

Bezdek, Barbara L. 2021. "To Have and to Hold? Community Land Trust as Commons." In *The Cambridge Handbook of Commons Research Innovations*, ed. Sheila R. Foster, and Chrystie F. Swiney, 164–175. Cambridge: Cambridge University Press.

Bratianu, Constantin. 2022. *Knowledge Strategies*. Cambridge: Cambridge University Press.

Choo, Chun Wei, and Nick Bontis, eds. 2002. *The Strategic Management of Intellectual Capital and Organizational Knowledge*. New York: Oxford University Press.

Deakin, Simon. 2012. "The Corporation as Commons: Rethinking Property Rights, Governance and Sustainability in the Business Enterprise." *Queen's Law Journal* 37(2): 339–381.

DeMattee, Anthony J., and Chrystie Swiney. 2021. "Ostromian Logic Applied to Civil Society Organizations and the Rule That Shape Them." In *The Cambridge Handbook of Commons Research Innovations*, eds. Sheila R. Foster, and Chrystie F. Swiney, 175–187. Cambridge: Cambridge University Press.

Forster, Sheila R., and Christian Iaione. 2016. "The City as a Commons." *Yale Law and Policy Review* 34(2): 281–349.

Foss, Nicolai J., and Snejina Michailova, eds. 2009. *Knowledge Governance: Processes and Perspectives*. New York: Oxford University Press.
Frischmann, Brett M., Michael J. Madison, and Katherine J. Strandburg, eds. 2014. *Governing Knowledge Commons*. New York: Oxford University Press.
Gindis, David, and Eva Micheler. 2024. "Institutional Theory for Corporate Law: An Invitation." *Journal of Corporate Law Studies* 24(2): 399–435.
Grant, Robert M. 1996. "Toward a Knowledge-Based Theory of the Firm." *Strategic Management Journal* 17(1–2): 109–122.
Healy, Stephen. 2018. "Corporate Enterprise as Commonwealth." *Journal of Law and Society* 45(1): 46–63.
Hiller, Janine, and Scott J. Shackelford. 2018. "The Firm and Common Pool Resource Theory: Understanding the Rise of Benefit Corporations." *American Business Law Journal* 55(1): 5–51.
Lundvall, Bengt-Åke, K. J. Joseph, Christina Chaminade, and Jan Vang, eds. 2016. *Handbook of Innovation Systems and Developing Countries: Building Domestic Capabilities in a Global Setting*. Cheltenham: Edward Elgar.
Madison, Michael J., Brett M. Frischmann, and Katherine J. Strandburg. 2009. "The University as Constructed Cultural Commons." *Washington University Journal of Law and Policy* 30(1): 365–403.
Madison, Michael J., Brett M. Frischmann, and Katherine J. Strandburg. 2010. "Constructing Commons in the Cultural Environment." *Cornell Law Review* 95(4): 657–709.
Madison, Michael J., Brett M. Frischmann, and Katherine J. Strandburg. 2019. "Knowledge Commons." In *Routledge Handbook of the Study of the Commons*, ed. Blake Hudson, Jonathan Rosenbloom, and Daniel H. Cole, 76–90. Abingdon: Routledge.
McNabb, David E. 2006. *Knowledge Management in the Public Sector: A Blueprint for Innovation in Government*. London: Routledge.
Megyesi, Boldizsár, and Károly Mike. 2016. "Organising Collective Reputation: An Ostromian Perspective." *International Journal of the Commons* 10(2): 1082–1099.
Myers, Paul S. ed. 1996. *Knowledge Management and Organizational Design*. Boston: Butterworth-Heinemann.
Nonaka, Ikujiro. 1991. "The Knowledge-Creating Company." *Harvard Business Review* 69(6): 96–104.
Nonaka, Ikujiro, and David J. Teece, eds. 2001. *Managing Industrial Knowledge: Creation, Transfer and Utilization*. London: Sage.
Nooteboom, Bart. 2009. *A Cognitive Theory of the Firm: Learning, Governance and Dynamic Capabilities*. New York: Oxford University Press.
OECD. 2000. *Knowledge Management in the Learning Society*. Paris: OECD.
Ostrom, Elinor. 1990. *Governing the Commons: The Evolution of Institutions for Collective*. Cambridge: Cambridge University Press.
Ostrom, Elinor. 2005. *Understanding Institutional Diversity*. Cambridge, MA: MIT Press.
Ostrom, Elinor. 2011. "Background on the Institutional Analysis and Development Framework." *Policy Studies Journal* 37(1): 7–27.
Ostrom, Elinor, and Charlotte Hess. 2007. "A Framework for Analyzing the Knowledge Commons." In *Understanding Knowledge as a Commons: From Theory to Practice*, ed. Charlotte Hess, and Elinor Ostrom, 41–81. Cambridge, MA: MIT Press.
Ridley-Duff, Rory, and Mike Bull. 2021. "Common-Pool Resource Institutions: The Rise of Internet Platforms in the Social Solidarity Economy." *Business Strategy and the Environment* 30(3): 1436–1453.

Sanfilippo, Madelyn R., Brett M. Frischmann, and Katherine J. Standburg. 2018. "Privacy as Commons: Case Evaluation through the Governing Knowledge Commons Framework." *Journal of Information Policy* 8: 116–166.
Tortia, Ermanno C. 2018. "The Firm as a Common: Non-divided Ownership, Patrimonial Stability and Longevity of Co-operative Enterprises." *Sustainability* 10(4): 1023–1041.
Viale, Riccardo, and Henry Etzkowitz, eds. 2010. *The Capitalization of Knowledge: A Triple Helix of University-Industry-Government*. Cheltenham: Edward Elgar.

2

Toward a Knowledge Commons Perspective on the Corporate Form

David Gindis and Daniel H. Cole

2.1 INTRODUCTION

As the idea that society's long-term prosperity requires replacing the extractive shareholder value model with a participative stakeholder approach that ensures the sustainable creation of shared value gains momentum, efforts to reimagine the business corporation are underway (Morrow et al. 2016; British Academy 2019; Alvarez et al. 2020; Mayer 2021; Meyer et al. 2022). In this context, Simon Deakin (2012a, 2019) has suggested that valuable insights can be found in Elinor Ostrom's (1990, 2005) work on natural resource management. If we think of the corporation not as shareholders' property but rather as a commons – as a shared but depletable resource which is collectively held and managed for the benefit of multiple interests – then the participative stakeholder model ought to follow.

Deakin's argument rests on two moves. First, Deakin shows that the legal system sees the firm as an organizational entity constituted around a pool of shared resources, which it seeks to preserve. Hence, the bodies of law shaping and regulating the economic operations of the firm (corporate law, employment law, commercial law, insolvency law, and so on) specify the conditions under which various stakeholders contribute to and draw on the firm's resources, while maintaining the firm's asset pool and going concern value. The partially overlapping rights stakeholders hold in the corporate context, Deakin argues, are analogous to the partially overlapping combinations of property rights (access, withdrawal, management, exclusion, alienation) various actors hold in natural commons (Schlager and Ostrom 1992).

Deakin then transposes Ostrom's design principles for the sustainable governance of common-pool resources from the natural resource to the corporate context. For Deakin, this implies that boards ought to be accountable to all stakeholders and that stakeholders ought to be involved in crafting the rules that govern them. And for such self-governance

We thank Pavel Kuchař for his valuable contributions to the ideas developed in this chapter. Comments on previous versions received from audiences at King's College London, the Ostrom Workshop at Indiana University Bloomington, and the WINIR Conference on Institutional Resilience and Recovery at the University of Pittsburgh are gratefully acknowledged. Special thanks to Paul Dragos Aligica, Joshua Getzler, Brett Frischmann, Mike Madison, Eva Micheler, and Ilia Murtazashvili.

to be sustainable, governance norms limiting the excessive extraction of resources by one stakeholder group (most notably shareholders) and relative immunity from global capital market pressures are required. There is more to Deakin's discussion, but for our present purposes, this outline of the argument will suffice.

We welcome Deakin's invitation to extend the Ostromian perspective to the firm and seek to advance it in this chapter. But we do not go about it in the same way. While the design principles may well be generalizable beyond the natural resource context (Wilson et al. 2013), we should not expect them to be transposable by intuitive analogy, without qualifications. Any design principles applicable to corporations or other types of business firms must be established empirically. A meta-analysis of a wide range of case studies is needed (Poteete et al. 2010; Cole 2014). We do not pursue this sort of worthwhile analysis here.

Nor do we take the property rights route with a view to weighing in on the corporate governance debate. The analogy between the rights of corporate stakeholders and those held by users in natural commons is not a sufficient justification for the stakeholder governance model. Not all those with ownership claims have ownership competence – the ability to match judgment about resource uses and governance with the firm's evolving environment under uncertainty (Foss et al. 2020). In any case, the property rights route is complicated by the fact that many of the firm's key resources are not appropriable. Some are even shared with other firms (Aoki 2010).

We propose that, to take the *corporation-as-commons* idea forward, we need to think about the kinds of shared resources firms rely on or manage and ask whether it makes sense to view the corporation as such a resource. If we take *commons* to be a kind of institutional arrangement enabling community governance of shared resources (Frischmann et al. 2014; McGinnis 2019) – which need not be common-pool resources – the challenge is to specify what we mean by *corporation* in this context. We also need to determine who shares the corporation and identify the rules and practices that enable its provision, production, and reproduction in relevant action arenas. This chapter is an attempt to chart this course.

Drawing on insights from the literature on the firm, we conceptualize firms as systems of shared heterogeneous resources and argue that the firm's most critical resource is what we call its *corporate mask*.[1] The corporate mask is a special kind of institutional resource that exhibits infrastructural and intellectual features, which the Governing Knowledge Commons (GKC) framework (Ostrom and Hess 2007; Madison et al. 2010, 2019; Frischmann et al. 2014) is well-suited to study. Its provision by the legal system enables the firm's members to operate as a singular actor in the legal and commercial spheres (Gindis 2016). This helps address collective action problems, reduces transaction costs, and unlocks an important source of economies of scale and scope.

The corporate mask, however, is not merely a legal construct – the social recognition of the firm as a corporate actor, a reliable business partner, a reputable producer

[1] This expression alludes to the etymology of the term *person*, which in Roman times denoted the mask worn by actors in the legal and social drama of life.

of goods or services, and so on, matters a great deal as well. The corporate mask is a legal and epistemic focal point (McAdams 2015) shared by insiders and third parties with whom the firm contracts and more generally interacts in a network of adjacent action situations (McGinnis 2011a), ranging from commercial negotiation to enforcement and dispute resolution in the courts or some other relevant forum. The boundaries of the communities that govern its production and reproduction are open and evolve with the firm's activities.

2.2 FIRMS AND CORPORATE MASKS

Ostrom frequently sought to remind us that commons are neither relics nor confined to nature but can instead be found all around us today. Ostrom listed corporate treasuries and income as examples of common-pool resources (Ostrom 1998), and noted that a corporation, though frequently thought of as the epitome of private property, was in fact an example of a common property regime featuring a mix of commonly and individually held property rights (Ostrom 2000).[2] Fundamentally, Ostrom (1990) observed, the firm is one institutional arrangement among others that addresses the problem of independent action in situations of interdependence. These limited statements require clarification and elaboration.

Though limited, these observations echo Ostrom's recurring insistence on the need to distinguish resources (or resource systems) from the institutional regimes that govern them. Any Ostromian perspective on the question at hand must differentiate these aspects. Conceptual and terminological clarity was of paramount importance to Ostrom (Cole 2014), so we should seek to emulate this stance here. But while a suitably Ostromian point of departure would be to think of *firms* as resource systems and *corporations* as institutional artifacts that enable their governance, this distinction, which works for natural resources that can exist independently of any institutional regime, breaks down for resource systems that only really come into existence thanks to the institutional regime. Firms are examples of the latter kind. Let us, nevertheless, first examine the idea of the firm as a resource system. A wealth of insights can be found in economics, management, and organization studies. We summarize these in the next two sections, before introducing the concept of the corporate mask.

2.2.1 *Thinking about the Firm*

The *contractual theory* of the firm builds on Ronald Coase's (1937) suggestion that the firm emerges when it can economize on the transaction costs of organizing production relative to the market. This is the case when resource owners choose to contract with a central agent – an entrepreneur – instead of contracting with each

[2] If so, the corporation is perhaps best understood not as commons but as semicommons (Fennell 2009) and we may wish to adopt the expression *corporation-as-semicommons*. We need not concern ourselves with this distinction here, as we do not follow the property rights route.

other, as would be necessary if production were organized exclusively through bilateral exchanges (Eggertsson 1990). The intrafirm cost of organizing production is further reduced because long-term authority- or fiat-based relationships (between the entrepreneur-employer and employees) are open-ended and do not require frequent renegotiations. These institutional features of the firm help resource owners create a greater joint surplus value than would have otherwise been possible.

While some resources used by the firm can earn just as much elsewhere, the value of others is enhanced through firm-specific investments, with the implication that they have a significantly higher value within the firm than outside it. Realizing the potential value of such resources sometimes requires mutually compatible specialization among the participants (Alchian 1984). But firm-specific investments are at risk because opportunistic participants can credibly threaten to withdraw their cooperation, with a view to capturing a greater share of surplus (Klein et al. 1978). Anticipating this hold-up risk, participants will tend to underinvest, such that at least some potential value will be foregone. Various kinds of institutional arrangements – ranging from monitoring to contractual incentives and career rewards – are needed to reduce the likelihood of this outcome (Rubin 1990).

The logic extends to interfirm supplier-buyer relationships, where one or both firms need to make relationship-specific investments: Each firm can use the threat of exit to extract a greater share of the surplus. Since both firms are likely to underinvest, institutional arrangements – ranging from contractual specifications of penalties to joint ventures and vertical integration – are needed (Williamson 1985).[3] The greater the value of a firm's specific investments, the more it stands to lose from the opportunistic behavior of its partner, and, therefore, the greater the likelihood that it will choose to eliminate the threat by buying out the other firm (Hart 1995). Expanding the firm's boundaries by turning outside parties into employees mutes their incentives to behave opportunistically, but does not eliminate opportunism, and free-riding and other collective action problems remain (Miller 1992).

A distinct though somewhat complementary explanation of how and why firms grow can be found in the *resource dependence approach* proposed by Jeffrey Pfeffer and Gerald Salancik (1978). In this view, given that some key resources the firm requires to fulfill its strategic objectives are not tied to or controlled by it, the firm will try to manage external resource dependencies – through mergers, joint ventures, or board interlocks, as well as through various forms of political or legal action (Hillman et al. 2009). By securing at least some control over external resources, firms both diminish their exposure to the power of other organizations and reduce environmental uncertainty. This insight is found across a broad range of literatures: The importance of access to external resources for the creation of value by firms is well understood (Aoki 2010; Mayer 2020; Berti and Pitelis 2022), as is the idea that not

[3] Williamson and other transaction cost economists talk about *asset*, as opposed to *resource*, specificity. We use these terms interchangeably here.

having the right kinds of resources at the right time can significantly hurt a firm's competitive prospects (Langlois 1992).

The focus on links between competitive advantage and the growth of the firm is the hallmark of the *resource-based view*. Stemming from Edith Penrose (1959), this approach revolves around the idea that the firm's productive resources are heterogeneous and must be specialized, combined, arranged, and organized by entrepreneurs or managers seeking to generate a surplus by selling a good or service that creates value for third parties in the market (Barney 1991).[4] The ability to reconfigure internal and external resources in rapidly changing environments matters (Teece et al. 1997). Novel resource combinations lead to innovation (Galunic and Rodan 1998), while excess capacity may lead to diversification and firm growth. Diversified or multiproduct firms benefit from economies of scope, as David Teece (1982) showed, when they are able to share some resources across production processes or businesses without congestion. Various kinds of governance arrangements – ranging from the sequentialization of production to the divisionalization of the firm – are needed to minimize the incidence of this collective action problem (Teece 1980).

We can retain five points from this brief survey of extant thinking about the firm. First, firms and markets are alternative institutional settings within which the transactions enabling the organization of production are negotiated and executed. Second, when resource owners come together in firms, the resulting institutional structure is characterized by the presence of a central contractual agent. Third, firm-specific investments can enhance the value of the firm's heterogeneous resources, at least some of which need to be shared to make the most of economies of scope. Fourth, some of the resources firms need to create value for both participants and third parties in the market lie beyond their boundaries. Finally, given the range of inevitable collective action problems, firms can only succeed (and perhaps even thrive) if they evolve adequate governance arrangements.

2.2.2 The Firm's Shared Resources

Firms rely on a range of shared resources. Whether tangible or intangible, specialized or not, a shared resource is effectively a common input into two or more production processes (Teece 1980, 1982). Some production processes require *shared tangible resources*, such as IT networks, buildings, office space, parking, and certain machines. These resources can be more or less excludable and more or less subtractable, depending on the institutional setup (Rayamajhee and Paniagua 2021). Crafting governance arrangements to prevent their exploitation, congestion, and overuse can be relatively straightforward by assigning different bundles of rights

[4] The idea that the firm's capital is made up of heterogeneous resources is also a premise of the Austrian approach (Bylund 2016).

to different people, that is, distinguishing, to use Ostromian terminology, authorized users (those with access and withdrawal rights), claimants (access, withdrawal, and management rights), proprietors (access, withdrawal, management, and exclusion rights), and owners (access, withdrawal, management, exclusion, and alienation rights).

The firm's production processes also rely on a range of *shared intangible resources*. This category includes software and things like legal, administrative, human resource, secretarial, procurement, or marketing services. Like many of the tangible resources listed above, services of this kind are *infrastructural resources*, which can be private, club, or common-pool, depending on the context (Ellig 2001). As they are inputs into many different intrafirm processes, they are often centralized to make the most of the economies of scale and scope. But such pooled interdependence means that they are easily congestible when demand is high (Frost and Morner 2005). Here, too, it may be relatively easy to devise suitable rules to prevent congestion and overuse by assigning different bundles of rights to different people.

The resources discussed so far are unlikely to determine the firm's competitive advantage, which stems from its ability to develop imperfectly imitable and non-substitutable resources to create value for third parties (Barney and Clark 2007).[5] From this perspective, the firm's distinctive know-how and knowledge base are vital. At the firm level, knowledge exhibits high degrees of non-excludability and non-subtractability (Frost and Morner 2010), not least because much of it is tacit and dispersed (Spender 1996; Foss 1999). Pieces of knowledge are held by individuals, who must be motivated to communicate and share their ideas and skills (Cabrera and Cabrera 2002; Osterloh and Frost 2002; Grandori 2009). The collective action problem arising from the fact that hoarding one's knowledge may be more rational than communicating it is more likely to be overcome when individuals share group norms or a collective identity (Argote and Kane 2009; Camera and Hohl 2021).

But the imperative to forge and maintain the firm's identity (Kogut and Zander 1996) or corporate culture (Engel and Güth 2006) is also vulnerable to collective action problems. A key governance challenge arises from the fact that it is difficult to assign specific bundles of rights to such *intellectual resources*. Different degrees of access to or control over artifacts and facilities representing or storing intellectual resources can be assigned to different people, but it is much more difficult to assign access to or control over knowledge or ideas themselves (Hess and Ostrom 2003). Anyone who contributes to the firm's know-how may have a property-like claim (Hess and Ostrom 2007), but what shape an individual claim may take, and how it may relate to others' claims, is far from obvious. It is perhaps more useful to think of these claims as held in common. Similar considerations apply to the firm's reputation (Tadelis 1999) and organizational memory (Olivera 2000).

[5] This includes not just value for customers but also goodwill and going concern value.

The intersubjective beliefs and mental models that underpin such intellectual resources express certain values, provide meaning, and inform the organized interactions of firm participants (Cohendet and Llerena 2008; Nooteboom 2009). A firm's identity and culture guide the participants' productive routines (Nelson 2009; Witt 2011) – which newcomers must learn through firm-specific investments – and are therefore constitutive of the firm's capabilities (Levinthal 2000). They are, at the same time, grounded in the participants' cognition and emergent properties of the firm.[6] Furthermore, these intellectual resources are both inputs into and outputs of the firm's operations: A shared understanding of "the way we do things" is not just a factor of production but also something that is instantiated and reproduced, unintentionally, with the ordinary process of production. Since the maintenance of shared intellectual resources thus rests on a process of *joint production*, there is a sense in which even a monoproduct firm is effectively a multiproduct firm (Lloyd 1983).[7]

In this process of joint production and reproduction, shared intellectual resources may be gradually transformed. For example, if we think of organizational routines as grammars of action (Pentland and Rueter 1994), routinized individual and group activities instantiate and replicate the routines. But because routine replication is not a high-fidelity process, which is to say that it often is imperfect and subject to local variation, whether by accident or design, evolutionary mechanisms kick in, as Geoffrey Hodgson and Thorbjørn Knudsen (2004) have shown. Accordingly, the firm's routines – its instructions for future growth (Kogut and Zander 1992) – effectively change over time. Evolutionary processes of this kind are relevant in explanations of the nature and transformation of the firm's other shared intellectual resources.

These resources are not private goods because they are indivisible, non-subtractable, and exhibit high exclusion costs, but they are not exactly public goods either. They are perhaps more akin to club goods shared by insiders. However, this presupposes institutional arrangements keeping them within firm boundaries. These will always be imperfect because, to paraphrase Kenneth Arrow (1996), knowledge and intellectual resources more generally are "fugitive." This affects their production and maintenance – a challenge that is compounded by internal problems of shirking and free-riding. Just as the revenue generated from employees' firm-specific human capital investments must be shared by employers and employees (Hashimoto 1981), the benefits of investments in intellectual resources must also be shared. It is easy to see why participants may have an incentive to reduce their contributions without a proportional reduction in their rewards.

6 The idea that shared mental models are important for human interaction and organization (Denzau and North 1994) is a feature of the recent literature on cognitive institutions (Frolov 2024) and has long been central in the sociology of organizations (Scott 1995).

7 While the concept of joint production, sometimes referred to as coupled production (Dyckhoff and Souren 2023), is today most frequently found in ecological economics (Baumgärtner et al. 2006), the idea can be traced back to classical political economy and early neoclassical economics.

To summarize, if we view the firm as a system of shared tangible, intangible, infrastructural, and intellectual resources, we must pay attention to different sorts of governance dilemmas that affect each of these resource subsystems. Some of the firm's resources are appropriable, others are not. Some can be private, common-pool, or public, depending on the institutional context, while others cannot possibly be private. This is the case of many of the important shared intellectual resources that enable firms to operate and attain or maintain competitive advantages. Firm participants jointly produce, reproduce, and gradually transform these intellectual resources, which should accordingly be seen as both inputs into and outputs of the firm's operations. We are now in a better position to think about the corporate form.

2.2.3 *The Firm's Corporate Mask*

Our initial distinction between firms as resource systems and corporations as the institutional artifacts that govern them should not lead us to confine the concept of the corporation to the separate legal entity created by incorporation under the corporate law of some jurisdiction. Likewise, while there is a sense in which the business corporation is a type of firm (Deakin et al. 2021), in the context of the present discussion, it would be unhelpful to limit the analysis to the corporation so understood. We do not wish to focus on incidental features like limited liability or tradable shares. A broader concept of the corporation *qua* corporate actor – used by philosophers like Christian List and Philip Pettit (2011) or sociologists like James Coleman (1990) – can help us maintain the discussion at a more general level. In principle, we should be able to extend the corporation-as-commons idea to any legal form the firm may take. Indeed, the idea ought to extend to all the types of business and nonbusiness organizations that enable societies to function.

The various legal forms a firm can take – including, besides the business corporation, partnerships of various sorts, limited liability companies, and cooperatives – are institutional artifacts enabling people to hold property or interests in common. But this characteristic of being a common property regime, as suggested by Ostrom, is not what matters the most to the corporation-as-commons idea as we envisage it here. For us, the more significant feature is that all legal forms provide the firm with a singular *vector for collective action*, effectively transforming a group of resource owners into a corporate actor. The firm is thus endowed with a capacity to act as a singular whole in the legal and commercial spheres, and it is legally recognized and regulated as such (Deakin et al. 2021).[8]

The firm's corporate capacity and legal identity are separate to some degree (depending on the legal form and the jurisdiction) from all the individuals involved. This is what enables resource owners to contract with the firm, rather than with each

[8] Legal recognition is not coextensive with incorporation and can take many forms, including recognition by tax or competition authorities and the courts.

other, and why internal employment or external commercial contracts are typically made with firms, not their shareholders or managers (Gindis and Hodgson 2026). Organizational law, which Henry Hansmann and Reinier Kraakman (2000) define as the law governing the standard legal forms used by business and nonbusiness organizations, supports this transaction cost-reducing institutional structure. It also enables autonomous organizational action (Micheler 2021; Gindis and Micheler 2024). The firm, as a result, is a self-governing entity.

Because the law distinguishes to some degree (depending on the legal form and the jurisdiction) the firm's business assets from the personal assets of its founders or shareholders, its contractual and financial commitments can survive changes in its membership (Spulber 2009). Removing the incentive for new participants to walk back on the firm's past promises or to use that threat to renegotiate existing deals supports the continuity of the firm's activities and makes it a more reliable business partner. And by vesting the ownership of shared tangible and intangible infrastructural resources in the firm, the law gives managers the authority to assign access, use, and other rights that help prevent (where possible) their exploitation, congestion, and overuse. The firm controls the internal rules of the game: It can design jobs, set working rules, assign tasks, decide on strategic plans, delegate authority, control information channels, or foster a particular corporate culture (Holmström 1999).

It follows that, absent some form of *legal recognition* of the firm's corporate capacity, the firm would be unable to operate effectively. But it is important to acknowledge that *social recognition* of the firm as a corporate actor likewise constitutes it as such and enables it to operate in the commercial realm (Adelstein 2010). As John Searle (2005) explained, official and social recognition of institutional facts go hand in hand. Firms are intentional objects (Searle 1983): They are the objects of our thoughts; we see them as singular actors in our individual and collective representations. This is aided by the fact that firms typically adopt distinctive identifiers, such as logos or mottos, that provide insiders with a sense of shared identity and project an outward appearance of unity. Ownership of such intellectual resources is also vested in the firm, such that it has significant control over how it presents itself to both insiders and outsiders. Legal and social recognition of the firm come together in our notion of *corporate mask*, which expresses the view that the firm is at the same time a legal and a social actor.

The corporate mask is represented in identifying legal and social artifacts – registration documents, company or employer identification numbers, contracts, bank accounts, annual reports, websites, logos, brands, mottos, and so on – but the mask itself is an intangible *institutional resource*. Several conceptions of institutional assets have been proposed in the literature. One approach sees them as a category of a firm's capabilities that enable it to deal with and take advantage of a given institutional environment (Jansson 2007). Another takes the view that they are the beneficial features of the environment itself (Teece et al. 1997). Institutional assets have also been conceptualized as the set of institutions governing value-generating processes both inside the firm and between the firm and its external stakeholders (Dunning and Lundan 2008). Our view relates to all three definitions: institutional resources, such as the corporate mask, are drawn from and are anchored in specific institutional environments, help actors navigate those environments, and govern a range of intrafirm and interfirm value-generating processes.

As such, the corporate mask combines features of infrastructural and intellectual resources. The *infrastructural dimension* comes into focus when we think of the role played by the central contractual agent highlighted in the Coasean tradition. The value of having a single referent for contracts that are bonded by a separate pool of assets is not merely that it helps reduce transaction costs, but that it unlocks an important source of economies of scale and scope. The firm grows by entering new contractual arrangements, so the centralization of the firm's legal infrastructure largely simplifies the simultaneous pursuit of multiple lines of business.[9] That the central contractual agent is an input into many different intrafirm and interfirm processes underpins the organizational capabilities of the firm (Deakin 2012b; Gindis 2016), which is to say its ability to acquire, specialize, and combine heterogenous resources in value-generating ways. But while the corporate mask shares some characteristics of mundane infrastructural resources (such as procurement services), it is not congestible, even when demand is high. Nor can it be depleted.

The nature of the corporate mask is further revealed when its *intellectual dimensions* are considered. Implicitly or explicitly, the notion of the firm as an identifiable and singular entity serves as a coordinating focal point (Basu 2018) for both insiders and outsiders. Insiders and outsiders refer to this "extended cognitive resource," as Masahiko Aoki (2010) put it, to position themselves vis-à-vis the firms they work for or deal with, and to interpret signals about and give meaning to the firm's activities. It is with an image of an identifiable and singular whole in mind that insiders and outsiders, who normally recognize the firm's boundaries (Santos and Eisenhardt 2005), impute objectives and actions to the firm when they interact with it and with each other. The identity of the firm enters into contracts made with it, expressing the expectation that it will honor its commitments (Pettit 2023), and is reproduced when those commitments are honored. This is how firms acquire and maintain reputations, and why these reputations attach to the firm itself, independently of the reputations any of its representatives may have.[10]

Overall, the firm relies on a legally and socially recognized identity to engage in the economic life of society. The legal recognition of the firm, which is essential for its centralized contractual structure, establishes it as a corporate actor. But the firm cannot operate based solely on its legal status. It must also be socially recognized as not only a corporate actor but also a reliable business partner, a reputable producer

9 This arguably remains true, albeit in more subtle ways, in the case of corporate groups.

10 Shared beliefs about firms can foster or hamper trust in them. This affects the transaction costs of dealing with them and, indirectly, the boundaries of firms. Parallel observations can be made about the extent of markets (Dekker and Kuchař 2021).

of goods or services, and so on. The firm's corporate mask is thus both legal and social: It is a special kind of shared institutional resource that combines the features of infrastructural resources (because it is as a pooled input in many intrafirm production processes) and intellectual resources (because it underpins and feeds into shared beliefs about the firm and its activities). We now need to take a closer look at how the provision, production, and reproduction of the corporate mask takes place across adjacent action situations.

2.3 CONSTRUCTING THE CORPORATE MASK ACROSS ADJACENT ACTION SITUATIONS

We have suggested that the corporation-as-commons idea requires thinking about the kinds shared resources firms rely on or manage and have argued that the corporate mask is an institutional resource of this kind. Our next task is to provide a clearer sense of who shares this resource and to specify some of the contexts within which it is shared. This requires zooming in on the rules and practices that govern its provision, production, and reproduction in the relevant *action arenas*. Action arenas, which are core units of analysis in both the GKC framework and the Institutional Analysis and Development (IAD) framework (Ostrom 2005; Cole 2017) upon which it is built, are broadly speaking interaction settings within which more specific action situations can be scrutinized.

We connect the discussion with the theory of the firm by translating into Ostromian terms the Coasean approach of viewing firms and markets as alternative "institutional matrices" within which transactions are negotiated and executed (Williamson 1996). However, contrary to the standard Coasean account, which misses the essential role played by the legal system in the constitution of the firm (Gindis and Hodgson 2026), we view the legal system as the third action arena of interest and characterize the legal system's role in the provision of the corporate mask. We then examine the analytically relevant *adjacent action situations* (McGinnis 2011a) in which the legal and social recognition of the firm produces and reproduces the corporate mask.

2.3.1 *The Firm and the Market as Adjacent Action Arenas*

To say that firms and markets are alternative institutional matrices within which transactions are negotiated and executed is to say that firms and markets are alternative action arenas within which specific action situations take place. But where transaction cost economists like Williamson (1985) focus the characteristics of a given transaction (primarily the degree of asset specificity involved) to determine the appropriate governance structure, an Ostromian does not presume to know which governance structures are appropriate and instead tries to gain a deeper understanding of internal structure of action situations. The relevant variables are

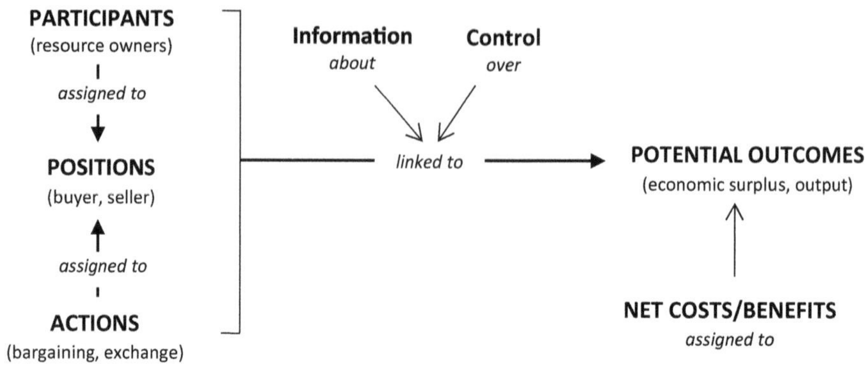

FIGURE 2.1 Market action situation. Source: Based on Ostrom (2005, 189).

the participants; the positions they fill; the set of actions they can take by virtue of their positions; the set of potential outcomes; the information participants have about actions, outcomes, and their linkages; the control participants can exercise over these linkages; and the criteria participants use to evaluate outcomes (Ostrom 2011). It is useful to express the Coasean theory of the firm in these terms.

Assuming that "in the beginning there were markets," as Oliver Williamson (1975) famously put it, we take the market as our initial action arena (Figure 2.1). Given the position, boundary, choice, aggregation, information, payoff, and scope rules governing this action arena,[11] market action situations involve participants (resource owners) in specific positions (buyer, seller), by virtue of which they can engage in certain kinds of actions (bargaining, exchange of property rights) and produce certain outcomes (economic surplus, if the action situation involves interpersonal exchange; output, if the action situation involves the Coasean scenario of organizing production through bilateral exchange). Note that participants must have some common information about their relative positions, their available actions, and the potential outcomes – otherwise they would not be in the *same* situation[12] – and that they also have some control over the allowable actions, outcomes, and their linkages.

The distribution of costs and benefits associated with outcomes may incentivize certain actions and deter others in the next iteration of the participants' interactions. Participants will exercise their control over the structure of the action situation when

[11] Position rules create positions; boundary rules define who is eligible to hold certain positions and how positions are assigned; choice rules prescribe actions actors in positions must, must not, or may take; aggregation rules specify how many and which actors must take part in collective decisions; information rules specify the information available to the holders of each position; payoff rules assign costs and benefits to actions or outcomes; and scope rules delimit the range of possible outcomes (McGinnis 2011b; Cole 2017).

[12] In game-theoretic terms, there is common knowledge about the basic structure of the action situation.

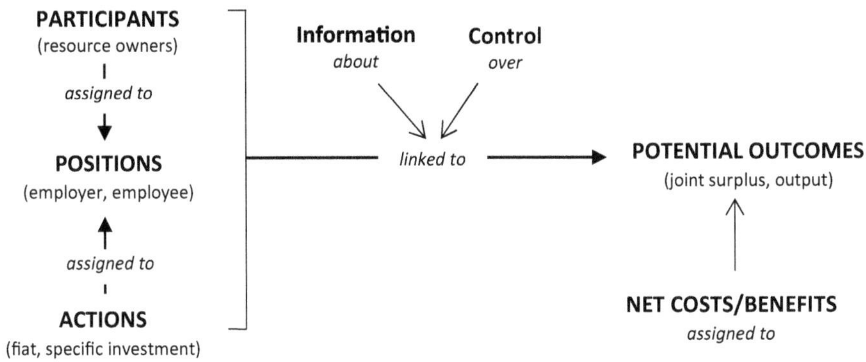

FIGURE 2.2 Intrafirm action situation.

costs exceed benefits, when benefits seem small relative to costs, or when potential benefits seem unrealized. They may, for example, rely on their bargaining power and threaten to withhold cooperation to get a better deal. But they may also switch to or create a new action situation, in the hope of realizing greater benefits. The rules of this new action situation place participants in different positions, by virtue of which they may engage in a new set of actions. Their control over the allowable actions, outcomes, and their linkages is exercised through different channels. We can think of the emergence of the firm from the market in these terms.

Our second action arena, and indeed our *focal* one, is inside the firm (Figure 2.2). The firm emerges from the market when one of the participants (resource owners) takes on the role of an entrepreneur. Positions change from buyer and seller to employer and employee, with a new set of permissible actions (fiat, specific investment) and outcomes (joint surplus, output). As before, participants have some common information about their relative positions, their available actions, and the potential outcomes – otherwise they would not be in the same action situation. They also have some control over the allowable actions, outcomes, and their linkages. Free-riding, hold-up behavior, and other collective action problems arise because they can act independently in situations of interdependence.

Per Coase (1937), it is only worth moving from a market action arena (Figure 2.1) to the intrafirm action arena (Figure 2.2) if the firm can produce the same outcome (output) at a lower cost. Since any productive activity can be contracted out to an outside supplier or be undertaken in-house – recall that firms and markets are alternative institutional matrices within which transactions are negotiated and executed – it should be clear that these action arenas are in fact *adjacent*, with the choice of moving from the market to the firm and vice versa guided by the comparison of net costs and benefits (Figure 2.3).

FIGURE 2.3 Make-or-buy.

That the firm and the market are adjacent action arenas is reinforced by the fact that the firm must return to a market arena as a seller and create value for buyers in excess of its production costs, if it is to make a profit. The firm will fail to sell its output if the price exceeds the benefits to buyers (firms, if the output is an intermediate good; consumers, if the output is a final good). In this case, the firm's evaluation of this signal sends it back to the drawing board: It uses its control over the structure of the action situation (fiat) to reduce costs before coming back to the market to try again. Both the make-or-buy decision and this ongoing process of responding to market signals suggest that one cannot understand action situations within our focal action arena without placing them alongside various action situations in the market arena. The analysis, however, is incomplete.

2.3.2 *The Legal System and the Provision and Coproduction of the Corporate Mask*

A significant shortcoming of most of the literature on firms and markets developed in Coase's footsteps is that the essential roles played by organizational law and the legal system more broadly are overlooked (Deakin et al. 2017; Gindis and Hodgson 2026). While participants in market action situations (Figure 2.1) may wish to switch to an intrafirm action situation (Figure 2.2) because output can be produced at a lower cost or because greater benefits can be realized, the move between the two situations requires an intermediate step. The firm can only engage in transactions in which the make-or-buy decision is relevant if it has its own legal identity and contracting capacity (Iacobucci and Triantis 2007; Kornhauser and MacLeod 2013). It follows that placing our focal action arena alongside the market arena is insufficient; a third action arena – the legal system – must be included in the discussion. Recall that, as an institutional resource, the corporate mask is drawn from and is anchored in the legal environment.

In Ostromian jargon, *provision* refers to the public availability of goods or services for collective consumption (McGinnis 2011b). The legal system provides a range of such goods and services (with varying quality across jurisdictions). Among other things, entrepreneurs or coalitions of resource owners have an array of legal forms to choose from when setting up firms; they can access a system of property and business registries; and they can turn to impartial courts in cases of disputes. The benefits of being able to simply "plug into" such shared legal platforms are enormous (Hadfield 2017), not least because the services provided are generic, partly modular, and adaptable, which makes them valuable in a wide set of context-specific circumstances. The legal system's services can be consumed non-rivalrously and their demand, as Brett Frischmann (2012) has argued, is driven by downstream activities requiring them as an input for the production of a range of private, public, or club goods and services.

In most jurisdictions, there is virtually no restriction on who counts as an authorized user (with access and withdrawal rights) of the shared business registration system. The firm becomes operational when its founder or founders plug into the relevant platform. Whether the firm is merely registered with tax authorities to separate business from personal income or is formally incorporated by a state registrar, this legal recognition of the firm (embodied for example in a company or employer identification number) is a process of *coproduction* (Parks et al. 1981), in the sense that the users' input is required for the institutional resource to be produced. The public authority records the users' input and gives it legal effect. The legal constitution of the corporate mask is therefore neither private nor public; it is "essentially hybrid," to borrow Katharina Pistor's (2013) expression.

These considerations have a broader relevance. Depending on the legal form and the jurisdiction, there may be a requirement to file any amendments made to constitutional documents (such as articles of association or incorporation) that intervene after the firm's initial registration. Likewise, there may be a requirement to register any variations of share capital or capital stock, as well as any charges or secured interests over the firm's assets. Each of these commonplace situations in the life of a firm involves a process of coproduction: Governance actions are initiated by the firm's managers, shareholders, or creditors, but registration gives them legal effect. Significantly, in each of these instances where the publicly available information about it is modified, the firm must be legally re-recognized: The registration authority must confirm the identity of the firm before changing its registered characteristics. The firm remains the same, but its properties or qualities evolve.

Because the legal system is in fact a set of subsystems (legislation, regulation, courts, registries), each producing distinct resource units (statutes, rules, decisions, identification numbers) in a large range of different action situations, capturing it in a simple illustration is going to be difficult. Suffice it to say that the rules-in-form promulgated by legislators and regulators expand, restrict, or qualify the position, boundary, choice, aggregation, information, payoff, and scope rules-in-use governing many action situations in firms and markets. Importantly, rules-in-form determine both who or what is to be registered and the legal effects of registration. It is not surprising that policymakers in many developing countries have liberalized access to business and property registries and sought to make these more accommodating and

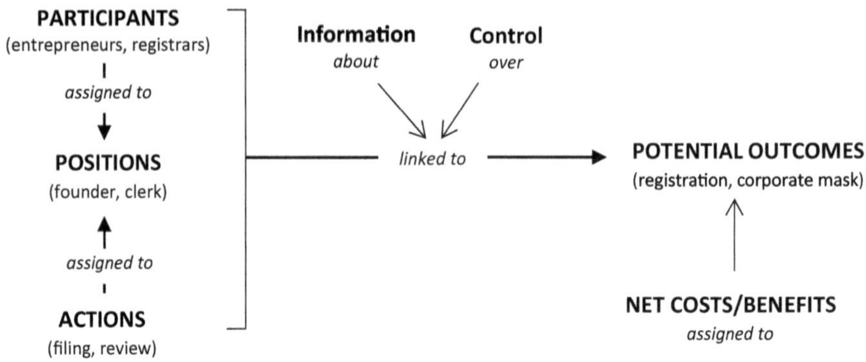

FIGURE 2.4 Provision and coproduction of the corporate mask.

cost-effective for users. Registries and third-party access to them for verification purposes are essential forms of institutional support for firms (Arruñada, 2010). Importantly, these systems involve the provision and coproduction of the corporate mask (Figure 2.4).

2.3.3 *Producing and Reproducing the Corporate Mask*

Once constituted and in possession of their own legal identity and contracting capacity, firms are participants in a range of analytically relevant market action situations. For example, they hire and fire workers in labor markets, buy and sell intermediate goods in producer markets, pledge assets and raise finance in capital markets, and acquire and sell intellectual property in the market for technology. All parties in such transactions will occupy a set of positions and have a set of authorized actions, some control over their actions and the linkages between these and the potential outcomes, and of course some common information about the situations they find themselves in. A key part of this common information is the mutual understanding that deals are being made with firms. Prospective employees know that the product of their labor will be appropriated by the firm and not the manager hiring them, and those negotiating interfirm deals know that the contracts thus entered into will bind not them but their firms.

While shared social perceptions and understandings are not backed by the state and thus may not bind in quite the same way as legal actions do (McAdams 2017), they nevertheless have the *constitutive force* captured in Searle's (1995) famous formula, "X counts as Y in context C." Note that this constitutive force is in operation whether we mean "a group of resource owners" counts as "a corporate actor" in context C1 or infer that "an authorized agent" counts as (represents, binds) "a corporate actor" in context C2. In both cases, a combination of formal rules, informal norms, and their *situational interpretations* comes into play. The process of interpretation is straightforward when formal rules are sufficient and informal norms are relegated to the background, but the weight of informal norms and situational interpretations increases when formal rules are insufficient (Cole 2017).

Compare first two contexts C1 where "a group of resource owners" counts as "a corporate actor." The first scenario, C1(a), is that of an incorporated firm, which unequivocally counts as a corporate actor, if the appropriate registration papers were filed with the state registrar, if various bureaucratic procedures (such as registration with the tax authorities) have been followed, and so on.[13] In this case, the provision and coproduction of the corporate mask occurs in an ex ante action situation (incorporation and registration), enabling the firm to operate legally as a corporate actor in the network of subsequent adjacent action situations. When the firm's trade name includes "Ltd." or some other such signifier that performs a semiotic mediation between the legal and social worlds (Bau Macedo and Herrmann-Pillath 2021), parties perceive it as such and deal with it accordingly.

The second scenario, C1(b), is that of the unincorporated partnership, which as a matter of rules-in-form is not a corporate actor in England (contrary to numerous other jurisdictions). Here, the beliefs and representations of both participants and third parties matter a great deal, as do the courts' norms of statutory interpretation and their attitudes toward context-specific business conventions. There is, for example, a long tradition of courts treating unincorporated partnerships as if they were corporate entities to uphold deals third parties struck with the firm in good faith, based on the firm's outward appearance of unity (Wells 2021). The corporate mask had already been produced and reproduced thanks to the parties' shared understandings and interpretations of the nature and effect of their business interactions, so when the court enforces contracts entered into on this basis, it recognizes this state of affairs by providing, so to speak, the corporate mask ex post.

That the social recognition of the firm as a corporate actor matters at least as much as its formal legal recognition is thrown into relief when we look at the set of contexts C2 where "an authorized agent" counts as (represents, binds) "a corporate actor." In any contractual negotiation between two firms, each firm's authorized agent presents themselves as having the capacity to bind a corporate actor and assumes that the other's analogous representation can be reasonably relied upon. The negotiation will proceed if both parties are satisfied that they are indeed in a C2 context and that the result will legally bind their respective firms. The idea of the firm as a corporate actor helps align the parties' shared beliefs and expectations and is therefore an input into the negotiation, while the actions and outcomes based on these beliefs and expectations instantiate and reproduce it. The corporate mask, in other words, is produced jointly with interfirm contractual agreements in markets (Figure 2.5).

The role played by shared understandings in this process means that it is vulnerable to *conflicting interpretations*. Where the parties' interpretations of their situations and

[13] Work on the constitutive power of document acts (Smith 2013) is relevant here.

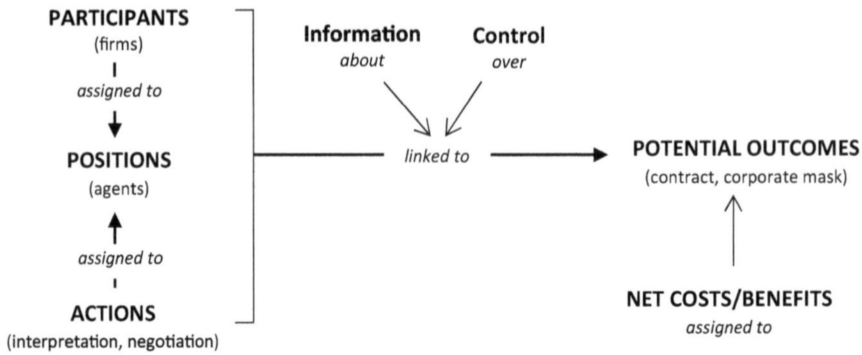

FIGURE 2.5 Joint production of the corporate mask.

positions differ, or where their understandings of the formal rules and informal norms in operation diverge, contractual negotiations can become more complicated. If one of the parties doubts that the other is properly authorized, there will be disagreement about whether they are in fact in a C2 context until further assurances can be made. The doubting party may proceed without further assurances, but if it then turns out that the counterparty lacked actual authority, it may be difficult to enforce the agreement. It is important to note that the governance of such disputes and the enforcement of agreements take place in a range of adjacent action situations – from the informal meeting of the parties to the courtroom – in which the firm's rights and duties are defined or redefined. It is the firm, not its agents, that is recognized as having standing to enforce agreements or adjudicate disputes in courts (Vining 1978). Its corporate mask is an input into and a jointly produced outcome of these processes.

The problem of conflicting interpretations also complicates the *distribution* of the joint surplus created by the firm, which exhibits, as Ostrom (1998) intimated, features of a common-pool resource. Distributional conflicts are compounded when outsiders also present themselves as legitimate claimants. While both insiders and outsiders have a shared understanding that the surplus belongs to the firm, they also have a shared understanding that many of the key resources that help produce, maintain, and enhance that surplus are not strictly speaking owned by the firm but can instead be said to be held in common. Insiders and outsiders will often justify their claims based on different evaluative criteria (contribution, efficiency, equity, legitimacy), and it is the central problem of corporate governance to resolve such disputes (Bridoux and Stoelhorst 2022). The corporate mask is ever-present in these debates.

2.4 CONCLUSIONS

We welcome Deakin's (2012a, 2019) corporation-as-commons idea and have sought to take it forward in this chapter. We have argued that this requires thinking about the kinds of shared resources firms rely on or manage and asking whether, and in what sense, we can view the corporation as such as resource. We have shown that the *corporate mask* is the firm's most critical resource, enabling it to operate as a singular actor in the legal and commercial spheres. The corporate mask functions as a legal and epistemic focal point shared by insiders and third parties with whom the firm interacts in a network of adjacent action situations both within and across firm boundaries.

More specifically, we characterized the corporate mask as a special kind of institutional resource that combines features of infrastructural and intellectual resources, because it is a pooled input in many intrafirm and interfirm processes, and at the same time underpins and feeds into shared beliefs about the firm and its activities. It is provided by the legal system when it recognizes (ex ante or ex post) the firm's capacity to act as a singular whole, and is coproduced through various forms of registration. It is also produced and reproduced jointly with the firm's interactions with third parties, including contracting parties and the courts. The shared understanding that a corporate actor is involved is both an input into and an output of these interactions, which we have examined in representative action situations.

We believe that the focus on adjacent action situations is a productive way to think about and extend the GKC research program. In this respect, despite some differences, this chapter is a continuation of Erwin Dekker and Pavel Kuchař's (2024) work on the governance of markets as knowledge commons. Further advances in this direction will require more detailed analyses of the connections between relevant action situations in the three action arenas. It will also be important to gain a better understanding of how resource and governance systems coevolve. And there is certainly much more to say about how the analysis relates to, or has bearing on, ongoing debates in corporate governance. Different versions of the corporation-as-commons idea should be proposed and compared, and case studies of specific types of corporations and other kinds of corporate knowledge commons should be developed. We look forward to the growth of this exciting new area of interdisciplinary institutional research.

REFERENCES

Adelstein, Richard. 2010. "Firms as Social Actors." *Journal of Institutional Economics* 6(3): 329–349.

Alchian, Armen A. 1984. "Specificity, Specialization, and Coalitions." *Journal of Institutional and Theoretical Economics* 140(1): 34–49.

Alvarez, Sharon A., Udo Zander, Jay B. Barney, and Allan Afuah. 2020. "Developing a Theory of the Firm for the 21st Century." *Academy of Management Review* 45(2): 711–716.

Aoki, Masahiko. 2010. *Corporations in Evolving Diversity: Cognition, Governance, and Institutions*. New York: Oxford University Press.

Argote, Linda, and Aimée A. Kane. 2009. "Superordinate Identity and Knowledge Creation and Transfer in Organizations." In *Knowledge Governance: Processes and Perspectives*, ed. Nicolai J. Foss, and Snejina Michailova, 166–190. New York: Oxford University Press.

Arrow, Kenneth J. 1996. "Technical Information and Industrial Structure." *Industrial and Corporate Change* 5(2): 645–652.
Arruñada, Benito. 2010. "Institutional Support of the Firm: A Theory of Business Registries." *Journal of Legal Analysis* 2(2): 525–576.
Barney, Jay B. 1991. "Firm Resources and Sustainable Competitive Advantage." *Journal of Management* 17(1): 99–120.
Barney, Jay B., and Delwyn N. Clark. 2007. *Resource-Based Theory: Creating and Sustaining Competitive Advantage*. New York: Oxford University Press.
Basu, Kaushik. 2018. *The Republic of Beliefs: A New Approach to Law and Economics*. Princeton: Princeton University Press.
Bau Macedo, Luís O., and Carsten Herrmann-Pillath. 2021. "Towards a Semiotic Theory of the Corporation." *Social Semiotics* 31(2): 282–304.
Baumgärtner, Stefan, Malte Faber, and Johannes Schiller. 2006. *Joint Production and Responsibility in Ecological Economics: On the Foundations of Environmental Policy*. Cheltenham: Edward Elgar.
Berti, Marco, and Christos Pitelis. 2022. "Open Team Production, the New Cooperative Firm, and Hybrid Advantage." *Academy of Management Review* 47(2): 309–330.
Bridoux, Flore M., and J. W. Stoelhorst. 2022. "Stakeholder Governance: Solving the Collective Action Problem in Joint Value Creation." *Academy of Management Review* 47(2): 214–236.
British Academy. 2019. *Principles for Purposeful Business: How to Deliver the Framework for the Future of the Corporation*. www.thebritishacademy.ac.uk/publications/future-of-the-corporation-principles-for-purposeful-business.
Bylund, Per. 2016. *The Problem of Production: A New Theory of the Firm*. Abingdon: Routledge.
Cabrera, Angel, and Elizabeth F. Cabrera. 2002. "Knowledge-Sharing Dilemmas." *Organization Studies* 23(5): 687–710.
Camera, Gabriele, and Lukas Hohl. 2021. "Group-Identity and Long-Run Cooperation: An Experiment." *Journal of Economic Behavior and Organization* 188: 903–915.
Coase, Ronald H. 1937. "The Nature of the Firm." *Economica* 4(16): 386–405.
Cohendet, Patrick, and Patrick Llerena. 2008. "The Role of Teams and Communities in the Emergence of Organizational Routines." In *Handbook of Organizational Routines*, ed. Markus C. Becker, 256–277. Cheltenham: Edward Elgar.
Cole, Daniel H. 2014. "Learning from Lin: Lessons and Cautions from the Natural Commons for the Knowledge Commons." In *Governing Knowledge Commons*, ed. Brett M. Frischmann, Michael J. Madison, and Katherine J. Strandburg, 45–68. New York: Oxford University Press.
Cole, Daniel H. 2017. "Laws, Norms and the Institutional Analysis and Development Framework." *Journal of Institutional Economics* 13(4): 829–847.
Coleman, James S. 1990. *Foundations of Social Theory*. Cambridge, MA: Harvard University Press.
Deakin, Simon. 2012a. "The Corporation as Commons: Rethinking Property Rights, Governance and Sustainability in the Business Enterprise." *Queen's Law Journal* 37(2): 339–381.
Deakin, Simon. 2012b. "The Juridical Nature of the Firm." In *The Sage Handbook of Corporate Governance*, ed. Thomas Clarke, and Douglas Branson, 113–135. London: Sage.
Deakin, Simon. 2019. "The Evolution of the Corporate Form: From Shareholders' Property to the Corporation as Commons." In *The Oxford Handbook of the Corporation*, ed. Thomas Clarke, Justin O'Brien, and Charles R. T. O'Kelley, 687–710. New York: Oxford University Press.
Deakin, Simon, David Gindis, and Geoffrey M. Hodgson. 2021. "What Is a Firm? A Reply to Jean-Philippe Robé." *Journal of Institutional Economics* 17(5): 861–871.

Deakin, Simon, David Gindis, Geoffrey M. Hodgson, Kainan Huang, and Katharina Pistor. 2017. "Legal Institutionalism: Capitalism and the Constitutive Role of Law." *Journal of Comparative Economics* 41(4): 1043–1061.

Dekker, Erwin, and Pavel Kuchař. 2021. "Introduction: Governing Markets as Knowledge Commons." In *Governing Markets as Knowledge Commons*, ed. Erwin Dekker, and Pavel Kuchař, 1–18. Cambridge: Cambridge University Press.

Dekker, Erwin, and Pavel Kuchař. 2024. "Markets and Knowledge Commons: Is There a Difference between Private and Community Governance of Markets?" *Public Choice* 201(3–4): 533–553.

Denzau, Arthur T., and Douglass C. North. 1994. "Shared Mental Models: Ideologies and Institutions." *Kyklos* 47(1): 3–31.

Dunning, John H., and Sarianna M. Lundan. 2008. *Multinational Enterprise and the Global Economy*, 2nd ed. Cheltenham: Edward Elgar.

Dyckhoff, Harald, and Rainer Souren. 2023. "Are Important Phenomena of Joint Production Still Being Neglected by Economic Theory? A Review of Recent Literature." *Journal of Business Economics* 93(6–7): 1015–1053.

Eggertsson, Thráinn. 1990. *Economic Behavior and Institutions: Principles of Neoinstitutional Economics*. Cambridge: Cambridge University Press.

Ellig, Jerry. 2001. "Internal Markets and the Theory of the Firm." *Managerial and Decision Economics* 22(4-5): 227–237.

Engel, Christoph, and Werner Güth. 2006. "Corporate Culture as a Resource for Management." *Journal of Institutional and Theoretical Economics* 162(1): 97–100.

Fennell, Lee A. 2009. "Commons, Anticommons, Semicommons." In *Research Handbook on the Economics of Property Law*, ed. Kenneth Ayotte, and Henry E. Smith, 35–56. Cheltenham: Edward Elgar.

Foss, Nicolai J. 1999. "The Use of Knowledge in Firms." *Journal of Institutional and Theoretical Economics* 155(3): 458–486.

Foss, Nicolai J., Peter G. Klein, Lasse B. Lien, Thomas Zellweger, and Todd Zenger. 2020. "Ownership Competence." *Strategic Management Journal* 42(2): 302–328.

Frischmann, Brett M. 2012. *Infrastructure: The Social Value of Shared Resources*. New York: Oxford University Press.

Frischmann, Brett M., Michael J. Madison, and Katherina J. Strandburg, eds. 2014. *Governing Knowledge Commons*. New York: Oxford University Press.

Frolov, Daniil. 2024. "The Economics of Cognitive Institutions: Mapping Debates, Looking Ahead." *Journal of Institutional Economics* 20: e28.

Frost, Jetta, and Michele Morner. 2005. "Corporate Commons: Sustaining Competitiveness through Public Goods in Multidivisional Firms." *International Journal of Learning and Change* 1(1): 28–45.

Frost, Jetta, and Michele Morner. 2010. "Overcoming Knowledge Dilemmas: Governing the Creation, Sharing and Use of Knowledge Resources." *International Journal of Strategic Change Management* 2(2/3): 172–199.

Galunic, D. Charles, and Simon Rodan. 1998. "Resource Combinations in the Firm: Knowledge Structures and the Potential for Schumpeterian Innovation." *Strategic Management Journal* 19(12): 1193–1201.

Gindis, David. 2016. "Legal Personhood and the Firm: Avoiding Anthropomorphism and Equivocation." *Journal of Institutional Economics* 12(3): 499–513.

Gindis, David, and Geoffrey M. Hodgson. 2026. "The Legal Nature of the Firm." In *Research Handbook on the Theory of the Firm*, ed. Josef Windsperger, and Aveed Raha. Cheltenham: Edward Elgar.

Gindis, David, and Eva Micheler. 2024. "Institutional Theory for Corporate Law: An Invitation." *Journal of Corporate Law Studies* 24(2): 399–435.
Grandori, Anna. 2009. "Poliarchic Governance and the Growth of Knowledge." In *Knowledge Governance: Processes and Perspectives*, ed. Nicolai J. Foss, and Snejina Michailova, 81–107. New York: Oxford University Press.
Hadfield, Gillian K. 2017. *Rules for a Flat World: Why Humans Invented Law and How to Reinvent It for a Complex Global Economy*. New York: Oxford University Press.
Hansmann, Henry, and Reinier R. Kraakman. 2000. "The Essential Role of Organizational Law." *Yale Law Journal* 110(3): 387–440.
Hart, Oliver D. 1995. *Firms, Contracts and Financial Structure*. New York: Oxford University Press.
Hashimoto, Masanori. 1981. "Firm-Specific Human Capital as a Shared Investment." *American Economic Review* 71(3): 475–482.
Hess, Charlotte, and Elinor Ostrom. 2003. "Ideas, Artifacts, and Facilities: Information as a Common-Pool Resource." *Law and Contemporary Problems* 66(1–2): 111–145.
Hess, Charlotte, and Elinor Ostrom. 2007. "Introduction: An Overview of the Knowledge Commons." In *Understanding Knowledge as a Commons: From Theory to Practice*, ed. Charlotte Hess, and Elinor Ostrom, 1–26. Cambridge, MA: MIT Press.
Hillman, Amy J., Michael C. Withers, and Brian J. Collins. 2009. "Resource Dependence Theory: A Review." *Journal of Management* 35(6): 1404–1427.
Hodgson, Geoffrey M., and Thorbjørn Knudsen. 2004. "The Firm as an Interactor: Firms as Vehicles for Habits and Routines." *Journal of Evolutionary Economics* 14(2): 281–307.
Holmström, Bengt. 1999. "The Firm as a Subeconomy." *Journal of Law, Economics and Organization* 15(1): 74–102.
Iacobucci, Edward M., and George G. Triantis. 2007. "Economic and Legal Boundaries of Firms." *Virginia Law Review* 93(3): 515–570.
Jansson, Hans. 2007. *International Business Strategy in Emerging Country Markets: An Institutional Network Approach*. Cheltenham: Edward Elgar.
Klein, Benjamin, Robert G. Crawford, and Armen A. Alchian. 1978. "Vertical Integration, Appropriable Rents, and the Competitive Contracting Process." *Journal of Law and Economics* 21(2): 297–326.
Kogut, Bruce, and Udo Zander. 1992. "Knowledge of the Firm, Combinative Capabilities and the Replication of Technology." *Organization Science* 3(3): 383–397.
Kogut, Bruce, and Udo Zander. 1996. "What Firms Do? Coordination, Identity and Learning." *Organization Science* 7(5): 502–518.
Kornhauser, Lewis A., and Bentley MacLeod. 2013. "Contracts between Legal Persons." In *Handbook of Organizational Economics*, ed. Robert Gibbons, and John Roberts, 918–957. Princeton: Princeton University Press.
Langlois, Richard N. 1992. "Transaction Costs in Real Time." *Industrial and Corporate Change* 1(1): 99–127.
Levinthal, Daniel A. 2000. "Organizational Capabilities in Complex Worlds." In *The Nature and Dynamics of Organizational Capabilities*, ed. Giovanni Dosi, Richard R. Nelson, and Sidney G. Winter, 363–379. New York: Oxford University Press.
List, Christian, and Philip Pettit. 2011. *Group Agency: The Possibility, Design and Status of Corporate Actors*. New York: Oxford University Press.
Lloyd, Peter J. 1983. "Why Do Firms Produce Multiple Outputs?" *Journal of Economic Behavior and Organization* 4(1): 41–51.
Madison, Michael J., Brett M. Frischmann, and Katherine J. Strandburg. 2010. "Constructing Commons in the Cultural Environment." *Cornell Law Review* 95(4): 657–709.

Madison, Michael J., Brett M. Frischmann, and Katherine J. Strandburg. 2019. "Knowledge Commons." In *Routledge Handbook of the Study of the Commons*, ed. Blake Hudson, Jonathan Rosenbloom, and Daniel H. Cole, 76–90. Abingdon: Routledge.

Mayer, Colin. 2020. "Ownership, Agency, and Trusteeship: An Assessment." *Oxford Review of Economic Policy* 36(2): 223–240.

Mayer, Colin. 2021. "The Future of the Corporation and the Economics of Purpose." *Journal of Management Studies* 58(3): 887–901.

McAdams, Richard H. 2017. *The Expressive Powers of Law: Theories and Limits*. Cambridge, MA: Harvard University Press.

McGinnis, Michael D. 2011a. "Networks of Adjacent Action Situations in Polycentric Governance." *Policy Studies Journal* 39(1): 51-78.

McGinnis, Michael D. 2011b. "An Introduction to IAD and the Language of the Ostrom Workshop: A Simple Guide to a Complex Framework." *Policy Studies Journal* 39(1): 169–184.

McGinnis, Michael D. 2019. "Connecting Commons and the IAD Framework." In *Routledge Handbook of the Study of the Commons*, ed. Blake Hudson, Jonathan Rosenbloom, and Daniel H. Cole, 50–62. Abingdon: Routledge.

Meyer, Renate E., Stefan Leixnering, and Jeroen Veldman, eds. 2022. *The Corporation: Rethinking the Iconic Form of Business Organization*. Bingley: Emerald.

Micheler, Eva. 2021. *Company Law: A Real Entity Theory*. Oxford: Oxford University Press.

Miller, Gary J. 1992. *Managerial Dilemmas: The Political Economy of Hierarchy*. Cambridge: Cambridge University Press.

Morrow, Paige, Filip Gregor, and Jeroen Veldman. 2016. *Revisioning the Corporation: A Short Guide Sustainable Corporate Governance*, 2nd ed. Brussels: Frank Bold.

Nelson, Richard R. 2009. "Routines as Technologies and as Organizational Capabilities." In *Organizational Routines: Advancing Empirical Research*, ed. Markus C. Becker, and Nathalie Lazaric, 11–25. Cheltenham: Edward Elgar.

Nooteboom, Bart. 2009. *A Cognitive Theory of the Firm: Learning, Governance and Dynamic Capabilities*. Cheltenham: Edward Elgar.

Olivera, Fernando. 2000. "Memory Systems in Organizations: An Empirical Investigation of Mechanisms for Knowledge Collection, Storage and Access." *Journal of Management Studies* 37(6): 811–832.

Osterloh, Magrit, and Jetta Frost. 2002. "Motivation and Knowledge as Strategic Resources." In *Successful Management by Motivation: Balancing Intrinsic and Extrinsic Motivation*, ed. Bruno S. Frey, and Magrit Osterloh, 27–51. Berlin: Springer.

Ostrom, Elinor. 1990. *Governing the Commons: The Evolution of Institutions for Collective Action*. Cambridge: Cambridge University Press.

Ostrom, Elinor. 1998. "Self-Governance of Common-Pool Resources." In *The New Palgrave Dictionary of Economics and the Law, Vol. 3*, ed. Peter K. Newman, 424–433. London: Macmillan.

Ostrom, Elinor. 2000. "Private and Common Property Rights." In *Encyclopedia of Law and Economics, Vol 2: Civil Law and Economics*, ed. Boudewijn Bouckaert, and Gerrit De Geest, 332–379. Cheltenham: Edward Elgar.

Ostrom, Elinor. 2005. *Understanding Institutional Diversity*. Cambridge, MA: MIT Press.

Ostrom, Elinor. 2011. "Background on the Institutional Analysis and Development Framework." *Policy Studies Journal* 37(1): 7–27.

Ostrom, Elinor, and Charlotte Hess. 2007. "A Framework for Analyzing the Knowledge Commons." In *Understanding Knowledge as a Commons: From Theory to Practice*, ed. Charlotte Hess, and Elinor Ostrom, 41–81. Cambridge, MA: MIT Press.

Parks, Roger B., Paula C. Baker, Larry Kiser, et al. 1981. "Consumers as Coproducers of Public Services: Some Economic and Institutional Considerations." *Policy Studies Journal* 9(7): 1001–1011.

Penrose, Edith T. 1959. *The Theory of the Growth of the Firm*. Oxford: Blackwell.

Pentland, Brian T., and Henry H. Rueter. 1994. "Organizational Routines as Grammars of Action." *Administrative Science Quarterly* 39(3): 484–510.

Pettit, Philip. 2023. "Five Elements of Group Agency." *Inquiry* 68(3): 1069–1089.

Pfeffer, Jeffrey, and Gerald R. Salancik. 1978. *The External Control of Organizations: A Resource-Dependence Perspective*. New York: Harper & Row.

Pistor, Katharina. 2013. "A Legal Theory of Finance." *Journal of Comparative Economics* 41(2): 315–330.

Poteete, Amy, Marco A. Janssen, and Elinor Ostrom. 2010. *Working Together: Collective Action, the Commons, and Multiple Methods in Practice*. Princeton: Princeton University Press.

Rayamajhee, Veeshan, and Pablo Paniagua. 2021. "The Ostroms and the Contestable Nature of Goods: Beyond Taxonomies and Toward Institutional Polycentricity." *Journal of Institutional Economics* 17(1): 71–89.

Rubin, Paul H. 1990. *Managing Business Transactions: Controlling the Cost of Coordinating, Communication, and Decision Making*. New York: Free Press.

Santos, Filipe M., and Kathleen M. Eisenhardt. 2005. "Organizational Boundaries and Theories of Organization." *Organization Science* 16(5/2): 491–508.

Schlager, Edella, and Elinor Ostrom. 1992. "Property-Rights Regimes and Natural Resources: A Conceptual Analysis." *Land Economics* 68(3): 249–262.

Scott, W. Richard. 1995. *Institutions and Organizations: Ideas, Interests, and Identities*. Thousand Oaks: Sage.

Searle, John R. 1983. *Intentionality*. Cambridge: Cambridge University Press.

Searle, John R. 1995. *The Construction of Social Reality*. New York: Free Press.

Searle, John R. 2005. "What Is an Institution?" *Journal of Institutional Economics* 1(1): 1–22.

Sloan Wilson, David, Elinor Ostrom, and Michael E. Cox. 2013. "Generalizing the Core Design Principles for the Efficacy of Groups." *Journal of Economic Behavior and Organization* 90(S): S21–S32.

Smith, Barry. 2013. "Documents Acts." In *Institutions, Emotions, and Group Agents: Contributions to Social Ontology*, ed. Anita Konzelmann-Ziv, and Hans B. Schmid, 19–31. Dordrecht: Springer.

Spender, Joseph C. 1996. "Making Knowledge the Basis of a Dynamic Theory of the Firm." *Strategic Management Journal* 17(S): 45–62.

Spulber, Daniel F. 2009. *The Theory of the Firm: Microeconomics with Endogenous Entrepreneurs, Firms, Markets and Organizations*. Cambridge: Cambridge University Press.

Tadelis, Steven. 1999. "What's in a Name? Reputation as a Tradeable Asset." *American Economic Review* 89(3): 548–563.

Teece, David J. 1980. "Economies of Scope and the Scope of the Enterprise." *Journal of Economic Behavior and Organization* 1(3): 223–247.

Teece, David J. 1982. "Towards an Economic Theory of the Multiproduct Firm." *Journal of Economic Behavior and Organization* 3(1): 39–63.

Teece, David J., Gary Pisano, and Amy Shuen. 1997. "Dynamic Capabilities and Strategic Management." *Strategic Management Journal* 18(7): 509–533.

Vining, Aidan R. 2003. "Internal Market Failure: A Framework for Diagnosing Firm Inefficiency." *Journal of Management Studies* 40(2): 431–457.

Vining, Joseph. 1978. *Legal Identity: The Coming of Age of Public Law*. New Haven: Yale University Press.
Waitzer, Edward J. 2018. "Rethinking the Purpose of the Corporation." *Journal of Applied Corporate Finance* 30(2): 18–21.
Wells, Harwell. 2021. "The Personification of the Partnership." *Vanderbilt Law Review* 74(6): 1835–1873.
Williamson, Oliver E. 1975. *Market and Hierarchies: Analysis and Antitrust Implications*. New York: Free Press.
Williamson, Oliver E. 1985. *The Economic Institutions of Capitalism: Firms, Markets and Relational Contracting*. New York: Free Press.
Williamson, Oliver E. 1996. *The Mechanisms of Governance*. New York: Oxford University Press.
Witt, Ulrich. 2011. "Emergence and Functionality of Organizational Routines: An Individualistic Approach." *Journal of Institutional Economics* 7(2): 157–174.

3

What Do Corporations Do?

Joshua Getzler

3.1 INTRODUCTION

Corporations are entities with purposes and patrimonies separate to their membership, presenting to and acting upon the world with a single will and voice distinct from the wills of the membership.[1] The law inveterately uses images or metaphors to convey the function of a discrete, univocal, and integrated group will and action belonging to the entity. Thus we have the corporate *persona*, or mask or face; the *corpore*, or body aggregate, wielding a fund or *universitatis* being a collection of partitioned and dedicated assets, and so on. These juridical metaphors articulate how the corporation can be a site of social action distinct from the extra-corporate behaviour of its members. At one extreme of legal analysis a "corporation sole," such as a monarch or bishop or another official, can act in an entirely different juridical and social space to the person who holds the office, and who will spend a good deal of life engaging in non-corporate activities outside the office; such persons have two bodies, or perhaps such bodies have two persons. At the other extreme we have the state or commonwealth, embracing a whole population within a single will and purpose gathered in the mind and body of a representative sovereign.

The extremes of the corporation sole as the vehicle of office and the state sovereign as universal representative are not our chief concern here, but rather the vast array of corporations aggregate that lie in between. Four historic models of corporate activity will be laid out, each searching for fresh metaphorical insight, and each feeding ideas into the modern conception of the corporation: the *cathedral* built by guilds, comprising organizations with a skilled membership self-regulating admissions and standards of conduct; the *factory*, connoting the classic hierarchical and bureaucratized corporation with highly specified division of labour and capital with membership determined contractually; the *bazaar*, being collations of nested

I thank David Gindis, Pavel Kuchař, and Eva Micheler who shared much time, attention, and knowledge to help me start and finish this study; and David Kershaw, Simon Deakin, Isabelle Ferreras, Hanoch Dagan, and Lorren Eldridge for many valuable observations.

[1] The title of this article is a straight-up homage to Stephen Marglin's (1974) "What Do Bosses Do?"

or adjoining enterprises such as a chamber of commerce or a stock market, providing a platform for interacting traders; and the *commune*, being an organization with personalized bonds and common purposes, found most intensely in family and religious enterprise.

These ideal types are not mutually exclusive and can be found across different time periods pursuing radically different profit and non-profit objectives; and they each persist in pure or hybrid form into the modern age. They are all affected by coordination problems that arise when members of a group take decisions, whether by direction, representation, or some other deliberative system such as voting. We can next stipulate an inductive conclusion: a group attains corporate status when it functions as a univocal entity, directing and backing the actions of its agents and reciprocally attributing agent action to the corporation. Real corporation theory then postulates that in these conditions of integrated direction and attribution the corporation thinks, purposes, and behaves as an agent or entity distinct from its membership. Much attention is given in law to the attribution of decision and conduct by corporate directors and servants to the corporate person as responsible agent. Collective agency should be broken into two parts: there must be collective knowledge as a precondition of collective conduct. In other words, there must be a system for processing relevant information about member, agent, and counterparty conduct, joined to observation of more objective facts about the state of the world. The corporation must have protocols to act upon this shared information to decide conduct – it must, in other words, create a *knowledge commons* governance structure.

The key argument of this chapter is that the corporation (thinking/acting through individual actors within the corporation) must be able to interpret facts largely comprising observations of other agents' conduct, both within and without the firm boundaries. In other words, the corporation must cultivate and embody *common knowledge*, allowing fissiparous agents with distinct levels of knowledge and contending goals to nonetheless successfully predict mutual conduct and evoke successful group heuristics (valuable knowledge-building canons) and thus have the capacity to form and execute plans that can deal with uncertainty and surprise founded on interactive rationalities. So we must look for two interlocking steps in the mental life of the corporation – hunting, gathering, and cultivating information about a world (including the corporation itself) populated by contending sentient agents (a knowledge commons), and then aligning interpretation of the fruits of the information harvest to permit mutual cooperation within and across firm boundaries (attaining common knowledge).

To articulate this framework of corporate analysis, we must move nimbly from legal and historical examples to more abstract tools of analytical philosophy and economics. The approach here links closely to the evolving Governing Knowledge Commons (GKC) framework (Madison et al. 2010; Frischmann et al. 2014; Strandburg et al. 2017) derived from the seminal work of Elinor Ostrom, which examines cooperation through a matrix of rule-following, community attributes, and patterns of interactions (Ostrom 1990, 2005, 2010, 2011). The GKC framework can be tested and enriched by taking the legal-historical record of corporate development seriously, and the best way to do that is by pursuing a case study of an important corporation that has not only had ups and downs but also left very good records describing what happened. The business history of the Boeing Company demonstrates quite starkly how shifts in the internal dynamics of corporate knowing and acting, of authority and cooperation, of consensus, loyalty, and dissent, can determine the success or downfall of an organization.

3.2 KNOWING AND ACTING: THE CASE OF THE BOEING COMPANY

William Edward Boeing (1881–1956) founded and registered his airplane corporation in Washington State in 1916 as the Pacific Aero Products Company, with a share capital of $100,000 divided into $100 shares, of which he controlled 98% (Boeing 2024). He re-registered the enterprise in 1917 as the Boeing Airplane Company. He used the engineering resources of a boatbuilding yard he had acquired in 1910 on the Duwamish River on the outskirts of Seattle. There he could enjoy the benefit of abundant supplies of local spruce joined to a strong craft tradition in the workshop, enabling the factory to produce excellent seaplanes of wood with bi-foil construction (Cloud 2011; Reed 2015; Robison 2021).

The company soon diversified into mail-courier, passenger, and military planes, and sold training planes to the Navy when the United States entered the First World War. In the interwar period, Boeing innovated with larger aircraft, including a twelve-passenger three-engine Model 80 in 1928, a harbinger of mass consumer travel later in the century. The corporation combined sophisticated engineering skills from MIT graduates with local craft manufacturing skills, and as it grew, it reincorporated in Delaware to access eastern sources of loan and equity capital. Boeing merged his company with various rival carriers and manufacturers to create a national airline in 1929 using his own planes, but was forced by antitrust actions in 1934 to split manufacturing from commercial flight services. Accordingly, United Airlines was split off from the Boeing Corporation, the latter now headquartered in Seattle, though the two corporations remained close with tie-ins of equipment orders.

A commercial breakthrough for Boeing came with the mono-foil two-engine 247 passenger plane in 1933. The company then grew rapidly, its industrial and engineering bases placed well to build heavy bombers, transports, and fighters in large quantity during the Second World War. After 1945, Boeing fell behind rival manufacturers more prominent in the civil sector, and with military contracts tailing, the Seattle company shrank its workforce and factories. Company fortunes revived with the 707 passenger plane in 1958, and then the innovative 727 jet plane in 1960, which sold over a thousand units. By the 1960s Boeing's engineering prowess and quality-assured manufacturing processes eclipsed its rivals. A host of technical innovations poured out of its Seattle laboratories, producing the ubiquitous 727 (1,823 units built) and the even more profitable 747 "Jumbo" jet (1,574 units built), the latter plane taking five years of investment and design effort to produce, including the building of a large bespoke manufacturing facility near Seattle. Remarkably, the 747 production ran from 1968 to 2023.

For engineers, scientists, and aviators, Boeing in the later twentieth century had become the premium workplace in the world, with engineering-led manufacturing sparing no cost to maintain technical excellence, and with staff encouraged to treat their work as a life-long vocation practised within intimate and loyal teams, buttressed by plentiful lifestyle benefits for workers and their families in the beautiful Northwest. The Boeing Company had become an exemplar of the American post-war imperial, economic, and lifestyle hegemony, ten times larger than that other exemplar of American technological prowess in the twentieth century, the National Aeronautics and Space Administration.

The fall of Boeing was seeded by the entry of rival manufacturers keen to challenge Boeing's dominance, notably Airbus Industrie founded in 1970, which combined technical excellence with cost-reducing industrial techniques. Boeing fought back by studying the best Japanese manufacturing processes, and promoting talented and committed scientist and engineers to design an exemplary product that would nullify the Airbus advantage. The team, backed by an $11 billion order from industrial ally United Airlines, produced the advanced passenger jet dubbed the 777, to date the most successful wide-body commercial plane in history with 1,701 units delivered and many hundreds more ordered and in production. Boeing allowed the 777 engineers unlimited resources in the Seattle facility to design the technologies, manufacturing systems, testing, and training to make sure of success against the excellent Airbus rival products.

The 777 team leader was a pilot and engineer named Alan Mulally. He worked closely with a group of eight purchasing airlines to determine need and operational demands, and cultivated loosely controlled and overlapping design and engineering teams whose members were encouraged to be outspoken in identifying issues. Mulally's managerial watchwords were "no secrets" and "the data will set you free." Workers at every stage of design and manufacture felt they were listened to wherever they were in the hierarchy and encouraged to evoke problems and plough effort and resources into solutions. His second in command recalled of Mulally that "Accountability is huge with him. Burying things and letting them fester – Darth Vader comes out." Less politely, an irate Mulally once threatened: "The only thing that will make me rip off your head and s**t down your neck is withholding information."

To prevent the necessity of such information withdrawal, Mulally put powerful and expensive computer terminals on every engineers' desk to enable complex 3D computer designs to be shared rapidly and worked on collectively. One of the installers of the comms network reflected: "No expense was spared. There was this feeling of camaraderie" (quotes from Robison 2021, 4546). Mullally also called lengthy quarterly meetings of the entire team, encouraging face-to-face communication across all parts of the enterprise, hunting for ideas to pursue and problems to solve. He invited the Federal Aviation Administration (FAA) regulators in regularly to inspect and understand Boeing's work, and he sought their feedback. Mulally swiftly absorbed all the details his system of information and audit fed through to him. He protected and advanced the team of skilled workers who entrusted their disclosures to him. Any prototype components or designs shown to have weakness were swiftly scrapped no matter the sunk costs. It was not only that an elaborate system of audit and report was in place; the staff were encouraged to produce meaningful, high-quality information identifying problems and solutions.

Meanwhile, as competition in aircraft manufacture intensified, Boeing management reacted to market pressures by merging in 1997 with McDonnell Douglas, a rival US manufacturer with a large military dimension but which had suffered humiliating civilian failures with the dangerously designed DC-10 large passenger carrier. The engraftment into Boeing of McDonnell Douglas executives who were used to ordering around their staff as dependent subordinates disrupted the close team or familial culture of the Seattle manufacturing headquarters, where collegiate relations ruled and where the best engineering solutions were sought regardless of time, source, or cost. The next step was the ingress of aggressive corporate executives drawn into the C-suite and mid-executive level from General Electric, 3M, and beyond that from the private equity world. These new executives typically had no connection to the engineering base of design and manufacture but were primed by the new business school cultures of financial assessment and manipulation of resources to yield shareholder value. The new executive class tended to see the firm labour and capital as fungible and always susceptible to reconfiguration in pursuit of profit; financial targets should lead engineering choices, not the other way round. Boeing's governance was quickly transformed: R&D investment was slashed and profits steered into share buy backs enriching shareholders and stock rewards for executives. Time horizons for product development tightened, with targets for delivery and cost containment the paramount drivers. Workers were forced to compete for their jobs, with regular culls of the least productive 10 per cent often younger workers still learning, or experienced greyheads with much to teach.

The managerial and financial executives decamped from Seattle in 2001 to a new corporate headquarters in Chicago, where efforts were increasingly bent towards lobbying the Pentagon for sales and the Federal regulators to relax standards to speed up production. Manufacturing was dispersed to southern parts of the United States or abroad where Boeing could use low-wage non-unionized labour, often employed by outside contracting enterprises. The crucial activities of testing new machines and training pilots and crew were spun off into subsidiaries or sold to new cost-cutting ventures outside the firm and beholden to Boeing for contract renewal.

Outsourcing was to be used wherever possible, so that union practices and craft traditions within the old firm could be evaded, and supply and demand made flexible without lengthy lock-ins. Contracts were redrawn with the core Seattle groups of engineers and test pilots, withdrawing benefits, tenure, and self-management, which in turn provoked renewed labour organization and strikes, further souring relations.

Worst of all, information flows were stymied as engineers feared reporting problems and asking for resources to distant executives, and workers failed to pass back data about component manufacturing problems coming from the factories and firms distant from Seattle. Outsourcing would often end up costing more than the old in-house production as specifications had to be very elaborate, there was no instant feedback between designers and makers, and mistakes required constant expensive revision and scrapping of useless inventory. Whistle-blowers pegging corruption and concealment in outsourcing, procurement, and sales were sacked, despite the management stating that they would run a clean company. In 2013, the latest Boeing CEO proudly told his alma mater, the Harvard Business School, "We understand that we are not going to get fiercely loyal people who will never leave like we did in the 1950s" (Robison 2021, 134). Atomizing and distancing the workforce was seen as a win for the management.

Two different projects showed how the rot had set in, with information flows interrupted, and the gathered and common knowledge of key interlocking teams dissipated. A high-tech 787 superjumbo plane was to be developed with precisely defined funding and targeted delivery dates, to face down the market-winning Airbus 330. Technical innovations were consciously to be subjected to cost limits – a constraint never applied in the older design regime for large-scale Boeing planes. When problems with the elaborate battery power system for the 787 emerged, with considerable danger of onboard fire or explosion, the problems were buried by executive command who argued that the risks were too small to redesign the plane with heavy shielding that would reduce efficiency and delay final implantation. Mulally, the most senior engineering executive, was by now demoralized and marginalized and failed to object; his malaise may have expressed itself with an extramarital affair with a co-worker that cost him the succession to the CEO post. He departed to head Ford Motor Company in 2006, where he achieved great engineering success, a horizon that had been denied to him at Boeing. In a moment of potent symbolism, his banner outside his office "Working Together" came down. A senior engineer commented: "The idealism just went out. It was no longer about working together, it was about something else – I guess shareholder value" (Robison 2021, 93). In due course, airplane fires caused by exploding batteries did blight the 787 causing recalls and expensive refits. Not only was money lost but also a system of trust and information exchange had been abandoned: get it out fast and cheap, spend on fixes if something goes wrong later, once the purchaser is locked in. A leading engineer and test pilot, Peter Morton, who had helped design with Mulally the successful 757 and 777 models, wrote from retirement to the Boeing executive that the company was now suffering from a "dysfunctional silo mentality" with "broken lines of communication … misunderstanding and confusion." The executives in Chicago did not bother to reply (Robison 2021, 239).

The tragic denouement came with the development of the 737-MAX (House Committee on Transportation and Infrastructure 2020). This plane model was maybe the tenth refurbishment by Boeing of a serviceable but veteran design for short and medium hauls, carrying 85–215 passengers in various configurations. The original 737 was a two-engine development of the 707 which had been introduced in 1956, and the 737 inherited the analogue instrumentation of the earlier plane. From 1967 over more than half a century, over 12,000 of these workhorses in various 737 model iterations were built, and many thousand remained in service into the next century, especially in poorer countries serviced by low-cost airlines. Pilots who grew up with the 737s were at home with the familiar flight technology, but the planes were heavy and fuel hungry, and again Boeing was losing out to newer and better Airbus and Bombardier models with modernized and computerized flight decks. The fateful decision was taken not to design a new smaller Boeing two-engine plane using advanced 777 and 787 technologies, but to drop new, fuel-efficient but heavy engines into the old 737 frame at a new forward position on the wings, adding in some updates to the plane's cosmetics and facilities, and engrafting digital dials onto a fundamentally analogue legacy control system. The engineers protested that if one changed one big thing – the drive mechanism and weighting of the aircraft – then one had to change everything, but they were overruled. The executives driving the 737-MAX project had two overriding commercial objectives: avoiding certification and retraining costs by presenting the plane as a smart variation on the old, and catching up with Airbus whose new planes were edging Boeing out of this sector of the market.

Boeing introduced what seemed like a clever shortcut to make the old 737 design balance in-flight with the heavier fuel-efficient engines – the "Maneuvering Characteristics Augmentation System" (MCAS). This was a software-controlled rear aerofoil that would react to sensors to lower the nose of the plane automatically during high-speed turns when the plane would otherwise buck upwards. Test pilot returns evidenced that MCAS could kick in destructively at lower speeds and low altitudes, notably at take-off, but these results were initially downplayed or suppressed by management as insignificant, as was evidence that any sensor failure could cause the MCAS to kick in hard during take-off so as to make pilot override in real time very difficult. To compound the risks, Boeing resisted the call to retrain tens of thousands of pilots in how to override MCAS if it behaved badly, and it sold stripped-down versions of the 737-MAX lacking reporting instruments and backup when the normal sensors had gone wrong. Boeing then made the impossibly bad decision to not even inform pilots of the new MCAS system and its foibles, lest this led to a call for expensive new training and delay or inhibit sales. After attending meetings where executives insisted on the inauguration of the plane without patient and thoughtful training and study of emergent flight problems, one manager reflected: "It's systemic. It's culture. It's the fact that we have a senior leadership team that understand very little about the business and yet are driving us to certain objectives. Its [sic] lots of individual groups that aren't working closely and being accountable … Sometimes you have to let things fail big so that everyone can identify a problem" (Robison 2021, 169). Some engineers surmised that they were not to communicate problems upwards in case this would leave a paper trail helping establish legal liability down the track, and so learned to keep silent; or at best to send in bland anonymized reports.

To make things worse, alongside these internal failings, there was no outside body to take audit and offer a second opinion. Under successive deregulating administrations, egged on by strident lobbying by airplane executives, including the Boeing team in Chicago, the FAA had been gutted of independent regulators charged to test and certify all new planes. Rather, the FAA staff were told to help manufacturers complete and sell units, and accept self-certification by the knowledgeable corporations who designed and made the machines. Any impedance to certification by an FAA officer had to be strongly justified, or would lead to withdrawn bonuses or even firing of that recalcitrant officer. Boeing's contempt for the FAA was shown by the manner of their submission of the MCAS system for scrutiny. The third MCAS revision allowed for a half percentage point in the change of plane stabilization at high speed, and this version was put forward to the FAA – without revealing that it was not the third but a *fifth* revision of MCAS that had in fact been installed on the planes, being a more radical mechanism making up to a 4 per cent shift for purposes of low-speed adjustment. In other words, the FAA were invited to approve a mechanism with eight times the tolerance of the version put forward for licencing. "When they changed the design it drastically changed the potential criticality of the MCAS feature," one FAA specialist said. "And that was not communicated to the FAA engineers who find compliance. In fact they didn't even know about it" (House Committee 2020, 56–84; Robison 2021, 39, 181). On the brink of launch, a senior engineer cognisant of the regulatory non-disclosures told his manager: "Frankly right now all my internal warning bells are going off. For the first time in my life, I'm sorry to say that I'm hesitant about putting my family on a Boeing airplane." He pointed out that the military where he used to work would not tolerate the poor safety margins of such a plane. The manager replied: "The military isn't a profit-making organization" (House Committee 2020, 85–137; Robison 2021, 170).

The risk of take-off low-velocity plane dives caused by the enhanced – and basically untested – fifth iteration of MCAS soon emerged in flights of the new model from its launch in late 2016, but Boeing again buried the adverse information, hoping for the best. When a new 737-MAX crashed in Indonesia on take-off in October 2018, losing all on board, Boeing blamed the pilots, and sent their lawyers to negotiate aggressively in the wake of the crash to force grieving and shocked families of little means to sign away standard rights to full compensation. A second 737-MAX plane then crashed in Ethiopia in March 2019 killing all crew and passengers, exhibiting the exact same instability observed to have been caused by overcompensation by MCAS at low speed with poor feedback to the pilot. After a total of 346 deaths in two crashes within six months, the plane was grounded in all territories outside the United States, but Boeing continued to resist claims that the plane was unsafe, blaming pilot error and failing to acknowledge the MCAS vulnerability. Finally, even the captive FAA was forced to ground the plane in its home country as whistle-blower evidence emerged of the flawed MCAS design, inadequate pilot training, and ensuing cover up.

At a Senate inquiry into the crash in October 2019, the concealment of the MCAS problems was fully aired. Dennis Muilenberg, the chief executive of Boeing, claimed that the problem had never surfaced at the top layer of management, despite abundance evidence that warnings from pilots and engineers had been suppressed within the organization. He claimed that the responsible executives had lacked the intellectual tools to make the correct judgements; that the very complexity of financing, building, and selling modern aircraft would inevitably lead to errors; that no-one could have known that a series of efficiency-driven decisions to maintain Boeing's commercial position would accumulate to cause the disasters; that lessons had been learned, and that every sympathy was felt for the grieving families. Senator Ted Cruz, hardly known for hostility to the corporate world, cut through Boeing's defences, noting with disbelief that even *after* the crashes Boeing had not publicized the MCAS problems nor warned the airline industry, fearing lest orders be cancelled, and market position lost. Cruz made this stark denunciation in confrontation with Muilenberg:

> You're the CEO, the buck stops with you. How did your team not put it in front of you, run in with their hair on fire saying, 'We've got a real problem here'? How did that not happen and what does that say about the culture at Boeing if they didn't give it to you and you didn't read it and say, 'I want to see what happened!' How did you not in February send out a 911 fire alarm to say we need to figure out exactly what happened, not after all the hearings, not after the pressure, but because 346 people have died and we don't want another person to die? (House Committee 2020, 122–137; Robison 2021, 222–23)

In the wake of the scandal there was an exodus of senior management – but no clawback of bonuses, and no prosecutions or disqualifications. Boeing had to mothball its inventory of 737-MAXs, and endure cancelled and withdrawn orders it could ill afford as it had run down its capital stocks to pay out its executives and shareholders. Total losses of over $11 billion caused by the 737-MAX disaster could have been used by Boeing to implement a newly designed model built around the latest safe and efficient technologies, with cash left over. Informing and training pilots properly in the 737-MAX controls to curb the dangers presented by MCAS and correcting the sensor risks that destabilized the system would have amounted to the cost of just one plane. But cost calculus turned out to be inadequate to discipline the company, whether ex ante or ex post. The share price fluctuated between $300 and $400 dollars per share across the key decades of corporate failure – the market seemingly shrugged, calculating that putting out cheapened and badly built planes and then paying out for ensuing death and loss was a cost of business, observing that Boeing's bottom line had remained strong throughout the 737-MAX saga. Boeing went on to lose half its corporate value in the travel freeze caused by Covid-19 and became a mendicant of the state via financial support to the prostrated airlines. The new executives hired to clean up the mess were almost grateful that the blows landed by the pandemic buried the news of Boeing's gross failings and frauds in making the 737-MAX.

Reflecting on what had gone wrong during the crash inquiries in 2019, one Boeing employee messaged: "I still haven't been forgiven by God for the covering up I did last year" (Robison 2021, 168). But the company forgave itself. By 2023 it had rebuilt its workforce to almost pre-pandemic levels, and after posting a $5.64 billion loss in 2020 was making over $3 billion in profit on revenues over $70 billion in each of 2021 and 2022. But its recovery was fragile. In 2023, its order book was depleted, its profit reduced by a third, as its rival Airbus supplanted it in market share. Through 2024 the company was a constant generator of bad news and controversy. In February, a door system manufactured for Boeing by a spinoff company failed; more lax work on 737 doors and fuselages betokening, and inadequate testing and oversight, were again exposed to view; airlines grounded the affected Boeing planes and a whopping 20% of share value was wiped out in just two weeks. In August, the Boeing Starliner, built to ferry astronauts to the International Space Station as a prestigious exercise in aerospace engineering, was grounded with faults, putting the space mission at risk. At least in these latest bouts of engineering failure no-one was killed.

The latter part of the year was marred by massive worker disaffection and widespread industrial action, costing the company close to $6 billion in losses. Debt soared, as money was set aside to improve engineering and production and settle the strikes, further depressing the share price and company value. The corporate leadership acknowledged failings and apologized, executives were moved around or sacked, and new corporate discipline was promised. The latest managers had to stave off a credit downgrade by making a massive issue of fresh stock, raising some $24.3 billion, and the markets absorbed this development with only a small markdown of share price. Hitherto twelfth in the S&P 500 index, by late 2024 Boeing had fallen to ninety-fourth, and on some measures was the worst performing stock of 2024 within the index. Facing new tariff wars, as well as stiff competition from Chinese and European manufacturers and deep unrest in the demoralized workforce, Boeing faces an uphill struggle to recover reliability, reputation, and profitability, with the financial press suggesting that its recent problems may prove terminal for the company, closing a rich chapter of American manufacturing and business history.[2]

Looking back over its proud history, Boeing could well claim to be one of the greatest of corporations of modern times, an exemplar of sophisticated enterprise in the era of American power and prestige. It was long regarded as the pre-eminent airplane manufacturer in the world, almost always leader in the market against its arch-rivals Douglas and Airbus. The corporation earned a superb reputation for engineering and safety, ascribed in large part to its internal organization and work cultures. Design and production teams were keenly focused on information flows and feedback between actors, overcoming the distinction between workers and decision-makers, and encouraging problem solving at all levels. Employees and managers considered themselves as stakeholders responsible for maintaining the corporate entity and enterprise, and were therefore prepared to share information generated from practice in order to construct a working knowledge commons. All of this was lost in the course of just one decade. In the wake of mergers bringing new managerial cultures from the mid 1990s, the independence and security of the workforce were reduced, and cooperation and information flows were disrupted with offshoring and dispersion of design and production – all changes made with a view to increasing shareholder value and executive profit. Lines of communication between teams were broken and worker initiative and input discouraged. Actors from the older information-sharing culture were pushed out, or retreated into internal exile.

Instead of investing in and advancing its proven work practices and technologies, in the 2000s Boeing cheapened all its processes and produced compromised aircraft designs, fraudulently concealing known risks in its products, and putting extraordinary efforts into subverting regulatory controls and cutting back on testing and training costs. Inquiries in the wake of the 737-MAX crashes showed how reduction of the corporation's internal management to a network of antagonistic transactions had displaced the beneficial operation of the corporation as a knowledge commons, defined as an organizational form in which the production and uses of shared knowledge and information is governed collectively and collaboratively. The results were literally fatal. Cost-cutting mistakes were not detected, or not reported, or not acted upon, or intentionally suppressed, and so flaws in design and operation were compounded until major systems failures emerged. So entrenched were the attitudes of mind producing these failures that corrective action proved extremely difficult; destruction proved a lot easier than recovery and fresh creation.

The Boeing history is particularly interesting in demonstrating the importance of information collection, dissemination, and the way in which group minds act on

[2] An event widely commented in the business press reporting: For example, "Fixing Boeing" *Financial Times* January 31, 2024; "Why the FAA Still Can't Fix Boeing" *Wall Street Journal*, February 6, 2024; "Understanding the Boeing Mess" *Wall Street Journal* 19 March 2004; "How Much Trouble is Boing In?" *Economist*, September 19, 2024; "Can Anyone Fix Boeing?" *Financial Times*, October 25, 2024.

available information. The story shows how important corporate cultures can be in permitting the corporation, as carried in the minds of its workers, directors, investors, and wider stakeholders, to know and think clearly, and to predicate well-judged collective action on properly integrated and weighted reasons. The rise and fall of the company may have been shaped by the course of technologies, military needs, consumer tastes, competitive rivals, and other factors specific to the aeronautics industry. But the Boeing history also illustrates transmogrifications in the very nature of the corporation. We need theoretical tools to work through how and why corporations exist, and how they evolve, using the tools of law, economics, philosophy, and history, going beyond the limits of a business case history.

3.3 THE LEGAL PHENOMENOLOGY OF THE CORPORATION

The corporation is an essentially contested concept (Gallie 1956) of legal theory, meaning theorists have proliferated models explaining what a corporation means and how it works, with each theory negating rival theories. We have well-developed fictive, concessionary, real, realist-functionalist, contractarian, proprietary, hierarchical, and fiduciary models of the corporation to choose from. But before this heated dispute can launch, theorists must tacitly agree certain premises that form the basis of everyday corporate life (Harris, 2006; Gindis 2009; Micheler 2021). The corporation acts as an entity created or recognized by law, and bestowed with representational, transactional, and asset-holding capacities. As "an independent person with its rights and liabilities appropriate to itself,"[3] it is legally distinguished from its shareholders, managers, and employees; and the liabilities of the company are not coterminous with those of its members, so that even a single-member company concentrating action and control in a single individual erects a strong legal distinction between the corporate person and its controller. The single-person company can usefully be distinguished from the corporation sole as a governmental or ecclesiastical office; the existence of both casts into doubt the stability of the opposed category of "natural" persons (Getzler 2016a, b).

The corporate form permits lawyers to marshal and coordinate inputs of share and bond capital, management, and labour, and to distribute risk, profit, liability, and control across various participant classes. Historically, the law provided a variety of associational forms (partnerships, trusts, "firms" combining elements of each) that had many attributes of entities, including partial asset partitioning and elaborated governance structures (Getzler and Macnair 2005; Hansmann et al. 2006). However, since the 1880s, with radical extensions of national and international trading, technology-intensive production, heightened division of labour, and intermediated finance, the corporation with discrete legal personality has grown to become the

[3] *Salomon v Salomon & Co Ltd* [1897] AC 22, 30, 51 (HL); Companies Act 2006, Section 16.

pre-eminent legal vehicle enabling collective enterprise and group decision-making, whether in the public, private, or voluntary spheres (Runciman 2023).

In the legal phenomenology of the corporation, we have noted how we typically deploy a distinctive metaphoric language to articulate the roles and responsibilities generated by group action. Juridical sources for this language include ecclesiastical bodies, factors and bailiffs, stewards and agents, trustees and partners, governmental organs, real and personal property forms, and a basic alphabet of private and public law (contract, tort, crime, fiduciaries, officers, etc.). Thus, we have a *body corporate*, founded or subscribed by *members* and run or operated by *directors* and *servants*, whose actions are *attributed* to the *corporate person*, which person may have a *constitution* with limiting and enabling *purposes*, *powers*, and *capacities*, residing in a *seat* but also enjoying *freedom of movement*. The corporate person is governed by a *board*, subject to *account* and *audit*, with steering and control from *shareholders* and *stakeholders*, and in extremis by *receivers* representing creditors, with corporate value embodied in *capital* denominated by *equities* and *bonds*, and with *separate personality* always maintained unless *veil piercing* can be justified.

All of these highlighted concepts are exactly metaphors – "removals" from one legal context to another to do fresh work in structuring collective action. These metaphors constitute the ideational reality in which corporate lawyers live and imagine, providing a means of communication and a reserve of rhetoric deployed to solve – or conceal – persistent problems in the distribution of risks, benefits, and burdens. The legal language is itself a type of common knowledge creating predictable cooperation. Yet problems cannot be wished away when metaphors collide, bringing doctrinal or decisional categories into conflict. For example, courts at the highest level have struggled to reconcile the theory of separate legal personality with the concepts of attribution and fraud-based veil-piercing.[4] Reliance on orthodox nominalist theories of legal meaning[5] has not provided any panacea as parties quarrel over directorial duties, principal–agent problems, conflicts of interest and tunnelling of value, distributional conflict between shareholders, creditors, employees and stakeholders, responsibility for corporate externalities in the physical and social world, and so on (Hart 1954; see also Micheler 2021, 2024).

Granted that it is crucial to master the lawyers' language games in understanding the institution of the corporation, we can usefully deploy social-scientific theories to understand the corporation as a site of social action, abstracting from legal form and consciousness (Deakin et al. 2021). In what follows, various models of the types of group action that underpin the legal corporation are offered up, drawing from business and economic history, microeconomics, rational choice theory, and the

[4] *Stone & Rolls Ltd v Moore Stephens (a firm)* [2009] AC 1391; *Prest v Petrodel Resources Ltd* [2013] 2 AC 415; *Jetivia SA v Bilta* (UK) Limited (in liquidation [2015] UKSC 23.

[5] *Meridian Global Funds Management Asia Ltd v Securities Commission* (1995) 2 AC 500 (PC), [6]-[18] per Lord Hoffmann.

GKC framework. The mutual exchange between legal theory and social scientific modelling can only benefit both modes of discourse (Gindis and Micheler 2024).

3.4 CATHEDRAL OR FACTORY, BAZAAR OR COMMUNE?

The modern idea of the corporation emerges from Fordist models of corporate organization, identified by Adolf Berle and Gardiner Means on the cusp of the New Deal (Berle and Means 1932) and later studied in depth by Alfred Chandler (Chandler 1977, 1990). It connotes a hierarchical organization with stated purposes and capabilities, run by personnel with clearly specified roles and authority, with tradeable or substitutable joint stock capital structure separating management from ownership, and above all bestowed by state law with separate legal personality, allowing a stable and focussed legal framework for corporate activity no matter what the present membership of the group, and moreover promoting a rational distribution of risk, liability, and profit between investors, operatives, and creditor classes. The Berle and Means ideal model was a creature of its time, and is only one of many possibilities thrown into play by legal evolution. Business history teaches us to take a longer and broader view of the phenomena of corporate organization, and decentre the hierarchical limited liability company from our account of collective enterprise (Deakin 2012). The classic corporation then takes its place as one of maybe four ideal types: the cathedral, the factory, the bazaar, and the commune.[6]

First imagine tightly knit work groups, embodying skills and craft built up by reiterative training and emulation, organized in self-regulating and cartelizing guilds, headed by the most senior and experienced workers with the knowledge and authority to plan joint effort – like the teams that built the great medieval cathedrals. The embedded skills and capital of the workforce take time to cultivate and are not interchangeable or easily summoned from the market, and so work relations must be consultative and cooperative (Epstein 1998). Cartel and craft traditions will guide admission to the group and the ensuing division of tasks and rewards and the maintenance of standards (Brentano 1870; see Ogilvie 2019); and there will be a strong ethos of shared values, rituals, and regard for colleagues holding the group together (Black 1984). In modern times, examples of such community governance may include a multiparty professional practice, an academic faculty or college, an orchestra, a joint venture, a closely held partnership.

A second class of enterprise will deploy a less-skilled workforce, stripped of craft and discretion, harnessed as contractually hired operatives of fixed-cost technologies. Such a labour force will surrender discretion and power to management, which is also contractually appointed, but on more advantageous terms. In the classical factory, the workforce submits to the organization in a centralized plant with strong

[6] Adapting metaphorical analysis from the maverick open-source programmer Eric Steven Raymond's (1999) book, *The Cathedral and the Bazaar*.

monitoring and discipline to coordinate inputs, maintain chains of production, and repress shirking. As the corporate enterprise grows in scale and scope, it will seek capital from external sources and insiders will share some level of control and profit with outside investors. Division of control leads to juridification or specification of rules distributing levels of profit share, managerial power, residual claims, and risk as between the various factions providing capital and labour to the enterprise. Here we have the classic corporation with highly specified division of labour and rigid separation of labour and capital, with control distributed between managers and investors with differential levels of profit, risk, and residual claims set down by rules, often highly juridified (for neoclassical, radical, and game-theoretic accounts building on the Berle and Means model, see respectively Alchian and Demsetz 1972; Marglin 1974; Clark 1994). The economic origins lie not only with the factory enterprise of early industrialism but also capital-intensive enterprises such as utilities and railways (Kostal 1997), then spreading across the economy by the early twentieth century as the conveniences of focused representation of the enterprise in the market as a capital-raising and contracting device become clear (Johnson 2010).

For our third ideal type, there are more open forms of group activity, uncoordinated and even rivalrous, with plenty of opportunities for voice, exit, and loyalty, yielding indeterminate personnel of varying commitment, together with changing assets, powers, and capabilities. For illustration take a bazaar or fair, comprising nested adjoining enterprises within a unifying market space and some acknowledged adjudicator to maintain standards (Milgrom et al. 1990). Examples can include construction and retail platforms, securities brokerages, and much of today's digital and gig economy (Buttrick 1952; Williamson 1975; Eccles 1981).

The fourth ideal type of communal organization is marked by personalized bonds and common purposes. It may be integrated by co-ownership, co-determination, and some level of shared life vision, often with the individual members subordinated to the power of a representative individual, such as the monastery of abbot and monks, the family with children and servants, the manorial or village community, the Roman *universitatis*, the ship and crew, military units and other arms of the state. Other forms may be less hierarchical, including various types of condominium from joint tenancies and associative trusts to cooperatives and kibbutzim (Ellickson 1993).

These four types are not mutually exclusive; a guild may buttress its identity by associative marriage (model 1 plus 4); a family firm may provide the nucleus for a wider professional practice or industrial enterprise with outside private investors (model 4 plus 2); and so on. Historical determinants of corporate organization will include types of technology, extent of market trades, division of labour, capital needs, risk pooling, integration of supply chains, demand structure, and so on. Modern monopolistic corporations can create vast hybrids of all four ideal corporate types, driven by new embedded technologies of industrial production and digital communication. Legal form is probative but not conclusive: associational forms deploy contractual, proprietary, fiduciary, chartered and statutory rights, duties, liabilities, and powers in any manner of combination. And the production of rules and norms to govern the collective can be internal/private/market; external/impersonal/state; communal/local/ collective; or a hybridization of all elements (Dekker and Kuchař 2024).

Historical stylizing of group action using these ideal types contrasts with neoclassical economic models of the "firm," which embraces almost any collective enterprise with a governance structure and representative agents, from a multinational corporation to a two-person household. The corporation is seen as a system to allow coordination and monitoring where reiterative contracting between sole agents cannot yield more complex and embedded cooperation (Coase 1937; Jensen and Meckling 1976; Becker 1981; Williamson 1985). Corporate hierarchy replaces costly and incomplete market transactions, but competition between interacting parties – management, owners, labour, suppliers, creditors, consumers – continues inside the corporation, yielding constant dynamic change in the corporate structure of accountability and control. The basic model does not map or explain the wide array of corporate forms that flourish and persist across time. One way to explain this complexity is to investigate the specific historical determinants of firms on a sectoral basis, and then generalize by induction as to the types of law, administration, and bonding needed to maintain effective collective enterprise (Chandler 1977, 1990; Ostrom 1990; Harris, 2000 & 2020; Hansmann et al. 2006; Cheffins, 2008, 2018; Ribstein 2010; Guinnane et al. 2017). Another way is to proceed deductively, exploring the kind of coordination problems that fall to be solved by firm or corporation structures. A productive dialogue can then follow, measuring the logical problems of collective coordination against the historical evidence of legal and business organization. We continue next on the more analytical and deductive track.

3.5 AGGREGATING PREFERENCES AND SOCIAL CHOICE

Thomas Hobbes early isolated the rational defection problem with his observation that transacting parties will be incentivized to breach cooperative covenants in order to forestall reciprocal breach and exploitation by the counterparty. Private monitoring and enforcement is expensive and uncertain and can lead to a fruitless arms race and diversion of resources to protection and even warfare rather than cooperative production and trade. A strong enforcing state was the dominant solution needed to repress defections most efficiently, though that state might itself become a source of disutility (Hobbes 1651, chs 17–22; see also Piccione and Rubinstein 2007). Economists and political scientists have softened this étatist logic by propounding models of how beneficent market trades and complex cooperation may be guaranteed where basic entitlements to bodily integrity and security of assets are secured by a mix of law or custom (Ostrom et al. 1992).

Ronald Coase's theory of the firm is a variant from or alternative to this post-Hobbesian school of thought. Economists such as Coase tend to use the term "firm" stylistically to mean any collective enterprise with a governance structure, from a family or a partnership to a multinational corporation or corporate group. For our purposes the firm and the corporation can be merged; the chief hallmark is the structured direction of resources, including labour inputs within the firm and univocal representation to counterparties without the firm, and it does not matter here that a firm may lack juridical corporate attributes such as perpetual succession, separate legal personality, limited liability, defensive asset partitioning, and so on; the law is apt to provide surrogate methods supplying the necessary tools (Hansmann et al. 2006).

Coase's seminal contribution to legal-institutional analysis was to identify transaction costs as intrinsic to the organization of collective action within the market economy. Bilateral and multilateral transacting may be impeded by search, negotiation, monitoring and enforcement costs, and beyond that by holdouts, free-riding, and incomplete contracting as impediments to efficient trades. Coase distanced himself from the rational defection or opportunism strand of analysis; people could rationally agree to cooperate if only given the right tools for the job. A limited state capable of providing the correct institutions for asset-definition enhancing production and trade should be devised as a constitutive order, for the citizenry themselves to then operate outside state discretion. The two pre-eminent solutions to transaction cost barriers identified by Coase were clear legal definition of assets to promote fluid trades and internalization of externalities, and the organization of more complex production through hierarchy within the firm. The first limb of fluid competition through trade would then discipline the larger corporate units summoned into existence under the second limb where it was necessary to displace contract entirely (Coase 1988).

The Coasean firm can be conceived as a miniature version of Hobbes' commonwealth, which solves the problems of fragile and ineffective covenanting by adding a factor of external enforcement by command, with the sovereign commonwealth itself constrained by competition with other like commonwealths. The genius of Coase was to create a suggestive and elegant model of how a combination of commercial and employment contracts with more hierarchical corporate governance could guarantee the liberal market economy without tipping into greater state regulation; his hostility to the state as expressed in his attack on Pigovian regulation of externalities does not extend to the state as a definer of property rights and guarantor of a private market for trading and reconfiguration of those rights.

Both the Hobbesian macro-model and the Coasean micro-model then regress to the question of how rational actors might aggregate preferences in the first place to make group action setting up the corporation/commonwealth as a form of durable cooperation. Even if we see the firm as a nexus of contracts taking place within a collective setting that makes complex multiplayer trades across time possible, we still have to explain how the group could be set up to discharge its mission in the first place, without defection, conflict, or chaos (cf. Posner 1993, who suggests that Coase himself did not fully grasp the strategic bargaining issues implicit in his transaction cost theory). How can an ordered group emerge in the first place through a process of aggregation of wills in the absence of a command system imposing order? Coase explains the need for, but not the genesis of the corporation.

So we must return to the basic question of group agency – how a collection of disparate wills can act with a unified intentionality where there are mutual effects from any one individual's decision-making in relation to others. Ostrom denoted interactive behaviour jointly producing outcomes as "action situations," suggesting a wide array of techniques to see how institutional and social factors govern such behaviours (Ostrom 2005, 32–68). One important caveat was evoked in Kenneth Arrow's impossibility theorem, showing that collective action logically cannot be evolved by a simple aggregation of individual wants. His analysis predicts that group decision-making by summation of ordinal or ranked preferences must decline into sterile cycling of choices and self-veto, since any possible choice set is matched by equivalent choice sets; summation of contending preferences simply produces decisional noise (Arrow 1951, precursed by Condorcet 1785). The collective fails because it cannot logically produce a collective will.

There are many solutions to the impossibility paradox, for example, a meta-choice architecture provided by compelling leadership, or a culture of give and take, or education and convergence of tastes. Furthermore, if preferences are given cardinal weights, then agents may sell or gift their lightly held choices to others and so build coalitions in order to achieve their weightier goals; a pricing mechanism is an obvious way to achieve this, permitting votes to be sold. Or A may wield charismatic (or traditional or rational or other species of) authority and persuade the others to emulate A's preferences or simply fall into line; or A may enjoy a weighted vote as the creator of the group; or members of a group may agree to take turns directing the group in a reiterative play, and this week is A's turn (Arrow 1974). The Arrovian model both articulates the frailty of aggregation as a foundation of collective choice, and hints at ways in which that frailty can be escaped and group action might emerge, and these insights have clear applications in understanding the functionality of the corporation. But we need more work to see how that function of successful aggregation can be achieved.

3.6 COLLEGIAL AND DISCURSIVE RATIONALITY

This theory, associated with Philip Pettit amongst others (List and Pettit 2011), goes beyond simple aggregation of wills as summative votes, instead postulating collegial decision-making by a group where any decision is passed through stages of simple voting concerning its articulated parts, a process denoted as "discursive rationality." To illustrate, imagine three partners in an aeroplane engineering firm voting on whether to invest in the sequential production activities shown in Table 3.1.

TABLE 3.1 *An illustration of discursive rationality*

	Plane engines (1)	Plane bodies (2)	Plane interiors (3)	Complete planes (1) + (2) + (3)
Andrew	NO	YES	YES	NO
Boris	YES	NO	YES	NO
Charles	YES	YES	NO	NO
Firm	**YES**	**YES**	**YES**	**YES**

We may stipulate as elements of the thought experiment that the members' votes are rational, informed, and committed, rather than arbitrary, anonymous, private, and unsystematic in the sense of non-interdependent (no vote trading or discussion leading to imitation or herding). In the instant case, none of the members have voted for all three ingredients or predicates that when summed would yield the fourth aggregate decision. And consistently with their two-out-of -three staged votes for the components, none choose individually to vote for the complete plane option. But at each stage of the voting, a majority assents to the production of each of the component elements; and when these discursive elements subjected to staged group votes are added together along the bottom row, the group has seemingly voted for the aggregate, even though no individual in the group subjectively wants that aggregate. So at the same time the group objectively wills by voting to make the complete planes, but none of the members of the group taken as individuals want to do so. This discursive reasoning paradox has been applied to the very different terrains of collegial judgement aggregation (Kornhauser and Sager 1986, 1993; Chapman 1994, 1998), and to corporate decision-making (Rock 2006, extended to unincorporated associations and trusts by Getzler 2008).

List and Pettit supply an external solution to the discursive rationality paradox based on a notion of the "group agent" (List and Pettit 2011). When a group cannot survive without speaking and acting as one in the world, minority reports are suppressed, that is, the group (or the external rule-maker constituting the group) does not allow dissents, splits, or vetoes by members negating aggregate decisions yielded by the discursive reasoning they each participated in; and as a result group responsibility for collective action is legitimated and enforced. To use a different nomenclature, loyalty not voice is the rule, perhaps with exit or dissolution of the group as a safety valve (Hirschman 1970). The group that functions as a univocal united entity behaves and thinks as a distinct agent; a group mind emerges distinct from its component minds, and is capable of forming motivations and representing those motives through conduct addressed outwardly; and those representations and motivations compel the members' accession and accountability even if not adopted by the members as individuals.

How this measure of univocalism as the essence of agenthood is generated may be an empirical question. There may be strong bonding conventions setting boundaries to the common sense action of the group, as in a religious community or guild or professional association, so that contrary thoughts cannot be formulated that are inconsistent with identity and belonging. Alternatively, there may be conditions of majoritarian dictatorship where minority reports and vetoes are suppressed coercively rather than suspended by agreement, and here no group mind truly emerges; only the leader's mind is expressed with the subjects falling into line. Distinguishing such a collective based on a dictatorial and coercive power as opposed to a cooperative group with agency may be difficult. Groups, in business and production as well as in political life, may oscillate between conditions of free and dominated relations. At its best, the legally regulated corporation may be seen as a device to maintain freedom of association, communication, and ratiocination within durable groups, applying discursive rationality both to maintain internal debate and to discipline and contain group thought and action. The group agent may thereby attain a real if limited personhood, a distinct collective mind yielding agent responsibility for collective conduct (List and Pettit 2011, 170–185; Chiao 2014). The discursive rationality model thereby offers solutions to some impasses left by the Coasean standard model, namely, how a command structure can exist compatible with the plurality of wills of free participants in the corporation.

3.7 FORMING SHARED KNOWLEDGE TO FOUND AND RUN THE FIRM

Another way to unpack the theory of the firm involves study of mechanisms for durable commitment of resources sufficient to attain larger collective goals over lengthier time frames (Offer 2022). Not only capital has to be locked into firm structure but also personal attention and efforts of members of the corporation (Blair 2003, Roberts 2004). Aligning scarce finance, fixed capital, know-how and technology, managerial and labour skills, and supply and distribution chains may require a stable, integrated corporation that slows circulation, builds and enforces loyalty, and regulates exit. Or to put the same point negatively, problems of strategic bargaining and defection can be limited if all parties must make an initial commitment of time and value to the group to join in the enterprise, and then police that commitment effectively (Alchian and Demsetz 1972). We can link this set of issues to the prior point about formation of a group agent – parties must know that there is a rewarding game to be played so that the effort of forming a group agent and then committing resources to it is worth more than the alternatives (just as committing to marriage and forming the "us" of a family can be superior to the freedom of continuous singlehood with constantly negotiated alliances).

This yields an epistemic problem: how can actors gather the information to conceive and construct a successful lock-in operation, and then make it run without disintegration? The problem can be divided into two steps: first, which information can be gathered to stipulate the form of corporation, its terrain of operation, and its necessary initial commitment of resources? And once up and running, how is information harvested by the corporate actors and rendered useful in the effective continuation of the corporation? Arguably, we need a theory of aggregation of information as a prior to a theory of successful group formation and administration. There are several theoretical possibilities, each with distinct implications for corporate organization.

3.7.1 *Dispersed Knowledge: No-One Knows*

Friedrich von Hayek postulated in 1945 that useful economic knowledge was *dispersed* through the economy in such chaotic or discontinuous bundles that it could not rationally be sampled, captured, processed, and computed by any single intelligence: "The peculiar character of the problem of a rational economic order is determined precisely by the fact that the knowledge of the circumstances of which we must make use never exists in concentrated or integrated form but solely as the dispersed bits of incomplete and frequently contradictory knowledge, which all the separate individuals possess" (Hayek 1945, 519).

This assertion of unknowability was partly a polemic against the omniscient state production planning and demand management advocated by socialists and social liberals, arguing that there could be no objective estimation of a knowable economic reality divorced from price observations cultivated by the spontaneous order of a market regulated wholly by the free interactions of supply and demand (Boettke et al. 2010). Hayek's price information epistemology took on a life of its own as a guide to economic life (Mirowski and Nik-Khah 2017). For Hayekians the decentralized free market was the superb solution to the intrinsic unknowability of reality, which unfolds as actors incrementally experiment with trades that uncover and generate information useful locally to themselves and others. The complex adaptive system of the larger economy was comprised of sites of useful local knowledge, where entrepreneurs could link up separate networks of information to produce larger production systems, up to a limit where market information failed and inefficiencies set in (Vaughn 1999). The brilliant model of decentralized experimentation with disordered and subjective knowledge, viewing cooperation between unknowing individuals as only possible through the price mechanism, perfected the Smithian metaphor of the invisible hand and gave renewed vigour to the anti-collectivist movement. The model explained away or ignored the salience of unpredictable and disruptive events, including wars, revolutions, market crashes, and natural disasters, or unforeseen ripples and cascades of reactive and interactive behaviour on a smaller or local scale.

Hayekian information economics does not instantly reveal reasons why the local processing of market information should be situated within vertically or horizontally integrated corporations. One answer is that the birth and death of firms is a constant exercise in group informational experimentation: when the group's structure prevents it from discovering or predicting relevant price information in changing circumstances, the corporation dies or is displaced by newcomers.[7] Hayek goes so far as to describe a "natural selection" of groups, mirroring individual market competition but also shaped by cultural evolution. Uncertainty and risk in internal price information flows are an aspect of the principal–agent problem, and firms must calibrate internal relations within the firm to maintain incentives for price discovery without rivalries destroying trust and cooperation (Dew et al. 2004; Lewis 2017). To sum up, *no-one* knows all relevant information in any complete form, but the market as a sum of traders' activities learning about each other's reactions "knows" in a heuristic impersonal sense as a group mind; and corporations as a subset of the market gather, interpret, and act on information productively until they fail.

As a lemma to the Hayekian theory, all state action and regulation presuming to know better than individuals and corporations engaging and experimenting in markets to generate profits was doomed to failure or worse; étatism driven by sectoral interests and distributional justice claims would only repress good information flows about profitable activity and so produce misleading hypotheses about social reality. Yet Hayek did not clearly explain how an unguided and decentralized process of pricing would always yield useful information promoting efficient aggregate allocations; the negative attack on planning was matched by unwavering confidence in the virtues of the price mechanism (Sunstein 2023).[8] This makes it difficult to account for the Coasean corporation displacing decentralized pricing with collective and hierarchical administration. Corporations might be useful simply by scaling up the automaticity of price arbitrage so that market cultures can be expanded into utilities and public goods more generally. But there remains doubt as to whether the scope and scale of the corporation can really be explained in a Hayekian world of dispersed knowledge as superior to a purely contractual world of individuals participating in factor markets, using principal–agent relations ad hoc rather than surrendering a good deal of freedom of contract by locking into corporate hierarchies. In a Hayekian world of dispersed knowledge, why does the corporation know what's best for the many individuals who comprise the group? (Foss 1999).

3.7.2 *Distributed Knowledge: The Wise Person Knows*

An alternative view of knowledge sees more room for both corporate–private-sphere and state–public-sphere aggregation and processing of information, yielding more fluent cooperation and rational planning based on that information. If we substitute *distributed* knowledge for Hayekian dispersed knowledge, we can model a set of actors

7 Examples besides Boeing losing to Airbus include English carmakers overtaken by Japanese, American, and German firms.

8 Although Hayek's basic epistemic argument in favour of the market does not typically engage with modern research into strategic bargaining, bounded rationality, and behavioural economics more generally, Hayek's later work made substantial room for the idea that ecological rationality and culture supplement the price mechanism in its guidance of choice (Rizzo 2016; Caldwell and Klausinger 2022).

who each have a degree of access to true and valuable information that they can interpret, providing them with a useful subset partaking of the total information that represents the opportunities and choices of the real economy. It is not that the world is an unknowable chaos; it is just difficult to assemble the interlocking information out there and process it into a rational account and basis for action. But a wise person (one skilled in interpretation of information, a kind of meta-knowledge as a basis of judgement) who is positioned at the central node of an organization receiving data from all the branches and extremities of the organization will be able to convert distributed and useless information into integrated and useful information, and then redistribute it to those who can use it best (Demsetz 1988; Casson 1994). Or actors within the corporation can more easily trade useful gathered and cultivated knowledge and so bind each into cooperation through mutually beneficial information sharing. This process of information exchange creates decision rules and practices that are themselves useful forms of internal corporate knowledge or meta-knowledge (knowledge about knowledge). The corporation as a bureaucratic hierarchy therefore exists as a mechanism to harvest and produce distributed knowledge and share its fruits effectively (Nickerson and Zenger 2004; Madison et al. 2010).

As an extrapolation of this model, the state can itself be an effective corporation making decisions based on distributed knowledge across the gamut of production, consumption, and regulation. The dark side of the model is the problem of asymmetric information and limited knowledge leading to principal–agent problems and conflicted interests, a deformation of the internal knowledge rules of the firm. But healthy corporate cultures promoting *knowledge commons* may spur the parties as information collectors and knowledge sharers to keep on the right side of cooperation. Trusted information interpreters can provide leadership for the group that curbs defections and promotes further information contributing to the knowledge commons (Aghion and Tirole 1997; Foss 1999; Ostrom and Hess 2007).

3.7.3 *Common Knowledge: Any Fool Knows*

The notion of *common knowledge* (which is quite distinct from the knowledge commons idea that closed the previous section) was developed by David Lewis, Robert Aumann, and John Harsyani in the mid twentieth century, and is a subtle tool of game theory addressing the problem of meta-knowledge. Common knowledge, sometimes described as nested knowledge, is defined by Ken Binmore as follows:

> Something is common knowledge if everybody knows it; everybody knows that everybody knows it; everybody knows that everybody knows that everybody knows it; and so on. Game theorists usually assume that the rules of the game and the preferences of the players are common knowledge. … [T]hey typically need also to assume that the fact that all the players subscribe to appropriate rationality principles is also common knowledge. (Binmore 1991, 150)

Common knowledge theory teaches two incompatible lessons. First, no plurality of actors can cooperate if they do not have at least some common knowledge of each other's rational principles for conduct, even if they do not share knowledge of the external world nor have congruent tastes and ambitions. The problem of finding cooperation between two actors whose minds are partially closed to each other is rapidly accelerated with multiple actors who may not be in bilateral proximity to all other members and must make delegations of trust to ensure that all parties in the group share basic protocols of rational action and cooperation/non-cooperation. If Johnny only has experience of people who predictably betray and expect others to betray, then he cannot easily cooperate with Mary, who naïvely believes that she will always be true and trustworthy and that others will reciprocate with trustworthiness. But how are parties like Mary to find other Marys to repose trust in – and how to avoid or sanction the low-trust Johnnys, who may simulate trust in order to practice the guile that comes more naturally? (Geanakoplos 1992; Fagin et al. 1995).

To explore the selection problem that disturbs the production of common knowledge, let us divert to a story by Zhuangzi, an intellectual from the time of the Warring States in ancient China c. 300 BCE and a founder of Taoism (Zhuangzi 2003, ch 17):

> Zhuangzi and Huizi were enjoying themselves on the bridge over the Hao River. Zhuangzi said, "The minnows are darting about free and easy! This is how fish are happy." Huizi replied, "You are not a fish. How do you know that the fish are happy?" Zhuangzi said, "You are not I. How do you know that I do not know that the fish are happy?" Huizi said, "I am not you, to be sure, so of course I don't know about you. But you obviously are not a fish; so the case is complete that you do not know that the fish are happy." Zhuangzi said, "Let's go back to the beginning of this. You said, How do you know that the fish are happy; but in asking me this, you already knew that I know it. I know it right here above the Hao."

As the friends probe each other's mental equipment they realize they cannot establish the conditions of common knowledge. Indeed, they cannot agree in the possibility of mutually understood belief and action; even believable communication between differently constituted actors may be out of reach. Only the most basic of mutual knowledge is available to us in everyday life – the stuff that "any fool knows" – and such basic shared and known-to-be-shared information may not be rich enough to mount decent cooperation and inter-subjective belief.

Another surprising common knowledge result was uncovered by Aumann in 1976. His "Agreeing to Disagree" model states that when A and B agree as to the *canons of interpretation* they use in estimating the probability of events in the world – and each knows the other knows they hold that canon, and knows of that mutual canonic knowledge, and so on – then they cannot disagree as to their *beliefs* about some fact or decision eventuating, even if they use private or exclusive, non-shared information in arriving at those beliefs (Aumann 1976; Aoki 2010; Deakin 2011). They must each assume that the other person will rationally converge on the same answer as they gather in more facts to trial using their prior shared heuristic. Thus, two investors with the same mental equipment would assume that their pricing of a stock will come out the same given enough information to process – even if they use variant information.

If Aumann's model is robust, then it disrupts Hayek's dispersed knowledge hypothesis; parties need not hold on to the same information to find agreement provided they can generate sufficient common knowledge. But if the common knowledge model does pertain in real life, then it does not explain why there is so much interpretative disagreement about facts in the world, resulting in failures to reach potentially beneficial market trades, or even outright destructive conflict. One rejoinder (not a solution) to Aumann's paradox is to acknowledge that there are not enough commonly known or shared heuristics in market society. A more menacing alternative conclusion is that there may be a good deal of common knowledge in the world, but that what is held in common is a mutual expectation that parties will be uncooperative or conflictual in their relationships. The challenge is then to evolve the shared heuristic so the parties can attain a common knowledge promoting cooperation.

Ostrom's field work (Ostrom 1990, 2010) showed how groups can overcome the "social dilemma" that rational strangers competing for resources might share a sensible belief that they ought not to trust each other. She described a number of instances where groups learnt how to enjoy a common pool resource together where it was difficult to stint access and impossible to monitor investment in the pool, averting a tragedy of the commons. High trust cooperation became possible where certain conditions were in place: easy multilateral communication, obvious means of monitoring reputations and defections, observation of how defection caused mutual harm and how cooperation caused mutual benefit, ability to exit and so not feel trapped by the misbehaviour of others, and finally internal sanctions that worked by invoking self-policing through mental and emotional commitment and not just through fear of external punishment. Ostrom showed how effective governance of commons in turn deepened the common knowledge of its participants, their ability to buttress each other's mutual belief in cooperation. The problem lies in finding how to engineer frameworks that promote such qualities and encourage the benign evolution and preservation of such a commons.

The corporation as a platform of communication (learning by speaking, and listening) and of exemplary interactive behaviours (learning by watching, and doing together) exists to establish a knowledge commons, which in turn cultivates common knowledge in the sense of trusted mutual prediction. The corporation as a knowledge commons thus makes complex cooperation possible where people know different things that they cannot explain to each other, yet can share sufficient mental equipment to help each other get along (Kogut and Zander 1996). The corporation makes business possible between those who would otherwise be strangers, extending the range of cooperation beyond tight family and friend memberships so as to embrace those distant to us in time, space, and culture. The corporation may be strongest when blurring the lines between cathedrals and factories, between bazaars and communes. The corporation succeeds as a knowledge commons with the key task of promoting common knowledge. It dies when the parties to the corporation no longer share what they know nor know what they share.

We began with the exemplary story of the rise and fall of Boeing. That story showed how important cooperative knowledge-sharing was in the long decades of success of the company, and how easily that success could be dissipated when information flows and frank communications were blocked, and fearless interpretations repressed. The knowledge commons was swiftly undone, and common knowledge within the corporation collapsed as participants fell into silent internal exile, blocking the potential for the group to recover itself.

3.8 ENVOI

What do corporations do? Conventional legal and economic analysis looking for rules and incentives to foster cooperation may not reveal the epistemic dimensions of this question. Amongst other activities, corporations teach individuals to think, to know, to communicate, and to predict together as a prelude to durable cooperation. The healthiest organizations may combine elements of each of the four identified types of corporative association under one roof, permitting a variety of epistemic forms, and not allow an exaggerated version of type 2, the deskilled hierarchical corporation, to dominate. The past thirty years of the cult of shareholder value as the dominant corporate purpose, and the reduction of the corporation's internal management to a network of antagonistic transactions, has caused obvious damage to the beneficial operation of corporations as information brokerages and decision vehicles. The self-evisceration of the Boeing Company demonstrates this decline all too starkly. We can multiply examples from the recent past of corporate failures to know and to act, and the inadequacy of regulation to maintain standards: Lehman and the rest of the rotten banking sector in 2008; Volkswagen in 2015; building cladding regulation in 2017; PPE procurement in 2019; and the British water industry now. The list of corporate pathologies is dauntingly long, but could it get worse? We face a world of transformed interconnectedness and information harvesting driven by the new data and media networks of the past two decades, shaped by algorithmic processing and machine learning that filters and orders social information in order to maximize profit and control for a corporate elite (Zuboff 2019; Eidenmüller and Wagner 2021; Bant 2023; Runciman 2023). It is possible to describe the new corporate world as an enclosure of the knowledge commons, yielding a common knowledge based not on respectful cooperation but on submission and hierarchy. Whether such a fifth type of corporation, whose ethos is spreading into the institutions of the state, can be durable or even workable will swiftly be put to the test.

REFERENCES

Aghion, Philippe, and Jean Tirole. 1997. "Formal and Real Authority in Organizations." *Journal of Political Economy* 105(1): 1–29.

Alchian, Armen A., and Harold Demsetz. 1972. "Production, Information Costs, and Economic Organization." *American Economic Review* 62(5): 777–795.

Aoki, Masahiko. 2010. *Corporations in Evolving Diversity: Cognition, Governance, and Institutional Rules*. Oxford: Oxford University Press.

Arrow, Kenneth J. 1951. *Social Choice and Individual Values*. New Haven: Yale University Press.

Arrow, Kenneth J. 1974. *The Limits of Organization*. New York: W. W. Norton.

Aumann, Robert J. 1976. "Agreeing to Disagree." *Annals of Statistics* 4(6): 1236–1239.

Bant, Elise, ed. 2023. *The Culpable Corporate Mind*. Oxford: Hart Publishing.

Becker, Gary S. 1981. A *Treatise on the Family*. Cambridge, MA: Harvard University Press.

Berle, Adolf A. and Gardiner C. Means. 1932. *The Modern Corporation and Private Property*. New York: Harcourt, Brace & World.

Binmore, Ken. 1991. *Fun and Games: A Text on Game Theory*. Lexington, MA: Heath.

Black, Antony. 1984. *Guild and State: European Political Thought from the Twelfth Century to the Present*. Ithaca: Cornell University Press.

Blair, Margaret M. 2003. "Locking in Capital: What Corporate Law Achieved for Business Organizers in the Nineteenth Century." *UCLA Law Review* 51(2): 387–455.

Boeing. 2024. *Boeing History Chronology*. www.boeing.com/content/dam/boeing/boeingdot com/history/pdf/Boeing-Chronology.pdf.

Boettke, Peter J, Emily C. Shaeffer, and Nicholas A. Snow. 2010. "The Context of Context: The Evolution of Hayek's Epistemic Turn in Economics and Politics." *Advances in Austrian Economics* 14: 69–86.

Brentano, Lujo. 1870. *On the History and Development of Gilds, and the Origin of Trade-Unions*. London: Trübner.

Buttrick, John. 1952. "The Inside Contract System." *Journal of Economic History* 12(3): 205–221.

Caldwell, Bruce, and Hansjoerg Klausinger. 2022. *Hayek: A Life 1899–1950*. Chicago: University of Chicago Press.

Casson, Mark. 1994. "Why Are Firms Hierarchical?" *Journal of the Economics of Business* 1(1): 47–76.

Chandler, Alfred D. 1977. *The Visible Hand: The Managerial Revolution in American Business*. Cambridge, MA: Harvard University Press.

Chandler, Alfred D. 1990. *Scale and Scope: The Dynamics of Industrial Capitalism*. Cambridge, MA: Harvard University Press.

Chapman, Bruce. 1998. "More Easily Done than Said: Rules, Reasons, and Rational Social Choice." *Oxford Journal of Legal Studies* 18(2): 293–329.

Chapman, Bruce. 1994. "The Rational and the Reasonable: Social Choice Theory and Adjudication." *University of Chicago Law Review* 61(1): 41–122.

Cheffins, Brian R. 2008. *Corporate Ownership and Control: British Business Transformed*. Oxford: Oxford University Press.

Cheffins, Brian R. 2018. *The Public Company Transformed*. Oxford: Oxford University Press.

Chiao, Vincent. 2014. "List and Pettit on Group Agency and Group Responsibility." *University of Toronto Law Journal* 64(5): 753–770.

Clark, Gregory. 1994. "Factory Discipline." *Journal of Economic History* 54(1): 128–163.

Cloud, Dana L. 2011. *We Are the Union: Democratic Unionism and Dissent at Boeing*. Champaign: University of Illinois Press.

Coase, Ronald H. 1937. "The Nature of the Firm." *Economica* 4(16): 386–405.

Coase, Ronald H. 1988. *The Firm, the Market and the Law*. Chicago: University of Chicago Press.

Condorcet, Nicolas de 1785. *Essai sur l'application de l'analyse à la probabilité des décisions rendues à la pluralité des voix*. Paris: Imprimerie Royale.

Deakin, Simon. 2011. "Legal Evolution: Integrating Economic and Systemic Approaches." *Review of Law and Economics* 7(3): 659–683.

Deakin, Simon. 2012. "The Corporation as Commons: Rethinking Property Rights, Governance and Sustainability in the Business Enterprise." *Queen's Law Journal* 37(2): 339–381.

Deakin, Simon, David Gindis, and Geoffrey M. Hodgson. 2021. "What Is a Firm? A Reply to Jean-Philippe Robé." *Journal of Institutional Economics* 17(5): 861–871.

Dekker, Erwin, and Pavel Kuchař. 2024. "Markets and Knowledge Commons: Is There a Difference between Private and Community Governance of Markets?" *Public Choice* 201(3–4): 533–553.

Demsetz, Harold. 1988. "The Theory of the Firm Revisited." *Journal of Law, Economics, and Organization* 4(1): 141–161.

Dew, Nicholas, S. Ramakrishna Velamuri, and Sankaran Venkatarama, 2004. "Dispersed Knowledge and an Entrepreneurial Theory of the firm." *Journal of Business Venturing* 19(5): 659–679.

Eccles, Robert G. 1981. "The Quasifirm in the Construction Industry." *Journal of Economic Behavior & Organization* 2(4): 335–357.

Eidenmüller, Horst, and Gerhard Wagner. 2021. *Law By Algorithm*. Tübingen: Mohr Siebeck.

Ellickson, Robert C. 1993. "Property in Land." *Yale Law Journal* 102(6): 1315–1400.

Epstein, Stephan R. 1998. "Craft Guilds, Apprenticeship, and Technological Change in Preindustrial Europe." *Journal of Economic History*, 58(3): 684–713.

Fagin, Ronald, Joseph Y. Halpern, Yoram Moses, and Moshe Y. Vardi. 1995. *Reasoning about Knowledge*. Cambridge, MA: MIT Press.

Foss, Nicolai J. 1999. "The Use of Knowledge in Firms." *Journal of Institutional and Theoretical Economics* 155(3): 458–486.

Frischmann, Brett M., Michael J. Madison, and Katherina J. Strandburg, eds. 2014. *Governing Knowledge Commons*. New York: Oxford University Press

Gallie, Walter B. 1956. "Essentially Contested Concepts." *Proceedings of the Aristotelian Society* 56: 167–198.

Geanakoplos, John. 1992. "Common Knowledge." *Journal of Economic Perspectives* 6(4): 53–82.

Getzler, Joshua. 2008. "Plural Ownership, Funds, and the Aggregation of Wills." *Theoretical Inquiries in Law* 10(1): 241–270.

Getzler, Joshua. 2016a. "Frederic William Maitland – Trust and Corporation." *University of Queensland Law Journal* 35(1): 171–190.

Getzler, Joshua. 2016b "Personality and Capacity: Lessons from Legal History." In *Finn's Law: An Australian Justice*, ed. Timothy Bonyhady, 147–178. Sydney: Federation Press.

Getzler, Joshua, and Mike Macnair. 2005. "The Firm as an Entity before the Companies Acts." In *Adventures in the Law*, ed. Paul Brand, Kevin Costello, and W. N. Osborough, 267–288. Dublin: Four Courts Press.

Gindis, David. 2009. "From Fictions and Aggregates to Real Entities in the Theory of the Firm." *Journal of Institutional Economics* 5(1): 25–46.

Gindis, David, and Eva Micheler. 2024. "Institutional Theory for Corporate Law: An Invitation." *Journal of Corporate Law Studies* 24(2): 399–435.

Guinnane, Tim, Ron Harris, and Naomi R. Lamoreaux. 2017. "Contractual Freedom and Corporate Governance in Britain in the Late Nineteenth and Early Twentieth Centuries." *Business History Review* 91(2): 227–277.

Hansmann, Henry, Reinier Kraakman, and Richard Squire. 2006. "Law and the Rise of the Firm." *Harvard Law Review* 119(5): 1333–1403.

Harris, Ron. 2000. *Industrializing English Law: Entrepreneurship and Business Organization, 1720–1844*. Cambridge: Cambridge University Press.

Harris, Ron. 2006. "The Transplantation of the Legal Discourse on Corporate Personality Theories: From German Codification to British Political Pluralism and American Big Business." *Washington & Lee Law Review* 63(4): 1421–1478.

Harris, Ron. 2020. *Going the Distance: Eurasian Trade and the Rise of the Business Corporation 1400–1700*. Princeton: Princeton University Press.

Hart, Herbert L. A. 1954. "Definition and Theory in Jurisprudence." *Law Quarterly Review* 70(1): 37–60.

Hayek, Friedrich A. 1945. "The Use of Knowledge in Society." *American Economic Review* 35(4): 519–530.

Hirschman, Albert O. 1970. *Exit, Voice, and Loyalty: Responses to Decline in Firms, Organizations, and States*. Cambridge, MA: Harvard University Press.

Hobbes, Thomas. 1651. *Leviathan or the Matter, Forme and Power of a Commonwealth Ecclesiasticall and Civil*. London: Crooke.

House Committee on Transportation and Infrastructure. 2020. *Final Committee Report on the Design, Development & Certification of the Boeing 737 Max*. Washington, DC: United States Congress.

Jensen, Michael C., and William H. Meckling. 1976. "Theory of the Firm: Managerial Behavior, Agency Costs and Ownership Structure." *Journal of Financial Economics* 3(4): 305–360.

Johnson, Paul. 2010. *Making the Market: Victorian Origins of Corporate Capitalism*. Cambridge: Cambridge University Press.

Kogut, Bruce, and Udo Zander. 1996. "What Firms Do? Coordination, Identity, and Learning." *Organization Science* 7(5): 502–518.

Kornhauser, Lewis A., and Larry G. Sager. 1986. "Unpacking the Court." *Yale Law Journal* 96(1): 82–117.

Kornhauser, Lewis A., and Larry G. Sager. 1993. "The One and the Many: Adjudication in Collegial Courts." *California Law Review* 81(1): 1–59.

Kostal, Rande W. 1997. *Law and English Railway Capitalism 1825–1875*. Oxford: Oxford University Press.

Lewis, Paul A. 2017. "The Ostroms and Hayek as Theorists of Complex Adaptive Systems: Commonality and Complementarity." *Advances in Austrian Economics* 22: 35–66.

List, Christian, and Philip Pettit. 2011. *Group Agency: The Possibility, Design, and Status of Corporate Agents*. New York: Oxford University Press.

Madison, Michael J., Brett M. Frischmann and Katherine J. Strandburg. 2010. "Constructing Commons in the Cultural Environment." *Cornell Law Review* 95(4): 657–710.

Marglin, Stephen. 1974. "What Do Bosses Do? The Origins and Functions of Hierarchy in Capitalist Production." *Review of Radical Political Economics* 6(2): 60–112.

Micheler, Eva. 2024. "Separate Legal Personality – An Explanation and a Defence." *Journal of Corporate Law Studies* 24(1): 301–329.
Micheler, Eva. 2021. *Company Law: A Real Entity Theory*. Oxford: Oxford University Press.
Milgrom, Paul R., Douglass C. North, and Barry R. Weingast. 1990. "The Role of Institutions in the Revival of Trade: The Law Merchant, Private Judges, and the Champagne Fairs." *Economics & Politics* 2(1): 1–23.
Mirowski, Philip, and Edward Nik-Khah. 2017. *The Knowledge We Have Lost in Information: The History of Information in Modern Economics*. Oxford: Oxford University Press.
Nickerson, Jack A., and Todd R. Zenger. 2004. "A Knowledge-Based Theory of the Firm – The Problem-Solving Perspective." *Organization Science* 15(6): 617–632.
Offer, Avner. 2022. *Understanding the Private-Public Divide: Markets, Governments, and Time Horizons*. Cambridge: Cambridge University Press.
Ogilvie, Sheilagh. 2019. *The European Guilds: An Economic Analysis*. Princeton: Princeton University Press.
Ostrom, Elinor. 1990. *Governing the Commons: The Evolution of Institutions for Collective Action*. Cambridge: Cambridge University Press.
Ostrom, Elinor. 2005. *Understanding Institutional Diversity*. Princeton: Princeton University Press.
Ostrom, Elinor. 2011. "Background on the Institutional Analysis and Development Framework." *Policy Studies Journal* 39(1): 7–27.
Ostrom, Elinor. 2010. "Beyond Markets and States: Polycentric Governance of Complex Economic Systems." *American Economic Review* 100(3): 641–672.
Ostrom, Elinor, and Charlotte Hess. 2007. "A Framework for Analyzing the Knowledge Commons." In *Understanding Knowledge as a Commons: From Theory to Practice*, ed. Charlotte Hess, and Elinor Ostrom, 41–81. Cambridge, MA: MIT Press.
Ostrom, Elinor, James Walker, and Roy Gardner. 1992. "Covenants With and Without a Sword: Self-Governance Is Possible." *American Political Science Review* 86(2): 404–417.
Pettit, Philip. 2001. *A Theory of Freedom: From the Psychology to the Politics of Agency*. Oxford: Oxford University Press.
Piccione, Michele, and Ariel Rubinstein. 2007. "Equilibrium in the Jungle." *Economic Journal* 117(522): 883–896.
Posner, Richard A. 1993. "Ronald Coase and Methodology." *Journal of Economic Perspectives* 7(4): 195–210.
Raymond, Eric Steven. 1999. *The Cathedral and the Bazaar: Musings on Linux and Open Source by an Accidental Revolutionary*. Sebastopol: O'Reilly Media.
Reed, Polly. 2015. *Capitalist Family Values: Gender, Work, and Corporate Culture at Boeing*. Lincoln: University of Nebraska Press.
Ribstein, Larry E. 2010. *The Rise of the Uncorporation*. Oxford: Oxford University Press.
Rizzo, Mario J. 2016. "F. A. Hayek and the Rationality of Individual Choice." *Advances in Austrian Economics* 21: 21–39.
Roberts, John. 2004. *The Modern Firm: Organizational Design for Performance and Growth*. Oxford: Oxford University Press.
Robison, Peter. 2021. *Flying Blind: The 737 MAX Tragedy and the Fall of Boeing*. London: Penguin.
Rock, Edward B. 2006. "The Corporate Form as a Solution to a Discursive Dilemma." *Journal of Institutional and Theoretical Economics* 162(1): 57–71.
Runciman, David. 2023. *The Handover: How We Gave Control of Our Lives to Corporations, States and AIs*. London: Profile.

Strandburg, Katherine J., Brett M. Frischmann, and Michael J. Madison. 2017. "The Knowledge Commons Framework." In *Governing Medical Knowledge Commons*, ed. Katherine J. Strandburg, Brett M. Frischmann, and Michael J. Madison, 9–18. Cambridge: Cambridge University Press.

Sunstein, Cass R. 2023. "Hayekian Behavioral Economics." *Behavioural Public Policy* 7(1): 170–188.

Vaughn, Karen I. 1999. "Hayek's Theory of the Market Order as an Instance of the Theory of Complex Adaptive Systems." *Journal des économistes et des études humaines* 9(2–3): 241–256.

Williamson, Oliver E. 1975. *Markets and Hierarchies: Analysis and Antitrust Implications*. New York: Free Press.

Williamson, Oliver E. 1985. *The Economic Institutions of Capitalism: Firms, Market, Relational Contracting*. New York: Free Press/Macmillan.

Zhuangzi. 2023. *Zhuangzi: Basic Writings* (trans. B. Watson), 3rd ed. New York: Columbia University Press.

Zuboff, Shoshanna. 2019. *The Age of Surveillance Capitalism: The Fight for a Human Future at the New Frontier of Power*. London: Profile.

4

Managing Knowledge in Bat'a Enterprises

Marek Hudik and Martin Komrska

4.1 INTRODUCTION

Hayek (1945) famously argued that the price system is a mechanism for communicating knowledge dispersed among many people. However, as developments in institutional economics and political economy have emphasized, this mechanism is not costless and is often replaced by other mechanisms, such as firms or collective decisions (Coase 1937, 1960; Buchanan & Tullock 1962; Williamson 1975, 1985). The question that thus arises is how knowledge is managed under arrangements that do not rely predominantly on the price system.

The present chapter attempts to answer this question in the context of corporations. In corporations, as in markets, knowledge is not only communicated but also produced and utilized. But while in markets these processes are organic and spontaneous, in corporations a complex set of mechanisms that address various collective action problems needs to be designed and implemented. Moreover, the types of knowledge produced and utilized in the market and in corporations differ. In markets, the relevant types of knowledge constitute the infrastructure for exchanges (Dekker and Kuchař 2021); corporations also rely on such knowledge infrastructure, but also produce and utilize other types of knowledge, especially technical knowledge (Foss and Michailova 2009).

We focus on the operation of these mechanisms in the case of Bat'a enterprises, a well-known Czech shoemaking company that experienced a dramatic growth in the early twentieth century. The focus on Bat'a enterprises is no coincidence: The company's adeptness in governing knowledge significantly contributed to Bat'a's success (Zeleny 2010). By examining the Bat'a case, this chapter aims to contribute to a broader understanding of mechanisms of knowledge governance in corporations and their limits.

Our analysis applies the Governing Knowledge Commons (GKC) framework (Hess and Ostrom 2007; Frischmann et al. 2014) in treating knowledge as a shared

The Czech Science Foundation Project No. 22–28539 S supported this chapter. We thank Pavel Kuchař and David Gindis for valuable comments.

resource, where multiple stakeholders have overlapping claims on its use. The commons perspective was applied to corporations by Deakin (2012), while the associated collective action problems that complicate the production and utilization of shared resources in firms are emphasized by Bridoux and Stoelhorst (2022). The latter authors identify three governance structures that address the collective action problems in different ways. We build on their analysis and show how Bat'a enterprises employed one of these structures – the Lead Role Governance – to deal with the specific challenges of knowledge governance.

In line with Bridoux and Stoelhorst (2022), collective action problems are assumed to emerge not only among "insiders" – between employees or between employees and managers – but also among a broader set of "outsiders" – that is, stakeholders ordinarily deemed to be outside the boundaries of the firm as traditionally understood. We show that Bat'a emphasized the harmony of the interests among various stakeholders, including suppliers and consumers, and that this harmony was embedded in Bat'a's system. The case of Bat'a's enterprises is thus relevant not only for GKC literature but also the stakeholder theory more generally (e.g., Freeman et al. 2010; Phillips 2003).

One of the challenges to the commons perspective on the firm is that firms are typically hierarchical, while we tend to think of commons in terms of the community governance of shared resources (Frischmann et al. 2014). Furthermore, firms are generally considered forms of private governance, while commons refer to a structure that is neither private nor public (Kuchar and Dekker 2024). Nonetheless, as Deakin (2012) argues, corporations cannot be reduced to shareholder-owned entities, as they are also constituted by legal rules that define participation, governance, and accountability. From this perspective, the hierarchical structure of the firm is not merely a technological but also a legal phenomenon. In Deakin's (2012) view, the commons perspective of the firm offers greater descriptive accuracy and has a greater explanatory power than alternative accounts. Indeed, the hierarchical structure of the firm, including the role of managers, is something that needs to be explained rather than assumed. Moreover, firms have varying degrees of hierarchy. While there is a recent interest in decentralized structures (Foss and Klein 2022), the case of Bat'a's enterprises shows that such structures are not exclusively a recent phenomenon.

While our starting point is Hayek's (1945) analysis of the price system as the knowledge-communicating device, our focus is different. In markets, prices are usually public, and therefore there is no issue regarding access to the knowledge embodied in the prices. In contrast, knowledge in firms can be shared with or withheld from others (Grant 1996; Cabrera and Cabrera 2002). Furthermore, knowledge embodied in the price system is necessarily condensed in order to be effectively communicated. The knowledge within firms is multifaced, which gives rise to additional governance issues. Some aspects of the use of knowledge in firms are discussed by Foss (1999), who focuses on the subjective nature of knowledge. We take this discussion forward by emphasizing the collective action problems associated with the production, transmission, and utilization of knowledge.

Various aspects of knowledge, including its various types, are discussed by Machlup (1962), who builds on the earlier contributions of Hayek (1945), Ryle (1949), and Polanyi (1958).[1] A good discussion of the role of knowledge from the management perspective can be found in Winter (1987). Drawing on these perspectives, the present chapter focuses primarily on *practical knowledge*, as this type of knowledge is routinely and actively managed in corporations. This does not mean that the other types of knowledge are irrelevant for organizations. For instance, Methot et al. (2021) show that the knowledge acquired through small talk at work enhances organizational citizenship behaviors but also disrupts employees' ability to engage in their work. In any case, we assume that practical knowledge is sufficiently independent from other types of knowledge so that it can be studied separately.

The rest of the chapter is organized as follows. The following section introduces a theoretical framework, while describing various collective action problems associated with the production, transmission, and utilization of knowledge within a business corporation. Three governance models addressing these problems are discussed. Next, the case of Bat'a enterprises as an example of one of these governance models is presented. The connections with Ostrom's design principles and the GKC framework are considered in the final section.

4.2 THEORETICAL FRAMEWORK

In line with the GKC framework, we think of knowledge as a resource, where knowledge is defined very broadly as a "set of intellectual and cultural resources" (Frischmann et al. 2014, 2). In the present context, we consider a firm as an institutionalized form of community governance that embodies the rules for managing these resources. Community here refers to various stakeholders, including employees, suppliers, and consumers. In our focus on practical knowledge, we follow Machlup (1962, 23) in including "all knowledge regardless of the strength of belief in it or warranty for it." In particular, we do not restrict practical knowledge to scientific or proven knowledge but include conjectures and unverified hypotheses.

4.2.1 *Collective Action Problems*

A conventional view of knowledge is that it is non-rival (Romer 1990; Grant 1996): Everyone can use a piece of knowledge, a new idea or method of production, without diminishing its usage by others. Knowledge can be even anti-rival, in the sense that its value increases the more people use it (Weber 2004). However, specific consumption or production plans that utilize knowledge can be rival. For example, everyone can learn principles of accounting without making it more difficult for someone else to learn these principles, but plans that utilize this knowledge can be

[1] A valuable summary of Machlup's views can be found in Godin (2010).

in conflict (Hudik 2024), as accountants with similar knowledge compete for the same jobs.

Furthermore, the production of knowledge involves rival inputs, such as time and effort, which are scarce and have alternative uses (Romer 1990). Additionally, although knowledge is non-rival in consumption and application, it is excludable and therefore it can be selectively withheld, either intentionally, due to personal incentives, or unintentionally, due to communication barriers or lack of trust. This creates coordination and incentive problems that may hinder optimal sharing and integration (Grant 1996; Osterloh and Frey 2000; Cabrera and Cabrera 2002).

If the knowledge is not strongly firm-specific, it can be used in ways that do not contribute to the firm's objectives. These issues give rise to various collective action problems. A typical characteristic of such problems is the conflict between collective and personal objectives (Cabrera and Cabrera 2002). For example, individuals can use the firm's reputation to obtain political influence, rely on the firm's know-how in their own business, or engage in other forms of knowledge misappropriation (Lerner and Malmendier 2010; Colombo and Piva 2019). They can contribute to the production of firm's knowledge or pursue other goals (Holmstrom and Milgrom 1991). They can communicate knowledge to others to enhance the firm's performance or they can withhold knowledge to avoid potential conflicts within the firm (Chatterjee et al. 2021; Gonçalves et al. 2023). Such counterproductive uses of knowledge (Serenko and Bontis 2016), and counterproductive work behaviors more generally (Marcus et al. 2016; Suseno et al. 2021), can give rise to inefficiencies if an adequate governance structure is not adopted.

4.2.2 *The GKC Framework*

Collective action problems are often analyzed with game-theoretic tools (e.g., Ostrom et al. 1994; Dixit et al. 2014). Such an analysis is extremely useful in studying the incentives and the stability of outcomes within the given rules of the game. However, it has several important shortcomings. First, individuals do not always take the rules of the game as given. They can often modify them and thereby transform one game into another (Ostrom 1990; Cole and Grossman 2010; Hudik 2021). Second, the game-theoretic analysis is too general. Once we consider particular resources, such as various types of knowledge, we can impose more structure on the interactions and provide more specific results. For instance, the cost of excluding others from using a resource or the degree of rivalry in consumption determines the possible parameters of rules that can be effectively used to manage the resource.

Third, interactions in the real-world are usually complex, such that collapsing them into a simple game may not capture all the relevant aspects of interactions. There are multiple levels of analysis and decisions made at one level that are influenced by choices made at higher levels (Ostrom 1990). This complexity is especially important in the case of corporations, where many kinds of resources are governed. Generally speaking, a firm cannot be collapsed into a single type of collective action problem. Instead, there are different types of collective action problems within a firm, and some of them are more common or more important for its operation than others.

To address these issues, it is useful to adopt a broader perspective represented by the GKC framework (Frischmann et al. 2014; Sanfilippo et al. 2018; Dekker and Kuchař 2021). This framework, which is derived from the Institutional Analysis and Development (IAD) framework developed by Ostrom and others in Bloomington (Ostrom 2005), draws attention to the characteristics of the relevant (knowledge) resources, the actors involved in its production and use, and the patterns of their interactions, given the rules-in-use, the attributes of the community, and a range of evaluative criteria. In comparison to the basic game-theoretical approach, this framework provides a more nuanced view of the relevant collective action problems and their solutions. In particular, the GKC framework can explain the emergence of various governance structures.

4.2.3 *Three Governance Structures*

One of the typical characteristics of firms is they are run by at least one manager. Even formally "bossless" companies develop informal hierarchical structures, with a dominant role assigned to one or several individuals (Foss and Klein 2022). Managers are thus in a privileged position to address both intra-firm and interfirm collective action problems by implementing various governance structures. Bridoux and Stoelhorst (2022) identify three such structures: Hub-and-Spoke Governance; Lead Role Governance; and Shared Governance. The three structures differ in particular in terms of their openness and control. Openness of a resource refers to the "extent to which there are barriers to possession or use" (Frischmann et al. 2014, 29). The Hub-and-Spoke Governance model exhibits the lowest degree of openness and the highest degree of control, while the Shared Governance model lies at the opposite end.

In the Hub-and-Spoke Governance model, the firm's central management acts as the "hub" that coordinates and controls the actions of various stakeholders, who are the "spokes." The firm ensures that stakeholders contribute to joint value creation by setting clear rules, monitoring compliance, and enforcing them. Centralization helps mitigate conflicts and ensures that individual actions align with the firm's overall objectives. By monitoring stakeholder activities and enforcing compliance, the firm reduces the likelihood of collective action problems and ensures that stakeholders contribute their share toward joint value creation. The firm can implement graduated sanctions for noncompliance, which discourages stakeholders from pursuing self-interested behaviors that could undermine collective goals. Centralized control ensures alignment and minimizes the risk of individual stakeholders prioritizing their own short-term interests over the collective good.

In the Lead Role Governance model, the management of the focal firm acts as the lead stakeholder and takes a central role. However, compared to the Hub-and-Spoke model, it allows more autonomy to other stakeholders. The lead firm sets the strategic direction and facilitates cooperation among stakeholders but does not control every action. Stakeholders have more freedom to act independently compared to the Hub-and-Spoke model, which can enhance their engagement and investment in joint value creation. The lead firm's role is to guide and support rather than command, which helps in resolving conflicts and ensuring stakeholder alignment. It leverages the lead firm's influence while allowing stakeholders some level of autonomy, which can foster more genuine cooperation and commitment to shared goals.

In the Shared Governance model, stakeholders collectively govern their interactions, with no single firm or stakeholder dominating the process. Decision-making is more decentralized, with stakeholders collaboratively setting rules, monitoring, and enforcing compliance. This inclusive approach ensures that all stakeholders have a voice in the governance process, which can increase buy-in and commitment. Stakeholders monitor each other's actions and enforce compliance through mutual oversight. This decentralized monitoring helps prevent free-riding and encourages equitable contributions to joint value creation. Sanctions and conflict resolution mechanisms are developed and applied collectively, which can lead to more contextually appropriate solutions and foster a sense of shared responsibility. By involving all stakeholders in governance, this model helps align individual actions with collective interests, addressing collective action problems through collaborative effort.

Bridoux and Stoelhorst (2022) highlight that the choice of the governance model primarily depends on the complexity and the dynamism of the value creation activities. Specifically, the Shared Governance model performs best at relatively high levels of complexity, at which the Hub-and-Spoke model performs the worst. Complexity here refers to a characteristic or a set of characteristics that affect individuals' ability to understand the link between their actions and the joint value creation. The Lead Role Governance model is the most efficient at high levels of dynamism in joint value creation activities, while the other two forms are moderately efficient. We emphasize some additional aspects affecting the performance of the three models.

The Hub-and-Spoke model tends to be efficient in cases where the collective action problems resemble a Prisoner's Dilemma and the collectively optimal outcome is not the Nash equilibrium. In such cases, the issue is not only how to achieve but also how to maintain the collectively optimal outcome. The Hub-and-Spoke model furthermore requires that management can monitor the other stakeholders at low cost. It also presupposes that in order to achieve the collectively optimal outcome, the most effective method is to modify the stakeholders' payoffs through sanctions and rewards, rather than modifying the rules of the game. Finally, the model assumes that management is benevolent. This assumption is reasonable in a competitive market, where it is relatively easy for the stakeholders to exit the relationship with an abusive management or replace it with a new one.

At the other extreme is the Shared Governance model. This more democratic model tends to be efficient when the market is not competitive and it is not easy for the stakeholders to exercise the exit option, and hence, the benevolence of management is difficult to achieve. The Shared Governance model is applicable in cases where monitoring by management is more costly than mutual monitoring of stakeholders via peer pressure. Collectively optimal outcomes are achieved not only through sanctions and rewards but also by tinkering with the rules of the game.

The Lead Role Governance model tends to be efficient in cases where there is a possibility of coordination failures, that is, in collective action problems with multiple equilibria. Management coordinates the activities in a way that helps to achieve the collectively optimal equilibrium. As in the case of the Shared Governance model, stakeholders have large autonomy, which corresponds to the situation where exit is costly and has to be replaced by stakeholder voice. Furthermore, monitoring by management is costly and the community thus relies on mutual monitoring and peer pressure.

While the Shared Governance model seems like the closest to the sort of commons arrangements famously studied by Ostrom (1990), Bridoux and Stoelhorst (2022) argue that the shared governance of shared knowledge can also successfully evolve under the Lead Role Governance model. In the following section, we show how the Lead Role Governance model was used to this effect by Bat'a enterprises in the early twentieth century.

4.3 THE CASE OF BAT'A ENTERPRISES

Bat'a shoe company stands out as one of the most compelling success stories in Czech business history. It was founded in 1894 in the poor agrarian village of Zlín in the eastern part of today's Czech Republic (formerly part of the Austro-Hungarian Empire). Its founder, Tomáš Bat'a, came from a family that had been making shoes for several generations, even though the shoemaking craft had long been perceived as socially inferior and poorly compensated. Over the span of less than forty years, under Tomáš Bat'a's leadership, the small shoemaking workshop blossomed into one of Central Europe's largest enterprises, employing 31,000 individuals by 1932, the year when the founder passed away.

During this period, Bat'a was one of the pioneers of globalization, managing to penetrate fifty-six countries on four continents. Its unique management system allowed it to flourish not only in its main business of shoe manufacturing but also in other industries, such as tire production, engineering, chemical manufacturing, agriculture, construction, and more (Pokluda 2015).

The company earned respect not only for its business success, high profitability, and above-average wages for employees but also for its socially responsible business activities, which were unusual for the time. It provided social housing for its employees and offered multilevel education, healthcare services, and public transportation. It employed people with disabilities and had its own social fund, which collected funds for charitable activities. The popularity of the company's founder and CEO, Tomáš Bat'a, eventually transcended the boundaries of the company, allowing him to stand in local elections in 1923 and become the mayor of Zlín. In the present chapter, we mainly focus on the organization and management system of the company as it was established under Tomáš Bat'a. Although the company experienced significant growth following its founder's passing, its operational principles remained largely unchanged.

4.3.1 *The Lead Role Governance Model of Bat'a Enterprises*

We argue that the remarkable success of the Bat'a enterprises was largely due to its organizational structure. The Bat'a system exemplified the Lead Role Governance model, as outlined in the previous section, where the company's leadership played a major role in designing rules, policies, and strategic decisions, but allowed significant degrees of autonomy to employees and other stakeholders. Bat'a applied these principles in its approach to knowledge management, which encouraged employee participation in the creation, transmission, and acquisition of knowledge. The system rested on two foundational pillars: a system of autonomous workshops and a corporate education system.

The organization in terms of autonomous workshops was characterized by an internal pricing and incentive system within the company, where departments conducted transactions with each other, thus pushing them toward greater efficiency. The internal pricing system quickly revealed poor managerial decisions and potential sources of loss within the company. Thanks to weekly accounting reports, this information was regularly accessible not only to management but also to all employees. Additionally, the profit-sharing scheme for employees motivated even ordinary workers to propose new, more productive work processes. Successful examples of these innovations could then be rapidly disseminated to other departments through the company's internal communication system.

The corporate education system was designed to enhance both technical expertise and soft skills across the company's diverse workforce. This program bridged gaps in educational backgrounds, equipping employees with the knowledge and capabilities needed to excel in their roles. The education system also served as a vehicle for transmitting not only technical knowledge but also the company's core values, fostering a cohesive corporate culture. Bat'a's education initiatives extended beyond traditional training, encompassing various modes of communication to ensure that shared knowledge and values permeated every level of the organization. This dual focus on technical proficiency and cultural alignment helped sustain productivity and innovation while reinforcing a shared sense of purpose.

4.3.2 *Autonomous Workshops*

Bat'a introduced a self-management system for workshops, characterized by the organizational and accounting decentralization of individual production departments. Echoing the sentiments of the company's founder, the primary objective was to establish a system that would autonomously incentivize the efficient functioning of the company "which – like the law gravity – will never fail" (Bat'a 1926). This innovative approach involved the separation of workshops from other company departments that were not directly engaged in the production. This separation facilitated independent transactions of goods between workshops and with other departments for purchases or sales. Consequently, each workshop gained the capability to assess its profitability on a weekly basis, a metric intricately linked to the material involvement of individual employees.

Since 1924, the company has implemented a profit-sharing system for the majority of its regular employees. The workshops were sufficiently small for everyone to be able to make an identifiable contribution to the outcome. Each employee was thus informed about their individual contribution to the company. At the same time, this approach provided an incentive for employees to enhance the firm's profitability, whether through the introduction of innovative production methods or through heightened industriousness.

If a workshop exceeded the planned output volume using the same amount of purchased materials (e.g., through reduced waste), it resulted in a profit. This profit, directly tied to the performance of individual employees, was reflected in their remuneration. The close relationship between employee efforts and financial gains not only fostered a sense of ownership and motivation but also aligned individual interests with the overall success of the company.

The higher level of autonomy granted to workshop managers also entailed increased responsibility. Unlike regular employees, they not only had a share of the profits but also bore a share of any losses incurred (Hodáč 2015). As Cekota (2016, 176) put it:

> It was a system that informed fifty-two times a year not only the top management of the company about the whole and all its parts but also the managers and employees of each unit about their results. The speed of information and its publication created a dynamic force to intervene exactly where it was needed. Losses, if they occurred, could thus be stopped at the outset.

The system of autonomous workshops illustrates that collective action problems characterized by potential misalignment between personal and collective goals can be mitigated when individual incentives are linked to the firm's overall performance. Bat'a's approach transformed the workplace into a cooperative environment where employees saw their own success as tied to the firm's success. At the same time, the system imitated the market in the sense that it provided signals through profits and losses and thereby helped to effectively manage resources.

While profit-sharing schemes were already in place in some American companies during that period (Langlois 2023), drawing inspiration from them, Bat'a introduced a distinctive approach. Unlike the conventional company-wide profit-sharing model prevalent at the time, typically distributed annually, Bat'a sought to create a system where every employee could actively and directly influence the outcome. Consequently, profits were calculated at the level of individual workshops and on a weekly basis (Urbanová and Dundelová 2012). Bat'a's overarching objective was to instill a sense in each employee that they could significantly shape the results. His vision entailed employees viewing their respective workshops as if they were the owners of their own businesses. This perspective not only encouraged a profound understanding of individual roles but also prompted employees to delve into the broader workings of their workshops and the company as a whole (Rybka 2016).

The decentralized self-management model proved immensely successful to the extent that even the communist regime that came to power in 1948 following the socialist revolution endeavored to implement it in large state-owned enterprises (Křeček 2015). This underscores the enduring impact and replicability of Bat'a's innovative approach to employee engagement and ownership.

The system of autonomous workshop represents a culmination of efforts to manage knowledge within the company as it encouraged its production and sharing. We now focus on the second pillar of Bat'a's governance, namely, the education system.

4.3.3 *Corporate Education System*

Given its significant size, even by European standards, Bat'a recognized the critical role of knowledge management in sustaining efficiency and productivity. We contend that Bat'a's success can be attributed, in part, to its exceptional ability to cultivate and expand knowledge in a markedly more intensive manner than was customary in corporate practices during that era.

The engagement with knowledge encompassed various levels, the foremost being technical knowledge and know-how, specifically in the context of workflows. Bat'a placed great importance on education. Beyond learning by doing, the company instituted a comprehensive internal training framework. This encompassed an extensive network of in-house educational establishments, ranging from foundational educational levels to specialized training units concentrating on specific business skills.

A critical organizational component in this regard was the Bat'a School of Labor, established in 1925 as a crucial element of the company's training infrastructure (Pokluda 2018). This three-year study program targeted young employees, typically around fourteen years old, seamlessly integrating factory work with academic pursuits. During their training, participants were exposed to a diverse array of tasks during their factory assignments, rather than being confined to a singular role. Upon successful completion of the program, participants were strategically placed based on their performance, with the option to continue their education within Bat'a schools (Rybka 2016). The significance of the Zlín apprenticeship's success and its instrumental role in the company was underscored by the replication of similar schools in Bat'a's foreign branches during the late 1930s (see Pokluda et al. 2020).

Beyond the formal training in company schools, there was also a model of lifelong learning, which allowed those already employed to further deepen or expand their knowledge or broaden their skill sets. In addition to technical courses and lectures spanning various disciplines, a notable emphasis was placed on language acquisition, particularly English (Pokluda 2018). Leveraging its extensive presence in international markets, the company actively promoted and facilitated its workforce to acquire foreign work experience through short-term internships. This approach not only enriched individual employees but also contributed to the company's overall global competence and adaptability.

Bat'a recognized that cultivating a sense of community requires more than just imparting technical skills. To foster healthy relationships within and beyond the workplace and to encourage participation in pro-growth initiatives, individuals need an understanding of how societal mechanisms function. This insight also aligns with "Tocqueville's challenge" (Ostrom 1997), which emphasizes the importance of equipping individuals with a capacity to actively engage in collective action and self-governance. By addressing this challenge, Bat'a's approach contributes to the creation of resilient, self-organizing communities, much like those envisioned in the Ostrom Workshop's studies of governance. As part of his educational initiatives, Bat'a strove to communicate that embracing a pro-business and pro-entrepreneurial mindset facilitates widespread prosperity. Bat'a (2016) recounted that he himself was raised in a society where socialist ideology prevailed. During his childhood, the notion of being a prominent factory owner was not deemed morally acceptable.

Bat'a's subsequent philosophical stance was markedly shaped by his travels to Germany and the United States. Shortly after establishing his business, Bat'a traveled to Frankfurt am Main, marking his initial exposure to a capitalistic mode of production. He recounted his astonishment upon witnessing factory workers who appeared not to be exploited by capitalistic proprietors. On the contrary, he observed individuals enjoying improved living standards and better health compared to Zlín. Wages were higher and working conditions more favorable, as machinery handled the most arduous mechanical aspects of the production process. Since then, Bat'a began to value the capitalistic mode of production and developed a heightened interest in the management systems of affluent Western countries.

Consequently, in 1904, Bat'a organized a trip to the United States for himself and a select group of Bat'a workers (Pokluda 2015). The objective was to secure employment as ordinary workers in the United States manufacturing industry and glean insights into the workings of these enterprises. Bat'a observed a stark contrast in the mindset of ordinary individuals in the United States and the Czech lands. In the United States, success was lauded, and affluent individuals were regarded as exemplary figures. Children were instilled with the belief, from a tender age, that they held their destinies in their own hands and should strive to accumulate capital at the earliest opportunity. This stood in stark contrast to the anti-capitalistic sentiment prevalent in Central Europe.

Bat'a recognized that prevailing misconceptions about capitalism and the market system were stifling the growth potential of Czech society. As part of his educational endeavors, Bat'a disseminated several speeches and even authored a book titled *Wealth to All* (Bat'a 1926), which, among other topics, elucidated the significance of entrepreneurship, wealth creation, and free trade. He realized that awareness of the benefits of free trade was actually one of the types of knowledge whose dissemination can have the most significant impact within both the company and the community.

4.3.4 *Communication*

Tomáš Bat'a believed that fostering a sense of belonging among employees necessitated a comprehensive understanding of the company's overall functioning, including its management. Indeed, the sense of belonging is crucial to overcoming collective dilemmas in systems that do not rely on external monitoring (Kandel and Lazear 1992). The first step toward achieving this was to make the company's economic results accessible to all employees. At the same time, regular updates on economic developments and company news were disseminated through the company magazine *Communication*, which commenced publication in May 1918 and was distributed on a weekly basis to employees at no cost (Pokluda 2018).

Later, the dissemination of specialized knowledge was further enhanced with the introduction of company-specific trade magazines, including *Technical Advisor*, *Shoe-Leather-Gum*, *Salesmen's Magazine*, and *Pioneer of Successful Business*. These publications served as conduits for conveying specific expertise and bringing the best practices from various departments directly to the employees, thereby fostering a culture of continuous learning and knowledge exchange within the company.

The company realized that information had to flow not only from the top down, from management to employees, but also from the bottom up. Traditionally, information about employee satisfaction, job challenges, and their expectations were funneled to top management through lower-level managers. However, Tomáš Bat'a foresaw the potential limitation of this approach in a large organization, where some information might remain concealed due to challenges in its transfer to the central level.

To address this issue, Bat'a implemented the role of "personnel clerks" to facilitate a more efficient upward flow of local information regarding the functioning, challenges, and atmosphere of each department. These personal officers, serving as representatives of the Personnel Department, spent most of their working week directly within individual workshops, assuming various roles to gain an in-depth understanding of the work processes (Končitíková 2022). This hands-on approach enabled them to acquire continuous firsthand insights into the workflow, identify obstacles to efficiency, gauge the shop floor atmosphere, and comprehend the most pressing issues perceived by employees.

Moreover, these personnel officers engaged in regular interviews with individual employees. These sessions went beyond soliciting feedback, as the officers actively assisted employees in their career paths and helped plan activities in their personal lives. This multifaceted interaction not only strengthened the bond of trust between the employees and the company but also facilitated a more nuanced and comprehensive understanding of the workforce dynamics.

The results of individual departments, inclusive of the disbursed profits, were disseminated weekly to all employees within the company, instigating a form of healthy competition and rivalry among the departments. At the same time, the stimulation of new innovations and the activation of local knowledge were actively fostered through the establishment of the Research Department. Its aim was to concentrate, document, and evaluate employee-generated ideas and inventions aimed at enhancing the company's operational efficiency. Successful ideas were not only financially rewarded but were also showcased in the company-wide newspaper to inspire dynamic engagement among other employees. According to Pokluda et al. (2020), Bat'a Company surpassed industry averages in innovations and their practical implementation due to this organizational design. This success was underpinned not only by the aforementioned Research Department but also by specialized research in engineering, chemistry, agriculture, and education.

Engineering research, in particular, yielded one of the most remarkable success stories in the field of shoe manufacturing productivity – the Bat'a moving belt introduced in 1927. The implementation of the automated processes resulted in an astounding 73 percent increase in production that year. This strategic integration of research initiatives, coupled with a robust rewards system for innovative ideas, fortified Bat'a's position as an industry leader in innovation and practical implementation.

4.4 BAT'A'S KNOWLEDGE COMMONS

Bat'a's governance structure, as described in the previous section, aligns with the Lead Role Governance model proposed by Bridoux and Stoelhorst (2022). This model grants considerable autonomy to employees and stakeholders, while maintaining central strategic direction and rule-setting responsibilities within management. Bridoux and Stoelhorst derive their governance models from Ostrom's pioneering work but do not explicitly apply the GKC framework. Analyzing the Bat'a case explicitly through the GKC framework enhances our understanding of the characteristics and management of knowledge in Bat'a's organizational structure.

Table 4.1 categorizes the key elements of knowledge governance at Bat'a along the dimensions emphasized in the GKC framework, namely: resource characteristics, goals and objectives, creation, communication, and governance mechanisms. Table 4.2 characterizes Bat'a in terms of Ostrom's design principles.

Bat'a's system recognized that important bits of knowledge were dispersed among numerous individuals throughout the organization (Foss 1999). To effectively harness and manage this dispersed knowledge, Bat'a implemented a decentralized governance structure based on autonomous workshops, which operationalized principles of congruence between appropriation rules and local conditions (Ostrom 1990; Hess and Ostrom 2007). The workshops incentivized grassroots innovation, experimentation, and continuous improvement by linking individual efforts directly to tangible outcomes (Urbanová and Dundelová 2012; Rybka 2016). Weekly profit-and-loss reports ensured transparency and enabled quick feedback, motivating individual contributions that aligned closely with broader organizational objectives.

Bat'a also addressed the non-rivalrous nature of knowledge highlighted by the GKC literature (Frischmann et al. 2014) by implementing mechanisms of knowledge creation and communication. For instance, Bat'a's corporate education initiatives, like the Bat'a School of Labor, provided learning opportunities that systematically reinforced knowledge-sharing and innovation across the enterprise (Pokluda 2018). Furthermore, regular internal publications such as the company magazine exemplified how Bat'a maintained open, continuous channels for effective knowledge-sharing.

The partial excludability of knowledge posed significant challenges in its governance, as individual motivations alone may not always lead to voluntary sharing (Cabrera and Cabrera 2002). Bat'a proactively addressed this by institutionalizing transparency and open knowledge exchange. The internal magazines and dedicated personnel officers facilitated bottom-up and top-down communication, creating an environment where knowledge-sharing became embedded in routine organizational practices rather than depending solely on individual initiative.

TABLE 4.1 *Knowledge governance in Bat'a*

Resource	Resource characteristics	Goals and objectives	Creation	Communication	Governance
Knowledge	Dispersed among individuals Non-rival or anti-rival Some excludable (e.g., technical knowledge), some non/excludable (e.g., company culture)	Potential misalignment between personal and collective goals Potential heterogeneity of values	Learning-by-doing R&D Grassroots engagement Imitation	Profits and losses Training Written materials Personal communication	Autonomous workshops Education system

TABLE 4.2 *Ostrom's design principles applied to Bat'a*

Design principle	Application to Bat'a enterprises
DP1: Clearly defined boundaries should be in place	Workshops had clearly defined boundaries, making it clear who contributes to value creation and at what stage of production process
DP2: Rules-in-use are well matched to local needs and conditions	All the rules were developed through gradual learning within the Bat'a organization itself; they were not adopted from external sources and were fully adapted to the local environment
DP3: Individuals affected by these rules can usually participate in modifying the rules	The rules of work processes and basic procedures were defined centrally, but all employees in Bat'a's factories were encouraged to come up with innovative ideas; the company's management was open to feedback, and employees had plenty of channels through which they could propose changes
DP4: The right of community members to devise their own rules is respected by external authorities	Each workshop had the freedom to introduce its own internal procedures, provided that it was able to meet the plan set by the central management
DP5: A system for self-monitoring members' behavior has been established	A self-monitoring system was the very essence and central pillar of Bat'a's management model; individual workshops had full autonomy in organizing their work and were motivated to maximize efficiency, as any improvement in the production process exceeding the plan was directly reflected in employee rewards through the established profit-sharing system
DP6: A graduated system of sanctions is available	Workshop leaders and company management were involved not only in profit sharing but also in sharing losses; penalties were applied automatically if workshops failed to meet the set plan; this was assessed on a weekly basis, with both profits and losses reflected directly in employees' wages
DP7: Community members have access to low-cost conflict-resolution mechanisms	The work organization system, based on internal weekly accounting, was designed to detect any errors or inefficiencies at an early stage; if conflicts arose, the company could quickly identify in the data; the final say in resolving them rested with the top management; since the company's director was also its sole shareholder, authoritative and irreversible decisions could be made in a very short time
DP8: Nested enterprises – that is, appropriation, provision, monitoring and sanctioning, conflict resolution, and other governance activities – are organized in a nested structure with multiple layers of activities	Bat'a management system was a multilayered decentralized structure comprising a large number of autonomous self-governing workshops contributing both locally and collectively to Bat'a's knowledge governance system

Note: Based on Hess and Ostrom (2007).

The autonomous workshop model featured clear rules that helped to align the incentives of workshop employees and the company management. The alignment was further reinforced by Baťa's profit-sharing rule, which fostered a strong alignment of personal and collective goals, reducing the risks of knowledge withholding and enhancing collaborative productivity (Cekota 2016). In line with Ostrom's design principles (Ostrom 1990, 2005; Hess and Ostrom 2007), these rules also defined clear boundaries between workshops as production units determining who contributes to the value creation in a particular workshop.

However, the system led to potential conflicts among workshops that were to some extent in competition. These potential conflicts were addressed through a strong company culture that emphasized shared values and collective success. The ethos instilled by Tomáš Baťa himself underscored entrepreneurship, personal accountability, and mutual prosperity, reinforced by slogans such as "One company – one interest – one goal" (Zeleny 1988). This explicit cultural alignment ensured cohesion and cooperation across the enterprise, reducing conflicts arising from internal competition.

Finally, the participatory governance model at Baťa significantly enhanced employee empowerment, aligning with the GKC's principles (Hess and Ostrom 2007; Frischmann et al. 2014). Employees directly participated in decision-making processes, gaining transparent access to operational results, which amplified their sense of ownership, agency, and commitment to collective outcomes. Overall, Baťa's case demonstrates how strategic management of knowledge commons, informed by clear governance principles, can lead to sustained organizational success.

4.5 CONCLUSION

Baťa Company is often regarded as one of the most successful examples of entrepreneurship in the Czech lands. In this chapter, we aimed to argue that its extraordinary success was not primarily due to harder work or the exceptional empathy of its founder, Tomáš Baťa. Instead, we have shown that Baťa's success was deeply rooted in an effectively structured management system centered around the production and use of shared knowledge.

We examined how knowledge resources were managed in Baťa and suggested that the firm adopted what Bridoux and Stoelhort (2022) described as the Lead Role Governance model that granted high autonomy to workshops and individual employees, while leaving the strategic decisions with the company's management. This decentralized knowledge governance model facilitated efficient problem-solving and cultivated a culture of continuous learning and knowledge exchange across all levels of the organization, while at the same time mitigating various collective action problems associated with the creation, communication, and utilization of knowledge (Hess and Ostrom 2007). It was this combination of decentralization and knowledge-sharing that played a crucial role in shaping Bat'a's innovative spirit and success during its glorious period.

Another cornerstone of Bat'a's success was education, and specifically its emphasis on lifelong learning. By investing in the continuous development of employees' skills and capabilities, the company not only enhanced their individual capabilities but also created a culture of knowledge-sharing. Tomáš Bat'a actively shaped its corporate culture to influence broader societal values. He became a public advocate for free trade, entrepreneurship, and personal responsibility. We contend that the successful penetration of the idea of shared benefit between employers and employees was another factor behind the company's success. Combined with above-average wages, a profit-sharing system, and a range of non-monetary benefits, this approach significantly contributed to a deeper sense of well-being and job satisfaction among workers. By emphasizing that every employee was also, in a sense, a capitalist, Bat'a cultivated a workplace culture where individuals felt genuinely valued and aligned with the company's broader mission.

Overall, the system of profit and loss within the framework of the workshop self-management system provided and disseminated information about economic activity and the efficiency of production processes within the company. Corporate education helped build essential work habits and procedures, while enlightenment regarding entrepreneurial values engaged a larger number of people in the production process and helped align individual interests with those of the company. The Bat'a model offers valuable inspiration for contemporary companies seeking long-term success through effective knowledge management and employee empowerment.

REFERENCES

Bat'a, Tomáš. 1926. *Zámožnost všem*. Zlín: T. & A. Bat'a.

Bat'a, Tomáš. 2016. *Úvahy a projevy*. Praha: Dobrovský s.r.o.

Bridoux, Fleur, and J. W. Stoelhorst. 2022. "Stakeholder Governance: Solving the Collective Action Problems in Joint Value Creation." *Academy of Management Review* 47(2): 214–236.

Buchanan, James M., and Gordon Tullock. 1962. *The Calculus of Consent: Logical Foundations for Constitutional Democracy*. Ann Arbor: University of Michigan Press.

Cabrera, Angel, and Elizabeth F. Cabrera. 2002. "Knowledge-Sharing Dilemmas." *Organization Studies* 23(5): 687–710.

Cekota, Antonín. 2016. *Geniální podnikatel Tomáš Bat'a*. Zlín: Nadace Tomáše Bati.

Chatterjee, Sheshadri, Ranjan Chaudhuri, Alkis Thrassou, and Demetris Vrontis. 2021. "Antecedents and Consequences of Knowledge Hiding: The Moderating Role of Knowledge Hiders and Knowledge Seekers in Organizations." *Journal of Business Research* 128: 303–313.

Coase, Ronald H. 1937. "The Nature of the Firm." *Economica* 4(16): 386–405.

Coase, Ronald H. 1960. "The Problem of Social Cost." *Journal of Law and Economics* 3: 1–44.

Cole, Daniel H., and Peter Z. Grossman. 2010. "Institutions Matter! Why the Herder Problem Is Not a Prisoner's Dilemma." *Theory and Decision* 69(2): 219–231.

Colombo, Massimo G., and Evila Piva. 2019. "Knowledge Misappropriation Risks and Contractual Complexity in Entrepreneurial Ventures' Non-Equity Alliances." *Small Business Economics* 53(1): 107–127.
Deakin, Simon. 2012. "The Corporation as Commons: Rethinking Property Rights, Governance and Sustainability in the Business Enterprise." *Queen's Law Journal* 37(2): 339–374.
Dekker, Erwin, and Pavel Kuchař, eds. 2021. *Governing Markets as Knowledge Commons.* Cambridge: Cambridge University Press.
Dekker, Erwin, and Pavel Kuchař. 2024. "Markets and Knowledge Commons: Is There a Difference between Private and Community Governance of Markets?" *Public Choice* 201(3–4): 533–553.
Dixit, Avinash K., Susan Skeath, and David H. Reiley Jr. 2014. *Games of Strategy*. New York: W. W. Norton.
Foss, Nicolai J. 1999. "The Use of Knowledge in Firms." *Journal of Institutional and Theoretical Economics* 155(4): 458–486.
Foss, Nicolai J., and Peter G. Klein. 2022. *Why Managers Matter: The Perils of the Bossless Company*. London: Hachette.
Foss, Nicolai J., and Snejina Michailova. 2009. *Knowledge Governance: Processes and Perspectives*. Oxford: Oxford University Press.
Freeman, R. Edward. 2010. "Managing for Stakeholders: Trade-offs or Value Creation." *Journal of Business Ethics* 96 (1S): 7–9.
Frischmann, Brett M., Michael J. Madison, and Katherine J. Strandburg, eds. 2014. *Governing Knowledge Commons*. Oxford: Oxford University Press.
Godin, Benoît. 2010. "The Knowledge Economy: Fritz Machlup's Construction of a Synthetic Concept." In *The Capitalization of Knowledge: A Triple Helix of University-Industry-Government*, ed. Riccardo Viale, and Henry Etzkowit, 261–290. Cheltenham: Edward Elgar.
Gonçalves, Tiago, Carla Curado, and Mírian Oliveira. 2023. "Clarifying Knowledge Withholding: A Systematic Literature Review and Future Research Agenda." *Journal of Business Research* 157: 113600.
Grant, Robert M. 1996. "Toward a Knowledge-Based Theory of the Firm." *Strategic Management Journal* 17(S2): 109–122.
Hayek, Friedrich A. 1945. "The Use of Knowledge in Society." *American Economic Review* 35(4): 519–530.
Hess, Charlotte, and Elinor Ostrom, eds. 2007. *Understanding Knowledge as a Commons: From Theory to Practice*. Cambridge, MA: MIT Press.
Hodáč, František. 2015. *Tomáš Bat'a: Život a práce hospodářského buditele*. Zlín: Nadace Tomáše Bati.
Holmstrom, Bengt, and Paul Milgrom. 1991. "Multitask Principal–Agent Analyses: Incentive Contracts, Asset Ownership, and Job Design." *Journal of Law, Economics and Organization* 7(1): 24–52.
Hudik, Marek. 2021. "Push Factors of Endogenous Institutional Change." *Journal of Economic Behavior & Organization* 189: 504–514.
Hudik, Marek. 2024. "Externality as a Coordination Problem." *Public Choice* 201: 495–510.
Kandel, Eugene, and Edward P. Lazear. 1992. "Peer Pressure and Partnerships." *Journal of Political Economy* 100(4): 801–817.
Křeček, Stanislav. 2015. *Má dáti – dal: účtoval jsem u Baťu*. Zlín: Nadace Tomáše Bati.

Končitíková, Gabriela. 2022. *Use of Bata Management System for Formation of Culture in Organizations*. Zlín: Universita Tomáše Bati.
Langlois, Richard N. 2023. *The Corporation and the Twentieth Century: The History of American Business Enterprise*. Princeton: Princeton University Press.
Lerner, Josh, and Ulrike Malmendier. 2010. "Contractibility and the Design of Research Agreements." *American Economic Review* 100(1): 214–246.
Machlup, Fritz. 1962. *The Production and Distribution of Knowledge in the United States*. Princeton: Princeton University Press.
Madison, Michael J., Brett M. Frischmann, Madelyn R. Sanfilippo and Katherine J. Strangburg. 2022. "Too Much for a Good thing? A Governing Knowledge Commons Review of Abundance in Context." *Frontiers in Research Metrics and Analytics* 7: 959505.
Marcus, Bernd, O. Anita Taylor, Stephanie E. Hastings, Alexandra Sturm, and Oliver Weigelt. 2016. "The Structure of Counterproductive Work Behavior: A Review, a Structural Meta-Analysis, and a Primary Study." *Journal of Management* 42(1): 203–233.
Methot, Jessica R., Efrat H. Rosado-Solomon, Patrick E. Downes, and Allison S. Gabriel. 2021. "Office Chitchat as a Social Ritual: The Uplifting Yet Distracting Effects of Daily Small Talk at Work." *Academy of Management Journal* 64(5): 1445–1471.
Osterloh, Margit, and Bruno S. Frey. 2000. "Motivation, Knowledge Transfer, and Organizational Forms." *Organization Science* 11(5): 538–550.
Ostrom, Elinor. 1990. *Governing the Commons: The Evolution of Institutions for Collective Action*. Cambridge: Cambridge University Press.
Ostrom, Elinor. 2005. *Understanding Institutional Diversity*. Princeton: Princeton University Press.
Ostrom, Vincent. 1997. *The Meaning of Democracy and the Vulnerability of Democracy: A Response to Tocqueville's Challenge*. Ann Arbor: University of Michigan Press.
Ostrom, Elinor, Roy Gardner, and James Walker. 1994. *Rules, Games and Common-Pool Resources*. Ann Arbor: University of Michigan Press.
Phillips, Robert A. 2003. *Stakeholder Theory and Organizational Ethics*. San Francisco: Berrett-Koehler.
Pokluda, Zdeněk. 2013. *Bat'a v kostce*. Zlín: Kniha Zlín.
Pokluda, Zdeněk. 2015. *Ze Zlína do světa – příběh Tomáše Bati*. Zlín: Nadace Tomáše Bati.
Pokluda, Zdeněk. 2018. *Bat'a – inspirace pro Československo*. Zlín: Nadace Tomáše Bati.
Pokluda, Zdeněk, Jakub Herman, and Miroslav Balaban. 2020. *Bat'a na všech kontinentech*. Zlín: Nadace Tomáše Bati.
Polanyi, Michael. 1958. *Personal Knowledge*. Chicago: University of Chicago Press.
Romer, Paul M. 1990. "Endogenous Technological Change." *Journal of Political Economy* 98 (5/2): S71–S102.
Rybka, Zdeněk. 2016. *Základní zásady Baťova systému řízení*. Zlín: Nadace Tomáše Bati.
Ryle, Gilbert. 1949. *The Concept of Mind*. Chicago: University of Chicago Press.
Sanfilippo, Madelyn, Brett Frischmann and Katherine Standburg. 2018. "Privacy as Commons: Case Evaluation through the Governing Knowledge Commons Framework." *Journal of Information Policy* 8: 116–166.
Serenko, Alexander, and Nick Bontis. 2016. "Understanding Counterproductive Knowledge Behavior: Antecedents and Consequences of Intra-Organizational Knowledge Hiding." *Journal of Knowledge Management* 20(6): 1199–1224.
Suseno, Yuliani, Chiachi Chang, Marek Hudik, Eddy Fang, and Na Liu. 2021. "Why Do Employees Engage in Counterproductive Work Behaviours? Cultural Values and White-Collar Employees in CHINA." *Motivation and Emotion* 45(4): 397–421.

Urbanová, Marie, and Jana Dundelová. 2012. "Work Culture of the Bata Company." *Acta Universitatis Agriculturae et Silviculturae Mendelianae Brunensis* 60(7): 487–494.

Weber, Steven. 2004. *The Success of Open Source*. Cambridge, MA: MIT Press.

Williamson, Oliver E. 1975. *Markets and Hierarchies: Analysis and Antitrust Implications*. New York: Free Press.

Williamson, Oliver E. 1985. *The Economic Institutions of Capitalism: Firms, Markets, Relational Contracting*. New York: Free Press.

Winter, Sidney G. 1987. "Knowledge and Competence as Strategic Assets." In *The Competitive Challenge*, ed. David J. Teece, 159–184. Cambridge, MA: Ballinger.

Zelený, Milan. 1988. "Bat'a-System of Management: Managerial Excellence Found." *Human Systems Management* 7(3): 213–219

Zelený, Milan. 2010. "Bata Management System: A Built-In Resilience against Crisis at the Micro Level." *Czech Economic Review* 4(1): 102–117.

5

Institutional Complementarities in the Governance of Corporate Knowledge Commons

Erkan Gürpinar

5.1 INTRODUCTION: HISTORY AND THEORETICAL BACKGROUND

The origins and evolution of institutional diversity in knowledge governance have preoccupied scholars from various disciplines over the past few decades. There are several factors that contribute to this growing interest. First and foremost, both theoretical and empirical studies have established that knowledge is the most critical input in the production process (Benkler 2006; Corrado et al. 2006). This is true across different levels of economic analysis ranging from firm-based micro approaches (Antonelli 2007; Fisk 2009; Stone 2013) to macro level studies of economic growth (Romer 1986). Second, given their lasting impact on knowledge production and dissemination, the role of institutions, both formal and informal, in governing today's knowledge-based economies is a subject of intense debate. In particular, some researchers express scepticism about legal arrangements such as intellectual property rights (IPR), arguing that they may hinder rather than promote the production and dissemination of knowledge (Fisk 2009; Elkin-Koren and Salzberger 2012; Benkler 2017).[1]

None of these ideas are new. The debate about the economic and legal nature of knowledge dates back to the nineteenth century, if not earlier. For example, at the firm level, current debates over the ownership of workplace knowledge in high-tech industries (Saxenian 1994; Hyde 2003; Stone 2013; Marx 2015) resemble the legal disputes over the ownership of workplace knowledge that emerged with the rise of the

This chapter is an extended and thoroughly revised version of a paper entitled "Capital, Workplace Knowledge and the Role of Intangible Assets in the Evolution of Modern Corporation" presented at the Governing Corporate Knowledge Commons workshop organized by the Centre for the Study of Governance and Society (CSGS) at King's College London in February 2024. An earlier version of parts of this paper, titled "Thorstein Veblen on capital as knowledge: some implications for the knowledge economy," was also presented at the Patents as Capital workshop organized by the ERC-funded project "Patents as Scientific Information 1895–2020" (PASSIM) in collaboration with the International Society for the History and Theory of Intellectual Property (ISHTIP) in Norrköping, Sweden, in May 2022. The author is grateful to the organizers and participants of both workshops. Last but not least, the author is grateful to David Gindis, whose insightful comments on earlier drafts were invaluable in shaping the final version of the chapter.

[1] Another strand of literature conceptualizes knowledge as a fictitious commodity. For further discussion, see Özveren and Gürpinar (2024).

factory system following the Industrial Revolution (Fisk 2009). In fact, as Pagano (2020) notes, the issue of the governance of workplace knowledge was first considered by scholars such as Adam Smith and Charles Babbage. They observed that the division of labour has complex implications for both the workforce and society. Depending on the extent – both in scale and scope – of the division of labour within the firm and the market, we could observe either *learning by doing* (as in Smith's work) or *deteriorating by doing* (as in Babbage's work, later echoed by F. W. Taylor). The adoption of technologies that promote the division of labour of the latter type – where learning and skill development are stifled – has significant consequences for workplace knowledge, including its legal ownership. This is why the rise of business corporation at the turn of the twentieth century coincided with a further erosion of workers' skills and expertise, along with the transfer of ownership of knowledge they produced on the shop floor to the business corporation itself (Fisk 2009).

Frederick W. Taylor (1911) was among the early analysts who highlighted the conflict inherent in knowledge governance within business firms, specifically regarding the distributional effects of controlling or owning workplace knowledge. The separation of intellectual and manual labour – and the relocation of the former almost exclusively to managerial authority, as advocated by Taylor's (1911) scientific management – exemplifies this kind of technological shift. In the process, attempts to increase productivity often reduced to machine-embedded technologies, neglecting the human knowledge components, that is, workers' expertise (Fisk 2009). The problem arises primarily from the *communal* nature of knowledge production, as emphasized by many scholars (Prendergast 2021). In this context, it was Thorstein Veblen (1899, 1908a, 1908b) who first argued that the common stock of knowledge and skills is an intangible asset that enables physical production processes.[2] However, this idea was lost as economists shifted the focus to the accumulation of tangible assets, that is, physical capital (Prendergast 2021).

As Veblen had explained, production units and indeed human groups more generally have always functioned as *communities*, whose coherence and continuity are matters of shared knowledge and habits of thought. In the earliest hunter-gatherer societies, for example, the general knowledge that enabled the quest of a livelihood was arguably at least as important as capital goods and equipment. The same holds true even in industrial societies: accumulated experience and knowledge are still transmitted within the community and are thus in a meaningful sense collectively owned. However, what has changed significantly since the Industrial Revolution is that ownership of physical capital goods and equipment has become

2 In classical economics, as represented by Adam Smith, David Ricardo, or Karl Marx, the possession and use of capital goods (such as machinery, tools, and equipment) are central to the organization of production, with the division between capitalists and workers based on this premise. Yet, this framework overlooks the role of knowledge or intangible assets used and controlled by firms. Veblen's more historically oriented perspective instead asks who controls and owns the useful knowledge within a community. This concern connects Veblen with the discussion on corporate knowledge commons.

TABLE 5.1 *Institutional arrangements for the creation of new knowledge*

	Ex ante	*Ex post*
Centralized	Public procurement	Prizes
Decentralized		IPR and the market

a prerequisite for effectively utilizing this shared common knowledge. The ownership of industrial equipment, as Veblen (1908a, 527) put it, became "an institution for cornering the community's intangible assets." Industrialization, accompanied by an ever-increasing production of tangible goods, thus became the dominant means of controlling immaterial wealth – and as a result a source of intra-firm conflict between capitalists and those in possession of usable knowledge, most notably technicians and engineers (Veblen 1904).

Debates about the communal and conflictual aspects of knowledge governance – particularly in business firms – have gradually lost prominence. This shift is partly due to the dominant focus of conventional economic analysis on markets, to the neglect of the internal organization of production.[3] In the basic economic model of competitive markets, atomistic firms, guided solely by the profit motive, do not genuinely need each other to produce new knowledge (Potts 2019). According to this view, the problem of knowledge production lies elsewhere. Once the intrinsic characteristics of knowledge – specifically its non-rivalry and non-excludability – are taken into account, an important implication emerges. Knowledge is a public good (Samuelson 1954; Ostrom and Ostrom 1977; Hess and Ostrom 2007). A well-developed body of literature on market failure in economics addresses potential remedies for managing public goods, and this framework is applied, usually uncritically, to knowledge governance as well. Since the conventional approach in economics is built on the dichotomy between market and state, the proposed solutions typically involve institutional arrangements that fall within one of these categories (Scotchmer 2004). These alternative arrangements are illustrated in Table 5.1.

The IPR system is considered as a distinct approach to incentivizing knowledge production, as it is the only *decentralized* mechanism that addresses the underinvestment problem by establishing an efficient market for various kinds of knowledge assets (Scotchmer 2004; Gans and Stern 2010; Gürpinar and Özveren 2024). On the other hand, centralized solutions typically involve some form of government intervention, depending on whether the reward is given before or after the creation of new knowledge. In this regard, the IPR system is not only an ex post mechanism but also the only system that is believed to charge only the consumers who are willing to pay for the creation of new knowledge. The theory that comes closest to the often-overlooked discussion of intra-firm dynamics concerning the control and ownership

[3] A now-seminal exception in this regard is Coase (1937).

of knowledge is human capital theory. This theory has been used to address dilemmas related to workplace knowledge by conceptualizing worker skills and competencies as valuable *assets* or resources (Romer 1986; Arrow 1962; Becker 1964). However, human capital theory primarily emphasizes individual decisions – such as those made by employees to acquire knowledge – and the impact of these decisions on productivity. What it tends to overlook is the inherently conflictual nature of knowledge governance, largely because it pays insufficient attention to the legal dimension of ownership and control.

In this context, one of the key contributions of the Governing Knowledge Commons (GKC) approach is its recognition of institutional arrangements that are largely absent from the traditional framework. The standard public goods perspective tends to overlook the importance of informal rules and community characteristics – such as social norms of sharing, cooperation, and reciprocity – in shaping knowledge governance (Hess and Ostrom 2007; Frischmann et al. 2014; Kealey and Ricketts 2014; Potts 2019; Dekker and Kuchař 2021; Prendergast 2021). This oversight stems from a failure to account for the *communal* nature of knowledge production, as emphasized in earlier literature, and from a lack of attention to how agents manage the conflicts that arise from this communal dimension of knowledge governance – conflicts that lie beyond the scope of the public goods paradigm. Meanwhile, developed during roughly the same period, the Institutional Complementarities (IC) approach sheds light on the inefficiencies and diversity that emerge from the interdependent and complex nature of knowledge creation. It redirects attention to the issue of the ownership of knowledge assets and how it may influence the evolution of knowledge governance in today's knowledge-based economies (Pagano and Rossi 2004; Pagano 2011; Landini 2013; Gürpinar 2016a).

Against this background, this chapter proposes a study of corporate knowledge commons that focuses on the micro-level interdependence between technological advancements and institutional diversity in IPR within business corporations. I integrate the IC approach with the GKC framework to explore the interplay between the characteristics of knowledge as a shared resource, the formal and informal rules governing its production and uses, and the strategic choices of the relevant actors. Section 5.2 outlines the theoretical foundations of the GKC and IC and discusses the possible benefits of their integration. Section 5.3 dwells into a micro-level analysis of the intra-firm evolution of and interdependence between the choice of IPR regimes and technological trajectories. Section 5.4 concludes the chapter.

5.2 INSTITUTIONAL COMPLEMENTARITIES AND ADJACENT ACTION SITUATIONS IN THE GKC FRAMEWORK

The GKC approach demonstrates that institutional arrangements for knowledge governance extend beyond IPR systems and government regulations. In other words, it highlights that the traditional framework – focused primarily on markets and state intervention – is incomplete. Several factors contribute to this limitation. First and foremost, the public goods approach overlooks the role of informal rules and the features of the community – such as social norms of sharing, cooperation, and reciprocity – in knowledge governance (Hess and Ostrom 2007; Kealey and Ricketts 2014; Benkler 2017; Potts 2019; Prendergast 2021). *Reciprocity* plays a particularly crucial role in this context, since access to shared knowledge usually requires prior contribution. The nature of reciprocity demands contribution to maintain membership in a community, that is, free riding generally is not sustainable in ongoing communal relationships. Moreover, as Prendergast (2021) points out, knowledge communities produce not only codified knowledge but also knowledge embodied in individuals. Production and dissemination of such tacit knowledge depend on specific norms of conduct, and usually evolve organically within the community. Therefore, the governance of knowledge production and dissemination operates not only through market-based systems with IPR and government regulation but also through community-based frameworks built on social norms. These governance structures determine the degree of openness with which knowledge can be accessed and shared. Importantly, alternative governance structures, which mediate the primary tension between technology and institutions in the governance of knowledge commons, are not mutually exclusive.

Second, shared knowledge is not usually easily accessible because its tacitness creates barriers. This further reinforces the value of the GKC approach and challenges the understanding of knowledge as originally proposed by the public goods approach (Polanyi 1958; Nelson and Winter 1982; Teece et al. 1997; Teece 1998).[4] Knowledge exhibits only partial excludability features (Kealey and Ricketts 2014, 2021). Setting aside the more philosophical debates on the nature of tacit knowledge (Cowan et al. 2000), its existence underscores the importance of community-based knowledge governance, that is, governance that involves neither recourse to public intervention nor IPRs as traditionally understood. In such alternative knowledge governance structures, contributors receive differential benefits compared with non-contributors (Kealey and Ricketts 2014; Aydogmus and Gürpinar 2022).

Third, knowledge is a unique asset in part because it is an intangible resource (Frischmann et al. 2014) whose production and reproduction require continuous interaction among agents. This process is subject to another qualification: the production of new knowledge almost always relies on existing knowledge as an input. Therefore, knowledge production is highly sequential and cumulative (Scotchmer 1991). These characteristics add to the complexity of knowledge governance, since the conditions under which new knowledge is produced are significantly shaped by prior knowledge and the institutional arrangements that enable them. In this context, the action arena (see below) in which knowledge-related decisions are made is influenced

[4] Further research is needed to demarcate the role of tacit knowledge and informal rules (in a unified framework). For such an effort, see Gürpinar and Aydogmus (2022).

by historical trajectories of both legal arrangements and technology. This process is path-dependent. Since pre-existing conditions exert a significant influence on the production on new knowledge, knowledge production and dissemination must be analysed within a *dynamic* framework, where past choices and strategies of agents exert a lasting influence on current and future decisions.

The GKC framework – like the Institutional Analysis and Development (IAD) framework upon which it is based – provides researchers with a powerful tool for analysing the diverse and often conflictual institutional arrangements that shape knowledge governance. It allows for the integration of key elements, such as the role of communities, social norms, tacit knowledge, and the dynamic nature of knowledge production, within a unified analytical structure. An important strength of the GKC framework is its ability to distinguish external variables – such as community attributes and rules-in-use – and the action arena, which includes the strategies and interactions of individual agents (Cole 2014). This distinction facilitates a more detailed analysis of how agents' actions both shape and are shaped by the formal and informal institutions in place.

In this formulation, the GKC framework highlights the complexity of knowledge governance that arises from the *interdependence* between various institutional arrangements. This interdependence was, in fact, a central concern for Elinor Ostrom. She argued that, at the configural level of analysis, the effect of a single rule is *dependent* on some other rules within a given situation (Ostrom 1986). Consequently, she rejected the idea of studying rules in isolation and instead emphasized the importance of studying the interdependence between rules-in-use as components of broader institutional context. Ostrom acknowledged the inherent complexity of institutional arrangements and identified game theory – an important foundation of the IAD framework (Ostrom 2010, 810) – as a useful tool for formalizing and understanding this complexity, particularly as it gives rise to various social dilemmas (Ostrom et al. 1994).

This is why incorporating adjacent actions situations into the GKC framework represents a fruitful conceptual innovation (Dekker and Kuchař 2024) that can deepen our understating of the corporation as an institution (Gindis and Cole 2026, this volume). As argued by Cole et al. (2019), no single action situation exists in isolation; instead, actions situations can be seen as a network. This means that actions as well as outcomes in one action situation influence other action situations. For example, as Dekker and Kuchař (2024) point out, various elements of market governance, most notably the formation and implementation of rules, constitute action situations that are adjacent to the primary action situation, which is market exchange itself. These adjacent action situations interact with and influence one another, thereby collectively determining the performance of outcomes of the market exchange itself.

The key idea underpinning the IC approach, namely that there are interdependent choice domains, links well with the Bloomington School's concept of adjacent action situations. Likewise, rooted in game theory, the IC framework provides a theoretical lens for examining the interdependence between institutions (Pagano and Rowthorn 1994;

Aoki 2001; Pagano 2007; Landini and Pagano 2016). Originally applied in the context of firm behaviour (Milgrom and Roberts 1990), the IC approach has since been used to explore the *complementarities* between technology and property rights within production processes. Specifically, it examines how the characteristics of tangible assets used in production interact with formal and informal institutional arrangements – those that govern the distribution of ownership and control rights – across the micro, meso, and macro levels of economic analysis (Hall and Soskice 2001; Landini and Pagano 2016).[5] More generally, the IC approach provides a valuable tool for analysing the origins and evolution of institutional diversity, where interdependence across domains lead to the emergence of multiple equilibria. Depending on initial conditions that shape the available choices in any one domain, suboptimal or inferior institutional arrangements may emerge (Aoki 2001; Nicita and Pagano 2005). This analytical strength of the framework aligns closely with the study of knowledge commons, since, as Benkler (2017) argues, institutional diversity is one of the defining characteristics of such knowledge commons.

The IC approach offers a framework for comparing and contrasting these alternative institutional arrangements in term of (Pareto) efficiency.[6] This framework helps explain why (or how) inferior institutional arrangements may *persist* under certain conditions in knowledge governance. While competition may effectively select for (Pareto) efficient technologies, given a set of formal and informal rules, it may also inhibit the emergence and development of more efficient technologies, which could thrive under alternative institutional arrangements (Pagano 2011). Such outcomes may arise from agents' inability to *strategically* coordinate their choices across different domains (Nicita and Pagano 2005) or from conflicts of interest regarding the division of the surplus generated by their interactions (Bowles 2004). In this way, the IC approach sheds light on phenomena like persistence, inertia, and diversity, which are frequently observed in the analysis of institutional change. This insight is especially relevant to the study of corporate knowledge commons, particularly in relation to the role of IPR in competitive corporate behaviour (Benkler 2002, 2017; Boldrin and Levine 2008). A key takeaway is that the viability of any technology is intrinsically influenced by existing property rights regimes, and vice versa.

These considerations suggest that a combination of the IC and GKC frameworks can yield valuable insights. Figure 5.1 combines the IC and the GKC frameworks in the context of the present discussion.

In the GKC framework, the knowledge creation action arena comprises several adjacent action situations in which agents interact. The IC approach is particularly informative in highlighting the interdependence between specific adjacent action situations. These include the choice of technology (technologies that either foster or hinder investment in human capital) and the selection of various forms of IPR (such

5 See Gagliardi (2014) for an extensive overview of the literature.

6 See Aoki (2001) and Landini and Pagano (2016) for a formal exposition of the IC framework. In game theory, "strategic complementarity" is used to address a similar concern (Bowles 2004).

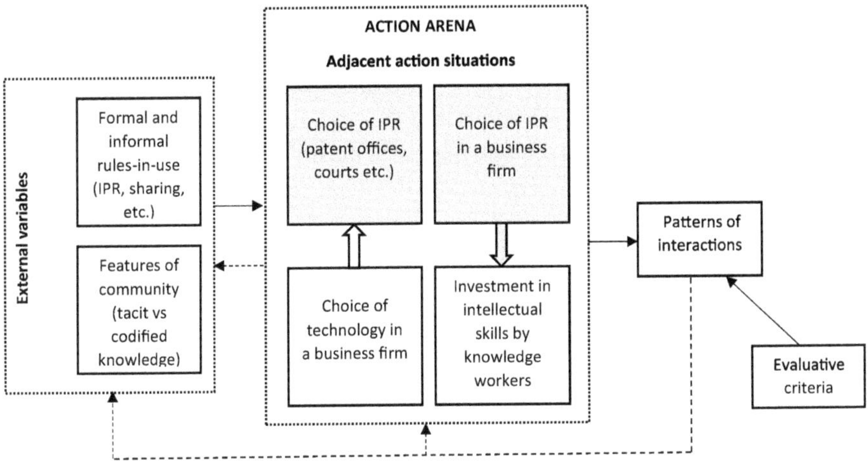

FIGURE 5.1 A combined GKC–IC framework.

as patents, trade secrets, and non-compete agreements) by firms. In the IPR domain (represented by the grey-shaded squares in Figure 5.1), the strategies of key actors include the provision of IPR forms by a government body (e.g. patent office), enforcement of IPRs by non-governmental public actors (e.g. courts), and the selection of IPR forms by firms. In the technology domain (represented by the white squares in Figure 5.1), the strategies of key actors revolve around the choice of technology (by firms) and investment in human capital (by firms and employees). The choices made by actors (patent office, courts, firms) in the IPR domain strategically interact with those in the technology domain (e.g. firms' investments in technology, workers' investment human capital).

These interactions within the action arena represent only part of the complexity of knowledge creation. External variables – such as the existing features of the community (including the prevailing codified and tacit knowledge encapsulated in technology), and formal and informal rules (including the IPR regime and social norms) – can also exert significant influence on the choice of technology and IPR within the action arena. Moreover, the choice of technology and IPR in the action arena can themselves become external variables that, in turn, affect the choices of agents in a dynamic framework. This dynamic and complex nature of knowledge governance is highlighted in the GKC framework.[7] In essence, as Cole et al. (2019) note, there is an almost *dialectical* process through which external variables in one period are transformed into outcomes, subsequently becoming the external variables for the next period. The block arrows in Figure 5.1 illustrate the interplay between these two domains.

[7] As illustrated in Figure 5.1.2 in Frischmann et al. (2014: 19).

The interdependence between the choice of technology and IPR operates through two channels. The first channel, highlighted by the GKC framework, is the *recursive* interdependence between adjacent action situations and pre-existing conditions. The second channel, underscored by the IC approach, emphasizes the interdependence that exists between these two broad domains within the action arena – technology and IPR – depicted by the white and grey boxes in Figure 5.1. A notable feature of the IC approach – and its key contribution to the present discussion – is its assertion that actors often struggle to strategically coordinate their decisions within this second channel of interdependence. This dynamic is a significant source of institutional evolution and diversity in knowledge creation, which also explains the potential source of persistence of certain institutional arrangements (e.g. an overreliance on IPR) that are often criticized in the literature (as explored further in the next section).

The analysis can be broken down as follows. As we have seen, the GKC framework highlights how feedback from outcomes of action situations affects, directly or indirectly, resource attributes, community attributes, and rules-in-use. As a result, all external variables are *endogenized* within the framework, forming sets of "initial conditions" that precede any particular social interaction. One example of this dynamic interdependence can be found in the evolution of the IPR regime. Central authorities have, over the last two centuries, made substantial investment in the establishment of the IPR regime as we know it today. Consequently, the legal environment is now primarily designed for inventors who seek exclusive rights to their innovations. As the pendulum has swung strongly towards private property and secrecy (Fisk 2009), there has been only a minimal effort to establish systems that promote knowledge sharing (Baldwin and von Hippel 2011). The potentially detrimental effects of the current IPR regime on new forms of business, including commons-based peer production, are well documented (Boyle 2003; Benkler 2006).

This suggests that existing legal rules exert a significant influence in shaping business firms' choice of technology. That is, these legal infrastructures can either facilitate or impede the accumulation of new knowledge by knowledge workers, as the ownership and control of knowledge assets – outcomes of past interactions – have a decisive impact on business firms' choice of technology today. Strict IPR, for example, may hinder investment in human capital by workers, while simultaneously promoting investment in technologies that favour codified technology by firms (Cowan et al. 2000; Foray 2004; Aydogmus and Gürpinar 2022). To put it differently, as Benkler (2006) argued, the legal regime functions as an institution that allows yesterday's winners to dictate the rules of competition today. This analysis can be extended to demonstrate how the set of initial conditions regarding the characteristics of technology – such as the prior choice of codification at the expense of workers' skills and abilities – can facilitate not only further investment in technologies that deepen reliance on codified knowledge but also the tightening of IPR in the realm of workplace knowledge, as documented by Fisk (2009). A clear example of this was found in Taylor's scientific management, which prioritized the codification of knowledge embedded in tasks over the development of worker's skills and expertise. Furthermore, this process can lead to systemic underinvestment in workers' intellectual skills and expertise, emerging from the mutually reinforcing relationship between technological choice and IPR regimes.

Yet, the role of IPR in our framework functions both as an external variable (i.e. a pre-existing condition) and as a strategic choice within the action arena. This dual role arises because the so-called intrinsic features of knowledge – such as its degree of tacitness – are themselves shaped by firms' strategic decisions concerning IPR. For example, when firms choose whether to rely on technologies embodied in workers' skills or to codify knowledge in ways that reduce reliance on workers' skills, they often *actively* use IPR to restrict the use of embodied knowledge created in the production process. In doing so, firms can strategically deploy legal instruments to prevent workers from using their tacit knowledge outside the firm. Thus, treating the legal framework solely as a set of initial condition risks overlooking how business firms continually use IPR not only in competition with other firms but also as a tool of control over workers, as illustrated by growing reliance on non-compete agreements (Marx 2015).

This unique feature of the ongoing interplay between technology and IPR in the knowledge economy was first recognized by Elkin-Koren and Salzberger (2004) and Pagano and Rossi (2004). These authors emphasize that neither technology nor IPR can be treated as fixed or purely external variables. Instead, their interdependence must be explicitly addressed in any meaningful analysis of knowledge creation. In line with this, and inspired by Gindis and Cole's (this volume) argument that the routine operations of business firms – embedded within a network of adjacent action situations – reinforce and are informed by the legal status of the corporation, the next section proposes an analysis that zooms in on relevant intra-firm relationships. Specifically, it focuses on strategic interactions among stakeholders, such as shareholders, managers, and knowledge workers.

5.3 THE CORPORATION AS COMMONS: IPR AND THE GOVERNANCE OF KNOWLEDGE IN FIRMS

Examinations of *corporate* knowledge commons, developed as part of the broader GKC research program, offer valuable insights into the governance of knowledge across various levels of economic analysis. Viewing the modern business corporation through the lens of commons arrangements, along the lines initially proposed by Deakin (2012), requires the identification of the types of *shared* assets or resources involved in corporate knowledge creation. Crucially, many of these intangible (knowledge) assets are created communally through the contributions of various stakeholders, such as shareholders, managers, and employees (Gindis and Cole, this volume). Thereby, it is important to recall that technologies utilized by business corporations are the product of cumulative interactions among various stakeholders over time (Allen 1983; Boyle 2003; Nuvolari 2004; Kealey and Ricketts 2021). It is this communal nature of accumulated knowledge that justifies analysing the business firm as corporate knowledge commons. Legal, but perhaps more crucially, social infrastructures – such as norms of sharing and cooperation – play a critical role when conceptualizing corporation as a commons.[8]

The value of communal cooperation notwithstanding, interactions among intra-firm stakeholders are often fraught with conflict. Moreover, as Milgrom and Roberts (1990) emphasized, the strategies of various stakeholders within business firms are not perfectly coordinated. Typically, managers shape the firm's technological trajectory, particularly thorough investments in codified knowledge; knowledge workers make decisions regarding the development of their intellectual skills; and shareholders influence the legal treatment of knowledge assets to reap the benefits (Gürpinar 2016b). The strategic interactions between these three sets of actors in different decision domains – which are increasingly acknowledged in the context of the knowledge economy (Landini 2013; Gürpinar 2016b) – underscore the value of the combined GKC–IC framework.

As noted in the introduction, a central conflict in business firms concerns the ownership and control of knowledge assets created during and used in the production process. While patents are the most viable form of IPR protection employed by firms, they may suit the codified portion of those assets but are generally insufficient for safeguarding the full range of knowledge developed internally within firms. Some of these knowledge assets are embodied in the skills, talent, and expertise of knowledge workers (Prendergast 2021), which poses a challenge to the traditional forms of IPR protection.

Assume that the circle in Figure 5.2 represents a technique – a specific technology that enables a firm to produce a given product. Since the codified portion of knowledge (which can be protected through patents) constitutes only a part of the total knowledge embodied in a technique, business corporations seeking to minimize involuntary knowledge spillovers related to the technique often employ a variety of additional legal strategies within the domain of IPR. Put differently, when patents prove inadequate, control over intra-firm knowledge assets are governed by other legal mechanisms, such as trade secrets and non-compete covenants (Marx 2015).

Such strategic choices made by firms interact closely with the choices of knowledge workers. A key consequence of efforts to safeguard intangible assets is that it may lead to underinvestment by knowledge workers, in response to perceptions that

[8] A valuable analysis of social infrastructures, broadly understood, can be found in Frischmann (2012). That markets rely on social infrastructure and function effectively, thanks to the interplay between physical and intellectual or knowledge infrastructures has been highlighted by Dekker and Kuchař (2019, 2021). This approach shows how such intangible infrastructures shape investment decisions in physical capital, and demonstrates the intricate relationships between institutions, functioning markets, and capital formation.

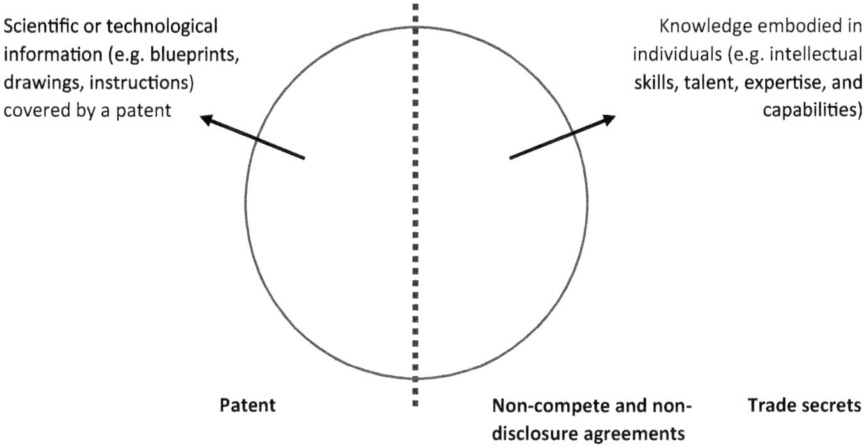

FIGURE 5.2 Complementary legal arrangements governing a technique.

their contributions are excessively controlled by their employers. Faced with less-than-fully cooperating employees, firms may further restrict workers from owning or using the knowledge assets they developed during their employment outside the firm. Non-competes thus restrict the productive uses of employees' occupational or industry-specific human capital outside the firm. Corporations often justify the use of such strategies by arguing that trade secrets alone are often insufficient; non-competes are also employed to prevent the leakage of trade secrets (Marx and Fleming 2012). These tools that strive to safeguard intangible assets beyond what the patent system can offer function not as substitutes to be used for different contexts, but as *complements* to patents. Outcome 1 captures this idea.[9]

> *Outcome 1*: Firms will extend and tighten IPR in the domain of employee human capital in order to safeguard patents.

This outcome explains, at least in part, how and why corporations have extended the scale and scope of IPR beyond their original intent – which was primarily justified on the ground of correcting market failures. In this context, it goes without saying that an institutional environment already favouring IPR not only facilitates but also further incentivizes business firms to expand the scale and scope of IPR protection, often at the expense of openness and sharing-based institutional arrangements.

[9] Outcomes, as specified in the GKC framework, are simply "patterns of interactions" and are in fact inseparable from patterns of interactions (Frischmann et al. 2014, 20). For the sake of simplicity, in the present discussion outcomes represent patterns that emerge from interactions in adjacent action situations.

Much of this expansion in IPR strategies centers on patents. However, since it is the skills and expertise of employees that create the knowledge-intensive outputs requiring protection, firms increasingly resort to additional legal mechanisms aimed at controlling employees' human capital. The overall effect is to control workplace knowledge in both its codified form (patents) and tacit dimensions (non-compete agreements).

A second set of strategies used by business firms focuses on technology. In the race to accumulate more patents, business firms can also increasingly invest in technologies that favour codified knowledge over tacit knowledge. Specifically, firms may choose to invest in technologies that facilitate the codification of knowledge, which in turn supports patenting efforts, as codification detaches knowledge from the individual who possesses it. This is summarized in Outcome 2. This strategy is employed because codification makes the object of protection more clearly identifiable (Cowan et al. 2000; Foray 2004; Arora and Gambardella 2010). As a result, the possibilities and prospects of patentability increase, allowing a greater extent of a technique to be covered by a patent.

> *Outcome 2*: Firms will invest in technologies that enable the codification of knowledge, which facilitates patenting and the broader extension of IPR.

This shift towards codified knowledge is detrimental to the accumulation of tacit knowledge. Thus, by investing in technologies that rely on and promote codification, firms reduce their reliance on tacit knowledge. This, in turn, diminishes the bargaining power of knowledge workers. Overall, such shifts in the domain of technology risks marginalizing the critical role of workers' intellectual skills and expertise in the production process, thereby altering the internal knowledge dynamics within the business corporation in ways that are potentially detrimental to knowledge workers (see Figure 5.3). Indeed, developments in technologies that significantly enhance codification (artificial intelligence, machine learning, and so on) further exemplify this outcome.

Patenting begets further patenting, creating a web of interactions across adjacent action situations that sustain and reinforce each other. While a possible justification for this overreaching control over all types of knowledge assets, including those embodied in workers' skills, could be that firms must protect themselves from the potential loss of knowledge assets, the feedback effect on the willingness of knowledge workers to invest in human capital can be detrimental, especially when they are unable to leverage the skills and capabilities in subsequent employment within the same industry. This is captured in Outcome 3, which is directly linked to the influence of IPR on employee incentives, which in turn shape the trajectory of technology development within business firms (Gürpinar 2016b).

> *Outcome 3*: The more firms invest in codification technologies and expand patentability, the more employees will be reluctant to develop their human capital.

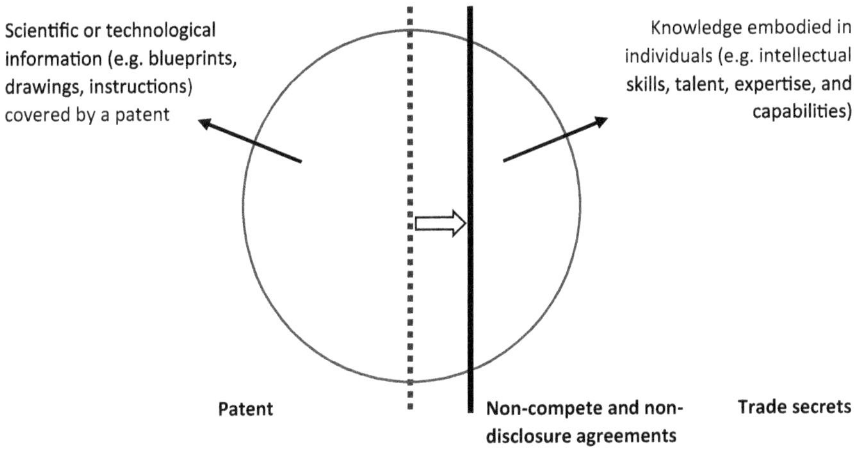

FIGURE 5.3 Changing IPR mix.

Overall, the chain of outcomes described here emerges from the interactions between stakeholders across multiple domains and depends on the configuration of adjacent action situations. The decision by firms to tighten IPR on employee-created knowledge leads to underinvestment in the development of intellectual skills among employees. What is crucial for knowledge workers is the industry and occupation-specific intellectual skills, which legal arrangements such as non-competes directly limit (Marx and Fleming 2012). Thus, efforts to limit knowledge spillovers often come at the expense of labour mobility and can undermine knowledge workers' motivation to invest in firm- and industry-specific intellectual skills (Gilson 1999; Hyde 2003; Fisk 2009; Marx and Fleming 2012). This is why some scholars argue that one reason behind the success of Silicon Valley is the non-enforcement of non-compete agreements by the state (Saxenian 1994; Gilson 1999; Hyde 2003). A contrasting example is the broader debate on non-compete agreements, which highlights how such legal arrangements can directly impact economic growth (Bjoerst 2019).

This discussion underscores another crucial implication of the combination of the IC approach with the GKC framework, augmented to include adjacent action situations. Adjacent action situations arise within a set of existing or external conditions, which are mainly shaped by the features of the resource systems within which they are embedded (Cole et al. 2019; Gindis and Cole, this volume). These conditions, which include the prevailing knowledge governance systems, in turn specify how actors are impacted by the existing conditions while interacting in the action arena. Yet, the choices made in the action arena – shaped by the prevailing knowledge governance systems, the characteristics of knowledge communities, and the legal status of knowledge – become part of the pre-existing conditions in every iteration of the web of interactions (see Figure 5.1). Therefore, to make sense of external variables (the outcome of past decisions) and to infer possible future configurations (outcome of interactions of adjacent action situations), it is crucial to examine the firm-level sources of IC within the GKC framework. As demonstrated here, this dynamic process within the business corporation emerges from two interrelated yet analytically distinct processes: first, the tightening of IPR arrangements in ways that constrain knowledge workers' autonomy over their embodied knowledge and skills; and second, increased investment in technologies that reduce reliance on tacit, worker-embodied expertise in favour of codified knowledge embedded in machinery, blueprints, software, and so on. Together, these choices create a feedback loop that discourages workers from developing their intellectual capabilities.

5.4 CONCLUSION

It has long been recognized that the primary capital of business corporations is immaterial, relying heavily on legal rights, contracts, and the process of purchase and sale in markets (Veblen 1908a: 163). Legal arrangements are therefore essential to understanding the nature of intangible assets, including knowledge, that firms utilize in the production process. This is why, in today's knowledge-based economies, there is a renewed interest in conceptualizing useful knowledge as an economic *asset*. In addition to the role of business corporations, there is a growing recognition that in the digital economy or the networked information economy, knowledge commons and innovation commons play central roles (Benkler 2002, 2006; von Hippel 2005; Hess and Ostrom 2007; Frischman et al. 2014; Potts 2019).

We now recognize that firms, industries, and indeed economies generate value by drawing on, creating, combining, and exchanging a range of intangible knowledge assets, including the codified knowledge embodied in blueprints, drawings, instructions, and software but also the tacit knowledge embodied in the skills and expertise of knowledge workers (Gürpinar and Özveren 2024). Many of these knowledge assets are inherited from the previous generations and are the result of their collective efforts (Boyle 2003; Jessop 2007). Business corporations take part in the shared collective efforts to create useful knowledge. This point directly relates to the idea of corporate knowledge commons. It is important, in this respect, to extend the discussion beyond community governance to the inherent conflicts within the business firm.

The combined GKC–IC framework proposed in this chapter offers valuable insights into the ongoing debate about how corporations can be understood as knowledge commons within today's environment – an environment that is increasingly defined by the extensive use of IPR in governing knowledge assets. A key dimension of the present discussion is the *conflictual* nature of ownership of intangible (knowledge) assets within business firms. The interdependence between adjacent action situations – particularly those involving IPR and technology – results not only in the exclusion of knowledge workers from accessing and utilizing the very knowledge they have produced but also in the gradual deterioration of their skills and expertise over time. This dynamic process creates a vicious cycle that may further erode the institutional diversity of corporate knowledge governance in favour of IPR-based governance mechanisms. Indeed, the IPR strategies employed by corporations can increase the costs of and barriers associated with the emergence of alternative, more collaborative forms of knowledge production. It is important to recognize that contemporary legal arrangements are primarily optimized for a market-based (and private property) system (Benkler 2017).

Of course, this does not imply that IPR as a tool should be abolished from the toolkit of policymakers. Rather, it suggests that IPR addresses only a portion of the broader landscape of knowledge governance in today's complex environment (Gürpinar and Özveren 2024), and that policymakers should bear in mind that current IPR-related governance mechanisms not only have the potential to extend beyond their traditional boundaries – as conceptualized by the public goods approach – but may also effectively inhibit the development of alternatives that place greater emphasis on the communal nature of knowledge production. Such alternatives would require paying due respect to the contributions in terms of skills, talent, and expertise of all stakeholders, especially knowledge workers. This perspective was highlighted in the early days of the knowledge-based economy (see, for example, Zuboff 1989). However, it has since been overshadowed by policy and scholarly debates focused on the tightening of IPR (Boldrin and Levine 2008) and the increasing codification of knowledge (Foray 2004), a trend that is likely to continue with the rise of artificial intelligence and machine learning.

As this chapter has shown, certain technologies may be seen as responses to the incentive mechanisms embedded in the existing institutional setup. Technology does not develop in an institution-free environment. Decisions about investment in technology by business firms, but also decisions regarding skill development by employees – key assets for firms – are made within an institutional environment shaped by past IPR decisions. Consequently, both prior investments in specific technologies and past decisions regarding the forms of IPRs can influence the trajectory of future technological development, by either facilitating or constraining subsequent investments in alternative technologies.

This chapter has also shown how technologies that significantly enable and enhance codification may depend, at least in part, on interactions between adjacent action situations. What this contributes to the emerging corporate knowledge commons literature is an understanding of how complementarities between various firm strategies, regarding the choice of technology and the choice of IPR, co-determine each other, and ultimately drive the evolution of technology in the system. An immediate policy implication follows. To the extent that the domains of IPR and technology complement and reinforce each other, coordinated interventions across multiple adjacent action situations are necessary to alter any institutional arrangement that is deemed suboptimal. Therefore, if scholars or public authorities identify such institutional arrangements that, for example, undermine commons aspects of knowledge governance, a combined set of policies – both in the domains of IPR and technology – is essential. Such an approach to policymaking would not only address undesired institutional arrangements but also foster greater institutional diversity in the governance of knowledge. Partial measures, such as adjusting IPR for greater openness and sharing, may be insufficient, since legal arrangements and technologies create self-sustaining equilibria.

REFERENCES

Allen, Robert C. 1983. "Collective Invention." *Journal of Economic Behavior and Organization* 4(1): 1–10.

Antonelli, Cristiano. 2007. "Technological Knowledge as an Essential Facility." *Journal of Evolutionary Economics* 17(4): 451–471.

Aoki, Masahiko. 2001. *Toward a Comparative Institutional Analysis*. MIT Press.

Arora, Ashish, and Alfonso Gambardella. 2010. "Ideas for Rent: An Overview of Markets for Technology." *Industrial and Corporate Change* 19(3): 775–803.

Arrow, Kenneth J. 1962. "Economic Welfare and the Allocation of Resources for Invention." In *The Rate and Direction of Inventive Activity: Economic and Social Factors*, ed. Richard R. Nelson, 609–626. Princeton: Princeton University Press.

Aydogmus, Özgur, and Erkan Gürpinar. 2022. "Science, Technology and Institutional Change in Knowledge Production: An Evolutionary Game Theoretic Framework." *Dynamic Games and Applications* 12(4): 1163–1188.

Becker, Gary S. 1964. *Human Capital: A Theoretical and Empirical Analysis, with Special Reference to Education*. Chicago: University of Chicago Press.

Benkler, Yochai. 2002. "Coase's Penguin, or, Linux and the Nature of the Firm." *Yale Law Journal* 112(3): 339–446.

Benkler, Yochai. 2006. *The Wealth of Networks: How Social Production Transforms Markets and Freedom*. New Haven: Yale University Press.

Benkler, Yochai. 2017. "Law, Innovation, and Collaboration in Networked Economy and Society." *Annual Review of Law and Social Sciences* 13: 231–250.

Bjoerst, Byrial. 2019. *Restrictive Covenants in Employment Contracts – An Unnoticed Hindrance to Growth in Europe*. www.europarl.europa.eu/cmsdata/86487/Bjorst_pres.pdf.

Boldrin, Michele, and David K. Levine. 2008. *Against Intellectual Monopoly*. Cambridge: Cambridge University Press.

Baldwin, Carliss, and Eric A. von Hippel. 2011. "Modelling a Paradigm Shift: From Producer Innovation to User and Open Collaborative Innovation." *Organization Science* 22(6): 1399–1417.

Bowles, Samuel. 2004. *Microeconomics: Behavior, Institutions, Evolution*. Princeton: Princeton University Press.

Boyle, James. 2003. "The Second Enclosure Movement and the Construction of the Public Domain." *Law and Contemporary Problems* 66(1): 33–74.

Coase, Ronald H. 1937. "The Nature of the Firm." *Economica* 4(16): 386–405.

Cole, Daniel H. 2014. "Learning from Nin: Lessons and Cautions from the Natural Commons for Knowledge Commons." In *Governing Knowledge Commons*, ed. Brett M. Frischmann, Michael J. Madison, and Katherine J. Strandburg, 45–68. New York: Oxford University Press.
Cole, Daniel H., Graham Epstein, and Michale D. McGinnis. 2019. "Combining the IAD and SES Frameworks." *International Journal of the Commons* 13(1): 244–275.
Corrado, Carol A., Charles R. Hulten, and Daniel E. Sichel. 2006. "Intangible Capital and Economic Growth." NBER Working Paper 11948. www.nber.org/papers/w11948.
Cowan, Robin, Paul A. David, and Dominique Foray. 2000. "The Explicit Economics of Knowledge Codification and Tacitness." *Industrial and Corporate Change* 9(2): 211–253.
Deakin, Simon. 2012. "The Corporation as Commons: Rethinking Property Rights, Governance and Sustainability in the Business Enterprise." *Queen's Law Journal* 37(2): 339–381.
Dekker, Erwin, and Pavel Kuchař. 2019. "Lachmann and Shackle: On the Joint Production of Interpretation Instruments." *Research in the History of Economic Thought and Methodology* 37B: 25–42.
Dekker, Erwin, and Pavel Kuchař, eds. 2021. *Governing Markets as Knowledge Commons*. Cambridge: Cambridge University Press.
Dekker, Erwin, and Pavel Kuchař. 2024. "Markets and Knowledge Commons: Is There a Difference between Private and Community Governance of Markets?" *Public Choice* 201(3–4): 533–553.
Elkin-Koren, Niva, and Eli M. Salzberger. 2004. *Law, Economics and Cyberspace: The Effects of Cyberspace on the Economic Analysis of Law*. Cheltenham: Edward Elgar.
Elkin-Koren, Niva, and Eli M. Salzberger. 2012. *The Law and Economics of Intellectual Property in the Digital Age*. London: Routledge.
Fisk, Catherine L. 2009. *Working Knowledge: Employee Innovation and the Rise of Corporate Intellectual Property, 1800-1930*. Chapel Hill: University of North Carolina Press.
Foray, Dominique. 2004. *Economics of Knowledge*. Cambridge, MA: MIT Press.
Frischmann, Brett M. 2012. *Infrastructure: The Social Value of Shared Resources*. New York: Oxford University Press.
Frischmann, Brett M., Michael J. Madison, and Katherine J. Strandburg, eds. 2014. *Governing Knowledge Commons*. New York: Oxford University Press.
Gagliardi, Francesca. 2014. "A Bibliometric Analysis of the Literature on Institutional Complementarities." Mimeo (on file with author).
Gans, Joshua S. and Scott Stern. 2010. "Is There a Market for Ideas?" *Industrial and Corporate Change* 19(3): 805–837.
Gilson, Ronald J. 1999. "The Legal Infrastructure of High Technology Industrial Districts: Silicon Valley, Route 128, and Covenants Not to Compete." *New York University Law Review* 74(3): 575–629.
Gindis, David, and Daniel H. Cole. 2026. "Toward a Knowledge Commons Perspective on the Corporate Form." In *Corporate Knowledge Commons*, ed. David Gindis. Cambridge: Cambridge University Press.
Gürpinar, Erkan. 2016a. "Organizational Forms in the Knowledge Economy: A Comparative Institutional Analysis." *Journal of Evolutionary Economics* 26(3): 501–518.
Gürpinar, Erkan. 2016b. "Institutional Complementarities, Intellectual Property Rights and Technology in the Knowledge Economy." *Journal of Institutional Economics* 12(3): 565–578.
Gürpinar, Erkan, and Özgur Aydogmus. 2022. "Investment in Knowledge Assets: The Role of Complementarity, Tacitness and Cooperation." https://ssrn.com/abstract=4294899.

Gürpinar, Erkan, and Eyüp Özveren, E. 2024. "Incomplete Contracts, Intellectual Property Rights and Incentives: Investment in Knowledge Assets under Alternative Institutional Configurations." In *Elgar Companion to Information Economics*, ed. Daphne R. Raban, and Julia Włodarczyk, 315–337. Cheltenham: Edward Elgar.

Hall, David A., and Peter Soskice, eds. 2001. *Varieties of Capitalism: The Institutional Foundations of Comparative Advantage*. New York: Oxford University Press.

Hyde, Alan. 2003. *Working in Silicon Valley: Economic and Legal Analysis of a High-Velocity Labor Market*. Armonk: M. E. Sharpe.

Hess Charlotte, and Ostrom, E. 2007, eds. *Understanding Knowledge as a Commons: From Theory to Practice*. Cambridge, MA: MIT Press

Jessop, Bob. 2007. "Knowledge as a Fictitious Commodity: Insights and Limits of a Polanyian Perspective." In *Reading Karl Polanyi for the Twenty-First Century*, ed. Ayşe Buğra and Kaan Ağartan, 115–133. Basingstoke: Palgrave Macmillan.

Kealey, Terence, and Martin Ricketts. 2014. "Modelling Science as a Contribution Good." *Research Policy* 43(6): 1014–1024.

Kealey, Terence, and Martin Ricketts. 2021. "The Contribution Good as the Foundation of the Industrial Revolution." In *Governing Markets as Knowledge Commons*, ed. Erwin Dekker, and Pavel Kuchař, 19–57. Cambridge: Cambridge University Press.

Landini, Fabio. 2013. "Institutional Change and Information Production." *Journal of Institutional Economics* 9(3): 257–284.

Landini, Fabio, and Ugo Pagano. 2016. "Institutional Complementarity." In *Encyclopedia of Law and Economics*, ed. Alain Marciano, and Giovanni B. Ramello, 1161–1164. New York: Springer.

Marx, Matt. 2015. "The Firm Strikes Back: Non-compete Agreements and the Mobility of Technical Professionals." *American Sociological Review* 76(5): 695–712.

Marx, Matt, and Lee Fleming. 2012. "Non-compete Agreements: Barriers to Entry ... and Exit?" *Innovation Policy and the Economy* 12(1): 39–64.

Milgrom, Paul, and John Roberts. 1990. "The Economics of Modern Manufacturing: Technology, Strategy and Organization." *American Economic Review* 80(3): 511–528.

Nelson, Richard R. 1959. "The Simple Economics of Basic Scientific Research." *Journal of Political Economy* 67(3): 297–306.

Nelson, Richard R., and Sidney S. Winter. 1982. *An Evolutionary Theory of Economic Change*. Cambridge, MA: Harvard University Press.

Nicita, Antonio, and Ugo Pagano. 2005. "Incomplete Contracts and Institutions." In *Elgar Companion to Law and Economics*, ed. Jürgen Backhaus, 145–164. Cheltenham: Edward Elgar.

Nuvolari, Alessandro. 2004. "Collective Invention during the British Industrial Revolution: The case of the Cornish Pumping Engine." *Cambridge Journal of Economics* 28(3): 347–363.

Ostrom, Elinor. 1986. "An Agenda for the Study of Institutions." *Public Choice* 48(1): 3–25.

Ostrom, Elinor. 2010. "The Institutional Analysis and Development Framework and the Commons." *Cornell Law Review* 95(4): 807–816.

Ostrom, Vincent, and Elinor Ostrom. 1977. "Public Goods and Public Choices." In *Alternatives for Delivering Public Services: Toward Improved Performance*, ed. Emanuel S. Savas, 7–49. Boulder: Westview.

Ostrom, Elinor, Roy Gardner, and James Walker. 1994. *Rules, Games and Common-Pool Resources*. Ann Arbor: University of Michigan Press.

Özveren, Eyüp, and Erkan Gürpinar. 2024. "More a Commons than a Fictitious Commodity: Tacit Knowledge, Sharing and Cooperation in Knowledge Governance." *Journal of the Knowledge Economy* 15(1): 3824–3843.
Pagano, Ugo. 2007. "Legal Positions and Institutional Complementarities." In *Legal Orderings and Economic Institutions*, ed. Fabrizio Cafaggi, Ugo Pagano, and Antonio Nicita, 54–83. London: Routledge.
Pagano, Ugo. 2011. "Interlocking Complementarities and Institutional Change." *Journal of Institutional Economics* 7(3): 379–392.
Pagano, Ugo. 2020. "Why Only Humans and Social Insects Have a Divison of Labour," *Cambridge Journal of Economics* 44(1): 1–15.
Pagano, Ugo and Maria A. Rossi. 2004. "Incomplete Contracts, Intellectual Property and Institutional Complementarities." *European Journal of Law and Economics* 18(1): 55–76.
Pagano, Ugo, and Robert Rowthorn. 1994. "Ownership, Technology and Institutional Stability." *Structural Change and Economic Dynamics* 5(2): 221–242.
Polanyi, Michael. 1958. *Personal Knowledge*. Chicago: University of Chicago Press.
Potts, Jason. 2019. *Innovation Commons: The Origin of Economic Growth*. New York: Oxford University Press.
Prendergast, Renée. 2021. "On the Social Evolution of Knowledge." In *Governing Markets as Knowledge Commons*, ed. Erwin Dekker, and Pavel Kuchař, 58–88. Cambridge: Cambridge University Press.
Romer, Paul M. 1986. "Increasing Returns and Long-Run Growth." *Journal of Political Economy* 94(5): 1002–1037.
Samuelson, Paul A. 1954. "The Pure Theory of Public Expenditure." *Review of Economics and Statistics* 36(4): 387–389.
Saxenian, AnnaLee. 1994. *Regional Advantage: Culture and Competition in Silicon Valley and Route 128*. Cambridge, MA: Harvard University Press.
Scotchmer, Suzanne. 1991. "Standing on the Shoulders of Giants: Cumulative Research and the Patent Law". *Journal of Economic Perspectives* 5(1): 29–41.
Scotchmer, Suzanne. 2004. *Innovation and Incentives*. Cambridge, MA: MIT Press.
Stone, Katherine V. W. 2013. "The Decline in the Standard Employment Contract: A Review of the Evidence." In *Rethinking Workplace Regulation: Beyond the Standard Labor Contract of Employment*, ed. Katherine V. W. Stone, and Harry Arthurs, 58–78. New York: Russell Sage Foundation Press.
Taylor, Frederick W. 1911. *The Principles of Scientific Management*. New York: Harper & Brothers.
Teece, David J. 1998. "Capturing Value from Knowledge Assets: The New Economy, Markets for Know-How, and Intangible Assets." *California Management Review* 40(3): 55–79.
Teece, David J., Gary Pisano, and Amy Shuen. 1997. "Dynamic Capabilities and Strategic Management." *Strategic Management Journal* 18(7): 509–533.
Veblen, Thorstein. 1899. *The Theory of the Leisure Class: An Economic Study in the Evolution of Institutions*. New York: Macmillan.
Veblen, Thorstein. 1904. *The Theory of Business Enterprise*. New York: Charles Scribner's Sons.
Veblen, Thorstein. 1908a. "On the Nature of Capital I." *Quarterly Journal of Economics* 22(4): 517–542.
Veblen, Thorstein. 1908b. "On the Nature of Capital II: Investment, Intangible Assets, and the Pecuniary Magnate." *Quarterly Journal of Economics* 23(1): 104–136.
von Hippel, Eric. 2005. *Democratizing Innovation*. Cambridge, MA: MIT Press.
Zuboff, Shoshana. 1989. *In the Age of the Smart Machine: The Future of Work and Power*. New York: Basic Books.

6

Who Owns a Corporation? Common-Sense Commons and Corporate Governance

Tanweer Ali

6.1 INTRODUCTION

This chapter concerns a specific type of knowledge resource, namely common sense. I will explore what types of knowledge, skills, and perspectives make up what is known as common sense and examine what might constitute a *common-sense commons* in the context of corporate governance. I will then focus on the apparently intuitive notion that shareholders own corporations, which is deeply embedded in public discourse, as an example of an idea that looks like common sense yet is by no means a matter of legal consensus. Using this example, and aided by concepts drawn from pragma-linguistics, I will show how common sense can be shaped to promote ideological precepts, in this case the ideology of shareholder primacy.

6.2 WHAT IS COMMON SENSE?

In a lecture in Edinburgh in 1965, the British philosopher Gilbert Ryle (1965, 3–4) related a conversation on a train with Bertrand Russell: "He said 'Locke was the spokesman of Common Sense.' Almost without thinking I retorted impatiently 'I think Locke invented Common Sense.' To which Russell rejoined 'By God, Ryle, I believe you are right. No one ever had Common Sense before John Locke – and no one but Englishmen have ever had it since.'"

I do not have the space here for a comprehensive history of the concept of common sense. Nevertheless, it is safe to assert that, with the greatest respect to Bertrand Russell, common sense over the ages has by no means been the sole preserve of Englishmen (nor English women, for that matter). The first known reference to common sense came from Aristotle (2012), who wrote in *De Animus* of *a common sense* through which we combine the information received from the five senses to perceive phenomena such as motion. Such phenomena involve the use of more than one of our senses, and without this common sense we would not be able to perceive them.

Our modern understanding of common sense dates back to Descartes, who wrote in *Discourse on the Method* about *le bon sens*, which "is, of all things among men, the most equally distributed" (Descartes 1912, 3). While the cognitive aspect of common sense concerns "such obvious truisms as not to be worth stating," as Moore (1925, 1) put it, early on ideas of common sense combined the cognitive dimension with the social. Drawing on Vico's (1990) thinking, Gadamer (2013, 19–20) stressed this point in his discussion of what he called *sensus communis*:

> The main thing for our purposes is that here sensus communis obviously does not mean only that general faculty in all men but the sense that founds community. According to Vico, what gives the human will its direction is not the abstract universality of reason but the concrete universality represented by the community of a group, people, a nation, or the whole human race.

Bergson (2002, 346) was even more emphatic about the social element:

> Our senses thus serve us, above all, to orient us in space; they are not turned towards science, but towards life. But we do not only live in a material milieu, but also in a social milieu. . . . It is thus indeed a sense in its own way; but while the other senses place us in relation to things, good sense presides over our relations with persons.

In a not-too-different vein, in an article describing a method for distinguishing thought process of machines and humans, Erion (2001, 33) explained that common sense concerns "the realm of familiar objects that we become acquainted with during ordinary experience." In this manner, common sense encompasses the knowledge, beliefs, and capabilities that allow us to "survive and thrive during our everyday lives" (Erion 2001, 33). Frischmann (2021), who cites Erion, seems to endorse this approach to defining and characterizing common sense, while also incorporating the social aspect. Common sense is essential for coping with everyday life, addressing common problems, and managing social systems. It is, therefore, an important component of knowledge that Strandburg et al. (2017, 10) characterize as "a broad set of intellectual and cultural resources."

A yet broader approach, echoing the work of Bourdieu, would view common sense as a product of social conditions and practices that are internalized by individuals through what he termed *habitus* (Bourdieu 1977). Such a view of common sense includes its role in creating and upholding social conventions, that is, practices and actions that are commonly regarded as acceptable or desirable (Choi 2021). A broad approach to common sense also encompasses its role in shaping discourse and makes a link between common sense and persuasion. Van Dijk (1998) has formulated a clear explanation of common sense that weaves together its cognitive and social aspects. Common sense consists of knowledge, beliefs, and opinions that are taken for granted in a society and therefore tend to be "presupposed" in discourse; it also applies to argumentation strategies as in "a common sense" argument, which is based on commonly shared premises; finally, it has a dimension which is "immediate, unreflected and untheoretical" (Van Dijk 1998, 104). Common sense is, then, "an implicit, naïve 'theory' of the world" (Van Dijk 1998, 104), which can be more or less right or wrong, and includes habits of thought and persuasion, as well as knowledge and skills.

Common sense thus conceived dovetails with the notion of a *common cultural ground*. As Van Dijk (1998, 105) summarizes:

> Common sense is then more or less what we try to conceptualize with the term "cultural beliefs," that is, the knowledge and opinions, as well as the evaluative criteria, that are common to all or most members of a culture. Like common sense, these cultural beliefs are also used as the basis for specific group beliefs, and also function as the general base of presupposed beliefs in all accounts, explanations and arguments.

Common sense includes what we, as a group, know (or think we know), along with all that we need for discourse to take place within a given social system.

Having explained common sense in terms of belief, knowledge, and skills, as well as the building blocks of discourse, I will now develop the idea of a *common-sense commons*. Before we examine the nature of what we might consider the *common-sense commons* related to corporate governance, we need to mark out the contours of the social system relevant for the study of corporate governance and this is what I will attempt to do in the next section.

6.3 THE FIELD OF CORPORATE CONTROL

We can describe the social system of interest for corporate governance with the help of Ostrom's Institutional Analysis and Development (IAD) framework (Ostrom 1990, 2005, 2011) if we consider the corporation itself as a shared resource. Deakin (2012) has set out the legal case for considering the corporation as a shared resource that is governed as a commons, grounding his argument in the commons literature. The action situations of concern are those relating to the governance and control of the corporation as a shared resource. They would include, for example, meetings of corporate boards; meetings of board committees (e.g. on the determination of executive compensation); annual general meetings; discussions on shareholder resolutions; reporting, disclosure, and compliance (e.g. production of financial and non-financial statements); other forms of communication between directors and managers; preparations for board meetings; and analyst conference calls. They would also include all forms of deliberation concerning potential mergers and acquisitions, as well as some communications with stakeholder groups besides voting shareholders. We can think of these as a nested system of interconnected action situations (Ostrom 2011; McGinnis 2020) and the set of all the actors as a community.

A useful analytical tool for conceptualizing such a social system, or community, is provided by the theory of strategic action fields (SAF) outlined by Fligstein and McAdam (2012).[1] An SAF is "a meso-level social order where actors (who can be individual or collective) interact with knowledge of one another under a set of common understandings about the purpose of the field, the relationships in the field (including who has power and why), and the field's rules" (Fligstein and McAdam 2011, 3). An SAF may be, for instance, a division within a firm, consisting of individual employees and their managers. It could also be the firm itself, comprising separate divisions. Or it could be the whole market, with different firms cooperating or competing against each other for business. Thus, fields may be contained within ever larger fields.[2] As a result, a society may have an unlimited number of SAFs, which may also overlap.

The theory of SAFs is helpful for our analysis in two ways. First, Fligstein and McAdam provide a clear method for determining whether a field exists, describing it, and, most importantly, setting its boundaries. For them, "field membership consists of those groups who *routinely* take each other into account in their actions" (Fligstein and McAdam 2012, 167). This sets a manageable boundary for our community, excluding those groups that are not routinely involved in deliberations regarding corporate control. The SAF related to corporate governance, then, comprises all the actors directly involved in the interconnected network of action situations in which matters of corporate control are resolved. This would include primarily corporate managers, directors, and shareholders (and their representatives).[3]

Parties not included in the SAF, so defined, but who are nevertheless involved include institutions (and individuals) that set standards and guide the work of boards and shareholder meetings, such as the Business Roundtable (BRT) in the United States, but also auditors, accounting standard setters, or proxy advisors. State structures, such as regulators, courts, and legislative bodies are also relevant, as are opinion formers and decision-makers, such as lawyers, academics, and the media. A narrower definition of the SAF does not preclude analysis of the influence of external actors. Fligstein and McAdam (2012) make clear that this would be a serious omission. They also emphasize the importance of examining the influence of state actors, such as the Securities and Exchange Commission (SEC), that are outside the SAF but nevertheless often play a key role.

Strategic field theory is useful for a second reason, namely that it provides a helpful analytical tool for studying social change within a community. Action

1 The theory of strategic action fields borrows the notion of fields from Bourdieu (Bourdieu 1990; Bourdieu and Wacquant 1992).

2 Fligstein and McAdam (2011) use the analogy of the Russian Matryoshka doll.

3 We should note that defining an SAF is not a normative judgement; there may be groups, such as employee representatives, that we do not place within the SAF but which we believe should have a greater degree of involvement in matters of corporate control.

situations change when the positions of and relationships between the various actors are transformed, resulting in the emergence of a new status quo. Fligstein and McAdam (2012) distinguish three types of actors in an SAF: incumbents, challengers, and governance units. Incumbents are those actors who hold power within the SAF and whose views are dominant. Challengers are those who are in a subsidiary position vis-à-vis the incumbents. Despite the designation, "challengers"' may accept their role and position, and are not necessarily in an adversarial relationship towards incumbents. Governance units are responsible for maintaining the rules within the SAF. This chapter looks primarily at incumbents and challengers.

Fligstein (2016) has described the field relating to corporate governance and refers to it "the market for corporate control,"[4] understood in a broad sense. I consider the use of the term "market" to describe this field as problematic for two reasons. First, the strategic action field concerns corporate control in a wider sense than the sale and purchase of shares in mergers and acquisitions transactions. This SAF also concerns the processes through which managers are held to account and the balance of power within corporations is maintained or changed. This includes the structure and functioning of boards, as well as the determination of who sits on boards. These aspects of the determination of control do not involve transactions where assets are exchanged, but encompass a broader range of social interactions than those necessarily associated with markets. When thinking about proxy contests as one means of establishing corporate control (Manne 1965), even if we use of term "market" in a metaphorical sense, there is a risk of unnecessary confusion.[5]

Secondly, even in the narrower domain of corporate mergers and acquisitions, the field entails a broader array of actors and institutions than simply the buying and selling of shares in market transactions. The process of takeovers is subject to a complex set of regulations in any developed market and involves an often-baffling range of issues and processes. To talk of a market for corporate control may imply a somewhat simpler perception of corporate mergers and acquisitions, and a greater level of transparency, than the often-messy reality merits. Moreover, we run the risk of exacerbating misconceptions about the link between shareholding and actual control. For this additional reason, I feel it would be preferable to use another term than "market." I prefer to think of the SAF as the "field of corporate control."

6.4 COMMON SENSE AND THE FIELD OF CORPORATE CONTROL

The common sense of a community is that set of common understandings, perspectives, and assumptions that are shared by all its members. Common sense is therefore part of the attributes of the community, contributing, as it does, to its

4 As Armour and Cheffins (2014) have explained, the term "market for corporate control" originated with Manne (1964, 1965).

5 In rejecting a potentially misleading overuse of the term "market" I have been guided by the work of Hodgson (2020).

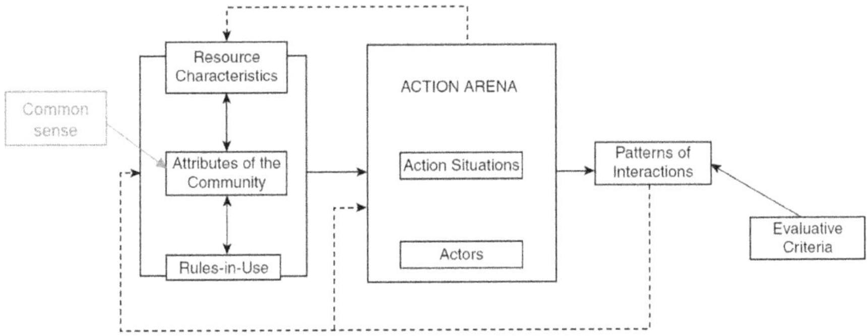

FIGURE 6.1 Common sense in the GKC framework. Source: Adapted from Sanfilippo et al. (2018, 10)

"shared understanding" (Ostrom 1986). As already explained with reference to the work of Van Dijk (1998), it also forms part of the *cultural repertoire* of the community (McGinnis 2020).[6] In an institutional analysis of corporate governance (with the corporation as the shared resource) relying on the governing knowledge commons (GKC) framework (Frischmann et al. 2014), the place of common sense is indicated in Figure 6.1.

Common sense enables both the field and the individuals within it to function. In the field of corporate control, it provides a set of background assumptions that enables discourse to take place, which either maintains stability in the field or drives a process of transformation. This holds for interactions pertaining to the composition and structure of boards, the recruitment of directors, the balance of power within governance systems, the setting of agendas for board meetings or shareholder meetings, the determination of performance metrics, and so on.

The key role of common sense in a social system or field suggests that, besides being part of the attributes of the community, common sense is itself a resource. Since it is a shared resource freely available to all within a social system, such that we can speak of a *common-sense commons*, the GKC framework appears to be an appropriate analytical tool. Frischmann (2021, 113) characterizes a common-sense commons as a "critical social infrastructure that shapes and enables various social systems." Action situations in the common-sense commons of corporate control are "adjacent," to borrow McGinnis's (2020) expression, to those of the field of corporate control.

6 The common or shared understanding can be defined via the following question: "What values and conceptual frameworks do the members of this community share, and specifically do most of them share at least some core values or goals as a member of that community?" (McGinnis 2020, 16). The cultural repertoire can be defined as the "set of strategies, norms, rules, organizational templates, and other remembered or imagined practices that are readily available to the members of that community for their use in processes of deliberation and implementation" (McGinnis 2020, 16).

In my doctoral dissertation (Ali 2024), I analysed the discourse of corporate governance in the United States during the 1980s and 1990s. In particular, I selected two genres for examination: speeches on corporate governance made by commissioners of the SEC over the period, and large samples of articles from the *Wall Street Journal* and *New York Times*. My analysis revealed how the discourse on corporations and their governance evolved during the period; importantly, the underlying assumptions and presuppositions behind the discourse changed. In other words, the common-sense commons of corporate control underwent a change. My research involved a detailed look at outputs of some of the action situations in the common-sense commons. The drafting of an SEC commissioner's speech was one such action situation involving the commissioner, their immediate staff, and possibly other SEC employees. The delivery and reporting of the speech to a public audience was another related action situation. The researching, writing, and editing of a newspaper article by a reporter was yet another. Moreover, the work of bodies such as BRT, which regularly publish and publicize statements on corporate governance, constituted a further nested set of action situations.

Common sense as a type of knowledge resource makes for a complex subject of analysis. A framework for analysing knowledge commons has been provided by Ostrom and Hess (2007) and developed further by the GKC research program (Frischmann et al. 2014; Strandburg et al. 2017; Sanfilippo et al. 2018). Special attention should be paid to the exogenous variables: material characteristics, the attributes of the community, and the rules-in-use. The material characteristics of a common-sense commons include the means of the dissemination of ideas. Changes brought by developments in technology and communication are of special importance.

A study of a common-sense commons would be concerned with not only the contents and nature of the knowledge but also with the rules-in-use that govern it. Unlike other forms of knowledge commons, it is not subject to clear and formal rules. Nevertheless, that is not to say that it is not subject to any rules. What constitutes common sense is determined – and changed – over time.

An important aspect of the rules-in-use relates to the selection of individuals and institutions – including journalists, academics, public officials, analysts, consultants, and business leaders – that are the most important in defining and refining what constitutes common sense. The views of some key actors enter the media – what Hall et al. (1978) term "primary definers." Some "experts" – and some opinions – are frequently quoted in prominent media and these are the actors who play an important role in defining mainstream opinion. Meanwhile other views are largely ignored. An important task of an analyst of the rules-in-use of the common sense of the field of corporate control is to identify the action situations in which the primary definers are chosen, and to examine whether there are any unspoken rules or criteria for such choices. This will include not only studying actions related to how journalists and editors select sources to quote but also understanding the media operations of influential organizations and the role of media ownership and control. The rules-in-use of the field of corporate control are closely related to the attributes of the community.

The GKC framework can be used to analyse changing as well as static situations. I will return briefly to questions about the governance of common-sense commons in the concluding section of this chapter. In the next section, I will examine how common sense can be made to include notions that are actually *ideological* in character. I will then present a case study of how an apparently common-sense notion served to support a transformation in the field of corporate control.

6.5 COMMON SENSE AND IDEOLOGY

As Frischmann (2021, 125) points out, common sense can be "biased and wrong." Common-sense assumptions can be misguided and even manipulative. Additionally, there are problems of scale and scope; simplifications and heuristics that may serve as reasonable approximations in one context may be misleading when applied elsewhere. This is a pertinent risk when heuristics that are effective in micro situations are extended to the macro context (Redekop 2009; Frischmann 2021).

Discourse analysts, such as Fairclough (2015), have explained that common sense can serve as a highly effective tool for promulgating ideologies. Ideology has been defined concisely by Reisigl and Wodak (2016, 26) as "a perspective (often one-sided), i.e. a world view and a system composed of related mental representations, convictions, opinions, attitudes, values and evaluations." It is also important to note that ideologies are "open to normative critique" (Fairclough 2015, 32). By far the most common conceptualization of ideology as used in Critical Discourse Studies draws inspiration from Gramsci's (1971) concept of hegemony, according to which ideologies serve to reinforce social and power relations, and are at their most effective when disguised and presented as common sense. This allows readers or listeners to be convinced of the necessity of the actions being supported without full deliberation. As Fairclough (2015, 108) explains:

> Ideology is most effective when its workings are least visible. If one becomes aware that a particular aspect of common sense is sustaining power inequalities at one's own expense, it ceases to be common sense. . . . And invisibility is achieved when ideologies are brought to discourse not as explicit elements of the text, but as background assumptions which on the one hand lead the text producer to "textualize" the world in a particular way, and on the other hand leads the interpreter to interpret the text in a particular way. . . . The more mechanical the functioning of an ideological assumption in the construction of coherent interpretations, the less likely it is to become a focus of conscious awareness, and hence the more secure its ideological status.

As Bourdieu and Wacquant (1992, 250) point out, ideology results in *habits of thought* which are often hard to overcome, even among scholars.

This explanation of what is meant by ideology and common sense is very much a traditional one used in the field of discourse analysis. But there is an alternative understanding of ideology that is superior in its explanatory power. This theory, developed by Van Dijk (1998), is based on social psychology, and takes greater account of the cognitive dimension of discourse (Forchtner 2018). Van Dijk (1998, 8) characterizes ideology as "the basis of the social representations shared by members of a group." This is not the same as a world view, as it encompasses the set of ideas upon which a world view is formed. Ideology does not equate to common sense; an ideology is shared among groups within the culture, whereas common sense pertains to the whole culture. However, an ideology may over time become – or cease to be – part of common sense.

In this conceptualization, the term ideology does not necessarily have the negative connotations of its use in the Marxist tradition. While ideologies may support power relations and inequality, they may also be emancipatory, in the sense of opposing power and its abuse, or indeed not involve power at all. One individual may be part of different groups sharing different ideologies. For instance, a person may work in the corporate sector and subscribe to the basic competitive profit-seeking ideology of modern business; they might at the same time be part of a religious group sharing a very different set of beliefs regarding charity. In any case, it should be clear that an ideology may change over time; it need not be static.

Van Dijk argues that ideology and common sense can be connected through the process of *legitimation*, that is, by providing a justification or motivation for actions that may be subject to criticism and challenge (or potential challenge). Of particular interest is the legitimation of action that is taken (or advocated) in an institutional context; legitimation may be provided by individuals as well as official bodies such as organizations, boards, or assemblies. As van Dijk explains (1998, 256): "legitimating discourses presuppose norms and values. They implicitly or explicitly state that some course of action, decision or policy is 'just' within the given legal or political system, or more broadly within the prevalent moral order of society." Ideology that encompasses a call for the adoption of a particular set of policies, especially when this entails a break from the past, will be more appealing if accompanied by legitimation that is effective. In summary, presenting claims that are founded on particular ideological assumptions as uncontroversial common sense can represent a powerful legitimation strategy. Effectively, this serves the purpose of "blocking one's rational device" (Saussure 2005, 128). Presenting or effectively disguising an idea as common sense blocks the normal critical faculties that would lead one to examine the validity of the idea.[7]

[7] Boltanski and Thévenot (1999) have usefully described the link between actions and justifications: presenting an idea as common sense serves to validate some justifications (and corresponding actions) and inhibit others.

6.6 THE IDEOLOGY OF SHAREHOLDER VALUE

For at least the period from the end of the Second World War to the late 1970s, the field of corporate control, dominated as it was by managers, was stable. In the framework of strategic field theory, during this era of what Chandler (1962) termed "managerial capitalism," managers were the incumbents and the prevailing view of corporate purpose was that the business corporation existed to serve broader social goals, beyond earning financial profits. The dominant view on the purpose of the corporation during the era of managerial capitalism was neatly summarized by the BRT in a statement on corporate responsibility in October 1981. The statement approvingly cited Reginald Jones, who had just completed his term as chairman and chief executive of General Electric (and had been chairman of the BRT until 1980): "Public policy and social issues are no longer adjuncts to business planning and management. They are in the mainstream of it. . . . Management must be measured for performance in noneconomic and economic areas alike" (The Business Roundtable 1981, 1).

However, the 1980s and 1990s saw a transformation in the field of corporate control. Fligstein (2016) cites the high inflation and economic stagnation of the 1970s as external shocks which set in motion the change that was to empower a set of challengers to incumbent corporate managers. Cheffins (2019) refers to numerous corporate scandals, a general decline in public confidence in managers to deliver economic prosperity, and increased competition from Japanese firms. Moreover, some external constraints on management, in the form of union power, regulation, and limited access to lending capital, were losing their saliency. As a result, the stability of the field was undermined, and new actors gained the ascendancy. Fligstein (2016), Heilbron et al. (2014), and Cheffins (2021) stress the important role played by so-called corporate raiders, who were relative outsiders in this transformation. Fligstein (2016) also describes the many in the financial community as challengers. The credo of the newly empowered actors was "shareholder value maximization" (or "shareholder value" for short), the idea summed up by Friedman (1962, 1970) that corporate managers were obliged to place the interest of shareholders above all other concerns.

Some scholars of corporate governance (Lazonick and O'Sullivan 2000; Stout 2012) have referred to shareholder value as an ideology. I believe it is reasonable and methodologically sound to treat it as an ideology. It certainly fits the description of a set of representations shared by a group. The argument made by adherents of shareholder value draws on a number of apparently common-sense assumptions and pre-suppositions, one of the most important of which being the premise that share owners jointly own the corporation.

6.7 SHAREHOLDERS AS OWNERS OF CORPORATIONS

The common sense of corporate governance tends to include the pre-supposition that corporations, including actively traded listed companies, are owned by their shareholders. Friedman (1970) predicated his argument for shareholder primacy on ownership in his famous *New York Times Magazine* article:

> A corporate executive is an employee of the owners of the business. He has direct responsibility to his employers. That responsibility is to conduct the business in accordance with their desires, which generally will be to make as much money as possible while conforming to the basic rules of the society, both those embodied in law and those embodied in ethical custom.

This is reflected in the BRT's position towards the end of the 1990s, which clearly links shareholder primacy with ownership (The Business Roundtable 1997, 1): "The Business Roundtable wishes to emphasize that the principal objective of a business enterprise is to generate economic returns to its owners. ... The Business Roundtable believes that good corporate governance practices provide an important framework for a timely response by a corporation's board of directors to situations that may directly affect stockholder value."

At the turn of the millennium Arthur Levitt, President Clinton's SEC chairman, summed up his view on corporate governance even more succinctly: "This system works brilliantly, provided those in control operate for the sole benefit of the true owners of public companies – the shareholders" (Levitt 2000).

None of these three statements are accompanied by any sort of discussion of ownership and corporations. That shareholders own the corporation is stated but not explained. Friedman, the BRT, and Levitt all simply use ownership as a starting point. It is presented as self-evident and as such is not debatable. In other words, that shareholders own corporations is introduced as common sense. This is to be found throughout the discourse on corporate governance and was especially notable during the rise of the shareholder value norm. Ownership is used as a legitimation strategy, to "shut down the argument" on the place of shareholders in the purpose of the business corporation.

Yet this notion, though frequently unchallenged in public discourse, does not align with specialist knowledge. Common sense is not necessarily the same thing as specialist (or scientific) knowledge, which may be restricted to people with specific educational and professional backgrounds and training. That said, to the extent that specialist knowledge has passed into the sphere of what is taken for granted among the population at large, there is an overlap with common sense. For example, the assertion that the Earth is round has been accepted as part of common sense (with the exception of a small but colourful minority), as has the heliocentric view of the solar system. Similarly, that smoking is an unhealthy habit has also been widely accepted. On the other hand, a significant part of the population and perhaps an even larger part of the political class in many countries have not as yet caught up with the dominant scientific view that climate change is a real phenomenon caused by humans.

While it is a prevalent assumption in management texts and media discourse that shareholders own corporations, it is certainly not an established view among legal scholars. I will explore this legal question of ownership and corporations in the next section.

6.8 THE CORPORATION AS A LEGAL PERSON

The separate legal personhood of the corporation is key to the argument that they cannot have owners. The meaning of this concept of legal personality is complex but is succinctly summarized in Worthington's (2016, 34) company law casebook: "We typically use the word 'person' to refer to an individual human being but in law the word has a more technical meaning: 'a subject of rights and duties.' In this sense it is possible to speak of a corporation as 'a person' and recognize its separate personality."

The characterization of a corporation as a legal person is not intended to suggest human qualities or agency but to denote legal status. As Gindis (2016, 508) explains: "when the law treats the firm as a 'person' nothing more than the fact that the firm *has* (not *is*) a point of imputation for rights and duties that arise in legal relations should be implied." The separate legal personality of the corporation has a number of important practical consequences.

One of the most important consequences of the corporation's legal personality is its ability to own assets. Besides having no claim to any of the assets nor a proportionate share, shareholders have no kind of equitable ownership interest of any kind relating to a corporation's assets (except in insolvency). Therefore, the property of a corporation is totally separate from that of its members or shareholders. This would be true even if there was only one shareholder holding 100 per cent of the equity.

By enabling the separation of the assets of the company from the assets of the shareholders, separate legal personality facilitates limited liability. Limited liability is enabled – though not legally required – for incorporated companies. (Again, this is unrelated to the level of dispersal of the equity holding, applying equally to companies with one shareholder.) Hansmann and Kraakman (2000), Hansmann, Kraakman and Squire (2006), and Kraakman et al. (2017) have shown that this is a two-way relationship, in the sense that assets of the company are also protected against the liabilities of the shareholders, and that the protection of the assets of the company is more significant in terms of enabling the corporation to create value. Shareholders also cannot unilaterally withdraw their equity contribution and cannot force partial liquidation. This is an important practical arrangement that lowers the cost of capital.

A corporation can enter into contracts and can bring cases to court in its own name. Furthermore, the company runs its own business, regardless of the dispersion of the control rights attached to equity holdings: "The fact that one person holds all, or substantially all, of the shares in a company does not, without more, make the company's business that person's business in the eyes of the law" (Worthington 2016, 47).

Finally, a corporation's existence is not subject to any time limits, since its duration is not constrained by the lifespan of any individual or group of individuals. As Bainbridge (2015, 5) explains, the corporation's "indefinite legal existence" is terminable only in the following circumstances: a voluntary dissolution, a merger, bankruptcy followed by liquidation or dissolution by a court.

There is a widespread view among legal scholars based on the separate legal personality of the corporation that it is an entity which cannot be owned. According to Davies (2010, 61), it is the "modern view that shareholders do not own the company, but only their shares." Indeed, "the old argument that shareholders have these rights because they are the owners of the company now carries little sway, because its premise is false: shareholders own their shares, not the company" (Davies 2010, 266). Dignam (2011, 256) is even more explicit in linking the conclusion that a corporation cannot be owned to the separation between the assets of the company and its shareholders, which results from the former's separate legal personality: "It is important to immediately cease to describe shareholders as 'owners' of the company as this is incorrect. Shareholders own their shares and the rights attached to them – nothing else. ... The company owns its own assets and the shareholders have no legal or equitable interest in the corporate assets."

In the UK, the clear judgment setting out the position of shareholders was made in *Short v Treasury Commissioners*,[8] in which the court ruled that the shareholders "were not part owners of the undertaking" (cited in Davies & Worthington 2016). This position was also underlined by the American Bar Association (2009, 5) in a report of its Section of Business Law Corporate Governance Committee on Delineation of Governance Role and Responsibilities:

> Shareholders are often referred to as the "owners" of the corporation. However, the corporation is a legal person in its own right rather than a mere asset. Once the separation of equity rights and control occurs in the formation of the corporate entity, the analogy of shareholders to "owners" of the corporate "asset" is imperfect at best. The asset that shareholders own is the stock that represents their investment interest.

The habitual use of the terms "owner" and "ownership" distorts the debate on corporate governance and the role of the corporation in modern society. As Blair (1995, 16) pointed out, the word "ownership" has highly persuasive emotional connotations: "the problem with calling shareholders the owners of corporations is that the word 'owner' has such a powerful, almost moralistic meaning in U.S. culture," such that "its use in this context cuts off debate by implying that certain rights and prerogatives should, by the very nature of things, flow to

[8] *Short v Treasury Commissioners* [1948] AC 534.

shareholders."[9] The emotional power of ownership strengthens its use as rhetorical tool. In addition, as Veldman and Willmott (2020) and Johnston (2024) have pointed out, the notion that shareholders own corporations in debates on corporate governance can play a performative role.[10]

Friedman (1962, 135) articulated an extremely influential argument for shareholder supremacy using the premise that shareholders are owners as a starting point: "the corporation is an instrument of the stockholders who own it." He did not feel the need to argue the case for ownership but was able to take it for granted that his readers also saw shareholders as owners of businesses. As a method of persuasion, the power of the idea of ownership, especially for ideological goals of promoting the interests of shareholders above all others, is compelling. This raises the question of why and how this notion that shareholders own corporations has proved to be so convincing. This is the question that I will explore in the next section.

6.9 OWNERSHIP AND "LOOSE TALK"

The concept of ownership as applied to businesses appears intuitive for at least two reasons. Firstly, seeing firms as having owners may serve as a useful mental shortcut in the case of small entrepreneurial companies, where one individual (or a small group of people) is tied to the enterprise in multiple ways and where the bond has a very personal dimension. It is then a short (and hidden) but flawed step to extend this line of thought to all corporations. Secondly, the historical evolution of the corporate form means that shareholders might indeed have been justifiably regarded as owners in the relatively recent past. Before we explore these reasons in deeper detail, it would be helpful to better understand what is actually going on in linguistic terms when we talk about ownership in the context of the business corporation.

It is perhaps tempting to consider talk of ownership of corporations as metaphorical in nature. Ali (2015) suggested that referring to corporations as being owned might fall into the category of an ontological metaphor, following the Kövecses's (2010, 38) recommendation to "assign a basic status in terms of objects, substances, and the like to many of our experiences." The categorization here rests on what Honoré (1961, 147) described as the "paradigm ... of a single human being owning, in the full liberal sense, a single material thing." Referring to a corporation as being owned would amount to (metaphorically) applying a concept more obviously suited

9 This applies to cultures and social settings other than the contemporary United States. It has been argued that ownership of some material possessions, namely those which have some sentimental significance, are an essential part of personhood and identity (Radin, 1982). This is an idea that was developed from Hegel (1991). Different types of ownership (for instance, precious personal possessions versus fungible financial assets) are not distinguished in language and terminology. This makes arguments based on ownership sound intuitively reasonable as well as psychologically and rhetorically compelling.

10 The idea of performativity, namely that words and statements can constitute a form of action and can initiate change, originated with the work of the philosopher Austin (1962).

to ordinary material objects – items in one's personal ownership – to relationships of an abstract nature.

However, this view fails to take into account the complex nature of legal ownership. Fully owning a single material object is just the most obvious and clearly understood instance of ownership, but there is a wide range of types of things that can be owned in varying degrees of complexity. Honoré (1961) outlines eleven "incidents" or aspects of ownership, stressing that there is no one single determining feature, and that it is not the case that all eleven incidents need be present for a relationship to constitute ownership. By contrast, authors such as Penner (1996, 1997), Smith (2011, 2012), and Merrill (1998) argue that there are some attributes or subsets of attributes of ownership that are decisive in determining whether ownership exists or not. For these authors, exclusion is the deciding characteristic of ownership. This is an important debate, but this still leaves us with forms of legal ownership that are more complex and abstract than a single material object fully owned by an individual. To characterize all forms of legal ownership besides the "full liberal" variety as metaphorical would stretch the concept of metaphor rather too far.

So how should we classify the habit of characterizing shareholders as owners of corporations? For our purposes, Sperber and Wilson (1986, 2008) provide a helpful account of the continuum between literal statements and looser expressions. Metaphors are only one part of this continuum, despite their importance and prevalence in language. And even seemingly literal statements can have different meanings (or implications) in different contexts. In order to understand the meaning of statements, literal or non-literal, context is key, as is *implicature*, namely the meaning that is contained in a statement though not fully stated (Grice 1975). Sperber and Wilson (1990, 145) propose the following principles of relevance:

(a) Everything else being equal, the greater the cognitive effect achieved by the processing of a given piece of information, the greater its relevance for the individual who processes it.
(b) Everything else being equal, the greater the effort involved in the processing of a given piece of information, the smaller its relevance for the individual who processes it.

> We claim that humans automatically aim at maximal relevance, that is, maximal cognitive effect for minimal processing effort.

In this scheme, characterizing shareholders as owners of a corporation falls under the category of *loose talk* (Sperber and Wilson 1986). Loose talk occurs when a speaker utters a statement that is not strictly correct but serves as an approximation or verbal shortcut. Much of the time, loose talk has clear meaning under the principles of relevance outlined here. If, for example, one were to say "Mary got lost in Pittsburgh and was walking around in a circle," it would be clear that the implication was not that Mary's route formed a geometrically perfect circle. What is meant (the implicature) is that Mary arrived at the point at which she started her walk. Arriving at this conclusion would satisfy the goal of arriving at the maximum cognitive result for the minimum input. Indeed, a more literal statement, describing Mary's exact path around Pittsburgh, would require a greater than necessary time and effort both for the speaker and the hearer. In this specific context, the loose meaning of "circle" has served a useful purpose in simplifying communication. However, this loose meaning is not necessarily useful in other situations. A loose meaning of the word "circle" would be problematic in a geometry textbook!

The key problem of the loose talk involved in characterizing shareholders as owners is that of scale. In the small entrepreneurial firm, this characterization may indeed work as a reasonable approximation. Consider a very small business, such as a restaurant, where one person owns 100 per cent of the equity of the business, has provided some of their personal property as collateral for the start-up loan that enabled the establishment of the business, is the manager, a worker, and is responsible for ensuring that health and safety laws and regulations are adhered to (so if, for instance, a customer were to be injured on the premises, this person could be held liable in tort). This person shares so many of the features (Honoré's incidents) of ownership besides owning the equity of the firm that it seems reasonable to label them as the "owner" of the business. None of this is to deny the legal personality of an incorporated company or to suggest that the ownership relationship is necessarily correct in a strict literal legal sense. (A term such as "founder" might be more accurate.) The point is that in such a situation, a reference to an "owner" outside a courtroom or classroom conveys a meaning about the relationship between the owner and the business which is shared by speaker and hearer alike. As loose talk, it serves a useful purpose, avoiding the effort of more complicated formulations, and is not manipulative in intent. This is something that we can consider as common-sense shorthand.

However, if we scale up this loose talk, and look at shareholders of large corporations, which are listed on stock exchanges, the looseness looks less reasonable. In many countries, shareholding is widely dispersed, and shareholders have little influence on management, no responsibilities, and no financial liability beyond their initial investment. Loosely terming one key individual the owner of a small entrepreneurial firm does not transfer well to the case of the large listed company, besides conveying a false sense of intimacy. This *common-sense shorthand* does not scale well.

The confusion is compounded by the problem of carrying the looseness of everyday conversation into formal academic discourse. In contexts where precision in language use and in defining concepts is important for clarity, loose talk can serve to cause obfuscation, akin to using less than precise definitions of a circle in geometry textbooks. This is what I claim has been achieved in discussions of corporate governance that are predicated on viewing shareholders as owners of corporations. It is probable that the looseness of the application of the concept of ownership in the corporate context has its roots in the historical development of the legal personality of the firm. Legal personality as an institution was not created in a single event but evolved into its present form over a long period of time. Davies and Worthington (2016, 29) comment on the relatively recent history of the full application of the legal personality of the corporation: "corporate personality became an attribute of the normal joint stock company only at a comparatively late stage in its development, and it was not until *Salomon v Salomon* at the end of the nineteenth century that its implications were fully grasped even by the courts." In other words, it took some time before even courts and judges fully understood the meaning and impact of separate legal personality, and made judgments and established precedents which realized the full potential of this concept. Until these precedents were established, many of the attributes of ownership would have fallen on shareholders.

Ireland (1999, 43) explains that the emergence of large corporations with limited liability and shares traded in liquid markets brought on the modern concept of separate corporate personality, accompanied by the idea that shareholders own shares as opposed to the company:

> In underlining the externality of the shareholder, these economic and legal changes laid the foundations for the emergence of the modern doctrine of separate corporate personality. The "complete separation" of company and members that this entailed was not, as company lawyers tend to assume, inherent in the legal act of incorporation. Rather, the legal meaning of incorporation in a business context was reinterpreted in the latter half of the nineteenth century to accommodate the radical economic separation of joint stock companies from their shareholders.

So conceptualizing shareholders as owners might have been a reasonably accurate representation in the past, when the relationship between the corporation and those who held equity positions was very different. Over time, as laws and their interpretations evolved, a new reality took shape; however, through force of habit, shareholders are still commonly thought of as owners. What might have been a correct part of common sense has long ceased to be an accurate representation of the actual legal position of corporate shareholders.

6.10 CONCLUDING COMMENTS: A RESEARCH AGENDA ON COMMON-SENSE COMMONS AND CORPORATE GOVERNANCE

This chapter has examined the concepts of common sense and the common-sense commons in the context of the business corporation and its governance. I have considered the role that common sense might play in the strategic action field related to corporate control. While common sense is an essential part of the knowledge infrastructure of a social system, in important ways it can also lead to confusion, manipulation, and a misconception of key relationships. What is generally recognized as common sense may not always be identical to scientifically accepted knowledge. In this chapter, I considered a key idea in the discourse of corporate control, namely that shareholders own corporations. This example, at the centre of recent and contemporary debates on corporate purpose and governances, is widely accepted as received common sense. Indeed, it presents an ideal subject of study, as an idea that seems intuitive, is rooted in everyday experience, has enormous persuasive force, and underpins a dominant ideology – but is nevertheless far from being an established truth in the academic discourse.

A research agenda to further our understanding of how the common-sense commons of the field of corporate control came into existence, and who determines its contents and how, requires the input of several disciplines and methodological approaches. This is why it is important to combine insights from the GKC framework with the strategic field approach of Fligstein and McAdam. The rules-in-use for a common-sense commons will present special challenges. The resource of common-sense is subject to non-rivalry and is not tangible. It does not require allocation mechanisms, but is widely disseminated, or shared, within the community. The sharing of common sense does not require regulating access to it or controlling its use. Neither does a common-sense commons involve proprietary rights like intellectual property. Nevertheless, the creation and dissemination of common sense is also not altogether spontaneous; the common-sense commons is not a free-for-all in which all actors have unlimited potential to influence what is accepted as presupposed knowledge by all or most of the given social system. In other words, informal governance through unwritten rules-in-use plays an important role in determining what is shared, subject to informal rules which determine how common sense is "produced, curated, sustained, and disseminated in social systems" (Frischmann 2021, 123).

A key task would be to identify which individuals and institutions are the primary definers, in the sense that they are the most important in defining and refining what constitutes common sense. Bibliometric analysis would contribute to understanding the spread of academic ideas but would need to be combined with media analysis to better understand how ideas from academia filter into public discourse. Ethnographic and anthropological methods, including conducting interviews with key participants, would also be an essential part of any investigation to understand the processes by which a common-sense commons is governed. The rise of the shareholder value ideology might serve as an ideal case study of the evolution of common sense and the underlying power structures.

REFERENCES

Ali, Tanweer. 2015. "Beyond Shareholders versus Stakeholders: Towards a Rawlsian Concept of the Firm." *Research in International Business and Finance* 34: 125–141.

Ali, Tanweer. 2024. *The Language of Ownership and the Rise of Shareholder Value: The Corporate Governance Discourse, 1980–1999*. Hatfield: University of Hertfordshire.

American Bar Association. 2009. *Report of the Task Force of the ABA Section of Business Law Corporate Governance Committee on Delineation of Governance Roles & Responsibilities.* https://apps.americanbar.org/buslaw/committees/CL260000pub/materials/20090801/delineation-final.pdf.
Aristotle. 2012. *De Animus* (trans. E. Gendlin). London: Penguin Classics.
Armour, John, and Brian R. Cheffins. 2014. "The Origins of the Market for Corporate Control." *University of Illinois Law Review* 2014(5): 1835–1866.
Austin, John L. 1962. *How to Do Things With Words*. Oxford: Oxford University Press.
Bainbridge, Stephen M. 2015. *Corporate Law*, 3rd ed. St. Paul: Foundation Press.
Bergson, Henr, 2002 [1895]. "Good Sense and Classical Studies." In *Henri Bergson: Key Writings*, ed. Keith Ansell-Pearson, and John Ó Mullarkey (trans. M. McMahon), 345–353. London: Continuum.
Blair, Margaret M. 1995. "Corporate 'Ownership'." *Brookings Review* 13(1): 16–19.
Boltanski, Luc, and Laurent Thévenot. 1999. "The Sociology of Critical Capacity." *European Journal of Social Theory* 2(3): 359–377.
Bourdieu, Pierre. 1977. *Outline of a Theory of Practice* (trans. R. Nice). Cambridge: Cambridge University Press.
Bourdieu, Pierre. 1990. *The Logic of Practice* (trans. R. Nice). Cambridge: Polity Press.
Bourdieu, Pierre, and Loïc Wacquant. (1992). *An Invitation to Reflexive Sociology*. Oxford: Polity Press.
Chandler, Alfred D. 1962. *Strategy and Structure: Chapters in the History of the Industrial Enterprise*. Cambridge, MA: Harvard University Press.
Cheffins, Brian R. 2019. *The Public Company Transformed*. New York: Oxford University Press.
Cheffins, Brian R. 2021. "Stop Blaming Milton Friedman." *Washington University Law Review* 98(6): 1607–1644.
Choi, Young B. 2021. "Conventions as Shared Cognitive Infrastructures." In *Governing Markets as Knowledge Commons*, ed. Erwin Decker, and Pavel Kuchář, 133–158. Cambridge: Cambridge University Press.
Davies, Paul. 2010. *Introduction to Company Law*, 2nd ed. Oxford: Oxford University Press.
Davies, Paul, and Sarah Worthington. 2016. *Gower's Principles of Modern Company Law*, 10th ed. London: Thomson Reuters.
Deakin, Simon. 2012. "The Corporation as Commons: Rethinking Property Rights, Governance and Sustainability in Business Enterprise." *Queen's Law Journal* 37(2): 339–381.
Descartes, René. 1912 [1637]. *Discourse On The Method* (trans. J. Veitch). London: Dent & Sons.
Dignam, Alan. 2011. *Hicks and Goo's Cases and Materials on Company Law*, 7th ed. Oxford: Oxford University Press.
Erion, Gerald J. 2001. "The Cartesian Test for Automatism." *Minds and Machines* 11(1): 29–39.
Fairclough, Norman. 2015. *Language and Power*, 3rd ed. Abingdon: Routledge.
Fligstein, Neil. 2016. "The Theory of Fields and Its Application to Corporate Governance." *Seattle University Law Review* 38(2): 237–262.
Fligstein, Neil, and Doug McAdam. 2011. "Toward a General Theory of Strategic Action Fields." *Sociological Theory* 29(1): 1–26.
Fligstein, Neil, and Doug McAdam. 2012. *A Theory of Fields*. Oxford: Oxford University Press.
Forchtner, Bernhard. 2018. "Critical Discourse Studies and Social Theory." In *Routledge Handbook of Critical Discourse Studies*, ed. John Flowerdew, and John E. Richardson, 259–271. London: Routledge.

Friedman, Milton. 1962. *Capitalism and Freedom*. Chicago: University of Chicago Press.
Friedman, Milton. 1970. "The Social Responsibility of Business Is to Increase Its Profits." *New York Times Magazine*, September 13, 1970.
Frischmann, Brett M. 2021. "Common Sense Commons: A Case of Commonsensical Social Norms." In *Governing Markets as Knowledge Commons*, ed. Erwin Decker, and Pavel Kuchář, 113–132. Cambridge: Cambridge University Press.
Frischmann, Brett M., Michael J. Madison, and Katherina J. Strandburg, eds. 2014. *Governing Knowledge Commons*. New York: Oxford University Press.
Gadamer, Hans-Georg. 2013 [1960]. *Truth and Method* (trans. J. Weinsheimer, and D. G. Marshall). London: Bloomsbury.
Gindis, David. 2016. "Legal Personhood and the Firm: Avoiding Anthropomorphism and Equivocation." *Journal of Institutional Economics* 12(3): 499–513.
Gramsci, Antonio. 1971. *Selections from the Prison Notebooks Method* (trans. G. Nowell-Smith, and Q. Hoare). New York: International Publishers.
Grice, H. P. 1975. "Logic and Conversation." In *Syntax and Semantics, Vol. 3: Speech Acts*, ed. Peter Cole, and Jerry L. Morgan, 41–58. New York: Academic Press.
Hall, Stuart, Chas Critcher, Tony Jefferson, John Clarke, and Brian Roberts. 1978. *Policing the Crisis: Mugging, the State, and Law and Order*. London: Macmillan.
Hansmann, Henry, and Reinier Kraakman. 2000. "The Essential Role of Organizational Law." *Yale Law Journal* 110(3): 387–440.
Hansmann, Henry, Reinier R. Kraakman, and Richard Squire. 2006. "Law and the Rise of the Firm." *Harvard Law Review* 119(5): 1335–1403.
Hegel, Georg W. 1991 [1820]. *Elements of the Philosophy of Right* (trans. H. B. Nisbet). Cambridge: Cambridge University Press.
Heilbron, Johan, Jochem Verheul, and Sander Quak. 2014. "The Origins and Early Diffusion of 'Shareholder Value' in the United States." *Theory and Society* 43(1): 1–22.
Hodgson, Geoffrey M. 2020. "How Mythical Markets Mislead Analysis: An Institutionalist Critique of Market Universalism." *Socio-Economic Review* 18(4): 1153–1174.
Honoré, Tony. 1961. "Ownership." In *Oxford Essays in Jurisprudence*, ed. A. G. Guest, 107–147. Oxford: Oxford University Press.
Ireland, Paddy. 1999. "Company Law and the Myth of Share Ownership." *Modern Law Review* 62(1): 32–57.
Johnston, Andrew. 2024. "The Bank of England and the 'Prehistory' of Corporate Governance." *Business History* 67(5): 1221–1246.
Kövecses, Zoltán. 2010. *Metaphor: A Practical Introduction*, 2nd ed. New York: Oxford University Press.
Kraakman, Reinier, John Armour, Paul Davies, et al. 2017. *The Anatomy of Corporate Law: A Comparative and Functional Approach*, 3rd ed. New York: Oxford University Press.
Lazonick, William, and Mary O'Sullivan. 2000. "Maximizing Shareholder Value: A New Ideology for Corporate Governance." *Economy and Society* 29(1): 13–35.
Levitt, Arthur. 2000. "Remarks Before the Conference on the Rise and Effectiveness of New Corporate Governance Standards. Federal Reserve Bank of New York," December 12, 2000. New York: Securities and Exchange Commission. www.sec.gov/news/speech/spch449.htm.
Manne, Henry G. 1964. "Some Theoretical Aspects of Share Voting: An Essay in Honor of Adolf A. Berle." *Columbia Law Review* 64(8): 1427–1445.
Manne, Henry G. 1965. "Mergers and the Market for Corporate Control." *Journal of Political Economy* 73(2): 110–120.

McGinnis, Michael D. 2020. "Updated Guide to IAD and the Language of the Ostrom Workshop: A Simplified Overview of a Complex Framework for the Analysis of Institutions and their Development." https://mcginnis.pages.iu.edu/iad_guide.pdf.
Merrill, Thomas W. 1998. "Property and the Right to Exclude." *Nebraska Law Review* 77(4): 730–755.
Moore, George E. 1925. "A Defence of Common Sense." In *Contemporary British Philosophy*, ed. John H. Muirhead, 191–224. London: George Allen & Unwin.
Ostrom, Vincent. 1986. "Constitutional Foundations for a Theory of System Comparisons: An Inquiry into Problems of Incommensurability, Emergent Properties, and Development. Workshop in Political Theory and Policy Analysis." W86-31. Bloomington: Indiana University.
Ostrom, Elinor. 1990. *Governing the Commons: The Evolution of Institutions for Collective Action*. Cambridge: Cambridge University Press.
Ostrom, Elinor. 2005. *Understanding Institutional Diversity*. Princeton: Princeton University Press.
Ostrom, Elinor. 2011. "Background on the Institutional Analysis and Development Framework." *Policy Studies Journal* 39(1): 7–27.
Ostrom, Elinor, and Charlotte Hess (2007). "A Framework for Analyzing the Knowledge Commons." In *Understanding Knowledge as a Commons: From Theory to Practice*, ed. Charlotte Hess, and Elinor Ostrom, 41–81. Cambridge: MIT Press.
Penner, James E. 1996. "The 'Bundle of Rights' Picture of Property." *UCLA Law Review* 43(3): 711–818.
Penner, James E. 1997. *The Idea of Property in Law*. Oxford: Oxford University Press.
Radin, Margaret J. 1982. "Property and Personhood." *Stanford Law Review* 34(5): 957–1015.
Redekop, Benjamin W. 2009. "Common Sense in Philosophical and Scientific Perspective." *Management Decision* 47(3): 399–412.
Reisigl, Martin, and Ruth Wodak. 2016. "The Discourse-Historical Approach (DHA)." In *Methods of Critical Discourse Studies*, ed. Ruth Wodak, and Michael Meyer, 23–61. London: Sage.
Ryle, Gilbert. 1967. "John Locke." *Crítica: Revista Hispanoamericana de Filosofía* 1(2): 3–19.
Sanfilippo, Madelyn R., Brett M. Frischmann, and Katherine J. Standburg. 2018. "Privacy as Commons: Case Evaluation through the Governing Knowledge Commons Framework." *Journal of Information Policy* 8: 116–166.
Saussure, Louis de. 2005. "Manipulation and Cognitive Pragmatics: Preliminary." In *Manipulation and Ideologies in the Twentieth Century: Discourse, Language*, Mind, ed. Louis de Saussure, and Peter Schulz, 113–146. Amsterdam-Philadelphia: John Benjamins.
Smith, Henry E. 2011. "Property Is Not Just a Bundle of Rights." *Econ Journal Watch* 8(3): 279–291.
Smith, Henry E. 2012. "Property as the Law of Things." *Harvard Law Review* 125(7): 1690–1726.
Sperber, Dan, and Deirdre Wilson. 1986. "Loose Talk." *Proceedings of the Aristotelian Society* 86: 153–171.
Sperber, Dan, and Deirdre Wilson. 1990. "Rhetoric and Relevance." In *The End of Rhetoric: History, Theory, Practice*, ed. John B. Bender, 140–155. Stanford: Stanford University Press.
Sperber, Dan, and Deirdre Wilson. 2008. "A Deflationary Account of Metaphors." In *The Cambridge Handbook of Metaphor and Thought*, ed. Raymond W. Gibbs, and David E. Wellbery, 113–146. Cambridge: Cambridge University Press.
Stout, Lynn A. 2012. *The Shareholder Value Myth: How Putting Shareholders First Harms Investors, Corporations, and the Public*. San Francisco: Berrett-Koehler Publishers.

Strandburg, Katherine J., Brett M. Frischmann, Michael J. Madison. 2017. "The Knowledge Commons Framework." In *Governing Medical Knowledge Commons*, ed. Katherine J. Strandburg, Brett M. Frischmann, Michael J. Madison, 9–19. Cambridge: Cambridge University Press.

The Business Roundtable. 1981. *Statement on Corporate Responsibility*. New York: The Business Roundtable.

The Business Roundtable. 1997. *Statement on Corporate Governance*. New York: The Business Roundtable.

van Dijk, Teun A. 1998. *Ideology: A Multi-Disciplinary Approach*. London: Sage.

Veldman, Jeroen, and Hugh Willmott. 2020. "Performativity and Convergence in Corporate Governance." *Competition and Change* 24(5): 408–428.

Vico, Giambattista. 1990 [1709]. *De Nostri Temporis Studiorum Ratione* (trans. E. Gianturco). Ithaca: Cornell University Press.

Worthington, Sarah. 2016. *Sealy and Worthington's Text, Case and Materials in Company Law*, 11th ed. Oxford: Oxford University Press.

7

Corporate Governance and Knowledge Commons

Jeroen Veldman

7.1 INTRODUCTION

In the past decade, Paul Polman, the then CEO of Unilever, and Emmanuel Faber, the then CEO of Danone, were held up as examples of CEOs who wanted to take account of stakeholders beyond shareholders.[1] And in that same decade, Larry Fink, CEO of Blackrock, used his annual "Letter to CEOs" to call for the inclusion of longer-term consequences of a company's strategy in the board's deliberations.[2] Likewise, Dutch pension funds, including ABP, PFZW, and PME, started to reduce or abandon their holdings in fossil fuel-related assets.[3]

But by the start of 2019, Polman had been replaced, and by early 2021 Faber was sacked. Likewise, the mandate of Dutch pension fund managers to pursue investments guided by environmental, social, and governance (ESG) criteria was questioned,[4] with the argument that they should prioritize near-term financial results. This last challenge followed a 2022 debate in the US, in which Fink was vigorously attacked by Senators who argued that he had overstepped the boundaries of what was permissible under US rules governing fiduciary duties.[5] In the wake of this attack, Fink stepped back from his earlier statements, while Blackrock, Vanguard, and many other asset managers dropped their support for ESG-oriented shareholder proposals and left initiatives like Climate Action 100+.[6]

[1] "Business, Society, and the Future of Capitalism," *McKinsey Sustainability*, May 1, 2014; "Unilever's Paul Polman: CEOs Can't Be 'Slaves' to Shareholders," *Forbes*, July 20, 2015; "Danone Adopts New Legal Status to Reflect Social Mission," *Financial Times*, June 26, 2020.

[2] "Laurence D. Fink's 2016 Corporate Governance Letter," *New York Times*, February 2, 2016.

[3] "Dutch Pension Giant ABP to Dump €15 bn in Fossil Fuel Holdings," *Financial Times*, October 26, 2001.

[4] "Aartsen: Wat de Pensioendeelnemer Wil Is Van Ondergeschikt Belang," Het Financieele Dagblad, September 25, 2024.

[5] "BlackRock Chief Larry Fink Pressured to Resign over ESG 'Hypocrisy'," *Financial Times*, December 6, 2022. See also "BlackRock Steps Up Security for Larry Fink After 'Anti-Woke' Backlash," *Financial Times*, April 21, 2024.

[6] "BlackRock's Fink Says He's Stopped Using 'Weaponised' Term ESG," *Reuters*, June 26, 2023; "BlackRock's Support for Climate and Social Resolutions Falls Sharply," *Financial Times*, August 23, 2023.

These cases raise several questions, including: What is the real-world mandate for CEOs seeking to engage with stakeholder and long-term interests? How can a shift in the interpretation of a concept like fiduciary duties silence the CEO of one the largest institutional investors in the world? And who determines the correct interpretation of the scope of such a concept, particularly when the emergence of systemic risks like climate change puts increasing pressure on the role of CEOs of companies and investors to engage with broader notions of risk and opportunities for broader types of audiences (Veldman 2024)? To address these questions, my starting point is the Governing Knowledge Commons (GKC) framework (Frischmann et al. 2014), which I connect with the Strategic Action Field (SAF) approach (Fligstein and McAdam 2012). Combining these approaches helps us think about both historical and current corporate governance debates.

7.2 STRATEGIC ACTION FIELDS AND THE GKC FRAMEWORK

The GKC framework is "an approach (commons) to governing the management and/or production of a particular type of resource (knowledge)" (Frischmann et al. 2014, 2) in order to focus on "the institutionalized community governance of the sharing and, in some cases, creation, of a wide range of intellectual and cultural resources" (Frischmann et al. 2014, 3). Adopting this framework introduces three specific concerns regarding shared knowledge production in the domain of corporate governance. Firstly, a knowledge commons approach focuses on a *description* of the production and management of (knowledge) resources, including rules, institutional designs, governance mechanisms, and technological infrastructures (Sanfilippo et al. 2018).

Secondly, the GKC framework introduces a series of questions regarding the *quality* of the processes by which (knowledge) resources are produced and managed, including who has a say in the production of such knowledge. Relevant issues here pertain to the degree to which a relevant community (or communities) is (are) included; the ways in which the goals and objectives of the commons and the relationships among various types of participants and with the general public are taken into account and conceived as legitimate; the selection criteria for decision-makers and the degree to which they are perceived to be legitimate by community members, other decision-makers, and impacted outsiders; the degree to which non-members are able to interact with the commons and the institutionalization of those interactions; and the degree to which impacted groups have a say in the governance of the knowledge commons (Sanfilippo et al. 2018).

Thirdly, the GKC framework highlights the *outcomes* of the content and processes that feed into the production and management of (knowledge) resources. Notably, the GKC framework underscores the relationship between the quality of the production of (knowledge) resources and the conditions that allow for the successful pooling and sharing of intellectual or cultural resources, including the roles of and impact on (non-)community members in relation to the design of those rules; the goals, objectives, and established norms that help facilitate common valuations and types of knowledge creation that help overcome of collective action problems; the provision of benefits to (non-)members, and engagement with externalities (Sanfilippo et al. 2018).

In sum, the GKC framework draws attention to the content, quality, and consequences of the production, the institutionalized (community) governance, and the sharing of knowledge. In the domain of corporate governance, the key knowledge that is produced, institutionalized, and shared concerns the rules, institutional designs and mechanisms, and technological infrastructures that enable corporations to be governed. The SAF approach developed by Fligstein and McAdam (2011, 2012) is a useful way of thinking about how such knowledge is governed. This is because the SAF approach introduces three further questions that help us dig deeper into the attributes of the relevant communities.

The first question is: what are the (diffuse) understandings of the actors about what is going on and what is at stake in the field of corporate governance? In Section 7.3, I provide an account of how different *imaginaries* of corporate status, architecture, governance, and purpose have been actively created, and in Section 7.4, I explore how these imaginaries provide differing grounds for the formation of the rules of corporate governance, understood in terms of the seven distinct categories identified by Ostrom (2005).[7] The second question is: how do actors develop divergent and persistent historical social norms regarding these imaginaries? In my overview of the history of corporate governance, I explore how specific interconnected *epistemic communities* (Haas 2001), comprising disciplinary specialists, standard setters, and practitioners, actively seek to create, maintain, legitimize, and institutionalize particular social norms that affect the scope for the adoption of ideas of corporate status, architecture, governance, and purpose.

The third and final question is: which interpretive frames do individual and collective actors bring to make sense of what others are doing? As Hirschman and Berman (2014, 783–784) explain: "Epistemic communities are networks of experts who share some set of beliefs. They have more ideological unity than a whole profession, and thus can strategically promote policies consistent with their beliefs." It follows that we need to identify the "conditions under which epistemic communities are able to exert such influence." I will develop several examples to show how actors are well aware of both the proactive nature of these processes of knowledge creation and the consequences of such processes on the foregrounding of specific rule-sets in corporate governance.

By engaging with these three questions, I show how the GKC framework may be used to understand the content, conditions, and consequences of processes of

[7] Ostrom recommended distinguishing the position, boundary, choice, aggregation, information, payoff, and scope rules governing action situations.

creation of knowledge resources, while the SAF framework helps explain the agency of epistemic communities in establishing specific *knowledge claims* regarding the promotion and institutionalization of specific rule-sets (Fligstein and McAdam 2011, 2012; see also Fligstein 2016). With these two lenses, I demonstrate how historical episodes of active creation and maintenance of notions of corporate status, architecture, governance, and purpose delivered contrasting foundations for the creation of Ostromian rules in the domain of corporate governance.

Settling the question of which rule-sets are dominant is important from the perspective of the relevant epistemic communities, because the adoption of specific rule-sets is linked to a broad set of organizational outcomes, specifically the capacity to decide, control, monitor, and sanction within the corporate domain (Klein et al. 2019); the recognition of the validity and salience of particular stakeholders and interests (Veldman 2025); and the ability to overcome commitment problems in relation to the successful pooling of assets and liabilities (Bridoux and Vishwanathan 2020; Aguilera et al. 2021; Clarke 2021). And beyond organizational outcomes, the examples given in the introduction show how the adoption of specific rule-sets lays out the conditions of possibility for practitioners to engage with "externalities," which include the overshooting of planetary boundaries, climate change, and growing social inequality (Metcalf and Benn 2012; Howard-Grenville et al. 2019).

7.3 IMAGINARIES OF CORPORATE STATUS, ARCHITECTURE, GOVERNANCE, AND PURPOSE

Since the invention of the corporation, but particularly in the last two centuries, there has been a very lively debate about the status, architecture, governance, and purpose of the corporate form. The debate has mobilized many types of actors, including legal, economic, accounting, and management scholars, entrepreneurs, shareholders, judges, lawyers, standard setters, accountants, financial advisors, politicians, journalists, and the broader public (Roy 1999; Johnson 2010; Winkler 2019). The widely accepted outcomes of these debates evolved over time.

7.3.1 *Developing a Social Norm*

The financing of major public works during the nineteenth century provides a key starting point for the development of significant new ideas about corporate status, architecture, governance, and purpose. As railroads, canals, turnpikes, and other large public works needed significant amounts of capital, minority shareholders started to be drawn into joint stock corporations set up to develop and manage these works. But rampant abuses by majority shareholders, enabled by the lack of power and knowledge on the part of these minority shareholders, led to significant public and political backlash (Freeman et al. 2011).

The realization that the involvement of many different types of shareholders created what today is referred to as "principal-principal problems" (Young et al. 2008), which needed to be mitigated, informed the development and institutionalization of new ideas regarding the status and the architecture of the modern corporation. The core of these changes revolved around the shift in the conception of the separate legal entity (SLE) towards a fully reified social construct – an "it" (Ireland 1996; Litowitz 2000). By interpreting the SLE in such terms, formal ascription of organizational assets and liabilities could be shifted from the shareholders to the SLE, making it possible to argue that "control over the firm's assets is not actually given to shareholders, but to the fictional legal entity of the firm itself" (Gelter 2009, 14).

Shifting the locus for the ascription of control over the organizational assets and liabilities to the SLE was the cornerstone for new ideas of *corporate status* and architecture. Shareholders, who do not have direct claims to the pooled organizational assets, convene at an annual general meeting, seen as a collective "body of shareholders," while the (supervisory) board is charged with managing the corporation, conceived as the SLE itself. In this framing, both the shareholder meeting and the board operate as separate reified "organs" with collegial governance. These corporate organs do not contract for their role, rights, duties, and claims, but receive these in the context of their role in the "corporate order" (Greenwood 2017; Lokin and Veldman 2019).

The reification of the SLE thus solves the principal-principal problems associated with the modern corporation (Robé 2011) by providing for a devolved authority and governance structure. This novel *organizational architecture* enables checks and balances and countervailing powers between corporate organs (Lokin and Veldman 2019), as it endows the (supervisory) board with the autonomy to fulfil its duty to promote the success of the corporation, as distinguished from the controlling or dominant shareholder (Bratton 1989; Ireland 1996; Stout 2012).

Novel ideas of corporate status and architecture not only helped solve principal-principal problems but also enabled significant new *organizational capacities* that either had not been available before or had been available but not to the same extent. The most notable capacities involved the authorization of corporate groups, which helped support transjurisdictional operations, and the grant of constitutional rights to corporations (Veldman and Willmott 2022). Although the development of these new notions was arguably highly consequential for (minority) shareholders, they also led to significant contestation from many societal groups (Horwitz 1992; Johnson 2010; Winkler 2019).

A key aspect of this contestation revolved around the interpretation of the representative status of the SLE. As directors' duties were directed towards the SLE conceptualized as a reified "entity," the question of what the SLE was, and how and to what extent this new social construct represented specific parts or aspects of "the corporation," became very important. If the representative status of the SLE extends only to the (original) shareholders, its representative value does not need to extend beyond the assets and liabilities that were brought in at the point of the original constitution of the corporation. But if its representative value extends to assets and liabilities brought into the corporation after it is constituted, this opens up the possibility that the SLE represents an evolving set of *organizational* assets and liabilities.

At the start of the twentieth century, extensive debates by legal, economic, and accounting scholars regarding the representative status of the SLE, but also the broader public debate about the significant socio-economic effects associated with the development of new ideas of organizational architecture and capacities, gradually led to the inclusion of the claims of stakeholders beyond the shareholders. In *The Modern Corporation and Private Property*, arguably the century's most influential book on corporate governance published in 1932, Berle and Means (2007, 311–312) stated that

> the controlling groups, by means of the extension of corporate powers, have in their own interest broken the bars of tradition which require that the corporation be operated solely for the benefit of the owners of passive property . . . it seems almost essential if the corporate system is to survive – that the "control" of the great corporations should develop into a purely neutral technocracy, balancing a variety of claims by various groups in the community and assigning to each a portion of the income stream on the basis of public policy rather than private cupidity.

The notion that claims of stakeholders beyond those of the shareholders are relevant for *corporate governance* has since found further support in the economic rendering of this position. Blair and Stout (1999), for instance, argued that employees are residual claimants because they often cannot reap the benefits of their firm-specific investments outside the context of the corporation. If stakeholders other than shareholders have valid (residual) claims on the corporation, the SLE can be conceived as "a single and unitary source of control over the collective property of its various participants" (Lan and Heracleous 2010, 2). And with directors' duties oriented towards such an enlarged representative status for the SLE, it may be argued that the board operates as a "mediating hierarch," which has the (relative) autonomy to mediate between claims and interests pertaining to many types of stakeholders, relating to longer time frames (Pickering 1968; Eisenberg 1975; Millon 2014; Stout 2015; Du Plessis 2016).

Exploring the history of ideas related to the modern corporation thus shows how novel ideas of corporate status, architecture, and governance that developed during the late nineteenth and early twentieth century helped solve principal-principal conflicts and deliver new organizational capacities. At the same time, these ideas provided the basis for ongoing contestation regarding the interpretation of the (representative) status of the SLE and corporate "organs"; claims to current and future (organizational) assets and liabilities; the development of organizational checks and balances; and the allocation and division of protections, authority, and control to specific groups (Horwitz 1992; Hatchuel and Segrestin 2019; Winkler 2019).

It was well-understood in public, academic, and practitioner debates that the stabilization and institutionalization of specific interpretations of these new ideas would have very significant socio-economic consequences. A social norm concerning *corporate purpose* emerged that those in charge of governing the corporation had a duty to weigh the interests of broad sets of stakeholders (Dodd 1931; Berle 1947, 1954; Berle and Means 2007; Mizruchi and Hirschman 2010; Ciepley 2013).

7.3.2 A New Social Norm

While the social norm described in the previous section held until the 1960s, from the 1970s onwards, specific epistemic communities started to institutionalize new ideas of corporate status, architecture, governance, and purpose rooted in agency-theoretic logic (Bratton 1989; Davis 2009). As these ideas became part of a new social norm, they laid the foundations for corporate governance as we now know it.

A new generation of financial economists and lawyers trained in economics – many associated with the University of Chicago – were instrumental in developing these new ideas (Gindis 2020a, 2020b). Drawing on a theoretical, deductive approach to business school research (Romano 2005; Fourcade and Khurana 2017), they argued that the *status* of the corporation could be understood as a nexus of contracts extending into the market, rather than as an "entity" providing the basis for an internal hierarchy and clearly defined external boundaries (Bratton 1989; Khurana 2007).

Building on this view of the status of the corporation as a "flat" nexus of contracts, a new view of *corporate architecture* was developed. Rather than a devolved authority structure, the relationship between shareholders and corporate management was reconceived as a direct contractual arrangement. It could thus be argued that shareholders, even if they did not hold outright "ownership" claims, still held prioritized residual claims (Aglietta and Rebérioux 2005). This was supported by the argument that shareholders only received a reward after all contractual claimants had been paid and were last in line in the case of insolvency or liquidation; in contrast, the risks of claimants like creditors, employees, and suppliers were covered by contracts. Therefore, since shareholders ran the greatest risk with the least amount of protection, they had the strongest incentive to monitor management closely. A combination of theoretical and functional arguments thus (re-)associated the shareholder franchise with the mandate, the incentives, and the capacity to monitor and enforce managerial duties (Gelter 2009).

Reconceptualizing ideas of corporate status and architecture in this way redirected the *corporate governance* role of managers towards an exclusive orientation on the near-term economic interests of shareholders (Sundaram and Inkpen 2004; Aglietta and Rebérioux 2005). This new *purpose* was reflected in the rapid spread of stock-based incentive schemes for managers, the changing fiduciary standards relating to hostile takeovers by the Delaware Supreme Court in 1985, the adoption of these views by the SEC, and the manifest reliance on these ideas in a slew of court cases (Bratton 1989; Avi-Yonah 2011), which produced "remarkable judicial opinions [that] used the learning of modern finance in fashioning legal rules" (Romano 2005, 351).[8]

The process that led to the restriction of "managers' defensive tactics against hostile bids, influenced by the finance literature" (Romano 2005, 351–352), provided the basis for the creation of the leveraged buyout market of the 1980s (Ireland 2009) and also led to changes in the Federal Trade Commission's merger guidelines (Davies 2010), as the new ideas were translated into law. Up until the 1960s, the rise of the modern corporation was associated with outsized market positions that warranted antitrust regulation and enforcement (Bratton 1989). But reconceptualizing the corporation as a nexus of contracts enabled a view in which corporations engaged in contractual relations as generic types of economic "agents." And as contracting plays out in markets among nominally equal agents, those markets could theoretically be seen as self-regulating. As a result, dealing with the issue of monopoly could be left to the operation of the market itself (Van Horn 2009; Van Horn and Mirowski 2009; Hirschman and Berman 2014).

The changes in conceptions of the status, architecture, and governance of the modern corporation were actively spread by their advocates, who among other things founded new scholarly reviews in economics, finance, and accounting; presented their views in practitioner-oriented publications such as the *Harvard Business Review* and editorials in the *New York Times* and the *Wall Street Journal*; and worked with consulting firms and served as expert witnesses in relevant court cases (Mirowski and Plehwe 2009; Fourcade and Khurana 2013; Smith and Rönnegard 2016; Gindis 2020a).

Summer courses in economics for law professors (Teles 2008; Gindis 2020b; Priest 2020) educated legal scholars about "the applicability of neoclassical ideas to antitrust law, corporate law, and other fields" (Jacoby 2008, 33), with the expectation that its participants would become "norm entrepreneurs" and teach deregulation as well as shareholder primacy to their students. All this revolutionized the field of corporate law (Bratton 1989; Allen 1992). The adoption of ideas from the economic theory of the firm and corporate finance led to a "sea change in corporate law scholarship and practice for legal education in the twenty-first century, especially for law schools where research plays a central role" (Romano 2005, 342).

[8] In *Edgar v. MITE Corp.*, 457 U.S. 624 (1982), for instance, the court cited leading Chicago school scholars in support of the complaint that "Shareholders are deprived of the opportunity to sell their shares at a premium. The reallocation of economic resources to their highest valued use, a process which can improve efficiency and competition, is hindered" (643–644).

Initially developed and implemented in the US, these ideas spread to Europe, for instance in deliberations surrounding the European Union's draft Takeover Directive in 1989 and the debates leading up to the UK Companies Act 2006 (Talbot 2008; Collison et al. 2014). A similar rationale underpinned many economic reforms in Germany between 1998 and 2000, including the legalization of stock options and share buybacks; the adoption of a semi-voluntary corporate governance code; the tax exemption on sales of blocks of shares; and comprehensive changes to securities regulation, company law, and taxation introduced in the 1998 KonTraG Act (Cioffi 2002; Lane 2003). The global spread of corporate governance and stewardship codes from the 1990s onwards promoted an agenda of minimizing statutory regulation, as such soft law instruments were meant to be monitored, evaluated, and enforced by market actors (Haxhi et al. 2013; Veldman and Willmott 2016; Katelouzou and Zumbansen 2020).

We thus see how active processes of *knowledge construction* introduced novel assumptions about the corporation (Davies 2010). While these ideas were initially considered "provocative [and] contrary to conventional wisdom" (Davis 2011, 1128), they eventually developed into a unified theoretical approach to organizations (Fourcade and Khurana 2017). This unified approach, and the attendant conceptions of accountability, transparency, compliance, and disclosure, gradually spread and gained acceptance across disciplinary fields (Bratton 1989; Biondi et al. 2007; Lan and Heracleous 2010; Segrestin and Hatchuel 2011; Stout 2012; Millon 2014).

Indeed, they soon became the cornerstone for wide sets of institutions – including listing rules, securities regulation, tax law, banking regulation, trade law, and investment treaties (Aguilera and Cuervo-Cazurra 2004; Yoshikawa and Rasheed 2009; Botzem 2014). By the 1990s, their acceptance and institutionalization had become so well-established in corporate governance theory and regulation that many considered that the social norm that had held until the 1960s had been displaced (Fligstein and Shin 2007; Gelter 2009; Aguilera and Jackson 2010; Bratton 2017; Rock 2013, 2020; Yosifon 2013; Lund and Pollman 2021). Yet the older social norm has not disappeared entirely and is in fact at the heart of today's ESG movement.

7.4 COMPETING IMAGINARIES, SOCIAL NORMS, AND RULE CONFIGURATIONS

The discussion thus far has drawn attention to two issues relating to the production of knowledge in corporate governance. The first is that two social norms underpinning diverging ideas of corporate status, architecture, governance, and purpose are today vying for dominance (Veldman and Willmott 2022). The second is that it is important to examine the role of active processes of knowledge construction within interconnected epistemic communities where these social norms and the *competing imaginaries* upon which they are built develop and are propagated.

To relate these issues to the GKC framework, I will explore them further using the Ostromian notion of action situations, where the establishment and interpretation of the content, scope, and operation of specific rules frame the assignment of rights to positions, define structures of authority and responsibility, and govern access to and use of resources (Gindis and Micheler 2024). An illustration of how such rules enable and constrain actors to undertake or refrain from undertaking specific actions can be found in the way in which a narrowing of the interpretation of fiduciary duties led Larry Fink to rescind his earlier commitments to ESG and stakeholders. This example elucidates how rules are subject to interpretation and the enforcement of social norms. Before linking this with a broader discussion of social epistemology, I assess how the *competing social norms* of corporate governance are expressed in Ostrom's (2005) typology of position, boundary, choice, aggregation, information, payoff, and scope rules.

Position rules create positions and roles, such as being a voter or a member of a legislature or a committee (Ostrom 2005, 193). In Section 7.3, I showed how the currently dominant social norm understands the corporate authority structure as based on a flat architecture, in which a contractual, dyadic, and exclusive relation between individual shareholders and board members provides the basis for the creation of positions. In contrast, the pre-1970s social norm was predicated on the view that corporate architecture was built around corporate organs. On this latter view, positions are created in relation to organs with a collegiate status and responsibility, which provides the basis for a devolved model for the allocation of authority and rights. The dominance of a specific social norm, therefore, informs very different starting points for our understanding of corporate positions, and these directly affect the interpretation of the key constructs operating in the corporate architecture, including the (supervisory) board, the general meeting, management, work councils, and so on (Johnson and Millon 2005; Segrestin et al. 2019).

Boundary rules define who is eligible to hold the position of member, the process by which this happens, and the rules for leaving it (Ostrom 2005, 194). Building on the position rules described above, the pre-1970s social norm established the content and the validity of a member of the corporation as a consequence of membership of a corporate organ. Such a view allowed for the affordance of collegiate rights, claims, and responsibilities to (supervisory) directors and shareholders, and the framing of the role and duties of such members in a devolved authority and rights structure (Greenwood 2017; Lokin and Veldman 2019). By contrast, the post-1970s social norm uses residual claim arguments to understand membership on a functional and individual basis, and on that basis understands the affordance of rights, claims, and responsibilities to shareholders as direct, rather than mediated by a corporate rights structure.[9] As with the position rules, the two social norms thus deliver very

[9] It is notable that the functionalist claim that other stakeholders, such as employees, can also be viewed as members insofar as they also have residual claims (Aguilera and Jackson 2010; Blair and Stout 1999,

different points of departure for the understanding of the boundary rules that establish the concept and validity of the notion of a member of the corporation (Vasudev 2012).

Choice rules specify what a participant occupying a position must, must not, or may do at a particular point in a decision process and thereby affect the action sets that are available in specific positions (Ostrom 2005, 195). An example of the influence of social norms on choice rules is the remarkable shift in monitoring and control by (institutional) shareholders. Direct institutional shareholders' engagement with boards was not accepted before the 1980s, and it was the shift in social norms that created a significant pressure to provide institutional shareholders with a more active role in corporate governance issues. This is what led to a much more pronounced capacity for institutional shareholders to engage directly with boards (Pye 2001; Davis 2009).

Aggregation rules concern collective decision-making and dispute resolution (Ostrom 1995, 202). These are particularly important in situations where choice rules assign partial control over the same set of action variables to multiple positions. As noted, different interpretations of position rules inform divergent assumptions regarding the status of various actors, the allocation of rights on a devolved or direct basis, and, relatedly, the role and function of countervailing powers, checks, and balances in a corporate architecture. Divergent social norms affect the interpretation of boundary rules that govern who exactly counts a member and receives legal standing in relevant corporate governance institutions, as well as the interpretation of choice rules that affect expectations regarding what a specific corporate organ or corporate member can or cannot do. Divergent position, boundary, and choice rules in turn lead to divergent views concerning the scope, content, and operation of collective decision-making and dispute resolution. The two social norms are visible in debates regarding the need to consult or engage with different types of stakeholders and resolve or mediate their competing claims (Grandori 2010). The two norms are likewise visible in debates about the capacity of stakeholders other than shareholders to bring claims in specialist corporate governance-oriented courts, like the Dutch Enterprise Chamber (Lokin and Veldman 2019).

This brings us to *information rules*, which determine the type and level of information available to participants (Ostrom 2005, 206). The importance of such information rules can be exemplified by looking at the position and operation of works councils. Based on the previously dominant social norm, co-determination structures found their way into corporate governance, particularly in continental Europe (Leixnering et al. 2022). However, while much of the debate on such co-determination structures focuses on nomination rights for supervisory board members, the practical effect of such structures is often linked to the mandatory nature of

2005; Grandori 2010) is made in accordance with the post-1970s social claim, that is, without reference to corporate organs.

information, consultation, and negotiation rights afforded to works councils, specifically in the context of changes in ownership structure (Vitols 2004; Van Bekkum et al. 2010; Veldman 2019). With this in mind, the place of employees in corporate governance is dependent on position and boundary rules that establish the status of the works council, and on the use of information rules that guarantee their access to specific types of information under specific circumstances. Arguably, the development of a new social norm that affects the position and boundary rules concerning the status of the works council also affects the operation of these information rules.

It goes without saying that *payoff rules*, which affect the benefits and costs assigned to outcomes given the actions chosen (Ostrom 2005, 207), will also be affected by shifts in the social norms that affect positions, memberships, choice sets, decision mechanisms, and information access rights. The consequences of a shift to the post-1970s social norm are clearly visible in the expanding use of stock options in executive remuneration over the last four decades, the legalization and subsequent growth of share buybacks, and so on (Lazonick 2014).

Finally, *scope rules* determine which outcomes must, must not, or may be affected within a domain (Ostrom 2005, 208). These outcomes are most clearly connected to ideas of corporate purpose. While the pre-1970s social norm linked corporate governance to the achievement of broad societal and stakeholder goals, the currently dominant social norm focuses managerial consideration exclusively on near-term shareholder results. The interests of a broader set of stakeholders and broader issues like planetary boundaries and climate change have become relegated to the status of "externalities" (Butzbach 2022).

Overall, the content of the seven types of rules identified by Ostrom is captured in two diverging rule configurations, which rest on the dominant social norms in the domain of corporate governance. This draws attention to the way in which the (re-) production of knowledge regarding these rules takes place.

7.5 DISCUSSION

To assess the conditions of *knowledge production* in the domain of corporate governance, it is notable that the contingent basis for notions of social ontology is well-recognized in the history of corporate law and corporate governance (Dewey 1926; Horwitz 1992). Relatedly, it is well-recognized that "at any particular time, corporate governance contains a number of contradictory pressures and points of conflict" (Aguilera and Jackson 2010, 48), and that the resolution of these debates is linked to significant socio-economic outcomes (Ireland 2005; Freeman 2011; Winkler 2019). The replacement of the social norms underpinning corporate governance in the 1970s was a process of displacement of alternative imaginaries in what Peck (2010) referred to as a "war of ideas" and Davies (2010, 10) called a "self-consciously epistemological and discursive" battle, aimed at subsuming legal expertise within economic expertise.

Both the process and the content of the profound changes in prevailing conceptions of corporate status, architecture, governance, and purpose have affected scholarship in company law, economics, management, and accounting (Bratton 1989; Blair 1998; Ghoshal 2005; Biondi et al. 2007; Davies 2010; Stout 2012). Commenting on the currently dominant norm, Millon (2014, 32–33) observed:

> However accurate it might have been in the earlier nineteenth century in an age of closely held firms, an agency characterization of management's relation to the shareholders has been completely inaccurate as a descriptive matter since the turn of the twentieth century and was still so in the later 1970s when corporate law academics first began to insist on it. Against this backdrop, the emergence of the agency claim and its widespread embrace as an assumed legal requirement are nothing short of astonishing.

In Section 7.2, I explored how the development, stabilization, and institutionalization of these new knowledge claims was based on the availability of academic, cultural, and financial resources, such as funding and media outlets, and on the formation of academic and practitioner networks comprised of disciplinary specialists, such as accountants, academics, judges, lawyers, journalists, consultants, standard setters, central banks, and financial advisors operating across "linked ecologies" (Fourcade and Khurana 2013).

The knowledge commons underpinning corporate governance practices were governed by and across these epistemic communities (Haas 2001; Hirschman and Berman 2014), whose members were well-aware of both the stakes involved and what others were doing to arrive at a joint interpretive frame that facilitated the institutionalization of a new social norm (Bratton 1989; Davis 2009). The creation of this *joint interpretive frame* enabled the "cognitive" or "cultural" capture of regulators and courts, as well as the strategic promotion of policies in arenas where the new rules of the game could be developed and reinforced (Hirschman and Berman 2014). Overall, then, the creation and displacement of rules and social norms in corporate governance can be seen as part of a "strategic project of professional colonization" (Davies 2010, 19) that can be studied using the SAF approach developed by Fligstein and McAdam (2011, 2012).

The combination of the GKC framework and the SAF approach to the shared production and shared governance of knowledge in the domain of corporate governance draws attention to four key issues.

To start with, the exploration of historical and contemporary debates delivers an inherently contingent epistemological basis for knowledge claims regarding ideas of corporate status, architecture, governance, and purpose (Veldman and Willmott 2022), which provides the basis for at least two diverging rule-sets in the domain of corporate governance. Reliance on divergent rule-sets provides a contested basis, particularly in an international comparative setting, for resolving claims concerning corporate ownership; corporate assets and liabilities; authority and control; and the mandate, role, and position of managers, directors, shareholders, creditors, employees, and broader stakeholders (Horwitz 1992; Hatchuel and Segrestin 2019). The question of how knowledge claims regarding these diverging rule-sets is formed and transmitted deserves further academic attention (Pistor 2019; Nordberg 2020; Gindis and Micheler 2024).

In addition, the contingent epistemological basis for knowledge claims invites research into the processes of contestation and stabilization, with special attention to the ways in which specific social norms and rule-sets become established as core, high-status, or legitimate knowledge (Fligstein and McAdam 2011, 2012; Hirschman and Berman 2014). Similarly, we need to know more about how systemic closure and self-referentiality of knowledge claims in corporate governance work (Deakin 2017, 2019), given high barriers for stakeholders operating outside the "small worlds of corporate governance" (Kogut 2012) to engage in meaningful debate concerning the formation of these knowledge claims (Veldman and Willmott 2020). What we need is anthropological and sociological research into how epistemic communities are organized, how they acquire and maintain *definitional control* over knowledge claims, and why they coalesce around specific rule-sets (Miller and Rose 1990; Latour 2010). Such approaches can be usefully connected with historical research (Gindis, 2020a, 2020b; Johnston 2024) and with studies of performativity in law and economics (Roy 1999; Van Horn 2009; Fourcade and Khurana 2013; Ash et al. 2025).

A third issue that a combined GKC–SAF approach brings to the fore is the exploration of alternatives. The rule-set associated with the pre-1970s social norm is very much compatible with the idea of the corporation as commons: "a shared resource whose sustainability depends on the participation of multiple constituencies in its governance (not just shareholders, but employees, core suppliers and customers)" (Deakin 2012, 339). Corporate governance, from this perspective, is a rule-set developed under a social norm that underpins notions of corporate status, architecture, governance, and purpose that help reconciliate multiple and overlapping ownership claims, through rules mutually agreed by all participants, for the preservation of the shared resource on which they all depend (Deakin 2019). In this framing, the purpose of the corporation is to "deliver benefits for all of its stakeholders and for society as a whole" (Deakin 2012, 339). Further exploration of the *corporation-as-commons rule-set* and the associated governance norms may in principle help understanding polycentric organizational designs, in which the orientation of managerial duties towards the interests of broader sets of stakeholders helps overcome collective action problems in our present organizational and societal context (Ostrom 1990; Wuisman 2018; Aguilera et al. 2021; Baldwin et al. 2024).

In this context, the final point to note here is that there is much to gain from the general GKC concern with the content, quality, and consequences of the production of knowledge resources. The adoption of specific position, boundary, choice, aggregation, and information rules in the domain of corporate governance is directly related to the relevance, salience, and distribution of roles and functions, the constitution and operation of (hierarchical) relationships, and the resources, claims, rights, obligations, protections, risks, liabilities, rewards, interests, time frames, and capacities of actors. Likewise, payoff and scope rules are directly related to the distribution of risks, liabilities, protections, and rewards. Knowledge claims about the rule-sets of corporate governance have definitional, positional, and exclusionary effects (Veldman 2025).

The creation and settling of knowledge claims regarding these rules is therefore intimately connected with very significant socio-economic effects at both the organizational and the macroeconomic levels (Perrow 2002; Ireland 2005). And beyond these organizational outcomes, the example of Larry Fink makes clear that the capacity to establish or change the content and scope of an abstract concept like "fiduciary duties" is closely related to the real-world mandate for CEOs seeking to engage with stakeholders and various long-term interests. The content, quality, and consequences of debates that settle contingent knowledge claims in corporate governance are thus closely associated with the capacity of practitioners to engage with externalities, notably "grand challenges" like climate change and the overshooting of planetary boundaries (Veldman 2024). The GKC framework, especially in combination of the SAF approach, enhances our analytical and empirical ability to explore the process of knowledge construction in interconnected epistemic communities. This can improve our understanding of how knowledge claims shape the conditions of possibility for actors in corporate governance to engage effectively with the grand challenges we face.

7.6 CONCLUSIONS

The GKC framework questions about the content, quality, and consequences of the creation of knowledge in corporate governance. Combined with the SAF approach, this framework can help reveal how the development and institutionalization of knowledge claims about corporate status, architecture, governance, and purpose are based on active and often strategic processes of knowledge formation taking place in interconnected epistemic communities. This perspective can usefully explain how two historically contingent social norms informed the formation of distinct configurations of corporate governance rules.

An exploration of these diverging rule-sets, as well as the agency involved in their adoption and institutionalization, contributes to advancing ongoing debates in management and organization studies, including those that focus on the connections between governance design and collective action problems (Klein et al. 2019); self-interest, collective interest, and short-term versus long-term interest (Olson 1965); team production, firm-specific investments, and holdup problems faced by specific stakeholders (Grandori 2010); and the ability of managers to motivate, foster, and maintain stakeholders' trust and cooperative relationships necessary for joint value creation (Bridoux and Stoelhorst 2022a, 2022b).

Beyond debates about (shared) value creation in individual organizations, developing applications of the GKC framework in the broader institutional context of corporate governance can contribute to research into the conditions for fostering cooperation in theories of market transformation (Nijhof et al. 2022). Ultimately, the GKC framework helps us link an epistemological discussion about the inherently contingent basis of knowledge formation and institutional design, and a justification for enhancing the participation of stakeholders in processes of knowledge creation, sharing, and governance.

REFERENCES

Aglietta, Michel, and Antoine Rebérioux. 2005. *Corporate Governance Adrift: A Critique of Shareholder Value*. Cheltenham: Edward Elgar.

Aguilera, Ruth V., J. Alberto Aragón-Correa, Valentina Marano, and Peter A. Tashman. 2021. "The Corporate Governance of Environmental Sustainability: A Review and Proposal for More Integrated Research." *Journal of Management* 47(6): 1468–1497.

Aguilera, Ruth V., and Alvaro Cuervo-Cazurra. 2004. "Codes of Good Governance Worldwide: What Is the Trigger?" *Organization Studies* 25(3): 415–443.

Aguilera, Ruth V., and Gregory Jackson. 2010. "Comparative and International Corporate Governance." *Academy of Management Annals* 4(1): 485–556.

Allen, William T. 1992. "Our Schizophrenic Conception of the Business Corporation." *Cardozo Law Review* 14(2): 261–281.

Ash, Elliott, Daniel L. Chen, and Suresh Naidu. 2025. "Ideas Have Consequences: The Impact of Law and Economics on American Justice." *The Quarterly Journal of Economics* (forthcoming).

Avi-Yonah, Reuven S. 2011. "Citizens United and the Corporate Form." *Accounting, Economics, and Law* 1(3): 1–54.

Baldwin, Elizabeth, Andreas Thiel, Michael C. McGinnis, and Elke Kellner. 2024. "Empirical Research on Polycentric Governance: Critical Gaps and a Framework for Studying Long-Term Change." *Policy Studies Journal* 52(2): 319–348.

Bebchuk, Lucian A., and Roberto Tallarita. 2020. "The Illusory Promise of Stakeholder Governance." *Cornell Law Review* 106(91): 91–177.

Berle, Adolf A. 1931. "For Whom Corporate Managers Are Trustees: A Note." *Harvard Law Review* 45(8): 1365–1372.

Berle, Adolf A. 1947. "The Theory of Enterprise Entity." *Columbia Law Review* 47(3): 343–358.

Berle, Adolf A. 1954. *The 20th-Century Capitalist Revolution*. New York: Harcourt, Brace.

Berle, Adolf A., and Gardiner C. Means. 2007. *The Modern Corporation and Private Property*. New Brunswick: Transaction Publishers.

Biondi, Yuri, Arnaldo Canziani, and Thierry Kirat, eds. 2007. *The Firm as an Entity: Implications for Economics, Accounting, and the Law*. London: Routledge.

Blair, Margaret M. 1995. *Ownership and Control: Rethinking Corporate Governance for the Twenty-First Century*. Washington, DC: Brookings Institution Press.

Blair, Margaret M. 1998. "For Whom Should Corporations Be Run? An Economic Rationale for Stakeholder Management." *Long Range Planning* 31(2): 195–200.

Blair, Margaret M. 2015. "Of Corporations, Courts, Personhood, and Morality." *Business Ethics Quarterly* 25(4): 415–431.

Blair, Margaret M., and Lynn A. Stout. 1999. "A Team Production Theory of Corporate Law." *Virginia Law Review* 85(2): 247–328.

Blair, Margaret M., and Lynn A. Stout. 2005. "Specific Investment: Explaining Anomalies in Corporate Law." *Journal of Corporation Law* 31(3): 719–744.

Botzem, Sebastian. 2014. *The Politics of Accounting Regulation: Organizing Transnational Standard Setting in Financial Reporting*. Cheltenham: Edward Elgar.

Bratton, William W. 1989. "The New Economic Theory of the Firm: Critical Perspectives from History." *Stanford Law Review* 41(6): 1471–1527.

Bratton, William W. 2017. "The Separation of Corporate Law and Social Welfare." *Washington and Lee Law Review* 74(2): 767–790.

Bridoux, Flore M., and Pushpika Vishwanathan. 2020. "When Do Powerful Stakeholders Give Managers the Latitude to Balance All Stakeholders' Interests?" *Business and Society* 59(2): 232–262.

Bridoux, Flore M., and J. W. Stoelhorst. 2022a. "Stakeholder Governance: Solving the Collective Action Problems in Joint Value Creation." *Academy of Management Review* 47(2): 214–236.

Bridoux, Flore M., and J. W. Stoelhorst. 2022b. "Stakeholder Theory, Strategy, and Organization: Past, Present, and Future." *Strategic Organization* 20(4): 797–809.

Butzbach, Olivier. 2022. "The Elusive Nature of Shareholders' Claims Over the Corporation, or the Strange Non-death of Shareholder Primacy." In *The Corporation: Rethinking the Iconic Form of Business Organization*, ed. Renate E. Meyer, Stefan Leixnering, and Jeroen Veldman, 31–55. Leeds: Emerald.

Ciepley, David. 2013. "Beyond Public and Private: Toward a Political Theory of the Corporation." *American Political Science Review* 107(1): 1–20.

Cioffi, John W. 2010. *Public Law and Private Power: Corporate Governance Reform in the in the Age of Finance Capitalism*. Ithaca: Cornell University Press.

Clarke, Thomas. 2021. *Corporate Governance: A Survey*. Cambridge: Cambridge University Press

Collison, David, Stuart Cross, John Ferguson, David Power, and Lorna Stevenson. 2014. "Financialization and Company Law: A Study of the UK Company Law Review." *Critical Perspectives on Accounting* 25(1): 5–16.

Davis, Gerald F. 2009. *Managed by the Markets: How Finance Re-shaped America*. New York: Oxford University Press.

Davis, Gerald F. 2011. "Twilight of the Berle and Means Corporation." *Seattle University Law Review* 34(4): 1121–1138.

Davies, William. 2010. "Economics and the 'Nonsense' of Law: The Case of the Chicago Antitrust Revolution." *Economy and Society* 39(1): 64–83.

Deakin, Simon. 2012. "The Corporation as Commons: Rethinking Property Rights, Governance and Sustainability in the Business Enterprise." *Queen's Law Journal* 37(2): 339–381.

Deakin, Simon. 2017. "The Corporation in Legal Studies." In *The Corporation: A Critical, Multi-disciplinary Handbook*, ed. Grietje Baars and André Spicer, 47–63. Cambridge: Cambridge: Cambridge University Press.

Deakin, Simon. 2019. "The Evolution of Corporate Form: From shareholders' property to the corporation as commons." In *The Oxford Handbook of the Corporation*, ed. Thomas Clarke, Justin O'Brien, and Charles R. T. O'Kelley, 687–710. New York: Oxford University Press.

Dewey, John. 1926. "The Historic Background of Corporate Legal Personality." *Yale Law Journal* 35(6): 655–673.

Dodd, E. Merrick. 1931. "For Whom Are Corporate Managers Trustees." *Harvard Law Review* 45(7): 1145–1163.

Du Plessis, Jean. 2016. "Shareholder Primacy and Other Stakeholder Interests." *Company and Securities Law Journal* 34: 238–242.

Eisenberg, Melvin A. 1975. "Legal Models of Management Structure in the Modern Corporation: Officers, Directors, and Accountants." *California Law Review* 63(2): 375–439.

Fligstein, Neil. 1996. "The Theory of Fields and Its Application to Corporate Governance." *Seattle University Law Review* 39(2): 237–262.

Fligstein, Neil, and Doug McAdam. 2011. "Toward a General Theory of Strategic Action Fields." *Sociological Theory* 29(1): 1–26.

Fligstein, Neil, and Doug McAdam. 2012. *A Theory of Fields*. New York: Oxford University Press.

Fligstein, Neil, and Taekhin Shin. 2007. "Shareholder Value and the Transformation of the US Economy, 1984–2000." *Sociological Forum* 22(4): 399–424.

Fourcade, Marion, and Rakesh Khurana. 2013. "From Social Control to Financial Economics: The Linked Ecologies of Economics and Business in Twentieth-Century America." *Theory and Society* 42(2): 121–159.

Fourcade, Marion, and Rakesh Khurana. 2017. "The Social Trajectory of a Finance Professor and the Common Sense of Capital." *History of Political Economy* 49(2): 347–381.

Freeman, Mark, Robin Pearson, and James Taylor. 2011. *Shareholder Democracies? Corporate Governance in Britain and Ireland before 1850*. Chicago: University of Chicago Press.

Frischmann, Brett M., Michael J. Madison, and Katherine J. Strandburg, eds. 2014. *Governing Knowledge Commons*. New York: Oxford University Press.

Gelter, Martin. 2009. "The Dark Side of Shareholder Influence: Managerial Autonomy and Stakeholder Orientation in Comparative Corporate Governance." *Harvard International Law Journal* 50(1): 129–194.

Gindis, David. 2020a. On the Origins, Meaning and Influence of Jensen and Meckling's Definition of the Firm." *Oxford Economic Papers* 72(4): 966–984.

Gindis, David. 2020b. "Law and Economics under the Palms: Henry Manne at the University of Miami, 1974–1980." https://ssrn.com/abstract=3567105.

Gindis, David, and Eva Micheler. 2024. "Institutional Theory for Corporate Law: An Invitation." *Journal of Corporate Law Studies* 24(2): 399–435.

Ghoshal, Sumantra. 2005. "Bad Management Theories Are Destroying Good Management Practices." *Academy of Management Learning and Education* 4(1): 75–91.

Goranova, Maria, and Lor Verstegen Ryan. 2022. "The Corporate Objective Revisited: The Shareholder Perspective." *Journal of Management Studies* 59(2): 526–554.

Grandori, Anna. 2010. "Asset Commitment, Constitutional Governance and the Nature of the Firm." *Journal of Institutional Economics* 6(3): 351–375.

Grandori, Anna. 2022. "Constitutionalizing the Corporation." In *The Corporation: Rethinking the Iconic Form of Business Organization*, ed. Renate E. Meyer, Stefan Leixnering, and Jeroen Veldman, 57–76. Leeds: Emerald.

Greenwood, Daniel J. 2017. "Neofederalism: The Surprising Foundations of Corporate Constitutional Rights." *University of Illinois Law Review* 2017(1): 163–221.

Haas, Peter M. 2001. "Policy Knowledge: Epistemic Communities." In *International Encyclopedia of the Social and Behavioral Sciences*, ed. Neil J. Smelser, and Paul B. Baltes, 11578–11586. Amsterdam: Elsevier.

Hatchuel, Armand, and Blanche Segrestin. 2019. "A Century Old and Still Visionary: Fayol's Innovative Theory of Management." *European Management Review* 16(2): 399–412.

Haveman, Heather A., and Nataliya Nedzhvetskaya. 2022. "Community, Enterprise, and Self-help: The Coevolution of Capitalism and Non-profit and For-Profit Businesses in Britain and Germany." In *The Corporation: Rethinking the Iconic Form of Business Organization*, ed. Renate E. Meyer, Stefan Leixnering, and Jeroen Veldman, 121–141. Leeds: Emerald.

Haxhi, Ilir, Hans van Ees, and Arndt Sorge. 2013. "A Political Perspective on Business Elites and Institutional Embeddedness in the UK Code-Issuing Process." *Corporate Governance* 21(6): 535–546.

Heemskerk, Eelke M., Jeroen Veldman, and Jan Fichtner. 2022. "Mandate Ownership: Power Concentration and Second-Order Agency Conflict in the Age of Passive Asset Management." https://ssrn.com/abstract=4015828.

Hirschman, Daniel, and Elizabth Popp Berman. 2014. "Do Economists Make Policies? On the Political Effects of Economics." *Socio-Economic Review* 12(4): 779–811.

Horwitz, Morton J. 1992. *The Transformation of American Law, 1870-1960: The Crisis of Legal Orthodoxy*. New York: Oxford University Press.

Howard-Grenville, Jennifer, Gerald F. Davis, Thoams Dyllick, et al. 2019. "Sustainable Development for a Better World: Contributions of Leadership, Management, and Organizations." *Academy of Management Discoveries* 5(4): 355–366.

Ireland, Paddy. 1996. "Capitalism without the Capitalist: The Joint Stock Company Share and the Emergence of the Modern Doctrine of Separate Corporate Personality." *Journal of Legal History* 17(1): 41–73.

Ireland, Paddy. 2005. "Shareholder Primacy and the Distribution of Wealth." *Modern Law Review* 68(1): 49–81.

Ireland, Paddy. 2009. "Financialization and Corporate Governance." *Northern Ireland Legal Quarterly* 60(1): 1–34.

Jacoby, Sanford M. 2008. "Finance and Labor: Perspectives on Risk, Inequality, and Democracy." *Comparative Labor Law and Policy Journal* 30(1): 17–61.

Johnson, Lyman P. Q., and David Millon. 2005. "Recalling Why Corporate Officers Are Fiduciaries." *William and Mary Law Review* 46(5): 1597–1654.

Johnson, Paul. 2010. *Making the Market: Victorian Origins of Corporate Capitalism*. Cambridge: Cambridge University Press.

Johnston, Andrew. 2024. "The Bank of England and the 'Prehistory' of Corporate Governance." *Business History* 67(5): 1221–1246.

Katelouzou, Dionysia, and Peer Zumbanse. 2020. "The New Geographies of Corporate Governance." *University of Pennsylvania Journal of International Law* 42(1): 51–153.

Khurana, Rakesh. 2007. *From Higher Aims to Hired Hands: The Social Transformation of American Business Schools and the Unfulfilled Promise of Management as a Profession*. Princeton: Princeton University Press.

Klein, Peter G., Joseph T. Mahoney, Anita M. McGahan, and Christos N. Pitelis. 2019. "Organizational Governance Adaptation: Who Is In, Who Is Out, and Who Gets What." *Academy of Management Review* 44(1): 6–27.

Kogut, Bruce, ed. 2012. *The Small Worlds of Corporate Governance*. Cambridge, MA: MIT Press.

Lan, Luh L., and Loizos Heracleous. 2010. "Rethinking Agency Theory: The View from Law." *Academy of Management Review* 35(2): 294–314.

Lane, Christel. 2003. "Changes in Corporate Governance of German Corporations: Convergence to the Anglo-American Model?" *Competition and Change* 7(2–3): 79–100.

Latour, Bruno. 2010. *The Making of Law: An Ethnography of the Conseil D'Etat*. London: Polity Press.

Lazonick, William. 2014. "Profits without Prosperity: Stock Buybacks Manipulate the Market, and Leave Most Americans Worse Off." *Harvard Business Review* 92(9): 46–55.
Leixnering, Stefan, Renate E. Meyer, and Peter Doralt. 2022. "The Past as Prologue: Purpose Dynamics in the History of the *Aktiengesellschaft*." In *The Corporation: Rethinking the Iconic Form of Business Organization*, ed. Renate E. Meyer, Stefan Leixnering, and Jeroen Veldman, 97–120. Leeds: Emerald.
Litowitz, Douglas. 2000. "Reification in Law and Legal Theory." *Southern California Interdisciplinary Law Journal* 9: 401–427.
Lokin, Manuel, and Jeroen Veldman. 2019. "The Potential of the Dutch Corporate Governance Model for Sustainable Governance and Long-Term Stakeholder Value." *Erasmus Law Review*, 12(4): 50–60.
Lund, Dorothy S., and Elizabeth Pollman. 2021. "The Corporate Governance Machine." *Columbia Law Review* 121(8): 2563–2634.
Metcalf, Louise, and Sue Benn. 2012. "The Corporation Is Ailing Social Technology: Creating a 'Fit for Purpose' Design for Sustainability." *Journal of Business Ethics* 111(2): 195–210.
Miller, Peter, and Nikolas Rose. 1990. "Governing Economic Life." *Economy and Society*, 19(1): 1–31.
Millon, David. 2014. "Radical Shareholder Primacy." *University of St. Thomas Law Journal*10(4): 1013–1044.
Mirowski, Philip, and Deiter Plehwe. 2009. *The Road from Mont Pèlerin: The Making of the Neoliberal Thought Collective*. Cambridge, MA: Harvard University Press.
Mizruchi, Mark S., and Daniel Hirschman. 2010. The Modern Corporation as Social Construction. *Seattle University Law Review* 33(4): 1065–1108.
Nijhof, Andre., Alice Wins, Aikaterini Argyrou, and Nicolas Chevrollier. 2022. "Sustainable Market Transformation: A Refined Framework for Analyzing Causal Loops in Transitions to Sustainability." *Environmental Innovation and Societal Transitions* 42: 352–361.
Nordberg, Donald. 2020. *The Cadbury Code and Recurrent Crisis: A Model for Corporate Governance*. Cham: Palgrave Macmillan.
Olson, Mancur. 1965. *The Logic of Collective Action: Public Goods and the Theory of Groups*. Cambridge, MA: Harvard University Press.
Ostrom, Elinor. 1990. *Governing the Commons: The Evolution of Institutions of Collective Action*. Cambridge: Cambridge University Press.
Ostrom, Elinor. 2005. *Understanding Institutional Diversity*. Princeton: Princeton University Press.
Peck, Jamie. 2010. *Constructions of Neoliberal Reason*. New York: Oxford University Press.
Perrow, Charles. 2002. *Organizing America: Wealth, Power, and the Origins of Corporate Capitalism*. Princeton: Princeton University Press.
Pickering, Murray A. 1968. "The Company as a Separate Legal Entity." *Modern Law Review* 31(5): 481–511.
Pistor, Katharina. 2019. *The Code of Capital: How the Law Creates Wealth and Inequality*. Princeton: Princeton University Press.
Priest, George L. 2020. *The Rise of Law and Economics: An Intellectual History*. Abingdon: Routledge.
Pye, Annie. 2001. "Corporate Boards, Investors and Their Relationships: Accounts of Accountability and Corporate Governing in Action." *Corporate Governance* 9(3): 186–195.
Robé, Jean-Philippe. 2011. "The Legal Structure of the Firm." *Accounting, Economics, and Law* 1(1): 1–86.

Rock, Edward B. 2013. "Adapting to the New Shareholder-Centric Reality." *University of Pennsylvania Law Review* 161(7): 1907–1988.
Rock, Edward B. 2020. "For whom Is the Corporation Managed in 2020? The Debate over Corporate Purpose." *Business Lawyer* 76(2): 363–396.
Romano, Roberta. 2005. "After the Revolution in Corporate Law." *Journal of Legal Education* 55(3): 342–359.
Roy, William G. 1999. *Socializing Capital: The Rise of the Large Industrial Corporation in America*. Princeton: Princeton University Press.
Sanfilippo, Madelyn R., Brett M. Frischmann, and Katherine J. Standburg. 2018. "Privacy as Commons: Case Evaluation through the Governing Knowledge Commons Framework." *Journal of Information Policy* 8: 116–166.
Segrestin, Blanche, and Armand Hatchuel. 2011. "Beyond Agency Theory, a Post-crisis View of Corporate Law." *British Journal of Management* 22(3): 484–499.
Segrestin, Blanche, Andrew Johnston, and Armand Hatchuel. 2019. "The Separation of Directors and Managers: A Historical Examination of the Status of Managers." *Journal of Management History* 25(2): 141–164.
Smith, N. Craig, and David Rönnegard. 2016. "Shareholder Primacy, Corporate Social Responsibility, and the Role of Business Schools." *Journal of Business Ethics* 134(3): 463–478.
Stout, Lynn A. 2012. *The Shareholder Value Myth: How Putting Shareholders First Harms Investors, Corporations, and the Public*. San Francisco: Berrett-Koehler.
Stout, Lynn A. 2015. "The Corporation as Time Machine: Intergenerational Equity, Intergenerational Efficiency, and the Corporate Form." *Seattle University Law Review* 38(2): 685–723.
Sundaram, Anant K., and Andrew C Inkpen. 2004. "Stakeholder Theory and 'The Corporate Objective Revisited': A Reply." *Organization Science* 15(3): 370–371.
Talbot, Lorraine. 2008. *Critical Company Law*. London: Routledge.
Teles, Stephen M. 2008. *The Rise of the Conservative Legal Movement*. Princeton: Princeton University Press.
Van Bekkum, Jaron, Steven Hijink, Michale C. Schouten, and Jaap W. Winter. 2010. "Corporate Governance in the Netherlands." *Electronic Journal of Comparative Law* 14(3): 1–35.
Van Horn, Rob. 2009. "Reinventing Monopoly and the Role of Corporations: The Roots of Chicago Law and Economics." In *The Road from Mont Pèlerin: The Making of the Neoliberal Thought Collective*, ed. Philip Mirowski, and Dieter Plehwe, 204–237. Cambridge, MA: Harvard University Press.
Van Horn, Rob, and Philip Mirowski, 2009. "The Rise of the Chicago School of Economics and the Birth of Neoliberalism." In *The Road from Mont Pèlerin: The Making of the Neoliberal Thought Collective*, ed. Philip Mirowski, and Dieter Plehwe, 139–180. Cambridge, MA: Harvard University Press.
Vasudev, P. M. 2012. "The Stakeholder Principle, Corporate Governance, and Theory: Evidence from the Field and the Path Onward." *Hofstra Law Review* 41(2): 399–466.
Veldman, Jeroen. 2019. "Boards and Sustainable Value Creation: The Legal Entity, Co-determination and Other Means." *European Business Law Review* 30(2): 279–300.
Veldman, Jeroen. 2024. *Board Agenda 2035: Corporate Governance for the Next Decade*. Breukelen: Nyenrode Business University. https://ssrn.com/abstract=4929982.
Veldman, Jeroen. 2025. "Stakeholder Salience, Corporate Governance, and Sustainability." In *The Corporation, Corporate Governance and the Green Transition*, edited by Mathias H. Jessen, Tessa Barnow and Benjamin. A. Popp-Madsen. Leeds: Emerald.

Veldman, Jeroen, and Hugh Willmott. 2016. "The Cultural Grammar of Governance: The UK Code of Corporate Governance, Reflexivity, and the Limits of 'Soft' Regulation." *Human Relations* 69(3): 581–603.

Veldman, Jeroen, and Hugh Willmott. 2022. "Social Ontology of the Modern Corporation: Its Role in Understanding Organizations." In *The Corporation: Rethinking the Iconic Form of Business Organization*, ed. Renate E. Meyer, Sferan Leixnering, and Jeroen Veldman, 165–189. Leeds: Emerald.

Vitols, Sigurt. 2004. "Negotiated Shareholder Value: The German Variant of an Anglo-American Practice." *Competition and Change* 8(4): 357–374.

Winkler, Adam. 2019. *We the Corporations: How American Businesses Won Their Civil Rights*. New York: Liveright.

Wuisman, I. 2018. "Twitter: Naar een multi-stakeholder coöperatie en de commons." In *Ars Notariatus; De coöperatie anno 2017*, ed. M. Debeuker et al., 87–98. Deventer: Wolters Kluwer.

Young, Michael N., Mike W. Peng, David Ahlstrom, Garry D. Bruton, and Yi Jiang. 2008. "Corporate Governance in Emerging Economies: A Review of the Principal–Principal Perspective." *Journal of Management Studies* 45(1): 196–220.

Yoshikawa, Toru, and Adbul A. Rasheed. 2009. Convergence of Corporate Governance: Critical Review and Future Directions. *Corporate Governance* 17(3): 388–404.

Yosifon, David G. 2013. "The Law of Corporate Purpose." *Berkeley Business Law Journal* 10(2): 181–230.

8

Venture Capital as a Commons

Simon Deakin and Hanna Sitchenko

8.1 INTRODUCTION

Venture capital should be a key case for the study of the corporation as a knowledge commons, given the significant degree of venture capital funding in certain economies (the US and the UK) and its growing extent in others (including mainland Europe, east Asia, and Latin America). Virtually all of the major corporations built out of the digital revolution began life as venture capital-funded startups or received venture capital funding at an early point in their evolution.

At first sight, however, venture capital does not look much like a commons. In a commons, norms for the governance of a shared resource emerge through a process of deliberation and experimentation between stakeholders; venture capital, by contrast, is characterised by bright-line rules which are precisely calibrated to manage risk. If the norms of the corporate commons are in part designed, and partly evolve, so as to ensure its sustainability over time, venture capital funding presupposes corporate failure as a highly likely, indeed on average the most probable outcome, resulting in the dissolution of the firm and reallocation of its assets, while the wider portfolio of firms making up a venture capital fund has a limited life of normally less than a decade. Where the legal structure of the corporate commons is one which acknowledges the contribution of employees and communities to knowledge creation and preservation, the legal structure of venture capital confers few if any voice and participation rights on these stakeholders, potentially exposing them to the costs of failure.

In this chapter, we take a closer look at the governance of venture capital (VC), at how it operates, and how it is legally structured. The basis of our analysis is recently completed interview-based fieldwork which focused on the European experience of VC and, specifically, on the prospects of developing a VC sector in Ukraine as part of its post-conflict reconstruction. This project provided us with the opportunity to explore the practical operation of VC through engagement with funds, startups, and their legal and financial advisers.

We find that the legal structure of VC is indeed highly transactional, with clearly defined property and contract rights at the core of a widely used legal template, the aim of which is to allow investors to benefit in proportion to the gains made by successful firms, while limiting their exposure (financial risks) to those which fail. On the other hand, there are many elements of VC practice which resemble a commons. VC funds operate as pooling devices, enabling downstream risks to be shared across a portfolio of firms. Knowledge spillovers generate positive externalities beyond the gains captured by entrepreneurs, funds, and investors, thereby benefiting producers and communities. Formal legal rules, expressing individualised and indivisible property rights, are intertwined or "braided" with informal and relational norms. Insofar as VC succeeds in generating innovation, understood as the application of knowledge to novel technological ends, it is because these commons-type elements operate alongside and in conjunction with the hard-edged legal and financial ones. This is recognised, among others, by VC trade bodies, which increasingly emphasise a VC model directed towards "sustainable business growth," and which aim to deliver "economic and social value to those involved in the businesses (from employees, management and owners on the one hand, to customers and suppliers on the other) and a wide group of stakeholders (from local communities and local and regional economies, to national policy makers focused on issues such as climate change, diversity and inclusion and social justice)" (British Venture Capital Association 2023, 2).

Thus there is more to VC, and to the idea of VC as a commons, than immediately meets the eye. Yet the story of VC that we more usually hear is one of "disruption" and "destruction," however "necessary" and "creative" these are deemed to be. That there is a disjunction between the practice of VC and the way it is frequently presented poses a challenge for innovation policy. Legal exceptions designed to promote VC innovation may create perverse incentives, leading to value destruction, rent seeking, and negative knowledge externalities.

To develop these points, we begin by setting out some theoretical considerations concerning VC and the corporate commons, respectively. We focus here on Masahiko Aoki's theory of the corporation, which is one of the few accounts to address VC within a model of multi-stakeholder enterprise (Aoki 2010). Section 8.2 sets out a theoretical framework for understanding VC as a type of commons, building on Aoki's theory of VC as a particular form of *embedded cognition*. Extending the logic of the corporation as commons (Deakin 2012), the governance of VC becomes a question of maximising the net social return, taking account of both positive and negative knowledge spillovers, from VC-led innovation. In Section 8.3, we present our empirical findings. These focus on the contemporary experiences of Europe-based VC funds, startups, and advisers. Alongside features of VC that are familiar from the current literature, which tends to stress the elements of investor control and transactional flexibility characteristic of the US experience, we report on less familiar relational aspects of networks and systems in European

VC. Section 8.4 brings together theory and evidence in an assessment of our findings, and Section 8.5 concludes the chapter.

8.2 VENTURE CAPITAL AND THE AOKIAN THEORY OF THE CORPORATION

The Aokian theory of the corporation contains the conceptual ingredients for a useful analysis of corporate knowledge commons, which can be seen as complementary to the Institutional Analysis and Development (IAD) framework (Ostrom and Hess 2007) and especially the Governing Knowledge Gommons (GKC) framework (Frischmann et al. 2014). In this section we explore Aoki's distinctive understanding of the corporation as a form of embedded cognition, which can be extended to encompass a theory of corporate law as an endogenously generated, public representation of the enterprise form. We then apply the same theoretical understanding to the case of VC.

8.2.1 *The Corporation as Embedded Cognition*

In contrast to the theories of the "firm" associated with new institutional economics, Aoki presents a theory of the "corporation," of which the business firm is one instance. Aoki defines corporations as "voluntary, permanent associations of natural persons engaged in purposeful associative activities, having unique identity, and embodied in rule-based, self-governing organisations" (Aoki 2010, 4). All corporations, so defined, embed knowledge, in the specific sense, developed by Aoki, of *associational cognition*. Cognition is "associational" when it is distributed across and retained within networks of actors. The structure of the business firm, and ultimately its legal form, are determined by the way in which certain forms of knowledge become essential to the firm's operations. Relational *essentialities* between corporate actors explain the degree of control which is conferred by law and practice on different stakeholders.

In the large, bureaucratically organised corporation, the *cognitive assets* held by management are "essential" or core for the operation for the firm, while those of workers are only "quasi-essential." This explains, in Aoki's view, the hierarchical control which managers exercise in the organisation of production: the distribution of cognitive assets explains, in a functional sense, the organisational hierarchy of the firm. Shareholders, as monitors, are in a position to autonomously oversee and evaluate the evolving relationship between managerial and worker cognitive assets. Although Aoki observes the tendency for external monitoring of reciprocal essentialities through the capital market to become the norm around the world since the 1980s, he notes the risk that boards, under external investor pressure, will alter the balance of returns between shareholders and workers to the detriment of the latter, in such a way as to destroy value. German-style codetermination provides one possible solution, he suggests, by giving workers representation on boards, so enabling them to engage directly with shareholders in developing the firm's strategy. The Japanese "community firm" achieves a similar result less formally, via a series of social norms and institutionalised practices which balance shareholder rights with worker voice.

According to Aoki, VC emerges in contexts where the hierarchical organisation of the firm gives insufficient weight to worker cognitive assets which are essential to value creation. In his version of Silicon Valley's origin story, the decomposition of digital systems into modular units, connected by open interface rules, favoured the outsourcing of innovation to entrepreneurial startups. With the move to VC-based governance, startups provide the worker cognitive assets which are essential for innovation. Decentralisation of production to individual firms allows for a higher degree of specialisation than is possible within the integrated corporation while competition between firms drives improvements. The outsourcing of innovation favours an industrial structure based on complementary cognitive assets: through modularisation, "technological and attribute complementarities between products" are designed in such a way "that the cognitions involved in the design effort can be encapsulated without hierarchical ordering" (Aoki 2010, 45).

Venture capital funding, in which funds build portfolios of startup firms through which to channel investments, has particular properties in Aoki's framework. The managers of the fund, acting as *information brokers*, possess knowledge which is valuable but only "quasi-essential" in Aoki's terminology. The essential technical knowledge remains that of the entrepreneur and core employees of the startup. However, the value encapsulated in the startup can only be realised over time, as the project on which the firm is engaged plays out. Staged or "step finance" allows the fund to monitor the creation of knowledge essentialities over time. The role of the fund is therefore "akin to that of a referee governing a tournament game played among [startup] firms rather than managing them with its own essential cognitive assets" (Aoki 2010, 45).

This structure has implications for the way in which the fund manages uncertainty. In its role as the central monitor of a group of startups, the fund allocates investments between firms over the course of the startup life cycle in a manner akin to creating "option values" on their "parallel development efforts" (Aoki 2010, 46). The fund treats the individual firms as a series of "experiments," not all of which, or depending on circumstances, very few of which, need to succeed for the fund to make a return for its investors. However, "failed" firms, those which do not make it to a successful exit via an IPO or trade sale, may nonetheless generate ideas which will come to fruition at some point.

In this account, VC structures are highly decentralised, atomistic, and individualised, while at the same time operating through a *virtual corporate architecture* which is centralised, relational, and collective. Through its decentralised elements, the structure allows gains from innovation to be captured by successful entrepreneurs at the point of a trade sale or IPO once the investment has been realised, with stock options providing a means of rewarding the wider body of employees. The same structure, in its relational mode, generates a net surplus across the portfolio, in the form of returns to the investors as a group and to the managers of the fund, if the gains from the listing or trade sale of successful startups exceed the written-off investments in those that failed.

The VC structure also generates positive externalities beyond the individual fund. These take a number of forms: innovations developed by firms which fail, but which are then put to use in other projects; knowledge spillovers between projects, which are diffused via a mobile workforce; and tax revenues supporting public institutions, including universities and hospitals, which serve as knowledge repositories and training organisations. By these means, a wider *VC ecosystem* comes into being, with a corresponding set of cognitive assets which extends beyond individual firms (Aoki 2010, 44).

Returning to Aoki's definition of the corporation as a voluntary, rule-based, and self-organising association with a continuing existence, the implication of his analysis of is that attention should be focused on the network as a whole if the properties of VC are to be fully grasped. To the extent that VC ecosystem operates through the sharing of cognitive assets and resources, it is in need of a distinctive legal and transactional governance structure, one that is capable of supporting distributed coordination and generating a net knowledge surplus. How far does the current legal framework of VC meet these needs?

8.2.2 *The Cognitive Structure of Corporate Law*

Alongside his theory of the corporation, Aoki also offers an account of corporate law. In his approach, legal concepts specific to the corporation, such as separate personality and limited liability, operate as *public representations* of the emergent rules of corporate practice. Corporate law, in common with law in general, is an "endogenous normative order," which both reflects and frames the wider economic environment in which it operates. Law coordinates expectations by providing the parties with information on the rules of the game in which shared knowledge is codified. Thus law itself is an instrument of associational cognition, with evolutionary properties.

In reserving the term *corporation* for his description of the firm as an economic entity rather than a legal one, Aoki risks confusion. As Jean-Philippe Robé has argued, the economic concept of the "firm" and the legal notion of the "corporation" are two very different things. The "firm," in the sense used in new institutional economics, refers to a continuing entity or (the term Robé prefers) "activity" which combines physical and human assets in the production of goods and services (Robé 2011). The "corporation" is a legal term which refers to an artificially created person endowed by law with juridical capacity, that is, the power to enter into legal relations with other persons. Robé suggests using the term "firm" to refer to the economic entity and "corporation" to refer to the legal form. In practice, however, it is hard to maintain such a clear division, and Aoki's use of the term "corporation" in the economic sense is not in itself wrong, since lawyers do not have a monopoly in the use of terms (Deakin et al. 2017, 2021). Robé is nonetheless right to insist on the difference between economic and legal meanings of the term.

What, then, is the connection between the "corporation" as association, in Aoki's sense, and the "corporation" as the legal form which, as he puts it, "publicly represents" the association, or features of it? Aoki does not go into detail, but it would be consistent with his framework to suggest that the legal form is not a direct copy or replica of the economic one, nor a simple description of it. There is no one-to-one correspondence.

Rather, the legal form, as itself a type of *embedded cognition*, contains information which is functional with respect to the operation of the economic entity. Through the medium of legal language, features of corporate practice come to be recorded, abstracted, and retained for future use. As practice evolves, throwing up novel claims and form, juridical language adjusts to the changing corporate environment. The autonomy of the law implies that legal evolution is incremental and gradual, and that it may well be out of synch with fast moving technological and organisational changes. But over time, coevolution of law and the economy gives rise to a certain degree of "fit" between them.

The concept of the "corporation as commons" (Deakin 2012) is an application of the idea of law as embedded cognition. The claim is that there are features of corporate law which capture or represent an associational logic, present in the practice of corporations, which is akin to that of a commons. For this purpose, a commons is a shared resource governed by emergent rules whose function is to sustain the resource over time by reconciling the interests of the different groups that depend on and contribute to it (Hess 2008; Albareda and Sison 2020).

In Elinor Ostrom's typology (Ostrom 1990; Ostrom and Hess 2007; Poteete et al. 2010), commons-sustaining rules include norms of access, withdrawal, management, exclusion, and alienation. It is in the balance or tension between these different rules that the governance of the commons takes shape. Where multiple interests have the opportunity to participate in the making of the rules, the prospects for the survival of the commons as a shared resource are enhanced.

Thus like any other commons, the corporation or firm, understood as the continuing activity or entity through which production is organised, is a shared resource which benefits multiple interests, and is sustainable over time when each of these interests has a say in its governance. This is reflected in the logic of the corporation in its legal sense, as the form through which enterprise is cognised and regulated through law. The totality of the firm cannot be owned by any single group (Robé 2011), including the shareholders, who have no direct access to the corporate assets, and do not contract directly with the suppliers of other inputs. Vesting the ownership of the firm's working capital in the juridical person, the corporation, which cannot itself be owned, is not a legal "fiction" or sleight of hand, but a functional device for capturing the associational dimension of corporate practice. In the same way that the Aokian corporation is an emergent totality which is greater than the sum of its parts, so a holistic view is needed to comprehend the legal structure of the firm in all its relevant aspects, which extend beyond the core of company law to embrace elements of insolvency, employment, tax, and competition law.

Granting that the idea of the corporation as commons has a certain traction in the context of the integrated business firm, can the commons concept also be applied to the context of VC? Adopting Aoki's position, the equivalent of the integrated firm in the VC context is not the single startup, but the virtual corporate architecture linking funds to investors on the one hand and startup firms on the other. The fund-managed VC portfolio is linked to other elements of a wider VC ecosystem which includes service providers such as specialist law and consulting firms and public research institutions. The social value of the ecosystem is not confined to the returns achieved by investors, or for that matter other participants in the VC funding cycle, including fund managers, founders, and employees. Aoki's account of VC emphasises that the system-wide benefits can accrue to the professional firms which service VC and the universities and (in the case of biotech) hospitals which combine basic research with the provision of public health and education goods.

Thus, a VC ecosystem, as a *type* of commons, may be said to be sustainable when it generates a net social surplus, taking into account not just financial returns but also the knowledge spillovers and other positive externalities generated by the system as a whole. Venture capital does not just generate positive externalities, however. Over-ambitious and fad-driven projects, inflated firm values, stock market bubbles, and corporate fraud are also features of VC, and can be traced to the same legal structures which support VC-led innovation (Pollman 2020).

8.2.3 *The Legal Framework of VC*

Venture capital financing is legally structured according to a template which was initially established in the US and has come to be regarded as an industry standard which other countries should seek to emulate or replicate. The key features of the legal template are generally interpreted as reflecting a principal–agent logic. In this approach, innovation is characterised by a high-risk, high-return dynamic. Startups begin as micro enterprises with few or no physical assets and so have no collateral of the type needed to raise credit. Under these circumstances, investors are willing to finance startups only if they can protect themselves against downside risks. Investors manage risk by delegating control to the fund managers, who leverage their knowledge and experience in selecting firms for funding and, when necessary, deselecting a certain proportion of them as the funding cycle proceeds. Staged financing gives the fund the power to exercise close control over the firms in the portfolio and the opportunity to exit if a project looks like failing.

A key legal feature of VC finance is convertibility, that is to say, the power of the fund to switch the legal form of its investment from debt to equity and back again at points in the VC funding cycle. The practice, originating in the US, of funds taking an equity interest in the form of convertible preferred stock has been explained as enabling the separation of cash flow and control rights (Kaplan and Strömberg 2003). The preferential nature of the shareholding gives the fund priority over the common shareholders in the event of insolvency, while its convertibility enables the fund to exchange its holding for the more liquid common stock in the event of the firm's success. More recently, instruments akin to convertible loans, such as the SAFE (secure agreement for future equity) or KISS (keep it simple security), have become widely used. Reflecting a wider trend in corporate finance (Lalafaryan 2023), these instruments blur the line between debt and equity.

When the fund converts preferred stock or a loan, as the case may be, into common stock if the startup succeeds, it is in a position to benefit in direct proportion to the firm's success through an IPO or trade sale. If, on the other hand, the project fails, the fund is in a better position, as a preferred shareholder or lender, to protect itself against downside losses, than it would be if it held an equivalent common equity stake. Enabling the fund to flip its interest from debt to equity in this way can be defended as a precondition of startups with limited assets or earnings getting access to capital. The same arrangement, however, enables the fund to offload risk on to other input providers.

Another feature of the legal structuring of VC is that funds can exercise close control by taking seats on the board of the startup, or by stipulating for observer rights. It is also common for shareholders' agreements, supplementing the terms of corporate charters (articles of association or bylaws), to grant funds veto rights over certain transactions and to prevent the dilution of their holdings downstream as other investors take equity stakes.

Several theories have been offered to explain the role of the IPO in structuring incentives. The need for the fund to recover its investments via a flotation or listing may be only part of the explanation for the centrality of the IPO in the VC model. If returns were all that mattered, a trade sale or share transfer might work just as well. According to some accounts, the IPO route has the additional feature of enabling the founder-entrepreneur to retain a significant role in the management of the firm post-flotation (Black and Gilson 1998). This has the dual effect of heightening founders' incentives to invest their skills and resources in the firm during the startup phase, while also incentivising founders to stay with the firm. Following a trade sale, which leads to the integration of the startup into a larger corporate structure, founders may choose to move on in preference to taking a junior role in the organisation of the acquirer. This can lead to the loss of essential knowledge on the part of acquiring firm.

Exit dynamics are not all positive. The so-called VC power law dictates a strategy for funds of seeking exponentially high returns from the small number of successful startups, to compensate for losses in the majority of the portfolio. However, the pursuit of exponential returns may lead startups to prioritise short-term expansion over sustainability. A number of high-profile scandals associated with high-tech startups, extending to cases of fraud, have put the power-law model into question. These cases suggest that board membership and observer rights can only offer partial solutions to information asymmetries in cases of innovative technologies, and that the promise of exponential returns can induce problematic moral hazard effects (Pollman 2023).

Opportunism also arises in the context of the large majority of projects which do not get to the IPO or trade sale stage. Founders may try to exit before the firm realises its full investment potential. Funds respond by using their veto powers to prevent "beach money exits," which are of low risk for founders but imply a limited return for investors (Wansley 2019). Conversely, a founder may hold out against liquidation beyond the point when the investment is feasible for the fund. In this situation, funds may induce founders to accept "acqui-hires," in which they and the employees are taken on by the acquiring company. Another form of "failing with honour" is a "soft-landing insolvency." In some US states, an "ABC" (assignment for the benefit of creditors), in which the company transfers assets to a trustee who organises a controlled liquidation, is one route to achieving this.

On the other hand, VCs may come under pressure to liquidate investments before the point at which the founder is ready. This can happen as funds are reaching the end of their duration. A seven year or similar term is normal, but since firms will join at different points in the life of the fund, they will not all have the same opportunities to develop products or services to their full potential. A growing body of litigation in the US courts has been addressing this type of conflict. Conflicts occur not just between funds and founders but also between funds and other shareholders. These "horizontal conflicts" (Pollman 2023) are common where outside investors take up equity stakes in the later rounds of financing. Although the fund may in principle be able to invoke anti-dilution provisions to preserve its position, it may in practice have to accept a loss of a controlling or dominant stake as downstream investments are made. "Pay to play" provisions, on the other hand, can be used to incentivise existing investors to participate in a new funding round. Examples of these are terms which require the conversion of preferred shares to common stock for shareholders who decline to take part in a new funding round, subordinating their interests to those willing to participate in the call.

As these "power law dynamics" have become more visible in the practice of VC and in litigation, contractual and governance devices have evolved in the direction of growing complexity. This has led some to argue that the role of the VC fund is changing from that of monitoring and overseeing firms' development to dynamic management of risk across the different relationships, both vertical and horizontal, which make up the VC architecture (Brougham and Wansley 2023).

If the distinctive transactional structure of VC is largely the result of private ordering, VC is also defined by certain trends in regulation. Investments in VC funds enjoy various tax reliefs, depending on the jurisdiction in question. Share options, widely used to remunerate employees in high-tech startups, often enjoy a similarly beneficial tax treatment. In order to minimise their labour law obligations, startups often characterise employees as independent contractors, a practice which courts may be prepared to condone and which legislation in some jurisdictions actively encourages.

Employment law plays a role in framing VC, depending on how strictly it regulates hiring and dismissal decisions. Ease of hire and fire on the part of firms is generally thought to mitigate investment risks (Armour 2002). At ecosystem level, on the other hand, knowledge spillovers may also depend on the ability of employees to move between firms at short notice, without the restraints imposed by non-compete clauses. There is uncertainty over how far California's near-complete ban on non-competes in employment contracts might have stimulated the "high velocity labour market" of Silicon Valley, but it does seem that California's liberal position on employment restrictions is a point of difference with other high-tech clusters, elsewhere in the US and in other countries, which have not experienced the same success in generating spillovers from VC (Hyde 2005). A lenient bankruptcy law, which avoids unduly penalising entrepreneurial failure, is another factor often cited to explain Silicon Valley's success (Armour 2002).

It is not entirely clear how far close adherence to the original US template is a precondition of attempts to build VC ecosystems elsewhere. The UK, which has had a sizable VC sector since the 1980s, if one that is still much smaller than its US equivalent, has a legal framework which is similar to that in the US, but also some significant differences (Armour 2002). It has a malleable common law foundation to its commercial and corporate laws, and is also similar to the US in providing extensive protections for minority shareholders in public companies, of the kind believed to be important for encouraging IPOs. Not everything in the UK mirrors US practice, however. UK dismissal law is less pro-employer than that in the US, where the contract at will rule mostly prevails. In a marked contrast to California, English courts regularly enforce employment non-competes in the form of restrictive covenants and garden leave clauses.

Certain features of the US VC model can only with difficulty be transplanted into the civil law systems of mainland Europe. The conversion of preferred to common stock is not as straightforward as it is in the US, and shareholders' agreements providing for veto rights and liquidation preferences may come into conflict with background rules of corporate law which are treated as non-waivable or at least as "strong defaults" in civil law doctrine (Perreira 2023). Substitutes for conversion may replicate some of its effects. In Italy, non-convertible participating preferred shares are used to give VC funds priority over other investors, and there are mechanisms for converting debt to equity. Co-sale mechanisms can also be observed. US-style "drag along" rights, which enable majority shareholders to require minorities to join in a sale or call, and "tag along" provisions, through which minority shareholders can enforce their participation against the wishes of the majority, can also be found in European practice. In the light of this evolution, it has been argued that "corporate practice is pushing the envelope," with the general law, through reforms to legislation governing private companies and other LLC equivalents, and modifications to corporate charters and contract terms, responding to the pressures for change in countries such as Italy (Giudici et al. 2023). An alternative view is that Italian corporate law is still "unable to accommodate (US-style) VC contracting," and that "bargaining in the shadow of the law and implicit mandatory provisions of Italian corporate law leads to the adoption of a contractual technology that is overall costlier and less effective than the US model" (Enriques and Nigro 2023).

Similar assessments have been made of the situation in China. Chinese VC uses a functional equivalent to convertible stock in the form of the VAM ("valuation adjustment mechanism"), a contractual device which allows the VC fund to adjust the valuation of a portfolio company on the occurrence of a stipulated event (Lin 2020; Giudici et al. 2023). However, barriers to the transplantation of US standards terms and practices into the Chinese context have been identified, including a "lack of serious investment tools and the legal restrictions in the Company Law, the lack of effective protection of investors by law, and the presence of less experienced and sophisticated venture capitalists and entrepreneurs in China" (Lin 2020, 42).

Insofar as legal regimes outside the US are unable to replicate aspects of the standard VC template, startups can access US structures by taking advantage of the rules of the conflict of laws, which allow firms to designate a foreign legal system as applicable for corporate structures and related commercial transactions. Since the 1990s, the Israeli VC sector has operated this way, with significant numbers of startups incorporating in Delaware law and listing on NASDAQ (Clarysse et al. 2009). An entity physically based in one jurisdiction, the "home" state or state of origin, can incorporate and list in another jurisdiction, which becomes then its corporate law "host," while remaining subject to tax and employment laws in the former jurisdiction.

In short, the law is imbricated with the operation of VC systems at all levels and stages of their operation. The distinctive legal template associated with US VC is believed to have been a causal factor in the success of Silicon Valley (Armour and Cumming 2006), to the extent that other countries have sought to emulate it, with varying degrees of success (Enriques and Nigro 2023), and startups based outside the US increasingly seek to access it, by taking advantage of flexible incorporation and listing rules (Clarysse et al. 2009). Yet the "contingent control" and "power law" dynamics which flow from the US template are also at the source of growing horizontal conflicts, leading to value destruction and negative knowledge spillovers, in the US context where they have reached their most advanced form (Pollman 2020, 2024). While it was until recently taken for granted that European VC should be seeking to replicate the US model, this is no longer so clearly the case.

8.3 EUROPEAN VC IN PRACTICE: EVIDENCE FROM A QUALITATIVE STUDY

Recognising venture capital as a commons-like structure clarifies the need for governance models that do not only institutionalise control over capital but also organise the associational cognition on which the success of the wider VC ecosystem depends. In understanding how venture capital operates in practice as a commons, it is helpful to focus on the European context, where institutional design varies but increasingly reflects an ecosystem-based approach which departs in significant respects from US practice.

8.3.1 *Scope of Study*

The initial focus of our empirical research was the potential role of venture capital in supporting Ukraine's post-conflict reconstruction. Since the summer of 2022 a number of VC partnerships based in London and New York have announced new funds to support early-stage investment in Ukrainian companies. The Ukraine Venture Capital and Private Equity Association (UVCA) issued a Redevelopment Plan which was discussed at the Davos World Economic Forum of January 2023, and the Ukraine Reconstruction conferences which took place in London in June 2023 and in Berlin in June 2024 also prioritised VC as an area for development. Ukraine's government has taken a number of steps to encourage VC-based innovation, including the creation in 2022 of "Diia City," a legal "free zone" intended to support IT-related startups. Entities opting into the Diia City legal regime benefit from an advantageous tax regime and can take advantage of a template customised for VC which includes convertible loan notes, option agreements, and standard-form representations and warranties.

With a view to understanding potential legal support for, and obstacles to, VC development in Ukraine, we conducted twenty-five interviews with VC specialists in funds, startups, law firms, and industry associations between June 2023 and June 2024. The interviewees were initially identified through industry associations and public sources, with further contacts being established through the snowballing method. The focus of the interviews was on the experience of Ukrainian VC funds and startups in using contractual and governance mechanisms to structure their relations and on their perceptions of the wider legal and institutional framework. The interviews also ranged more widely to cover the current state of VC practice in the UK and other European countries. By these means we were able to obtain an insight into the current state of European VC.

Most studies assessing the role of the legal framework with respect to VC have taken a quantitative approach, using surveys and publicly available datasets to track the use of particular terms and devices in corporate charters and agreements, and building indices to benchmark developments in the formal content or substance of legal rules. Relatively few analyses have used qualitative approaches, which has resulted in something of a gap in the literature. There is a disconnect between the understanding that informal norms structure the operation of formal ones, and that the interaction or "braiding" of the formal and the informal is often key to understanding the way that innovation systems work in practice, and the lack of qualitative evidence of the kind needed to assess the role of informal factors (Grilli et al. 2019, 1115).

Quantitative studies tend to be thought of as the gold standard in law and finance research, since they possess features of objectivity and replicability which are consistent with general understandings of the need for external validity in social science research. However, surveys or reviews of the texts of corporate charters and contracts are rarely able to establish that they are representative of wider practice, much of which remains hidden from view, and they can quickly become dated, given how quickly VC evolves. Regression analyses can establish statistical associations between the terms of charters and contracts, on the one hand, and quantifiable variables such as magnitudes of investments flows and returns, on the other, but establishing a reliable causal connection can be more difficult, given that causal relations could, in principle, flow either way; laws and practices might well be responses to investment flows, for example, rather than an exogenous cause of them (Grilli et al. 2019, 1110).

Qualitative methods also have some well-known drawbacks. Representativeness is even more of a problem here, and replicability is an issue given the temporal and spatial specificity of individual interview settings. On the other hand, interviews can enable researchers to identify the causal mechanisms and sequencings which are mostly invisible to more quantitative approaches (Poteete et al. 2010).

A qualitative approach may be needed for understanding the *braiding* of formal and informal elements of VC architecture. The braiding hypothesis was first developed in the study of research and development agreements and similar contracts involving innovation (Jennejohn 2008; Gilson et al. 2009, 2020, 2011). While knowledge sharing and information diffusion are understood to be an essential aspect of innovation systems, the risk of opportunism grows the longer a relationship continues and according to the number of actors involved. Formal contract terms may be one way of reducing the risk of opportunism, but parties seeking to rely on them may face high enforcement costs (Perreira 2023). Reputation, on the other hand, may be an effective way of constraining moral hazard, particularly in contexts of repeat trading, or in the context of an innovation ecosystem where behaviours can be publicly observed (Aoki 2010, 100). Extending the braiding concept to the context of VC, what needs to be understood is how the complex "palette" of charter terms and contractual devices (Giuidici et al. 2022, 791) interacts with the parties' strategies and behaviour to shape outcomes. Interview-based research, allowing a "deep dive" into the lived experiences of participants, may provide access to information which would otherwise remain hidden from view or at least inaccessible from outside the sector.

We begin by examining a number of issues of general interest for understanding the operation of VC in its European (including Ukrainian) context: the relational dimension of the control exercised by funds, the blurring of equity and debt, approaches to exit, and the management of less successful firms. We then consider the issue of system-wide effects, and address the question of how far the limitation of the legal environment for VC in Europe can be overcome through a US incorporation or is a strategy of creating legal exceptions for VC within domestic law, as in Ukraine's Diia City model.

8.3.2 "VERY MUCH NOT ABOUT CONTROL": RELATIONAL MONITORING AND OVERSIGHT

For the funds we spoke to, how to ensure effective monitoring and oversight over portfolio firms was a key issue. However, funds rarely sought a controlling equity stake or a majority of board seats. Some of our interviewees rejected the language of "control" altogether: "The venture model is very much *not* about control, it is not like private equity, [venture capital] is very much, here are the funds, you deal with it don't do anything very structural without our consent, private equity is not like that" (Lawyer, UK).

Funds saw an arm's length relationship as necessary to preserve founder autonomy:

> How much equity would the venture capital fund hold? Typically 20% depending on the valuation. Venture capital funds are focused on being founder friendly. They will want to determine how to proceed based on the number of founders and their current holders, they have to work out what would be reasonable in order to incentivize the founders and keep them on board. (Lawyer, UK)

Investors were cautious not to demand too much from founders. Even in a downturn when they "have more power, they are in a better position to command terms," funds would avoid taking majority stakes because "the founder needs to be motivated, a founder with tiny pieces doesn't work" (VC fund, Ukraine).

In place of a majority holdings, funds relied on other mechanisms than majority stakes to protect their position: "Keeping control is important, but venture capital is about minority ownership, normally 20–30%, so a control mechanism is needed, a combination of a shareholders' agreement, reserved matters at board level and shareholder levels being specified, you might have for example the right to appoint a director, the board is not allowed to do certain things" (Lawyer, UK).

Pre-emption rights, board-level veto rights for the director nominated by the fund, and investor consents contained in the shareholders' agreement operate as negative constraints or guardrails:

> Imagine a road that could be straight or curvy, that road is the role of the management, they drive it forward, put on the brakes, the accelerator, they are driving it, the investors are the guardrails on the road, investor vetoes and investor consents. These work at two levels, two strata, they are negative controls, the fund can't force the company to do something but they can prevent it from doing certain things, bifurcation is at board level and at shareholder level so at board level most VC [funds] will want to have a board representative, board level consent is an issue, the board can't take certain actions without the consent of that director, at shareholder level, the shareholders can't do something without certain investors agreeing. My aim would be to keep operational matters at board level but keep matters affecting value at shareholder level. (Lawyer, UK)

The "guardrails" were about stopping certain things from happening rather than making them happen:

> Venture capital is about negative covenants, you can't do something without our consent, not positive covenants, so the founder is only exposed if the investors control the board which is a risk for them, and the second line is if investors control the share structure, but that's not very likely, as VC companies grow there is a cycle, and there is a cycle with many rounds, series A, B, at each stage they release more funding, the founder is slowly diluted over time, so the concern only comes in after many dilutions. (Lawyer, UK)

Consents were seen as becoming increasingly common in the European context and were more important there than in the US, where there was greater reliance on the liquidation preference route to safeguard the fund:

> In the US the key economic lever is in the investment document, the liquidation preference. The US is based on a one-time non-participating liquidation preference. It means that if the company does not do well I may get my money back and if it does well we share, and that is becoming the norm in Europe, but not always, and downside protection is one times participating preference, the investor gets their money back first and then shares, that is fading away, it is much more about guardrails now, the US VC has low guardrails, but the European VC has high guardrails, in the US the number of consents matters. Maybe 8–10 issues whereas it can be as many as 30 for a European one. (Lawyer, UK)

While some funds preferred to take board seats, others were content with observer status, as this would be sufficient to generate the information they needed, and put them in a position to use their veto power when necessary:

> Being a board observer is important, we will go along to meetings, if after a couple of years we have reason to believe there is no problem we might then give up that right

> because we are adding more companies, even if some go bust the fund grows, and some of the board meetings can go on, the optimal meeting is one and a half hours but some are three hours if we have to go 60 meetings, well, it is not worth it. Getting this right is tricky, we often have to compete to get into good deals. (VC fund, UK)

8.3.3 *Debt and Equity: "Don't Over-complicate It"*

Debt and equity were seen as increasingly interchangeable, with investors switching from one to another at different points in the funding cycle, according to changing risk profiles. Rather than take convertible preference shares, UK-based funds tended to supply convertible debt at initial seed stage and early stage. Convertible loans had "become more popular since the bubble burst in 2021" with the result that share prices were generally depressed and firms wanted to defer having an equity round (VC fund, UK). US-style SAFEs and their equivalents, advanced assured agreements, were also used. These instruments were seen as useful for the way they combined elements of debt and equity:

> For early stage, debt or access to debt is a luxury as they are not making any money at that point. Convertible debt, a quasi-debt instrument, means that the investors can invest without taking an equity stake. It is a way to deal with uncertainty, and if all goes well we can convert at a discount, it is about risk management, it is not debt per se, it is structured as debt to allow the investment to go forward, an Advanced Assured Agreement is like a US SAFE, a simple agreement for equity. (Lawyer, UK)

The flexibility of debt was emphasised:

> Debt is different. Venture capital equity is like gambling, you've got to be prepared to lose your money so don't over complicate it. ... If you talk about debt, is it low risk, well it ranks above equity on a liquidation ... so debt is a broad instrument. (Lawyer, UK).

Other interviewees emphasised the relational aspects of debt:

> If you are an investor, you won't get majority ownership, it is not how the model works, it is not private equity. The whole model is based on being not active investors but being a basic investor, you can influence how you can use informal methods to build relations, it's not really legal leverage. ... When Series A round [early stage] companies try to raise money through convertible notes and safe notes, then investors have no rights, it is founder friendly. (VC fund, UK)

The logic of this last observation is that with convertible notes and SAFEs, investors have little or no control over the company until conversion happens; during this period, founders retain decision-making power.

8.3.4 *Exit Dynamics: "Control the Downside"*

Exit via an IPO might be an ideal for funds and startups alike, but it was easier to "fantasise" about it than to "plan it," there had to be a very specific "window of opportunity" in terms of market conditions and the size of the deal. Conditions at the time of the interviews (2023–24) were not right: "the IPO is super-dependent on cash flow and rates of return, not good in a high interest rate world" (VC fund, Ukraine). The IPO route was seen as "hard," "super complicated," "very expensive, a bit broken" (VC fund, Ukraine). Early-stage investors were unlikely to get to the listing stage very often; they would more likely be selling out to a larger firm in the same sector, or, as was becoming more common in the UK market, a private equity fund. Trade sales were seen as flexible for founders if they could remain involved post-merger. For the shareholders, a trade sale was often preferred as it could give them a "full exit" in contrast to a listing or share sale. Taking up shares in a merged company was not risk-free for a fund:

> "A big US venture-backed company bought [one of our portfolio companies], there was some uplift, a good story, a validation of our approach, that was for shares, so now we have shares in the US company, for that we had to give up anti-dilution and observer rights, and that can be tricky" (VC fund, UK).

Elements of a power-law dynamic could be observed:

> We very much expect some [portfolio firms] to fail and one or two to make 10 times our money back, or more since over time, the majority will fail, or we will exit for less than we invested so we are looking for an investment that will make up for that, one that goes up 25 times by value, if you have 4% then everyone gets their money back, and that is nirvana, that is why we are always looking at the product market, if there a big market that is the first thing we look at, a £100 million market is too small if the market share is only 5%. We haven't had one like that yet [as the fund was relatively new] but that is our model. (VC fund, UK)

> Out of 10 startups, one will super perform, maybe 2, then 2–3 on average get their money back, maybe 4, and the rest will fail, and there is an acceptance of this, a high proportion will fail, and with different investors involved, it's straight betting. (Lawyer, UK)

Achieving a portfolio-wide return from just one or two investments was seen as unusual. More likely in practice was a situation in which returns could be obtained from a proportion of portfolio firms, rather than a few hyper-successful ones: "we are not just aiming for a single successful exit" (VC fund, Ukraine). In some funds, in less high-risk sectors, the goal was to achieve moderate to high returns in a sizable segment of the portfolio firms:

> How many startups actually succeed? It varies hugely from fund to fund. Some are investing at very early stage in deep tech. Very, very risky, but when it works it pays

> big time, one in ten, in AI for example. Some funds will want less spectacular returns from a larger number of companies, a slightly different bet, maybe a third do very well, a third ok, a third fail. Later stage [investment] is less of a risk, less lucrative. (Lawyer, UK)

Some interviewees perceived a difference in the approaches of US and European funds:

> How many actually succeed? There is a difference in approach between US and Europe, it is a different philosophical approach. With US VCs, there is some change over time but a US VC out of Silicon Valley, they would invest in ten and of those five will go belly up and they expect that out of the remaining five, two may do ok, and get your money back, another one or two, twice your money back, and just one or two will make your returns. The European approach is to invest in ten, you don't want to lose money on most of them, even if only one or two on average get you your money back. It's a different risk-reward profile, so what that means is, when you draft the documents, the US focus is on the upside, the European approach is on the downside, control the downside risk. (Lawyer, UK)

8.3.5 *Managing Less Successful Firms: "Ticking Over"*

This diversity of outcomes within a portfolio was reflected in the way that funds managed their less successful investments. Funds accepted the need for patience in assessing portfolio firms, and would sometimes emphasise the need to avoid becoming profitable too soon:

> Some companies will be cash flow positive, that may be ok, they may have a partial exit. We expect one or two to work out. But it's not good if some make a return straight away, it would be too soon. They won't grow. Maybe some will exit in the next two to three years. We will wait, and it is a game we are playing. In some funds, one in fifty, one in a hundred may be really big, and five or six may make five times the investment, but that is not a target for us. We are aiming for fifty companies to invest in eventually. (VC fund, UK)

Less successful firms were not simply written off. A significant proportion of companies in a portfolio could end up as "zombie or lifestyle companies, no exit, doing well but never looking to have an IPO or sale, perfectly fine, they tick over, but the investors get frustrated" (Lawyer, UK). While there might be a redemption term in a shareholders' agreement allowing the fund to redeem its shares or force the company to do so, this was not regarded as normal and might be difficult to enforce in practice. Funds would try to avoid an insolvency ("like Voldemort, it shall not be named") and it was becoming more common to see acqui-hires, "an insolvency which is masked as a sale . . ., an acquisition where you are effectively hiring the engineers, the buyer will pay £1 to take over the human skills" (Lawyer, UK).

8.3.6 *Employment Law: "Who Wants to be a Bad Leaver?"*

European labour law systems offer varying levels of flexibility in terms of how they regulate the substance of hiring and dismissing workers, and to what extent they allow forms of gig work contracting and consultancy agreements to be made which take the supply of services outside the scope of labour laws. However, very few of them observe the US employment at will rule, under which the default position is that the employer has the right to terminate the employment contract on no or minimal notice, without needing to show a reason for doing so. The relative inflexibility of employment laws in some mainland European jurisdictions, including France, Germany, and Italy, was cited by some of our interviewees as a reason for the limited growth of VC in those systems. However, none of our interviewees was prepared to accept the quid pro quo of US employment at will, namely the ban on non-competes which operates in California and which the US Federal Trade Commission was at the time of the interviews attempting to regulate out of existence on the grounds of its anti-competitive effects.

On the contrary, European funds use employment contracts strategically as a way of locking in the founder and core staff of the startup. The employment contract agreed with the founder will generally contain intellectual property clauses and covenants which are designed to penalise their premature departure. In English law, garden leave clauses and restrictive covenants are regularly enforced and can shape negotiations when the fund first invests and subsequently over the funding cycle:

> Employment contracts are important, they have to be governed by English law, this is important along with founder shares. Employment contracts get enforced, yes. If the founder leaves there is negotiation, it is rare to go to all the way to enforcement. You can have good leavers and bad leavers, who wants to be a bad leaver? We had a case where we got to the final negotiation to invest and the company was arguing about various things we were debating with them, one of the three co-founders wasn't sure but we weren't giving up, we knew we would look like idiots if the founder left three months later. Then they left the room, 45 minutes later they came back, they told us that the chief technology officer was handing in his notice and would leave in three months! We did not invest, the employment contract issue had flushed out potential risk. (VC fund, UK)

UK funds can also seek a covenant in the shareholders' agreement as a way of stopping the founder "upping sticks." Since the founder will also be a shareholder, a restrictive covenant in the shareholders' agreement will further mitigate the risk of hold-up: "you can take shares away from the founder if they leave, at unattractive prices, so they are locked in" (Lawyer, UK).

In addition, European-based startups have several options available to them if they want to avoid the application of the general labour laws. Several countries allow de facto exemptions from labour laws by permitting IT workers to incorporate as micro enterprises, or to make use of civil contracts for services. These arrangements generally attract a lower rate of income tax. However, interviewees also cited the downside of using contractors whose knowledge and skills were essential to the firm:

> If you employ independent contractors, you don't pay tax, but it can be complex, the independent contractor must have a legal entity, and it is hard to control them, and in any case the employer must have the control right, so then you may end up paying the tax anyway. (Startup, Ukraine).

Using workarounds was seen as potentially problematic from the point of view building sustainable businesses:

> You can work informally, through independent contractors, before you register a company, but this year we decided, as a value decision, to set up the company with employees, we may lose a part of the profit now but in future we will make more, so now we have a real company with employees not independent contractors, it is an opportunity to lose now but earn much more in future. (Entrepreneur, Ukraine)

In short, using contractors and workarounds could often be insufficiently protective of the *employer* interest.

8.3.7 *Ecosystem-Wide Effects: "Essential for an Onshore Industry"*

The benefits of having an ecosystem containing interlinked networks of public and private sector institutions were emphasised by several interviewees. Important elements of ecosystems were accelerators, such as Y Combinator in the US and Enterprise First in the UK. These were important as focal points for bringing together funds and companies, often entrepreneurs who set up funds after having succeeded with a startup: "what do they do, in an ecosystem they condense or focus the energy, founders who made money come back in, VC funds, it's a melting pot, you are more likely to create a successful company this way, they are very important where the VCs keep an eye on this channel of credible companies" (Lawyer, UK).

Also important were universities. Technology transfer offices and incubators helped create a community-based approach through alumni help and networking, adding to the credibility of startups: "there is some signalling" (Lawyer, UK). In addition, trade associations could assist in developing term sheets and standardised documentation, which helped establish a common knowledge base and build trust. In the UK context, "The BVCA [British Venture Capital Association] term sheets were very important, people coalesced around them, to avoid people going back to first principles, they were very helpful in avoiding the situation in which people just have to start from a blank piece of paper" (Lawyer, UK).

A further dimension of ecosystem effects concerned the need to build networks and structures that were not based wholly offshore. It was recognised that using an overseas law as the basis for corporate and commercial forms ran the risk of missing out on the network effects of having an onshore legal sector and local role models:

> Having a suitable vehicle is essential for an onshore industry. ... If you want a thriving local industry you need this for the economy of the country, it attracts not just the head office but also, advisers, UK lawyers benefit if the structure is UK, accountants, etcetera, the ecosystem develops around the jurisdiction, and there is some evidence that funds do invest closer to home, so UK funds do invest locally. So there is an argument for potential benefits there. Most jurisdictions do try hard to get this right. (Lawyer, UK)

It was thought to be important over time for successful entrepreneurs to return to Ukraine to support local networks:

> The tech ecosystem is driven by founders, and VC money attracts more money, it becomes a living system, you find concern over outflow of funds but that is minimised by having local champions, because the local champions will want to get back to Ukraine, to build and to contribute, now the US VCs may have capital that flows back to LLPs, but still there is money in the system. (Lawyer, UK)

In the "short term," European countries with developing VC sectors would have a need for foreign law to support inbound investment, but in the "long term you do need to develop the local legal framework, in the long term you can't really have this bifurcation" between domestic and foreign law (Lawyer, UK). There was some scepticism concerning the suitability for Ukraine of the Israeli model of VCs relying on foreign law and a US listing: "So I am not a proponent of that kind of model which is the Israeli model, the startup fund, if it is not registered in the Ukraine you can't get it financed, well that is outdated, it does not correspond to reality now, and ignores the wider context of fund-raising" (Entrepreneur, Ukraine).

Questions were also raised over the strategy of creating a legal enclave, within which the standard VC template could be accessed and common law approaches to transactional flexibility applied. The Ukrainian Diia City regime was seen as offering advantages in terms of legal flexibility by some of the Ukraine-based funds we interviewed. However, there were other views: "we would prefer general Ukrainian law to be of good quality," and using foreign law ran the risk of the country missing out on network effects: "the country loses if everyone leaves Kyiv for Lisbon, just taking their laptop" (official, Ukraine). Some saw the use of carve-outs as potentially detrimental to the process of building trust in local institutions and processes:

> We can outsource 20 people and it is cheaper that way and we operate at a discount but I don't want this, I want to build a business with everything official, I want to pay all my taxes and sleep well at night, I don't want to be part of corruption, part of some optimization scheme, of course I could optimize, I won't pay tax if my expenses are more than my income. ... I pay zero tax that is ok, but if I work with only independent contractors that is not ok, I need talented people for modern European and US markets, I don't need to hide my revenue, I don't need to optimize my revenue in a grey way, I want to go the US like a businessman not a tourist. (Entrepreneur, Ukraine)

8.4 ASSESSMENT

Our interviews suggest that the formal elements of VC contracting, which can appear to emphasise the control and monitoring roles of the fund, coexist or are "braided" with informal elements based on repeat trading between entrepreneurs, investors, and advisers, assisting reputation-based enforcement, and the generation of trust at ecosystem level. In practice, the VC fund startup has to be at least partly relational, rather than exclusively control-orientated if it is to work. As debt and equity become increasingly interchangeable, the relationality of debt-based forms of governance are coming to the fore. While exit dynamics in Europe reflect the need to obtain high returns from a small minority of firms as they do in the US, the power law is tempered in the European context, with less extreme outcomes at either end of the distribution, and greater tolerance for investments that do well enough to survive without generating hyper-profitable outcomes. European VC funds are willing to support lifestyle companies and arrange exits via acqui-hires, alongside more spectacular successes. In the conditions of a market downturn, which prevailed when we conducted our interviews, IPOs are rare compared to the trade sale route to exit, but it would seem that even in better times the IPO is no longer the sole or even more common route to realising investments.

There are several respects in which mainland European legal systems are not aligned with the US model of VC. Convertible preferred stock, the predominant investment mode for US VC, is not always available to European investors, and shareholder agreements may not be straightforwardly enforceable where they conflict with background rules of company law. Although it is believed that misalignment of European corporate law regimes with the US template puts European VC at a disadvantage (Enriques and Nigro 2023), this may be to put too much emphasis on the role of particular US legal and contractual arrangements in driving VC. Functional equivalents to convertible preferred stock, including convertible debt various kinds, are in wide use in Europe, along with local equivalents to the US-origin SAFE and KISS.

With respect to employment law, few European labour law systems come close to the flexibility of the US contract at will model. On the other hand, non-competes are more straightforwardly enforceable in the European context, and funds are not slow to use them to protect their interests. Using contractors in place of a directly employed workforce is not always straightforward from the point of view of additional transaction costs and a potential loss of access to essential knowledge.

Insofar as European legal systems nevertheless remain out of line with VC needs, the gap may be filled by reliance on access to the US legal system and to a lesser extent English law, to supply the basic VC template. Many European startups are either incorporated in US or English law or operate through a US or English-law holding company. Thus, in common with startups in other European countries, startups in Ukraine are in a position to take advantage of the transactional flexibility of US corporate and commercial contract law. Use of foreign law for corporate and commercial transactions may offer a plausible route for the development of European VC in the short term, but its positive effects may be time limited. The same point applies to legal "free zones" such as Ukraine's Diia City. Overreliance on foreign law and legal carve-outs runs the risk of missing out on the wider ecosystem benefits of VC, as knowledge-essential legal and financial skills remain offshore.

8.5 CONCLUSION

Venture capital seems at first sight to be an unpromising case study for the hypothesis of the corporate knowledge commons. The portfolio structure of the VC tournament pits startup firms against each other in a race that only a few can win. Exponential returns for the occasional successes balance losses in the vast majority that fail. Staged financing allows funds to dictate terms to startups and to decide the form and timing of their exit. Underlying the VC "power law" is a legal structure decisively tilted towards the interests of investors, who can flip their interests from debt to equity and back again to maximise their returns from successful projects while minimising their losses from failures. This hyper-flexible structure can leave other stakeholders out in the cold. Founder-entrepreneurs may be in a position, by virtue of their shareholdings, to benefit on the upside, and share option schemes enable employees to do likewise, at the cost of a loss of control over the form and timing of exits, and exposure to downside risks. The standard legal template for VC, once regarded as a causal factor in the success of the US model and a precondition for its dissemination to other countries, is increasingly seen as generating perverse incentives, which are reflected in rent-seeking (costly litigation) and value destruction (high-profile frauds).

If, however, the US-origin legal template is coming under question, this is arguably because it is at odds with features of VC practice which more closely resemble a commons than is generally supposed. As Aoki's model of VC emphasises, knowledge essentialities are tied up within startup firms; the knowledge possessed by the fund is only quasi-essential. Thus funds have to temper their control rights in ways which acknowledge the interests of founders and employees. Our interviews show how formal legal rights are "braided" with the practice of relational monitoring in order for individual projects to be brought to fruition and wider knowledge spillovers generated. In European VC, the search for exponential returns goes on, but there tends to be a more supportive attitude towards portfolio firms which are sustainable without being hyper-successful. Treating employees as a disposable resource while seeking to control their mobility through non-competes, an option unavailable in the US, is a hazardous strategy in a context where the workforce represents the firm's core cognitive asset.

In the final analysis, VC is no less a commons, dependent on the input of multiple stakeholders and on their shared participation in the emergent rules of the game, than other corporate settings. Venture capital relies heavily on the spillovers created by various ecosystem players, including locally based venture firms, trade associations, angel investors, legal advisors, startup networks, and informal mentors. Informal, culturally rooted elements significantly impact the performance of European VC ecosystems. However, they are frequently underrepresented in formal legal frameworks, particularly those originating in or borrowed from US practice.

An excessive emphasis on investor control and the formal properties of bright-line legal rules is currently putting the much-vaunted VC model into question in its system of origin, the US. The divergence of European VC from the original US form may be not so much a cause for concern, as the occasion for reflection on the persistence of diversity in corporate law and governance.

REFERENCES

Albareda, Laura, and Alejo J. G. Sison. 2020. "Commons Organizing: Embedding Common Good and Institutions for Collective Action. Insights from Ethics and Economics." *Journal of Business Ethics* 166(4): 727–743.

Aoki, Masahiko. 2010. *Corporations in Evolving Diversity*. New York: Oxford University Press.

Armour, John. 2002. "Law, Innovation and Finance: A Review." Centre for Business Research Working Paper No. 243. Cambridge: University of Cambridge.

Armour, John, and Douglas Cumming. 2006. "The Legislative Road to Silicon Valley." *Oxford Economic Papers* 58(4): 596–635.

Black, Bernard S., and Ronald J. Gilson. 1998. "Venture Capital and the Structure of Capital Markets: Banks versus Stock Markets." *Journal of Financial Economics* 47(3): 243–277.

Bonini, Stefano, and Senem Alkan. 2012. "The Political and Legal Determinants of Venture Capital Investments around the World." *Small Business Economics* 39(4): 997–1016.

Bottazzi, Laura, Marco Da Rin, and Thomas Hellmann. 2016. "The Importance of Trust for Investment: Evidence from Venture Capital." *Review of Financial Studies* 29(9): 2283–2318.

Bratton, William W. 2002. "Venture Capital on the Downside: Preferred Stock and Corporate Control." *Michigan Law Review* 100(5): 891–945.

Bratton, William W., and Michael L. Wachter. 2013. "A Theory of Preferred Stock." *University of Pennsylvania Law Review* 161(7): 1815–1906.

Broughman, Brian J., and Jesse M. Fried. 2013. "Carrots and Sticks: How VCs Induce Entrepreneurial Teams to Sell Startups." *Cornell Law Review* 98(6): 1319–1358.

Broughman, Brian J., and Matthew T. Wansley. 2023. "Risk-Seeking Governance." *Vanderbilt Law Review* 76(5): 1299–1378.

Bruton, Garry D., and David Ahlstrom. 2003. "An Institutional View of China's Venture Capital Industry." *Journal of Business Venturing*, 18(2): 233–259.

Bruton, Garry D., Vance H. Fried, and Sophie Manigart. 2005. "Institutional Influences on the Worldwide Expansion of Venture Capital." *Entrepreneurship Theory and Practice* 29(6): 737–760.

British Venture Capital Association. 2023. *BVCA Report on Investment Activity 2023*. London: British Private Equity & Venture Capital Association.

Clarysse, Bart, Mirjam Knockaert, and Mike Wright. 2009. *Benchmarking UK Venture Capital to the US and Israel: What Lessons Can Be Learned?* London: British Private Equity & Venture Capital Association.

Cumming, Douglas. 2011. "Misinforming the Public about Public Policy towards Venture Capital." *Venture Capital* 13(1): 99–102.

Cumming, Douglas, and Sofia A. Johan. 2014. *Venture Capital and Private Equity Contracting*. 2nd ed. London: Elsevier.

Da Rin, Marco, Giovanna Nicodano, and Alessandro Sembenelli. 2006. "Public Policy and the Creation of Active Venture Capital Markets." *Journal of Public Economics* 90(8–9): 1699–1723.

Deakin, Simon. 2012. "The Corporation as Commons: Rethinking Property Rights, Governance and Sustainability in the Business Enterprise." *Queen's Law Journal* 37(2): 339–381.

Deakin, Simon, David Gindis, Geoffrey M. Hodgson, Kainan Huang, and Katharina Pistor. 2017. "Legal Institutionalism: Capitalism and the Constitutive Role of Law." *Journal of Comparative Economics* 45(1): 188–200.

Deakin, Simon, David Gindis, and Geffrey M. Hodgson. 2021. "What Is a Firm? A Reply to Jean-Philippe Robé." *Journal of Institutional Economics* 17(5): 861–871.

Enriques, Luca, and Casimiro C. Nigro. 2023. "Corporate Law and Venture Capital in Italy: What Does the Empirical Evidence (Really) Tell Us?" *Oxford Business Law Blog*. November 16, 2023. https://blogs.law.ox.ac.uk/oblb/blog-post/2023/11/corporate-law-and-venture-capital-italy-what-does-empirical-evidence-really.

Frischmann, Brett M., Michael J. Madison, and Katherine J. Strandburg. 2014. *Governing Knowledge Commons*. New York: Oxford University Press.

Gilson, Ronald J. 2003. "Engineering a Venture Capital Market: Lessons from the American Experience." *Stanford Law Review* 55(4): 1067–1103.

Gilson, Ronald J., and Bernard S. Black. 1999. "Does Venture Capital Require an Active Stock Market?" *Journal of Applied Corporate Finance* 47(4): 243–277.

Gilson, Ronald J., and David M. Schizer. 2003. "Understanding Venture Capital Structure: A Tax Explanation for Convertible Preferred Stock." *Harvard Law Review* 116(3): 874–916.

Gilson, Ronald J., Charles F. Sabel, and Richard E. Scott. 2009. "Contracting for Innovation: Vertical Disintegration and Inter-Firm Collaboration." *Columbia Law Review* 109(3): 431–502.

Gilson, Ronald J., Charles F. Sabel, and Richard E. Scott. 2010. "Braiding: The Interaction of Formal and Informal Contracting in Theory, Practice, and Doctrine." *Columbia Law Review* 110(6): 1377–1447.

Gilson, Ronald J., Charles F. Sabel, and Richard E. Scott. 2011. "Contract, Uncertainty and Innovation." In *Rules for Growth: Promoting Innovation and Growth Through Legal Reform, Kauffman Taskforce on Law, Innovation and Growth*, 223–255. Kansas City: Ewing Marion Kauffman Foundation.

Giudici, Paolo, Peter Agstner, and Antonio Capizzi. 2022. "The Corporate Design of Investment in Startups: A European Experience." *European Business Organization* Review 23(4): 787–820.

Gompers, Paul A. 1995. "Optimal Investment, Monitoring, and the Staging of Venture Capital." *Journal of Finance* 50(5): 1461–1489.

Grilli, Luca, Gresa Latifi, and Boris Mrkajic. 2019. "Institutional Determinants of Venture Capital Activity: An Empirically Driven Literature Review and a Research Agenda." *Journal of Economic Surveys* 33(4): 1094–1122.

Hain, Daniel, Sofia A. Johan, and Daojuan Wang. 2016. "Determinants of Cross-Border Venture Capital Investments in Emerging and Developed Economies: The Effects of Relational and Institutional Trust." *Journal of Business Ethics* 138(4): 743–764.

Hess, Charlotte. 2008. "Mapping the New Commons." https://ssrn.com/abstract=1356835.

Hyde, Alan. 2005. "Silicon Valley's High Velocity Labour Market." *Journal of Applied Corporate Finance* 11(2): 28–37.

Jennejohn, Matthew. 2008. "Collaboration, Innovation, and Contract Design." *Stanford Journal of Law, Business and Finance* 14(1): 83–150.

Kaplan, Steven N., and Per Strömberg. 2003. "Financial Contracting Theory Meets the Real World: An Empirical Analysis of Venture Capital Contracts." *Review of Economic Studies* 70(2): 281–315.

Kaplan, Steven N., Frederic Martel, and Per Strömberg. 2007. "How Do Legal Differences and Learning Affect Financial Contracts?" *Journal of Financial Intermediation* 16(3): 273–311.

Lalafaryan, Narine. 2023. "Private Credit: A Renaissance in Corporate Finance." *Journal of Corporate Law Studies* 24(1): 41–95.

Lerner, Josh. 1995. "Venture Capitalists and the Oversight of Private Firms." *Journal of Finance* 50(1): 301–318.

Lerner, Josh, and Antoinette Schoar. 2005. "Does Legal Enforcement Affect Financial Transactions? The Contractual Channel in Private Equity." *Quarterly Journal of Economics* 120(1): 223–246.

Lin, Lin. 2020. "Contractual Innovation in China's Venture Capital Market." *European Business Organization Law Review* 21(1): 101–138.

Martin, Ron, Peter Sunley, and Dave Turner. 2002. "Taking Risks in Regions: The Geographical Anatomy of Europe's Emerging Venture Capital Market." *Journal of Economic Geography* 2(2): 121–150.

Nigro, Casimiro A., and Luca Enriques. 2021. "Venture capital e diritto societario italiano: un rapporto difficile." *Analisi Giuridica della Economia* 2021(1–2): 149–206.

Nigro, Casimiro A., and Demeterio Maltese. 2022. "Private equity, fusioni e rinuncia all'appraisal right: note su un caso statunitense con cenni all'esperienza italiana." *Rivista di diritto societario* 2022(3): 631–678.

Nigro, Casimiro A., and Jörg R. Stahl. 2021. "Venture Capital-Backed Firms, Unavoidable Value-Destroying Trade Sales, and Fair Value Protections." *European Business Organization Review* 22(1): 39–86.

Ostrom, Elinor. 1990. *Governing the Commons: The Evolution of Institutions for Collective Action*. Cambridge: Cambridge University Press.

Ostrom, Elinor. 2005. *Understanding Institutional Diversity*. Princeton: Princeton University Press.

Ostrom, Elinor, and Charlotte Hess. 2007. "A Framework for Analyzing the Knowledge Commons." In *Understanding Knowledge as a Commons: From Theory to Practice*, ed. Charlotte Hess and Elinor Ostrom, 41–81. Cambridge, MA: MIT Press.

Owen-Smith, Jason, and Walter W. Powell. 2004. "Knowledge Networks as Channels and Conduits: The Effects of Spillovers in the Boston Biotechnology Community." *Organization Science* 15(1): 5–21.

Perreira, Alvaro. 2023. "The Law of Contingent Control in Venture Capital." *Columbia Business Law Review* 2023(2): 675–727.

Pollman, Elizabeth. 2019. "Startup Governance." *University of Pennsylvania Law Review* 168(1): 155–221.

Pollman, Elizabeth. 2020. "Private Company Lies. *Georgetown Law Journal* 109(2): 353–403.

Pollman, Elizabeth. 2023. "Startup Failure." *Duke Law Journal* 73(2): 327–386.

Pollman, Elizabeth. 2024. "Dynamic Views of Startup Governance and Failure." In *Research Handbook on the Structure of Private Equity and Venture Capital*, ed. Brian J. Broughman and Elisabeth D. de Fontenay. Cheltenham: Edward Elgar.

Poteete, Amy R., Marco Janssen, and Elinor Ostrom. 2010. *Working Together: Collective Action, The Commons, and Multiple Methods in Practice*. Princeton: Princeton University Press.
Robé, Jean-Philippe. 2011. "The Legal Structure of the Firm." *Accounting, Economics and Law* 1(1): Article 5.
Saxenian, AnnaLee. 1994. *Regional Advantage: Culture and Competition in Silicon Valley and Route 128*. Cambridge, MA: Harvard University Press.
Wansley, Matthew. 2019. "Beach Money Exits." *Journal of Corporate Law* 45(1): 151–202.

9

Investor Alliances as Knowledge Commons

Amelia Miazad

9.1 INTRODUCTION

This chapter analyzes Investor Climate Alliances (ICAs) as a form of knowledge commons. "Knowledge commons" are not bounded physical commons, like forests or fisheries, but a systematic methodology for understanding the governance of knowledge resources. Stated simply, "knowledge commons is governance" (Madison 2024, 308). More specifically, the phrase "knowledge commons" refers to governance of shared knowledge, information, and data resources by a community.

Knowledge commons are often prompted by a community's need to manage complex and interconnected types of knowledge. Examples include the Human Genome Project, medical research consortium, Wikipedia, or patent pools. The knowledge, information, and data related to financially material climate risks are also complex, incomplete, opaque, and vast. Effectively managing these knowledge resources requires a collaborative governance system to generate, organize, and utilize the data and information. To satisfy this demand, private and public actors have formed Investor Climate Alliances (ICAs) such as Climate Action 100+[1] and Net Zero Asset Managers Alliance.[2] ICAs have proliferated in response to the impact of climate risk on investment returns, particularly for diversified investors. While ICAs have been mischaracterized as "climate cabals," a closer examination reveals that they are *collective-based governance institutions* for generating, sharing, and utilizing knowledge about how corporations can minimize their financially material climate risk. Crucially, the information that ICAs elicit, synthesize, interpret, and share is publicly available, and not proprietary.

I thank David Gindis and Pavel Kuchař for excellent suggestions and edits. I also thank Michael Madison for introducing me to, and guiding me through, the Knowledge Commons literature. Finally, thank you to all the participants at the symposium for this volume hosted at King's College London in February 2024.

[1] https://www.climateaction100.org/about/.

[2] https://www.netzeroassetmanagers.org/.

It is important to understand ICAs for several reasons. First, they have proven effective at generating knowledge resources about climate risk, an urgent global issue. However, their fate hangs in the balance due to a lack of understanding, which has led to hasty policy interventions. ICAs currently face mounting legal and political risks, driven by the misapplication of antitrust law, securities regulation, and investor fiduciary duties. These paradigms mistakenly assume that the production of knowledge resources requires either market incentives or government mandates. ICAs challenge this assumption, demonstrating that knowledge is often produced and utilized collaboratively by communities of heterogeneous actors following formal and informal rules, norms, and customs. Corporate law seeks to fit ICAs into its familiar paradigms, which draw sharp distinctions between the public and private sectors and rely on agency theory to explain the relationship between shareholders and directors. Rather than starting from theory, the Governing Knowledge Commons (GKC) framework observes how ICAs function in practice. This approach reveals that ICAs are governed by a range of formal and informal (sometimes conflicting) laws, rules, social norms, and customs.

However, as Elinor Ostrom (2010) often noted, commons governance is "no panacea" and presents its own unique social and ethical challenges. Consistent with knowledge commons research, this chapter will not draw normative conclusions or make policy recommendations about ICAs. Instead, it is intentionally descriptive and not prescriptive. We must first refine our understanding of ICAs before we can accurately assess their potential and limitations.

9.2 CASE STUDY OF CLIMATE ACTION 100+

ICAs are a relatively new phenomenon. They are rapidly morphing in response to increased regulatory scrutiny. This case study will focus on the first and largest ICA, Climate Action 100+, as it exists at the time of writing, while acknowledging that its future is far from certain. In addition to shedding light on Climate Action 100+, the GKC framework will help us identify the social dilemmas and vulnerabilities that affect ICAs in general, potentially offering insights into their future direction.

9.2.1 *Background Environment*

The study of knowledge commons often begins with an examination of the background environment, including the cultural and legal context. ICAs were not created by any one organization at a single point in time; their emergence is rooted in a broader sociohistorical context.

9.2.1.1 Phase 1: Climate Risk Incentivizes Diversified Investors to Collaborate

The convergence of two major developments, seemingly unrelated, created the impetus for wide-scale collaboration on climate risk. First, due to index investing, investors today are highly diversified. These diversified investors are often referred to as universal owners (Condon 2020). They do not use the same strategies as undiversified investors, who pick individual companies and try to "beat the market" by selecting winners and losers. Instead, universal owners – such as pension funds or sovereign wealth funds – maintain diversified portfolios specifically to avoid idiosyncratic risks (Quigley 2020). Indeed, many universal owners are required to do so by law; the State of California's Constitution, for example, requires the state's pension funds to diversify. In other words, universal owners' highly diversified portfolios are exposed to systemic risks *by design*. That fact immediately changes the incentive for diversified investors from competition to collaboration, at least insofar as it relates to reducing systemic or portfolio-wide risks (Condon 2020; Gordon 2022).

But investors are not, obviously, the only ones who are focused on climate risk, nor can they reduce that risk on their own. Other actors, including governments and NGOs, are also motivated to pressure corporations to reduce their climate risk, prompting the need for institutional infrastructure to support collaborative efforts. This level of collaboration is starkly at odds with corporate law's long-standing norms, rooted in the law and economics tradition. Collaboration resists two narratives that permeate corporate law: the private market narrative and the competition narrative. The private market narrative supposes that individual private market actors exist only to generate profits and externalize costs, and that the public sector must place limits or price tags on those externalities through regulation or taxes (Friedman 1970). Adherents of this view characterize ICAs as a form of "private regulation," reflecting that government has been captured by private interests, or is too weak or inept to address the externalities (Bebchuk and Tallarita 2020). Under the private market narrative, the public and private sectors are presented not only as separate but also as rivals.

The competition narrative is similarly adversarial, telling us that the desire to outperform competitors animates most, if not all, of the decisions that market actors make. Consequently, we cannot count on private firms to invest in minimizing externalities, particularly if the benefits of the externalization also inure to their competitors. At the same time, we can absolutely count on private firms to externalize their costs onto society if it means that they can outperform their competitors. Competition is not just accepted as a natural part of "free markets" but is also valorized as a normative goal, because it (purportedly) addresses concentrations of market power (Miazad 2022). Accordingly, adherents of the competitive narrative have described investor alliances as corporate governance cartels that need to be broken up (Chaim 2025). Thus, the dual narratives underlying corporate law scholarship either villainize collaboration outright or view it with a high degree of suspicion.

Viewing ICAs through these theoretical paradigms has obscured their reality. In fact, ICAs comprise both public and private actors that are creating and adhering to public and private rules and norms to govern information. Certainly, this reality is far messier than a caricature that arbitrarily assigns roles and incentives to "market" actors versus "public" actors. It is neither surprising nor novel that ICAs are a combination of public and private actors and resources. To the contrary, financial markets have always been sustained by *shared intellectual infrastructure* (Frischmann 2012; Dekker and Kuchař 2022). This infrastructure is not exclusively private or public but rather is created through collaborative efforts by public and private actors. ICAs are also a type of infrastructure that is co-created and shared by public and private actors.

This infrastructure was not built from scratch. The history of ICAs can be traced back to less systematized forms of investor collaboration, such as principles and stewardship codes initiated by the United Nations. Most notably, the UN's Principles for Responsible Investment (PRI) was formed in 2006 by the UN Global Compact, the UN Environment Programme (UNEP) Finance Initiative, and a group of large institutional investors. The PRI was the first time that large, diversified investors jointly agreed that oversight of environmental and social risks is essential to securing the long-term sustainability of their investment portfolios, marking a turning point in sustainable finance.

By participating in the PRI, these investors formally acknowledged their mutual interest in mitigating long-term systemic risks, creating a norm that laid the foundation for more robust investor collaboration. The next step was the creation of several PRI-supported "climate networks" of investors, organized regionally or by investor type. Examples include the Institutional Investors Group on Climate Change (IIGCC) or the Investor Group on Climate Change (IGCC) Australia/New Zealand. These networks evolved, adding systems for collaborative stewardship as investors worked together to draft stewardship codes. They created a forum to share information, engagement priorities, and strategies. Indeed, the PRI's "Collaboration Platform," described as "a unique private forum that allows signatories to pool resources, share information, and enhance their influence on ESG issues,"[3] is itself a knowledge commons.

These investors acutely recognized that their collaboration and long-term orientation was in tension with more traditional view of fiduciary duties and other legal norms. To strengthen the legitimacy of their approach, the PRI partnered with law firms and advisors to establish and proliferate norms within the global legal community, clarifying that investor fiduciary duties in most major jurisdictions require collaboration to mitigate systemic risks (Elliott et al. 2019).

Investor stewardship codes marked another significant milestone in the evolution of ICAs. The UK was the first country to adopt a stewardship code, leading to a proliferation of global stewardship codes. The US does not have a formal

[3] https://collaborate.unpri.org/.

stewardship code and relies instead on private ordering. In 2016, a group of asset managers created the Investor Stewardship Group, which established a "Framework for U.S. Stewardship and Governance."[4] This approach aligns with the cultural context in which corporate law serves as an enabling mechanism for private ordering rather than public regulation (Millon 1990).

9.2.1.2 Phase Two: Climate Action 100+ Introduces More Robust Infrastructure for Collaboration

ICAs emerged from this polycentric background environment, characterized by overlapping institutions made up of both public and private actors. While this approach may seem inefficient compared to centralized governance, as Ostrom (2010) recognized, these redundancies offer several advantages. Polycentricity enables non-state actors, such as businesses and nongovernmental organizations, to overcome the problem of insufficient government regulation. This is especially true for large-scale, transnational issues like the climate crisis.

Although these early collaborative arrangements were foundational, the climate crisis demanded more sustained and systematic collaboration than informal stewardship codes and principles could offer. This realization prompted investors to create Climate Action 100+, the first and largest of investor alliances focused on climate risk. Climate Action 100+'s origin story reflects the economic logic of commons governance. The alliance originated in 2017 when Anne Simpson, then director of CalPERS, the largest pension fund in the United States, conducted a carbon audit of the pension fund's $400 billion portfolio. This audit revealed that about 100 companies contributed to about 85 percent of the emissions in CalPERS' highly diversified portfolio. This led to a key insight: CalPERS could concentrate its engagement efforts on a small number of companies, and it could also collaborate with other investors, as the highest-emitting firms were likely the same across their portfolios.

In response, a group of about a dozen investors held meetings at the United Nations and created Climate Action 100+, the largest voluntary initiative for investors addressing climate change. This alliance was also polycentric and benefited from these investors' long-standing participation in past collaborative efforts. Climate Action 100+ was cofounded by five global investor networks: Asia Investor Group on Climate Change (AIGCC); IGCC (Australia and New Zealand); Institutional Investor Group on Climate Change (IIGCC) (Europe); Ceres Investor Network in Climate Risk and Sustainability (North America); and the Principles of Responsible Investment (global). What began with a small coalition of investors in 2017 has now expanded to over 600 investors across more than 30 countries.

Notably, Climate Action 100+ is not a legal entity; rather, it is a voluntary system of rules and norms for creating knowledge resources about climate risk.

4 https://isgframework.org/.https://isgframework.org/

9.2.1.3 Phase Three: Cultural, Political, and Legal Norms Threaten ICAs

In 2017, addressing climate risk and other ESG risks, such as diversity, was emerging as a business and investment norm. By 2020, the business community seemed to embrace the importance of responding to climate change, with Larry Fink famously writing in his 2020 letter to CEOs that "climate risk is investment risk" (Fink 2020). That same year, the World Economic Forum released the Davos Manifesto, outlining the obligations companies owe to their stakeholders. To fully address the financial harms of climate risk, firms turned to collaboration – and diversified investors seemed to be on board.

Despite this apparent convergence, the background cultural context was never entirely copacetic. For one thing, corporate law varies by jurisdiction, and ICAs are transnational. More important than legal mandates, corporate law narratives and norms differ, and norms drive behavior. As Mark Roe (1991, 33) has noted, in the US, there is a "widespread attitude that large institutions and accumulations of centralized economic power are inherently undesirable and should be reduced, even if concentration is productive." Antitrust law is often used as a tool to reinforce this norm, even when the actual collaboration is *procompetitive* (Miazad 2022).

It should come as no surprise, then, that the financial institutions that are departing from ICAs are overwhelmingly US-based, and reacting to US regulators' and lawmakers' (misguided) claims that collaboration is synonymous with collusion. The general mistrust of international law in the US exacerbates this – the US has repeatedly stepped into and out of the Paris Climate Accord, to which these ICAs are tethered. Additionally, there is a lack of consensus in the US about the extent to which climate risk is financial risk, with many noting that climate risk is a social preference or a contested value, and therefore outside the scope of what fiduciaries may consider.

As this chapter will explore, this increasingly discordant background environment has both facilitated and constrained ICAs. The GKC framework allows us to examine how these conflicting legal regimes materialize into social conflicts within Climate Action 100+, including high-profile departures of asset managers, from BlackRock to Goldman Sachs. First, though, it is important to detail the various knowledge resources that ICAs produce and manage, which the next part turns to.

9.2.2 *Relevant Knowledge, Information, and Data Resources*

Broadly speaking, ICAs produce and govern knowledge about financially material climate risk, which includes transition risk, physical risk, and liability risk. The GKC framework helps to delineate the different types of resources that fall under this broad umbrella, which includes data, information, and expertise. This type of knowledge cannot be produced unilaterally and demands knowledge commons governance for several reasons.

When an individual corporation discloses information about its climate risk to investors, that information is useful only to the extent that it is *comparable* to other corporations. This fundamental idea underlies financial accounting, which requires comparability, made possible through standardized accounting rules and guidelines such as Generally Accepted Accounting Principles (GAAP) or International Financial Reporting Standards (IFRS). To be decision-useful, financial information must also be specific and accurate. These three attributes – comparability, specificity, and accuracy – are made possible through standard-setting. They transform the resource from financial data into *knowledge and expertise* about financial risk. Importantly, the financial standard-setting process is ongoing, and financial standards can only be produced and maintained collectively by public and private actors.

Outside of financial markets, many types of information become significantly more valuable when considered in aggregate. Take the Human Genome Project, for example. Genomic Data Commons create knowledge by pooling genetic health data, then "drawing statistical inferences based on which variants and health conditions appear to occur together in the same individuals" (Evans 2017, 77). Thus, an individual human's genome sequence may be valuable to that person and researchers, but it is only in *aggregate* that it becomes a knowledge resource for the broader scientific community (Gregg, this volume).

Climate risk data is analogous. An individual corporation's climate risk disclosure is valuable to investors, regulators, and other stakeholders only if they can interpret how the data relates to other corporations, and to the financial system more broadly. Investor demand for consistent climate risk data has been driven by years of advocacy for mandatory climate disclosures. Investors emphasize that these disclosures should be "consistent, comparable, reliable, and decision useful" (Ceres 2020).

Managing financially material climate risk demands knowledge commons governance because it is a new and uncertain area. There is little consensus on which specific corporate governance reforms minimize transitional, physical, and litigation risks linked to climate change. Successfully navigating these challenges will require collaboration among investors, corporations, regulators, and society. Key questions remain unanswered, such as: What level of board oversight is most effective at minimizing climate risk? Do net zero commitments lead to real reductions in greenhouse gas emissions? What level of capital allocation is sufficient for transitioning from fossil fuels?

9.2.2.1 Categories of Knowledge Resources Produced by ICAs

We begin applying the GKC framework by examining the types of resources that knowledge commons produce. With ICAs, there is much to unpack. While the end goal of ICAs is to protect the value of their diversified asset pools, the resources that ICAs produce and utilize are *knowledge resources*. As the knowledge commons tradition recognizes, unlike physical resources, information can be generated and consumed (notwithstanding technological constraints like data storage) without being depleted. In economic terms, information and knowledge are non-rivalrous resources. Thus, Garett Hardin's "tragedy of the commons," which arises from the overconsumption of a finite resource, generally does not occur in knowledge commons (Frischmann et al. 2014). However, a key insight of the GKC framework is that other social dilemmas, such as collective action problems, information asymmetries, and misaligned incentives, can, and often do, impact knowledge commons.

The foregoing discussion synthesizes the types of resources that ICAs create and maintain. Each of these resources are *intangible knowledge resources*, such as data, information, and expertise, or other intangible resources like trust and time.

9.2.2.1.1 SHARED NORMS AND GOALS At the highest level, ICAs offer a set of shared objectives to organize activities and evaluate outcomes under a common framework. Climate Action 100+'s overarching goal is to reduce emissions "in line with the goals of the Paris Agreement to pursue efforts to limit warming to 1.5°C."[5] This shared goal is itself a resource because it aligns investor preferences and incentivizes corporations to produce more information, even absent regulatory obligations to do so (Bond and Zeng 2022). Moreover, the fact that this goal is linked to the Paris Agreement creates another resource: legitimacy. The investors are not unilaterally articulating this goal as so-called private actors. Rather, they are adhering to international law and norms (Gordon 2023). This allows for corporations to keep in line with the growing body of regulations which implement the Paris Agreement, even when the US is hesitant to adopt regulations that adhere to international norms.

Curiously, these shared norms and goals are also a liability. In the polarized landscape in the US, there is a high degree of criticism of international law and norms. This is evidenced by the US's fickle commitment to the Paris Agreement, which has changed with each administration. Moreover, there is disagreement as to whether the Agreement is binding international law, given that the US Congress has not ratified it. Critics have also argued that voluntary collaborative efforts by investors represent private regulatory efforts that lack democratic legitimacy (Lund 2022). There are concerns that the consolidation of economic power in large organizations is inherently undesirable, even if it offers benefits. And other critics claim that Climate Action 100+'s requirement that corporations adhere to an international treaty is inconsistent with individual investors' claims that they are developing their investment strategies unilaterally. In sum, while alignment allows US investors to consistently adhere to international norms despite shifting domestic policy, it also presents social dilemmas.

5 https://www.climateaction100.org/about/.

9.2.2.1.2 THREE ASKS FROM COMPANIES Managing climate risk can be amorphous and is exceedingly complex. An additional resource that Climate Action 100+ provides is consistency in its message to companies about what, specifically, investors want from companies. Climate Action 100+ has synthesized this into three "asks":

1. Implement a strong governance framework that clearly articulates the board's accountability and oversight of climate change risk.
2. Take action to reduce greenhouse gas emissions across the value chain, including engagement with stakeholders such as policymakers and other actors to address the sectoral barriers to transition. This should be consistent with the Paris Agreement's goal of limiting global average temperature increase to well below 2°C above preindustrial levels, aiming for 1.5°C. Notably, this implies the need to move toward net zero emissions by 2050 or sooner.
3. Provide enhanced corporate disclosure on and implement transition plans to deliver on robust targets. This should be in line with the final recommendations of the Task Force on Climate-Related Financial Disclosures (TCFD) and other relevant sector and regional guidance, to enable investors to assess the robustness of companies' business plans and improve investment decision-making.[6]

When investors ask for the same type of information, climate disclosure becomes a norm within the investor community, and companies are likely to disclose more information. However, converging on similar goals has also subjected ICAs to increasing antitrust scrutiny. Critics have characterized shared goals, like net zero commitments, as veiled "group boycotts" of the fossil fuel industry. These threats have manifested in legal and regulatory investigations. For example, in 2023, a group of state attorneys general accused ICAs of exerting "coordinated pressure" on companies to reduce emissions. The House Judiciary Committee has also issued subpoenas to organizations involved in Climate Action 100+ on the theory that they facilitate collusion.

9.2.2.1.3 KNOWLEDGE OF ENGAGEMENT BEST PRACTICES. Climate Action 100+ offers infrastructure for investors to share information about best practices on effective engagement strategies. This information is neither proprietary nor commercially sensitive; investors had previously been sharing best practices in more ad hoc and informal forums. Climate Action 100+ enables investors to share this information in a systematized way, making the information useful to investors. While CA100+'s procedures have evolved, the initial structure enabled lead investors – those who volunteer to engage a specific company – to share their annual

[6] https://www.climateaction100.org/the-three-goals/

engagement plans and periodic progress updates with other Climate Action 100+ members. This information was stored in a members-only portal and organized in a standardized format to enhance its usefulness to investors engaging with the same or other companies on the focus list.

9.2.2.1.4 MORE RELIABLE COMPANY SPECIFIC INFORMATION AND DATA. Compared to its other two asks from companies, Climate Action 100+ has been most successful in increasing corporate disclosure. More disclosure is not, of course, always a good thing for investors. Indeed, more data and information can sometimes impede investors' ability to use that data, and voluntary disclosures have also been associated with less reliability, or "cheap talk." Here, too, Climate Action 100+ improves the quality of corporate disclosures. A recent study found that companies engaging with Climate Action 100+ provided more reliable and actionable climate disclosures, with significantly less "cheap talk" (Bingler et al. 2022).

9.2.2.1.5 THE NET ZERO BENCHMARK. To ease the monitoring burden on investors, Climate Action 100+ launched the Net Zero Company Benchmark in 2020.[7] This benchmark utilizes both publicly available and self-reported data to track the progress of targeted companies. It consists of two main components: the Disclosure Framework, which assesses the quality of disclosures, and the Alignment Assessments, which determine whether a company's actions are consistent with its net zero commitments. The benchmark was developed in collaboration with external NGOs, academics, and technical experts, so that it could ensure the data's validity. Moreover, the specific standards in the benchmark are regularly updated. Importantly, to elicit "buy-in," updates to the benchmark incorporate feedback from Climate Action 100+ members. Still, the Net Zero Benchmark faces legitimacy challenges; some claim that the connection between carbon emissions and climate change is tenuous, or at the very least extremely difficult to measure.

9.2.2.1.6 SCIENTIFIC KNOWLEDGE AND EXPERTISE. We are far from fully understanding how carbon emissions impact investor portfolios, or what "net zero" means. These are scientific questions as much as they are financial or political ones. Climate Action 100+ provides the infrastructure for investors to collaborate with experts in the scientific community, including the Transition Pathway Initiative Centre (TPI Centre), Carbon Tracker Initiative (CTI), and InfluenceMap, to create specific indicators and sub-indicators in the Net Zero Benchmark. In doing so, Climate Action 100+ creates scientific knowledge and expertise within the investor community, and financial expertise within the scientific community.

7 https://www.climateaction100.org/net-zero-company-benchmark/.

9.2.2.1.7 LEGAL COMPLIANCE. Climate Action 100+ creates knowledge resources about compliance with a growing body of regulations on climate risk, particularly those governing corporate disclosure. In 2017, corporate disclosure of climate risk was voluntary in all jurisdictions. Since then, global securities regulators have required disclosure. These disclosure mandates have converged to recognize the voluntary TCFD framework as compliant with regulatory mandates. Since its inception, Climate Action 100+ has been working with the highest emitting companies to enhance their TCFD reporting, facilitating legal compliance.

In addition to knowledge resources, Climate Action 100+ provides its members with other intangible resources, including administrative support, time, and, perhaps most importantly, trust.

9.2.2.1.8 SHARED INFRASTRUCTURE FOR ADMINISTRATION. Collecting and synthesizing climate risk data and information requires administrative and logistical support. Thus, one key resource that Climate Action 100+ provides is the shared infrastructure, coordinated by the five founding investor networks. This infrastructure makes it easier for investors to communicate and overcome long-standing collective action problems that institutional investors have faced.

9.2.2.1.9 TIME. Monitoring, engagement, and voting rely on bespoke information, which is time-consuming (and costly) to obtain. Climate Action 100+ streamlines stewardship by focusing on the companies in investors' portfolios that emit the most greenhouse gasses. Therefore, an important intangible resource that Climate Action 100+ provides its members is the time to engage with companies in a meaningful way.

9.2.2.1.10 TRUST. The shared infrastructure enables institutional investors to engage in more "repeat play" than ever before. As Ostrom (2010) recognized, market actors often collaborate when they can communicate repeatedly and build trust, and this can function more effectively than externally imposed regulation or market sanctions. Lynn Stout and Margaret Blair (2001) also emphasized the power of repeat play to build trust among corporate actors, which underscores their Team Production Theory of the Corporation. Therefore, perhaps the most important resource that ICAs provide is trust, which incentivizes the participants to continue producing more knowledge resources.

9.2.2.2 Characteristics of Climate Action 100+'s Knowledge Resources

9.2.2.2.1 SCARCE AND ABUNDANT. While policymakers and scholars focus most often on scarcity, information resources – unlike finite natural resources – also suffer from problems related to abundance. Similarly, climate risk information is both scare and abundant. Indeed, investors backing the SEC's climate risk disclosure rule highlighted that there is insufficient information on how companies manage climate risk, yet also too much immaterial information. The SEC has acknowledged this, noting that "high levels of immaterial disclosure can obscure important information or diminish incentives for market participants to trade or create markets for securities."[8] This abundance necessitates intermediary systems like ICAs.

9.2.2.2.2 NON-RIVAL, ANTI-RIVAL, AND NON-EXCLUDABLE. The GKC framework clarifies that intangible information and knowledge resources, unlike physical resources, are often (but not always) non-rival and non-excludable. Therefore, knowledge resources generally do not suffer from problems of overconsumption; rather, they struggle with underproduction or coordination. With respect to underproduction, the concern is that intangible resources, such as creative works, will not be produced if access is not restricted. This concern undergirds intellectual property laws, such as those protecting copyrights and patents, which create production incentives by precluding access. But these concerns do not apply to climate risk information for several reasons.

Most of the information managed by ICAs either consists of publicly available climate disclosures or knowledge about how to obtain more such disclosures from corporations. For investors that are highly diversified, there is no competitive advantage in exploiting informational asymmetries to reduce systemic risks. To the contrary, it benefits CalPERS to invest in producing and sharing (at no cost) information about climate risk governance with other diversified investors. That is true even if the other investors in Climate Action 100+ fail to participate in or invest time or money into *generating* the resource.

While it might be optimal if all investors were contributing to generating knowledge resources, it still benefits CalPERS if other investors utilize the knowledge resources that CalPERS creates. In this way, climate risk information is akin to public health information – the more individuals voluntarily adopt health and hygiene guidelines, like wearing masks or handwashing, the better it is for the overall community. This is different from commercially sensitive information that can be leveraged for individual profit.

Certain types of information are not only non-rival but also anti-rival. In other words, the information becomes *more* valuable as more people use it (Weber 2005; Cooper 2006). This is evident in Artificial Intelligence (AI) platforms or open-source software programs where increased data input enhances the AI's learning model and, over time, makes the data more reliable or more useful. The knowledge and information resources that Climate Action 100+ produces are similar. Climate risk knowledge resources, both at the company and investor levels, are anti-rival.

[8] Business and Financial Disclosure Required by Regulation S-K, 81 Fed. Reg. 23,916, 23,919 (Apr. 22, 2016).

The more investors and corporations utilize the information and data, the more valuable it becomes.

Climate risk disclosure is both non-rival and anti-rival. It is a non-rival good because it can be used by multiple stakeholders without diminishing its availability to others. At the same time, it is anti-rival because the more people use climate risk data and information, the more valuable and useful it becomes for everyone. More specifically, the broader the participation in sharing and using climate risk information, the more comprehensive and accurate the data becomes.

9.2.2.3 Key Actors and Stakeholders

In contrast to trade associations or industry alliances, Climate Action 100+'s members and key players are a myriad of public and private actors, including investors, NGOs, scientific experts, civil society, and international organizations like the United Nations. Even within the investor community, the actors are far from homogeneous – private asset managers, public pension funds, and sovereign wealth funds are all investors. However, this diverse membership brings with it different incentives, legal obligations, rules, cultures, and norms, as this part details.

9.2.2.3.1 CA 100+ INVESTOR MEMBERS. While there are different individuals and organizations involved in Climate Action 100+, only three types of entities can join as official members: asset owners, asset managers, and engagement service providers.[9] Recognizing these entities are distinct, the Climate Action 100+ Signatory Handbook outlines different roles for each.

Asset managers and service providers join Climate Action 100+ as "investor participants," whereas asset owners have the option to join as "investor supporters." Investor participants engage directly with designated companies, while investor supporters are encouraged to advocate for their investment managers or service providers to join the initiative. These classifications acknowledge that certain legal and contractual barriers prevent asset owners from participating directly in engagements with focus companies. However, asset owners are still encouraged to persuade their asset managers and engagement service providers to participate in Climate Action 100+. In practice, of the 600 investors who comprise the Climate Action 100+, most are asset owners or asset managers like CalPERS and AXA Investment Managers. However, most of the engagement service provider members are either faith-based investor groups or ESG and sustainability advocacy and advisory organizations such as As You Sow.

Unlike investor supporters, investor participants engage directly with focus companies. Their engagement can take one of three forms: (1) lead company investors, (2) contributing company investors, and (3) individual participants. Lead company investors serve as the main liaison between focus companies and other investors

[9] https://www.climateaction100.org/wp-content/uploads/2023/06/Signatory-Handbook-2023-Climate-Action-100.pdf.

involved in Climate Action 100+. They gather and relay information regarding the focus companies, and their primary task is to create an annual engagement plan that is shared with alliance members. The Climate Action 100+ signatory handbook emphasizes the importance of lead investors developing "deep knowledge" of their focus companies through consistent engagement. Contributing company investors support the lead investors to implement the engagement plan. Some investors prefer to join as individual participants, which means that they engage with companies without the participation of other Climate Action 100+ members. Individual investors must also, however, ensure that their engagements are "aligned with the goals of the initiative and with the collaborative approach" that Climate Action 100+ fosters. All three participant types exchange information about the focus companies with other members of the alliance. Although this information is neither nonpublic nor proprietary, it can be difficult for individual investors to gather such information from each corporation unilaterally. Therefore, Climate Action 100+ also serves as a mechanism to govern access to this information.

Beyond these formal designations that are outlined in the signatory handbook, Climate Action 100+'s members are extremely diverse. For one thing, they are transnational, comprised of entities that operate in 35 countries. These jurisdictions have different corporate law rules and norms. In addition to these jurisdictional differences, the asset owners are different types of legal entities. At a high level (Figure 9.1), there are four different types of asset owners: (1) public entities; (2) private corporations; (3) socially responsible or impact organizations; and (4) religious organizations.

Some asset owners and managers are private entities, whereas others are government pension funds or sovereign wealth funds. Private asset managers are governed by their own boards, elected by shareholders. Private asset managers are governed by their own corporate boards and are accountable to their shareholders. Moreover, private asset owners can be publicly traded or privately held, leading to vastly different incentives and accountability structures.

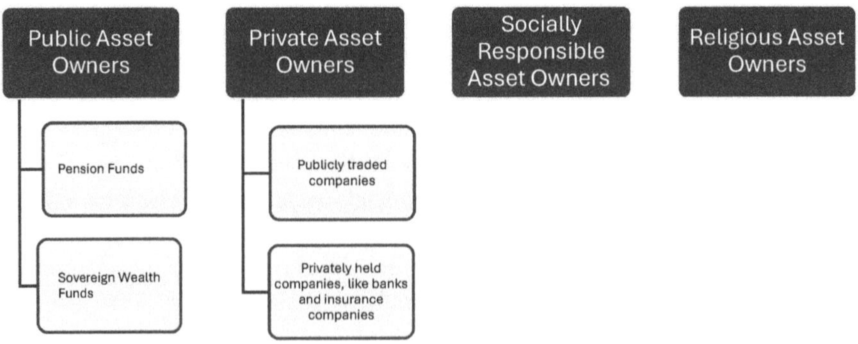

FIGURE 9.1 Types of asset owners.

In contrast, public asset owners, like state pension funds and sovereign wealth funds, are political entities, and accountable to the political process. While it varies by jurisdiction, the leadership of public pension funds is either elected by beneficiaries or appointed by state officials (such as the treasurer), or a combination of the two (Fisch and Schwartz 2024). In contrast, other members, including various impact and socially responsible investors, operate under different motivations. Likewise, religious asset owners are guided by religious orders that authorize and monitor their investment decisions through established governance processes (Miazad, 2026).

This diversity extends beyond mere legal frameworks and motivations; many of these investors do not function as market competitors in the traditional sense. While large asset managers like BlackRock and State Street may compete for clients, a pension fund such as CalPERS does not vie with another state's pension fund for beneficiaries. Instead, relationships among pension funds are typically collaborative, reflecting a shared interest in promoting ethical and sustainable investment practices. Similarly, faith-based investors, like the pension funds associated with the Catholic and Baptist churches, do not compete for clients but are incentivized to work together on pressing ethical issues, such as climate risk.

9.2.2.3.2 FOCUS COMPANIES. When the initiative was first founded, the investor members used data from the MSCI All Country World Index (MSCI ACWI) and Carbon Disclosure Project (CDP) reports to identify companies that are responsible for roughly two-thirds of annual industrial carbon dioxide emissions. The MSCI ACWI is an index that tracks performance in both developed and emerging nations, while CDP reports provide sustainability ratings to companies based on their voluntarily disclosed carbon emissions data. Climate Action 100+ originally comprised 100 of these focus companies. Today, that number stands at 168 focus companies. These companies are effectively the data subjects for the initiative, as each individual company's climate risk information is the data that gets incorporated into the Net Zero Benchmark.

Certainly, there are similarities among the focus companies, as they are all classified as "high emitting." However, these companies span various industries, including agriculture, airlines, automobiles, electric utilities, oil and gas, paper, shipping, and steel. Each industry requires a tailored engagement approach, which is why Climate Action 100+ has recently launched sector-specific strategies. In addition to industry variability, cultural differences also play a role, often reflecting norms around investor engagement. While it may be overstating the case to say corporations "welcome" the opportunity to become focus companies, Climate Action 100+ case studies highlight that many corporations recognize the value in it. These companies not only provide data about their own operations but also leverage data to learn from best practices among their peers.

More recently, Climate Action 100+ has shifted its perspective to view individual focus corporations more as research partners and collaborators, rather than as adversarial targets of investor scrutiny. Some companies, like Total, have embraced this collaborative role, while others, like Exxon, have resisted, even suing Climate Action 100+ members to block information gathering about their climate risk mitigation plans. Thus, while all focus companies are high-emitting, they exhibit significant heterogeneity in their approaches to shareholder engagement. While corporate law traditionally views the relationship between investors and corporations through agency theory, scholars argue that we are entering an era of collaborative information sharing. They suggest that "collaboration offers a mechanism for enhancing firm value that unilateral decision-making by either insiders or shareholders cannot provide" (Fisch and Sepe 2020).

9.2.2.3.3 LAWMAKERS AND REGULATORS. Global regulators have enacted laws that align with the goals of the Paris Agreement. Climate Action 100+ facilitates compliance with these legal frameworks. This eases the burden on regulators to monitor corporate adherence to climate-related commitments. Insights gained from Climate Action 100+ can help regulators identify gaps in existing legislation and inform the development of new regulatory measures that better support the transition to a low-carbon economy. Climate Action 100+ also encourages companies to disclose how their lobbying efforts align with the Paris Agreement. This transparency not only sheds light on corporate influence but also exposes the role of trade associations, holding legislatures accountable by disclosing when there is corporate influence in the legislative process. Finally, regulators benefit from Climate Action 100+ efforts to help harmonize global climate disclosure standards.

9.2.2.3.4 THE SCIENTIFIC COMMUNITY. The scientific community is in the process of defining precisely what "net-zero" means. As noted, this community contributes to the knowledge commons by providing inputs into Climate Action 100+'s standard-setting process, particularly the Net Zero Benchmark indicators. At the same time, the scientific community also benefits from the knowledge commons, as corporate disclosures provide valuable data and knowledge resources that would be challenging to access.

9.2.2.3.5 THE PUBLIC. The public is a key stakeholder in climate risk governance, which has garnered significant public attention and is frequently covered in the media. Climate risk affects the public in numerous ways, and thus, climate risk information and data are regarded as a public good. Research and mitigation efforts, as well as responses to climate disasters, are often funded by taxpayer dollars. Therefore, even if the public does not actively engage with data from the Net Zero Benchmark or other resources, it still gains from the overall reduction of climate risk.

While large asset managers and major financial institutions can hire analysts to perform private climate-risk assessments, the public relies on accessible data.

Resources like the Net Zero Benchmark, corporate disclosures, and TCFD reports enhance transparency in the public domain. US securities law uses disclosure requirements as the main tool of addressing information asymmetries. Disclosure requirements enable the public to make investment decisions that address their financial needs, which includes information about climate risks. In this sense, disclosure requirements enable the market to address climate change more effectively and competitively, and financial securities disclosures are often considered a public good (Sale 2019). Climate risk reports and data share similar characteristics: They are non-rivalrous and non-excludable, meaning that individuals cannot be prevented from accessing them (Samuelson 1954). However, climate risk reports may more aptly be described as *contribution goods*; while they are technically accessible to all, barriers such as limited expertise can prevent the public from meaningfully consuming this information (Kealey & Rickets 2014). Nonetheless, even when not widely consumed, scientific insights still benefit society. Indeed, a specific resource that is created for a private benefit often has "downstream" benefits and generates public and/or social goods (Frischmann 2012).

9.2.2.4 Governance

Governance refers to the methods or tools that members of a community use to meet their goals or resolve conflicts. For Climate Action 100+, this consists of a combination of laws, norms, rules, and socio-technical devices which are administered through polycentric governance by the following five coordinating networks.

1. Ceres: A sustainability nonprofit organization working with the most influential investors and companies to build leadership and drive solutions throughout the economy.
2. Principles for Responsible Investment: A UN-supported international network of investors working together to implement its six aspirational principles.
3. Asia Investor Group on Climate Change: A network dedicated to creating awareness and encouraging action among Asia's asset owners and financial institutions about the risks and opportunities associated with climate change and low carbon investing.
4. Investor Group on Climate Change: A collaboration of Australian and New Zealand investors focusing on the impact that climate change has on the financial value of investments.
5. Institutional Investor Group on Climate Change: The European membership body for investor collaboration on climate change and the voice of investors taking action for a prosperous, low-carbon future.[10]

[10] https://www.climateaction100.org/.

Some of these networks are regional, whereas others are nonprofits or intergovernmental organizations. Moreover, it is common for investor participants to be members of several of these networks – most investors are members of PRI and Ceres, for example. Ostrom (2010) recognized that duplication or redundancy is a feature, and not a bug, of polycentric governance systems.

It is important to recall that Climate Action 100+ is not a separate legal entity. Members join the alliance by signing an agreement and adhering to the informal rules set forth in the signatory handbook. Therefore, the alliance's members have voluntarily adopted a governance structure for coordinating their communications and activities. They have opted for shared governance and dispersed power throughout the five global investor networks. The alliance delegates formal oversight to a Global Steering Committee, which includes one investor network representative and two investor representatives from each global network. To ensure that one investor network does not have outsized power, the Steering Committee Chair and Vice Chair rotate each year. Legal institutions and norms, which we will turn to next, both enable and constrain the alliance's activities.

9.2.3 *Legal Institutions, Structures, and Norms*

Climate Action 100+'s members are transnational, subject to various and sometimes conflicting regulatory regimes. The corporations on the Climate Action 100+ focus list are also multinational, such as Exxon (incorporated in Texas with operations in over 60 countries) and Nestlé (incorporated in Switzerland with operations in 188 countries). This diversity necessitates navigating a complex web of laws, regulatory frameworks, and legal norms.

The legal environment for Climate Action 100+ is therefore highly complex, incorporating both "soft law" norms and an increasing number of hard law requirements. Climate risk oversight is becoming an integral part of board and investor fiduciary duties, reinforcing pro-climate regulatory trends that help legitimize Climate Action 100+. While regulatory frameworks are increasingly aligning globally, the legal environment remains fragmented. Corporate law paradigms, cultural norms, and a partisan anti-climate agenda in the US threaten the viability of Climate Action 100+ and similar alliances. Addressing the full legal complexity is beyond the scope of this chapter, so we will focus on the key legal rules and norms.

9.2.3.1 Legal Rules and Norms that Foster Climate Action 100+

On December 12, 2015, nearly 200 nations adopted the Paris Agreement, which aims to limit global warming to well below 2°C, with an aspirational target of 1.5°C. The agreement is unique in that it invites non-state actors to participate, resulting in over 13,000 commitments from myriad entities, from corporations to cities. It has also been incorporated into national, state, and local legislation. For example, carbon markets are mandatory in the EU, UK, and California, and many countries have submitted Nationally Determined Contributions (NDCs) detailing their climate actions. Additionally, twenty-four US states require pension funds to align their portfolios with the Paris Agreement's emissions targets.

On the other hand, the legitimacy of the Paris Agreement as binding international law remains hotly contested in the US, where it was never ratified by Congress, raising questions about enforceability. Unlike the United Nations Framework Convention on Climate Change (UNFCCC), which was ratified by Congress, the US enters and exists from the Paris Agreement via executive agreements. Despite this, the Paris Agreement operates as a form of soft law in the US, shaping the framework for Climate Action 100+. While soft law is not always legally enforceable through traditional means, it creates norms that shape corporate and investor behavior even without legal enforcement. Moreover, soft law can, and often does, have legal consequences if adopted through contracts.

For transnational institutional investors in particular, soft law is appealing because it involves minimal cost for amending voluntary commitments. In many jurisdictions, it is impractical to pass legislation quickly, particularly on addressing climate risk, which is a rapidly changing area, making soft law an attractive alternative.

Soft law also paves the way for future hard law by testing norms in the market. An example of this is net zero commitments, which arose from the Intergovernmental Panel on Climate Change (IPCC). These voluntary commitments are driving the development of reporting frameworks, benchmarks, and climate disclosure methodologies. Also, these soft law norms are increasingly being incorporated into hard law, particularly through mandatory climate disclosures. California has taken a lead with the Climate Corporate Data Accountability Act, which mandates public disclosure of Scope 1, 2, and 3 emissions for large companies. Other laws, such as the Climate-Related Financial Risk Act and the Voluntary Carbon Market Disclosures Act, also impose disclosure requirements. Globally, the UN launched the International Sustainability Standards Board to develop standards for sustainability disclosures, while the EU's Corporate Sustainability Reporting Directive, effective in January 2023, requires all listed companies to disclose ESG data. These regulations will likely have a lasting impact on sustainability reporting. However, these legal frameworks often conflict with traditional corporate law paradigms, which we will explore next.

9.2.3.2 Legal Rules and Norms that Constrain Climate Action 100+

The impetus for forming Climate Action 100+ was to help investors meet their fiduciary duty to oversee the risk of climate change. Recall that the alliance was formed when legal advisors and regulators were emphasizing that, as fiduciaries, investors not only have the right but also the obligation to manage it. Managing climate risk requires investors (and directors) to look beyond the profits of a single firm and toward the impacts that firms have on the rest of investors' portfolios. While investors' portfolios are not analogous to a common-pool resource like a fishery, there is a commons governance logic at play. As Climate Action 100+ explains, "[climate change] has the potential to harm all economies, asset classes and industries, whether directly or indirectly, with escalating consequences for all financial market actors."[11] Climate Action 100+ members are broadly diversified, which means they are invested in the same companies which span the economy. Its members invoke commons governance logic to justify their collaborative efforts. Members of investor alliances recognize that investing in "dirty assets" is a short-term gain that comes at the expense of long-term, portfolio-wide sustainability, much in the same way that overfishing or overharvesting timber threatens future abundance. This metaphor analogizing the physical commons to the financial commons is also woven throughout "universal owner" theory. Consider the words of Rick Alexander, founder of the Shareholder Commons: "Thus, like the villagers who are each rationally incentivized to overgraze the common meadow, leading to failure for the entire village, rational companies make decisions not to audit supply chains or use renewable energy because they have no rational reason to do otherwise. How can we [as investors] instill the value of an honorable harvest?"

While the basic economic logic of "portfolio primacy" for diversified investors is obvious, it is in tension with corporate law norms underlying fiduciary duty, antitrust, and securities law (Miazad 2025). I use the word *norm* intentionally – Climate Action 100+'s collaborative efforts have been carefully designed to ensure compliance with corporate law. Notwithstanding the legal merits, investors are still leaving the alliance because conservative lawmakers are equating collaboration with collusion, claiming it violates antitrust and securities regulations that limit investor communication. These lawmakers also argue that investors' efforts to reduce climate risk prioritize social values over economic returns, which they view as a breach of investors' fiduciary duty. Certainly, partisan politics is at play here. But the fact that investors are departing highlights that corporate law norms and theoretical paradigms are fundamentally in tension with collaborative efforts. These legal paradigms operate as institutional impediments to communication, which is necessary to shift from a competitive game to a collaborative one (Ostrom et al. 1994).

As Ostrom (2010) often stressed, real-world collaborative governance systems are complex and messy, in contrast to the neat theoretical models favored by economists. It is difficult to fit the real world into rigid legal frameworks. This may explain why corporate law begins with the assumption that individual directors and shareholders aim to maximize the value of their own firms, with the idea that, in aggregate, this will increase the overall value of investors' portfolios. But this overlooks the complex reality of systemic risks like climate change. One company

[11] https://www.climateaction100.org/approach/business-case/.

may increase its own value by externalizing costs, which may reduce the value of other companies – all of which are in the portfolio of the diversified investor.

There are two reasons why diversified investors do not simply divest from high-emitting companies. First, many are legally required to diversify, or are invested in index funds, which makes exit impossible or highly costly. But even if they *could* exit, other shareholders would readily purchase shares in the same high-emitting corporations. Worse, these other shareholders may not be diversified and therefore benefit from certain corporations, like Exxon, externalizing its climate impacts. Since divestment is often not economically rational for diversified investors, they have opted to collaborate on nudging high-emitting companies to reduce their emissions. The problem is that these emission reductions could reduce the share price of individual corporations. This reality exposes that the fiduciary duties of diversified investors are in tension with the fiduciary duties of other investors and the duties of directors.

For example, the Uniform Prudent Investor Act mandates that "[t]he standard of prudence is applied to any investment as part of the total portfolio, rather than to individual investments."[12] The Act further requires trustees to consider "general economic conditions," "inflation or deflation," and "the role that each investment or course of action plays within the overall trust portfolio."[13] But this is fundamentally at odds with the single-firm fiduciary duties of directors and officers, as the Delaware court recently reiterated in *McRitchie v. Zuckerberg*.[14] In that case, the Delaware Court of Chancery addressed a fundamental question of corporate governance: whether directors owe fiduciary duties to stockholders as diversified investors or specifically as stockholders in one company. The plaintiff argued that Meta's directors breached their duties by focusing solely on the company's interests without considering the broader impact on their diversified investors' portfolios. The court held that the directors' fiduciary duties are firm-specific, meaning that they owe their duties only to stockholders in their capacity as stockholders of that company, not as diversified investors. This ruling reinforced the principle that fiduciary duties are inherently tied to the specific company, not the individual stockholder's broader investment portfolio.

The tension between the single firm and the wider economy is also apparent in antitrust law. The argument that ICAs are anticompetitive centers on the claim that net zero commitments are a veiled group boycott of the fossil fuel industry because they result in decreased output of fossil fuels – ultimately harming consumers through higher prices or reduced availability of that product. But if we apply a portfolio-wide or commons lens to the problem, it becomes apparent that collaborative investor stewardship can increase the availability of multiple products for consumers in the long term. Consider home insurance – many consumers of

[12] Adding that the term "'portfolio' embraces all the trust's assets." See Uniform Prudent Investor Act 1994, Prefatory Note, § 2(b).

[13] Uniform Prudent Investor Act 1994, Section 2.

[14] *McRitchie v. Zuckerberg*, C.A. No. 2022–0890-JTL (D. Del. 2024) (order granting motion to dismiss).

insurance are either not able to secure coverage at all or are priced out of home insurance markets. If we acknowledge that climate change resulting from greenhouse gas emissions has increased the frequency and severity of natural disasters, it follows that the increase in greenhouse gas emissions has already reduced the output of insurance. Thus, a portfolio-wide approach makes it clear that even if we assume that the goal of antitrust law is to enhance consumer welfare, collaborative efforts could further impede that goal.

Finally, securities regulators across jurisdictions impose restrictions on shareholder collaboration through "acting in concert" rules. These rules were designed to alert boards when shareholders are forming a group for the purpose of a hostile takeover. However, these rules are also chilling efforts by shareholders who seek to file shareholder proposals asking corporate boards for better oversight of climate change risk. This highlights a key issue: shareholder collaboration is being restricted in areas that could benefit long-term corporate sustainability, such as tackling climate-related risks (Miazad 2024; Puchniak and Varottil 2024).

In sum, certain corporate law norms are in tension with investor collaboration. At the same time though, regulatory regimes around the world are placing more pressure on investors to oversee climate risk. ICAs are still evolving and will ultimately be shaped by these external regulatory forces.

9.3 OUTCOMES AND CONCLUSION

Corporate governance encompasses the methods for mediating between competing claims on who has the right to provide inputs into and extract benefits from the corporation. Those methods can take numerous forms, from shareholder primacy to stakeholder theory. But these simple distinctions belie the fact that even shareholder primacy is infused with polycentricity. Shareholders represent the diverse interests of a wide set of stakeholders. When shareholders were dispersed, rational apathy and the separation between ownership and control were the dominant concerns of corporate law. As institutional investors rose in number and prominence, the heterogeneity of investor preferences were being mediated by these investors. ICAs represent an evolution of this infrastructure for mediating this heterogeneity in more sophisticated ways.

Importantly, this is not a rebuke of agency theory. As Adolf Berle (1932) envisioned it, the corporate share still provides a superior accountability mechanism for shareholders to express their voice. That is what ICAs help facilitate – the use of the share, and the shareholder proposal process, as a vehicle for aligning and expressing shareholder preferences on climate risk.

Though collaboration is out of sync with the neoliberal economics that have dominated corporate law since the 1970s, it is in harmony with Ostrom's (2009, 2010) "polycentric" theories of governance and Berle's collaborative or "corporatist" theory of corporate governance (Bratton and Wachter 2008). While many credit Berle for laying the foundation for agency theory, his normative preference for collaboration over competition and groups over individuals would surprise many. Berle recognized that, in addition to legal mandates, companies were limited by "inchoate laws" or a set of community expectations for corporate behavior (Pollman 2019). ICAs reflect Adolf Berle's conception of collaborative governance shaped as much by norms and expectations as by formal legal mandates.

REFERENCES

Alexander, Frederick. 2019. "An Honorable Harvest: It Is Time for Universal Owners to Take Responsibility for Their Portfolios." https://theshareholdercommons.com/wp-content/uploads/2018/07/Honorable-Harvest-Time-for-Universal-Owners-to-Take-Responsibility-for-Their-Portfolios.pdf.

Bebchuk, Lucian A., and Roberto Tallarita. 2020. "The Illusory Promise of Stakeholder Governance." *Cornell Law Review* 106: 91–178.

Berle, Adolf A. 1932. "For Whom Corporate Managers Are Trustees: A Note." *Harvard Law Review* 45(8): 1365–1372.

Bingler, Julia, Mathias Kraus, Markus Leippold, and Nicolas Webersinke. 2022. "How Cheap Talk in Climate Disclosures Relates to Climate Initiatives, Corporate Emissions, and Reputation Risk." *Swiss Finance Institute Research Paper Series* No. 22–01.

Blair, Margaret M., and Lynn A. Stout. 2001. "Trust, Trustworthiness, and the Behavioral Foundations of Corporate Law." *University of Pennsylvania Law Review* 149(6): 1735–1810.

Bond, Philip, and Yao Zeng. 2022. "Silence Is Safest: Information Disclosure When the Audience's Preferences Are Uncertain." *Journal of Financial Economics* 145(1): 178–193.

Bratton, Willliam W., and Michael L. Wachter. 2008. "Shareholder Primacy's Corporatist Origins: Adolf Berle and the Modern Corporation." *Journal of Corporation Law* 34(1): 99–152.

Ceres. 2020. "Addressing Climate as a Systemic Risk: A Call to Action for U.S. Financial Regulators." www.ceres.org/resources/reports/addressing-climate-systemic-risk.

Chaim, Danielle A. 2025. "Investor Coalitions through an Antitrust Lens." *UC Irvine Law Review*, 15(3): 969–1023.

Condon, Madison. 2020. "Externalities and the Common Owner." *Washington Law Review* 95(1): 1–81.

Cooper, Mark. 2006. "From Wi-Fi to Wikis and Open Source: The Political Economy of Collaborative Production in the Digital Information Age." *Colorado Technology Law Journal*. 5(1): 125–158.

Dekker, Erwin, and Pavel Kuchař, eds. 2022. *Governing Markets as Knowledge Commons*. Cambridge: Cambridge University Press.

Elliott, Rebecca, Elodie Feller, Will Martindale, Margarita Pirovska, and Rory Sullivan. 2019. *Fiduciary Duty in the 21st Century (Final Report)*. UN Environment Programme, Finance Initiative. www.unepfi.org/industries/investment/fiduciary-duty-in-the-21st-century-final-report/.

Evans, Barbara J. 2017. "Genomic Data Commons." In *Governing Medical Knowledge Commons*, ed. Katherine J. Stranburg, Brett M. Frischmann, and Michael J. Madison, 74–101. Cambridge: Cambridge University Press.

Fink, Larry. 2020. "Letter to CEOs: A Fundamental Reshaping of Finance." BlackRock. www.blackrock.com/corporate/investor-relations/2020-larry-fink-ceo-letter.

Fisch, Jill E., and Jeff Schwartz. 2024. "Principals and Agents: The Anomalous Role of Public Pension Funds in Corporate Governance." Unpublished.
Fisch, Jill E., and Simone Sepe. 2020. "Shareholder Collaboration." *Texas Law Review* 98(5): 865–920.
Friedman, Milton. 1970. "The Social Responsibility of Business Is to Increase Its Profits." *New York Times Magazine*, September 13, 1970.
Frischmann, Brett M. 2012. *Infrastructure: The Social Value of Shared Resources*. New York: Oxford University Press.
Frischmann, Brett M., Michael J. Madison, and Katherine J. Strandburg, 2014. "Governing Knowledge Commons." In *Governing Knowledge Commons*, ed. Brett M. Frischmann, Michael J. Madison, and Katherine J. Strandburg, 1–43. New York: Oxford University Press.
Gordon, Jeffrey N. 2022. "Systematic Stewardship." *Journal of Corporation Law* 47(3): 628–673.
Gregg, Benjamin. 2025. "The Human Genome as Knowledge Commons." In *Governing Corporate Knowledge Commons*, ed. David Gindis. Cambridge: Cambridge University Press.
Jeffrey N. Gordon, "Unbundling Climate Change Risk from ESG," CLS Blue Sky Blog (Columbia Law School, 26 July 2023), https://clsbluesky.law.columbia.edu/2023/07/26/unbundling-climate-change-risk-from-esg/
Kealey, Terence, and Martin Ricketts. 2014. "Modelling Science as a Contribution Good." *Research Policy* 43(6): 1014–1024.
Lund, Dorothy S. 2022. "Asset Managers as Regulators." *University of Pennsylvania Law Review*, 171(1): 771146.
Madison, Michael J. 2024. "Knowledge Commons Past, Present, and Future." *Lewis & Clark Law Review* 28(2): 307–331.
Miazad, Amelia. 2022. "Prosocial Antitrust." *Hastings Law Journal* 73(6): 1637–1696.
Miazad, Amelia. 2025. "Investor Climate Alliances." *Washington University Law Review* 102(3): 797–857.
Miazad, Amelia. 2026. "Faith Investors." Minnesota Law Review (forthcoming).
Millon, David. 1990. "Theories of the Corporation." *Duke Law Journal* 1990(2): 201–262.
Ostrom, Elinor. 2009. "A Polycentric Approach for Coping with Climate Change." World Bank, Policy Research Working Paper 5095.
Ostrom, Elinor. 2010. "Beyond Markets and States: Polycentric Governance of Complex Economic Systems." *American Economic Review* 100(3): 641–672.
Ostrom Elinor, Roy Gardner, and James Walker. 1994. *Rules, Games, and Common-Pool Resources*. Ann Arbor: University of Michigan Press.
Pollman, Elizabeth. 2019. "Quasi Governments and Inchoate Law: Berle's Vision of Limits on Corporate Power." *Seattle University Law Review* 42(2): 617–639.
Puchniak, Dan W., and Umakanth Varottil. 2024. "Climate-Related Shareholder Activism as Corporate Democracy: A Call to Reform Acting in Concert Rules." *Journal of Corporation Law* 50(3): 618–651.
Quigley, Ellen. 2020. "Universal Ownership in Practice: A Practical Investment Framework for Asset Owners." https://ssrn.com/abstract=3638217.
Roe, Mark J. 1991. "A Political Theory of American Corporate Finance." *Columbia Law Review* 91(1): 10–67.
Sale, Hillary A. 2019. "Disclosure's Purpose." *Georgetown Law Journal* 107(4): 1045–1069.
Samuelson, Paul A. 1954. "A Pure Theory of Public Expenditure." *Review of Economics and Statistics* 36(4): 387–389.
Weber, Steven. 2005. *The Success of Open Source*. Cambridge, MA: Harvard University Press.

10

Data Commons, Data Oligopolies, and Consumer Financial Data Trusts

Alberto R. Salazar and Andi Rezda Rezal

10.1 INTRODUCTION

The rapid digitalization of capital markets and the expansion of financial technology have significantly enhanced the efficiency of the financial sector. However, this progress has also introduced new risks, particularly concerning financial data concentration. Financial companies are increasingly leveraging advanced technologies to consolidate control over public-generated financial data, leading to the rise of financial data oligopolies. This is part of a concerning trend. For instance, reports in recent years indicated that Google, Microsoft, and Yahoo together dominated 98 percent of the US search engine market, whereas Amazon accounted for 43 percent of US online retail sales and Facebook and Google controlled 73 percent of all digital advertising in the US (Shkabatur 2019, 358). This growing data concentration problem exposes the serious limitations of the prevailing individual consent model of data protection. Even in jurisdictions such as the European Union, where data subjects have greater protection and rights, most users accept cookies automatically to gain access to websites (Houser and Bagby 2023, 122). Neither the General Data Protection Regulation (GDPR) nor the California Consumer Privacy Act (CCPA), widely considered the two strongest privacy laws, has resulted in meaningful improvements in citizen's privacy protection and legal compliance by companies (Lancieri 2022).

This is largely due to information asymmetries, consumer rationality failures, and market power in data markets (Blankertz 2020, 6, 8; Solove 2021, 5; Lancieri 2022), as well as poor enforcement that relies on consumers' abilities to bring complaints and is often underfunded (Fisher and Streinz 2022, 902; Houser and Bagby 2023, 127). In fact, it appears that data concentration by big tech companies has increased after the introduction of robust privacy laws such as the GDPR (Blankertz 2020, 12; Johnson et al. 2023). Furthermore, while focusing on individual data rights, current data protection laws often overlook the negative impact of concentrated control over data and data-generating infrastructures (Fisher and Streinz 2022, 833, 906), including the internet, search engines, cloud services, operating systems, platforms, data centers, and other emerging technologies. As a small number of entities amass vast quantities of data, ostensibly to maximize profits and enhance their societal influence, it becomes imperative to critically examine the consequences of this data concentration.

The data concentration problem is evident in the financial sector. BlackRock's Aladdin platform serves as a potential example of the data oligopoly problem. BlackRock Inc., the world's biggest asset management company, to a significant extent owes its success to its operating system, Aladdin. This centralized platform collects and analyzes data on client portfolios, trades, risks, operations, performance, compliance, and accounting worldwide to predict market behavior and provide optimal information for effective investing decisions.[1] However, like other data-driven technologies, Aladdin must continue to scale the amount of data it collects and analyzes to maintain its competitive advantage. This expansion raises troubling concerns about the limits of BlackRock's access to data and the types of data it should be allowed to acquire. A critical concern with the emergence of financial data oligopolies such as Aladdin relates to their negative impact on financial consumers. Financial companies concentrating vast amount of data – including consumer behavior data – and empowered by financial technologies may facilitate financial exclusion and exploitation, including predatory and discriminatory lending, in addition to privacy breaches. While Aladdin mainly serves investors, it may enable or facilitate investors' decisions to engage in such problematic practices.

The Governing Knowledge Commons (GKC) framework (Frischmann et al. 2014; Madison 2024) provides a valuable lens through which to analyze the policy response to the emergence of financial data oligopolies. Viewed through this framework, financial data can be considered a shared resource that *could* be governed by a community of members. From this perspective, the monopolization of financial data by a select few entities may be viewed as eroding the fundamental principles of community governance that underpins the concept of data as commons. This process not only excludes important community members or stakeholders who contribute to the data ecosystem but also distorts the rules-in-use (Crawford and Ostrom 1995; Sanfilippo et al. 2018) that govern data sharing and utilization. The outcome is a system that disproportionately benefits a small group of actors while potentially undermining the broader societal benefits that could be derived from a more equitable and participatory approach to financial data management. Financial consumers, as important members of the governing community, are vulnerable to potential abuses by data oligopolies. However, they also have the capacity to act collectively to protect their data rights and interests and actively participate in the governance of *financial data commons*. One effective strategy involves consumer associations' activism, which can serve as a form of collective action to co-govern their financial data. This approach is akin to the concept of

[1] www.blackrock.com/aladdin.

consumer data trusts, where consumers band together to manage and safeguard their data collectively (Blankertz 2020).

Drawing on insights from the data commons approach (Shkabatur 2019), this chapter posits that consumer associations, acting as data trusts, can play a crucial role in overseeing financial data oligopolies while fostering the development of a community governance of data commons. In doing so, these associations can promote the attainment of valuable outcomes beyond addressing privacy harms, notably preventing predatory and discriminatory lending, mitigating financial exploitation, and expanding access to financial capital. By leveraging and shaping both formal and informal rules-in-use to facilitate these efforts, consumer associations or consumer data trusts contribute to *reinstitutionalizing* community governance that ultimately enhances the legitimacy of financial data commons.

This argument is discussed in the context of a case study, namely, BlackRock's Aladdin platform. Drawing on secondary sources, the analysis hypothesizes that Aladdin's massive financial data collection in various action situations may lead to the formation of data oligopolies that primarily benefit elite investors and potentially facilitate consumer financial exclusion and exploitation. Furthermore, by adopting a polycentric view of financial data governance and exploring the potential of consumer-led activism, this chapter discusses how consumer associations acting like data trusts can aggregate consumer data rights, enhance collective bargaining power, and negotiate more equitable terms with data oligopolies. Drawing on recent legal developments in Europe, particularly a case involving a German consumer association's action against Meta-Facebook, the chapter highlights the potential of such associations to address not only data privacy and value distribution concerns but also issues of financial exclusion and exploitation amid the emergence of financial data oligopolies.

10.2 A DATA COMMONS APPROACH TO FINANCIAL DATA AND FINTECH

Knowledge commons is the community governance of shared knowledge, information, and data resources (Madison 2024). Governance, whether the product of design or path-dependent accidents, consists of systems of formal and informal rules – ranging from law to social norms that may be mediated through socio-technical devices – by which members of that community achieve their goals and resolve problems and disputes. The GKC framework identifies instances of shared knowledge resources, highlights the problems or social dilemmas arising from the shared character of such resources – "conflicts between self-interested individual behavior and social or collective interests" (Madison 2024, 309) – and analyzes the rules communities can adopt to mitigate these problems. The important point is that the rules-in-use govern the production, contribution, sharing, use, appropriation, preservation, and even destruction of the shared resource (Madison 2024, 307–8).

A *data commons* can form around "a collection of data that is shared as a common resource" (Houser and Bagby 2023, 140). As a valuable knowledge resource, data is produced by market participants and can be considered a shared resource (Madison 2024: 308). These stakeholders – namely, companies, investors, consumers, employees, the environment, local communities, and governments – are involved in the creation, collection, management, and use of data. They can be part of a data commons (Shkabatur 2019: 383, 385) and often participate in the community governance of data. Rules-in-use – formal regulations, social norms, market practices, compliance strategies, and enforcement mechanisms, including those at the societal level (Crawford and Ostrom 1995; Sanfilippo et al. 2018) – affect their interactions in various practical action situations. For instance, the "transmission principles" that define the terms for information transfer and various informal norms regarding commercial sharing of information are examples of rules-in-use applied to specific interaction situations (Sanfilippo et al. 2018, 139). A data commons approach to financial data and fintech offers a nuanced framework for understanding and developing different mechanisms governing data. It addresses both top-down regulations and bottom-up practices and strategies, capturing the complexities of financial data creation, sharing, and management.

10.2.1 *The Monopolization of Financial Data*

Community governance of data is becoming an imperative. Community members are increasingly demanding not only protection of their interests, notably privacy, voice, and profit-sharing associated with data commercialization, but also *data sovereignty*. Data, from this perspective, should benefit not only companies that often provide the infrastructure for data collection and management but also all stakeholders involved and the public (Shkabatur 2019, 383). Such demands are growing, as current privacy laws are failing to provide significant protection of data subjects' rights, largely due to information asymmetries, rationality failures, and market power in data markets (Lancieri 2022), not to mention concentrated control over data infrastructures. These problems are compounded by poor enforcement that relies on consumers' abilities to bring complaints and is often underfunded (Houser and Bagby 2023, 127). Furthermore, the environmental cost of data governance imposed on community members and society at large provides additional reasons for the collective governance of data as shared resource. Data governance, including the use of financial technology, requires increasing consumption of energy and water, which worsens the ongoing climate crisis, affecting community members and the public in general. Recognizing this problem further warrants not only community members' entitlement to the benefits of data but also to participating in its collective governance.

Applying the GKC framework to financial data and fintech reveals several critical considerations. The community involved in creating, collecting, managing, and using shared financial data includes financial companies, investors, creditors, financial consumers, local communities, regulators, and other stakeholders. While these community members appear to somewhat participate in the collective governance of financial data, their involvement in financial data commons is limited in practice. The nature of the resource is such that financial data is non-rivalrous but excludable (Jones and Tonetti 2020; Purtova and van Maanen 2024). While it can be duplicated and shared at minimal marginal cost, access can be restricted through technical and legal measures, as well as by social norms and practices (Frischmann et al. 2014, 1–2). And notable power imbalances and information asymmetries exist among community members.

Specifically, financial and fintech companies are increasingly *monopolizing* the collection, storage, use, and commercialization of financial data to the detriment of other members of the governing community (McIntosh 2019; Chakravortl 2021; Houser and Bagby 2023). This situation gives rise to a critical social dilemma. Thanks to their control of financial technologies or infrastructures, financial companies absorb ever-growing amounts of financial data, while relying on formal and informal rules to largely exclude data subjects – notably small investors, creditors, and companies as well as financial consumers – from its governance (Sanfilippo et al. 2021, 268, 278; Fisher and Streinz 2022, 832). Consumer data is overshared with some and undershared with others (Houser and Bagby 2023, 116). Excluded community members have limited influence over how their data is collected, managed, and used, and are often excluded from governance (Sanfilippo et al. 2021, 268). This can be viewed as data subjects' involuntary contribution, which questions the legitimacy of data commons (Sanfilippo et al. 2021, 285–86). Interactions in this context are predominantly transactional, with, for instance, consumers exchanging data for services with minimal transparency or collective decision-making regarding data practices. Such practices by data oligopolies are often driven by commercial interests rather than public benefit. The primary benefits from financial data exploitation accrue mainly to financial and fintech companies, whereas several risks and harms fall on powerless community members such as consumers. While financial data is produced by all, it is largely under private control and mainly serves to maximize the benefits of private data controllers (Fan 2021, 1444), sometimes to the detriment of data subjects (MacCarthy 2011; Houser and Bagby 2023, 115). For instance, financial companies may use collected financial data to facilitate predatory and discriminatory lending practices.

These data oligopoly practices undermine the potential for a community governance of financial data. Concentrations of power prevent community governance, as the political economy of commons suggests (Madison 2024, 323–24). The GKC framework can thus reveal both the oligopolistic tendencies of financial companies and the need to heed community members' neglected interests and voices. Otherwise, data commons governance may be deemed ineffective and illegitimate (Sanfilippo et al. 2021, 268, 283). Furthermore, financial data oligopolies can erode the attainment of outcomes (Martens 2018; Houser and Bagby 2023, 116) that data commons can favor and that community members may value. These include preventing privacy harms, cybersecurity risks, and financial exclusion and exploitation; expanding access to credit and funding; sharing profits from data commercialization; stimulating financial innovation and enabling collaborative development of solutions; enhancing financial competition and facilitating the rise of new competitors; and reducing barriers to financial data access.

The nature of financial data as a shared resource, community members' involvement in financial data production and dissemination, and the desired outcomes may call for the need to both address the financial data oligopoly problem and seek the building of effective and legitimate community governance of financial data commons. Barriers to implementation include resistance from financial companies prioritizing profit maximization and proprietary technological platforms that limit community members' participation in financial data governance. Among other things, it seems imperative to encourage the development of rules that may facilitate the effective involvement of community members in creating financial data commons.

10.2.2 *The Promise of Consumer Data Trusts*

The activism of community members may play a crucial role in developing financial data commons, challenging the dominance of data oligopolies, and implementing a community governance of financial data. Specifically, financial consumer groups, as one important community member, can actively foster a collective governance of financial data. These groups can represent consumers or evolve into consumer data trusts (e.g., Zarkadakis 2020), serving the interests of consumer data subjects. *Data trusts* can be defined as governance devices that place an independent fiduciary intermediary between companies and data subjects (Houser and Bagby 2023). They can be viewed as a form of data commons (Scassa 2020; Madison 2024, 328), wherein consumers pool their data, assert their voice as data subjects, and govern it as shared resource. In this capacity, these trusts can play a crucial role in overseeing financial data oligopolies (Delacroix and Lawrence 2019; Houser and Bagby 2023), thus revealing the polycentricity of financial data governance (Sanfilippo et al. 2021, 270). These contestation efforts can lead to the development of more legitimate new rules-in-use (Sanfilippo et al. 2021, 281).

By aggregating consumer data rights and enhancing collective bargaining power, consumer data trusts and trustees acting on behalf of consumers can negotiate more equitable terms, enforce robust privacy safeguards (Delacroix and Lawrence 2019; Blankertz 2020; Ruhaak 2021; Fisher and Streinz 2022, 835; Houser and Bagby 2023, 140, 144, 152), and ensure a fair distribution of the economic value derived from financial data. Key features of consumer data trusts may include pooled data rights, democratic governance, professional management, and stringent privacy and ethical standards. Taken together, these elements offer greater negotiating power, stricter data protections, and a platform for collaborative decision-making on data policies, including efforts to attain valuable outcomes (Houser and Bagby 2023, 174). The emergence of such trusts represents a paradigm shift in data governance, addressing the limitations of individual consent models (MacCarthy 2011; Delacroix and Lawrence 2019) and potentially rebalancing power dynamics between individual consumers and data oligopolies (Van Geuns and Brandusescu 2020; Houser and Bagby 2023, 140). This model not only tackles immediate concerns about data privacy and value distribution but also lays the groundwork for a more participatory and equitable data commons.

Consumer data trusts may be enabled by formal rules and in turn help develop and implement informal rules to pursue outcomes that consumers deem valuable, including social norms, strategies, and practices seeking to protect consumers' interests and to undo data oligopolies' rules that are not conducive to building data commons. This combination of data subjects' participation and voice with legal regulation may address the governance failures of illegitimate and socially problematic commons governance (Sanfilippo et al. 2021, 283). For instance, granting a consumer association a right to bring a representative action, utilizing consumers' right to an explanation of companies' use of data or financial algorithms or to data portability, and embracing emerging open banking laws and policies legally empower these associations to oversee data oligopolies, including preventing discriminatory or exploitative lending practices (Anidjar and Mizrahi-Borohovich 2019, 201), and help build a community governance of data commons. By consolidating the data rights of numerous consumers and enhancing their collective bargaining power, consumer data trusts can negotiate with financial companies to oversee the development and implementation of new informal and formal rules. These rules, while fostering community governance, also safeguard consumers' interests. This is particularly important as financial companies are likely to resist external oversight and accountability, for instance by opposing financial algorithm and data disclosure and audits.

Data trusts can develop *strategies* to push for more favorable terms concerning data collection, usage, monetization, and access, including privacy and transparency (Houser and Bagby 2023: 144, 160). This is consistent with the idea that consumers have some ownership over their financial data and accessing it serves to attain positively valued outcomes (Fracassi and Magnuson 2021: 330, 346; Jurcys et al. 2021). For instance, trusts can develop and promote the enforcement of ethical guidelines for the use of financial data. These guidelines may include prohibiting the use of consumer data for predatory lending practices, ensuring that data is not used to unfairly discriminate in financial decision-making, and requiring transparency about the extent to which consumer data influences investment recommendations. Similarly, data trusts could promote data portability and interoperability standards. Trusts could advocate for standards that make it easier for consumers to transfer their data between different platforms. This could involve requiring financial companies to provide data in standardized, machine-readable formats, ensuring that consumers can easily move their financial data to competing platforms. Additionally, trusts could promote the development of open application programming interfaces (APIs) that foster greater competition within the financial technology sector. These standards could reduce the lock-in effects that help entrench data oligopolies. All these strategies by data trusts can help ensure that powerful financial companies and their financial technology also operate in the best interests of consumers and smaller companies.

Furthermore, consumer data trusts may provide *oversight* of financial companies, and in particular their financial technologies and data. Financial companies rely heavily on complex algorithms to analyze data and make decisions. Data trusts could demand transparency of how algorithms use consumer data, review them for potential biases or unfair practices, and require human oversight for certain types of algorithmic decisions. This oversight can help prevent algorithmic bias and discrimination (Shkabatur 2019, 383), ensure fair treatment of consumers, and exemplify the power of data trusts to "reveal 'black box' algorithms that leading technology firms use to concentrate their power and perpetuate injustices" (Houser and Bagby 2023, 118). Consumer data trusts could also conduct regular audits of financial and fintech companies' access and use of consumer financial data (Blankertz 2020; Houser and Bagby 2023, 179). These audits may involve reviewing data sharing agreements between financial companies and data users, analyzing data flows to ensure they comply with agreed-upon terms, and verifying that data access is limited to authorized purposes (Blankertz 2020, 16–17). By performing these audits, trusts can help ensure that financial data oligopolies are not overstepping bounds or misusing consumer data. Furthermore, consumer data trusts can set and enforce stricter privacy and security standards than individual consumers or regulators might be able to achieve. This could mean mandating specific encryption and data protection protocols, requiring regular third-party security audits and imposing penalties for data breaches or unauthorized access. The trust's ability to terminate agreements with companies and withhold access to member data gives it leverage to enforce these standards (Blankertz 2020, 17).

In terms of value distribution and compensation, consumer data trusts could negotiate for more equitable sharing of profits generated from consumer financial data (Mulgan and Straub 2019; Houser and Bagby 2023, 175). They could, for instance, require financial and fintech companies to share a portion of revenues derived from consumer data analysis, negotiate reduced fees or improved services for trust members, and ensure that insights from aggregated data are made available to consumers. This approach ensures that consumers receive a fairer share of the benefits generated by their data, rather than allowing large financial institutions to monopolize those gains. This aligns with the growth of data marketplace organizations that assist consumers in collecting and selling their data (Blankertz 2020, 11).

Moreover, consumer data trusts can establish mechanisms for resolving disputes related to data use and for sanctioning violations (Houser and Bagby 2023, 179). For financial companies, this might involve creating independent arbitration panels to handle complaints, establishing escalating penalties for repeated violations of agreed-upon terms, and providing consumers with the ability to challenge decisions made using their data. These processes offer consumers recourse if they believe their data has been misused.

While the implementation of such strategies and practices will likely face challenges, including resistance from financial companies and technical complexities, they offer a promising path forward. By *empowering consumers* collectively, consumer data trusts could provide a much-needed counterbalance to the growing power of financial data oligopolies, promoting fairer, more transparent, and more equitable use of consumer financial data. This can help build an effective community governance of financial data that could achieve important social goods such as privacy, quality, security, and innovation while enhancing competition. Collaborative data governance may spur innovation, improve access to financial services, and facilitate the emergence of new market players. Achieving these benefits, however, requires the cooperation of financial companies, regulators, and consumers to address challenges effectively.

Despite their potential, consumer data trusts face practical obstacles, such as achieving the necessary scale, developing effective engagement and internal governance among consumer members, having sustainable funding models, accessing appropriate technologies to manage shared consumer data, protecting against security risks associated with centralizing data within trusts, and navigating technical and regulatory landscapes. In particular, the legal status of consumer data trusts remains uncertain, and trusts' above-mentioned strategies and practices are likely to require facilitative laws and policies. Nonetheless, consumer data trusts offer a promising avenue for experimenting with participatory and equitable data governance models. Ultimately, consumer data trusts should be viewed as part of a broader data governance ecosystem. Data commons are part of polycentric data governance systems or multiple different governance centers (Sanfilippo et al. 2021, 270; Madison 2024, 325). Consumer data trusts' effectiveness could be enhanced when combined with community members' cooperative practices, thoughtful regulation, technical standards, and efforts to improve data literacy. As financial companies expand their data practices, novel governance approaches like data trusts will be crucial. Further research and pilot projects are necessary to refine these models and assess their long-term impact.

10.3 BLACKROCK AND ALADDIN: A CASE STUDY

There are two things that make *data-opoly* (Fisher 2021; Stucke 2022) possible under BlackRock: motive and capability. In the new digital age of finance, BlackRock must remain proactive in beating competitors to not suffer the same fate as other big players, such as Eastman Kodak or Blockbuster (Baxter et al. 2023). New financial technology used by the likes of Robinhood Markets Inc. can be a threat to BlackRock, as fintech makes investment more accessible to a more diverse population of investors.[2] According to Ananth Madhavan, the Global Head Research for ETFs and Index Investing at BlackRock, the best way to remain competitive is by investing in artificial intelligence (AI) and data technology, whose quality output depends on the amount of data available.[3] Better information output regarding risk management and investment will ensure the security of investors and the continuance of business. Better service also attracts more clients, who aid in further advancing BlackRock in the financial industry. Hence the key to survival and success is data collection – and this makes data-opoly a very attractive goal for BlackRock to achieve.

Not only is data-opoly desirable, but it is also achievable for BlackRock. Thanks to Aladdin, BlackRock has become the default option in the financial marketplace. According to BlackRock, "approximately 55,000 investment professionals around the world" from almost all industries rely on the Aladdin platform.[4] These investors include Google, Apple, Facebook, and Amazon (otherwise known as GAFA) – whose dominance over the information market is undeniable (Chakravortl 2021) – they all depend on BlackRock to manage their investment portfolios.[5] Furthermore, BlackRock is a major shareholder in 18,000 companies, banks, and financial services firms around the world.[6] As one executive of a large European insurer commented: "if you are looking to buy anything, or sell anything, or invest anything, it's very difficult to get around BlackRock."[7] Therefore, BlackRock can clearly use its position to gain virtually unlimited access to data – including to the databases of other dominant players in the data market – and to generate and exploit network effects to achieve data-opoly. At BlackRock's AI Labs, leading researchers, data scientists, and engineers are preparing for the processing and analysis of the ever-growing data the company is planning to accumulate.[8] This strategy may enable BlackRock to become the ultimate data-opoly. The next section elaborates on the direct and indirect methods BlackRock employs to collect different kinds of big data.

2 "The Four Biggest Ways That Robinhood Changed Investing," *Bloomberg Businessweek*, July 29, 2021.
3 "MIT AI Conference 2018: Staying Competitive in the World of AI in Finance." May 15, 2019. www.youtube.com/watch?v=0583lIm428A at 0'50"-2'06" and 10'50"-12':42".
4 www.blackrock.com/aladdin/offerings/aladdin-overview.
5 "BlackRock's Black Box: The Technology Hub of Modern Finance," *Financial Times*, February 23, 2023; "In Aladdin We Trust." *Queens Business Review*, September 18, 2023.
6 BlackRock, *Investor Stewardship Annual Report* 2023. www.blackrock.com/corporate/literature/publication/annual-stewardship-report-2023-summary.pdf.
7 "Aladdin and the Genius that is Larry Fink", *Cognitive Finance*, October 2020. www.cognitivefinance.ai/single-post/aladdin-and-the-genius-that-is-larry-fink.
8 www.blackrock.com/corporate/ai.

10.3.1 *BlackRock's Data Collection Capabilities*

BlackRock can acquire data through its massive client base via its Aladdin platform without needing countless permissions from clients to hand over various forms of data (Zetzsche et al. 2023). The ease of such data retrieval supports BlackRock's AI and machine learning technologies. Machine learning is an inductive approach to computing, in which AI systems analyze data to find the best solution to a problem, as opposed to following strict instructions coded by the programmers beforehand (Armour and Eidnmuller 2020). Machine learning is possible if the AI systems can act as a central nervous system and form a neural network with other information technologies and computers to communicate and deliver data between densely interconnected processing nodes, where the data is analyzed and an output created. In order for AI to work effectively, it must have access to as much relevant and accurate information as it can from one centralized database. Since any type of data may have the potential to be relevant in the long run, AI is designed to not be restrictive in data collection.

Similarly, Aladdin is designed to store, centralize, and convert various unstructured data – data mined from numerous sources – into readable data that is easier to analyze and utilize to make effective decisions concerning portfolios, risks, trades, operations, performance, compliance, and accounting management. In other words, it is the central nervous system that is equipped with the ability to connect with other data technologies and extract as much information from them as possible. BlackRock simply needs to obtain permission to initiate data collection from clients' information databases via the terms and conditions clients must consent to when signing up to use Aladdin. The terms include conforming to Aladdin's privacy policy, which covers the collection of personal information, including identification data, contact data, electronic monitoring data, financial data, and even sensitive personal information data (information regarding dietary restrictions, sexual orientation, disabilities, and political affiliation, among other things, taken from public sources such as social media or other third parties such as credit card providers). GAFA privacy notices confirm this by stating that third parties are able to gain access to their users' personal information collected by them; this is part of their own terms and conditions. Hence, the sharing of data between BlackRock and GAFA is inevitable because upon agreeing to Aladdin's privacy policies, users also consent to the sharing of their GAFA information with BlackRock. Users who consent to data sharing when using GAFA services may unknowingly authorize these companies to provide data to third parties, potentially including BlackRock when GAFA companies engage it for institutional investment services or analytics. GAFA companies themselves are clients of Aladdin, subjecting them to the same data-collecting terms and conditions as other clients, thus providing BlackRock access to even more data (Steele 2020, 23).

In addition, the upgrade to Aladdin Data Cloud – an investment platform developed in partnership with SnowFlake – further exacerbates BlackRock's collection capability by enabling Aladdin to "host all of the [clients'] data – from both inside and outside Aladdin."[9] This feature is heavily supported by clients who tend to pull "their own data sources from other places" to centralize their data for convenience and to maximize their use of the platform.[10] As clients of BlackRock, it is plausible that GAFA provides BlackRock with additional data not initially collected by Aladdin at registration in order to receive better results. When combined with the sheer volume of public market data – global economic data stock quotes, climate data, government decisions, alternative data like geolocation and consumer activity – it is clear that the data BlackRock has access to make investment decisions far exceeds the type of data outlined in Aladdin's privacy policy. While this can benefit clients, who now have all their information in one place, by enabling them to make more accurate and successful investment decisions, it is also very profitable for BlackRock, which effectively now has all of GAFA's information in one system.

Thanks to its partnership with Snowflake, the system can now integrate external data into its platform by using Snowflake's data technology, which can process unstructured and raw data at a rapid speed, converting that raw data into structured data that can be integrated and read by Aladdin.[11] As part of the agreement, BlackRock has access to Snowflake's Data Cloud, which can be used in Aladdin's analysis. This is not the first partnership BlackRock entered into with a view to improving Aladdin Data Cloud. In 2020, BlackRock and Microsoft formed a strategic partnership to host Aladdin on Microsoft's Azure cloud platform, providing BlackRock with access to Microsoft's data centers around the world.[12] BlackRock was also able to leverage Microsoft's scale in computing and expertise in cloud computing and data analytics, as part of the collaboration. While the partnership did not give BlackRrock access to other Azure users' data, BlackRrock can use Microsoft's computers to collect new data globally. Aladdin's main cloud partner, Amazon's AWS, provides another access point into Amazon's database, including users' purchasing behavior and other data provided by Amazon's Internet of Things devices.[13] Being the top e-commerce company in the world that is also advancing into many lines of business, Amazon is providing BlackRock access to a plethora of information (Khan 2017, 754–767).

9 www.blackrock.com/aladdin/products/aladdin-data-cloud.

10 "Snowflake Inc. (SNOW) Q4 2020 Earnings Call Transcript." March 2021. www.fool.com/earnings/call-transcripts/2021/03/04/snowflake-inc-snow-q4-2020-earnings-call-transcrip/

11 www.snowflake.com/blog/blackrock-and-snowflake-partner-to-unlock-the-value-of-data-for-the-investment-management-industry/?utm_source=blackrock&utm_medium=referral&utm_campaign=powered-by-snowflake-blackrock.

12 "https://news.microsoft.com/2020/04/07/blackrock-and-microsoft-form-strategic-partnership-to-host-aladdin-on-azure-as-blackrock-readies-aladdin-for-next-chapter-of-innovation/.

13 https://aws.amazon.com/what-is-aws/.

Aladdin can acquire even more data from portfolio companies through BlackRock's investments. This starts even before the purchase of any shares, when BlackRock is given access to prospective companies' information, which may include all types of information that can be used to assess the opportunities and risks of investing in those companies.[14] When applied to GAFA, this can include any type of users' information. As the head of the product group for Aladdin, Jody Kochansky noted almost a decade ago, given that untapped data – such as GPS locations, customers' online behavior, and transaction histories – is tremendously valuable for quality investment analysis, the strategy is to access as much untapped data as possible.[15] BlackRock's Aladdin can thus collect increasing amounts of data from all the four platforms before and after investing in them.

While BlackRock has utilized its Aladdin platform to collect data directly from GAFA in new and unconventional ways in order to optimize its AI technology and big data collection capacities, it also employs an indirect method of data collection: the exploitation of shareholder power to control corporate decisions and push for joint ventures, which ultimately aid its direct data collection. BlackRock's investments across vast segments of the market – it is among a small group of institutional investors that own large stakes in most US corporations (Azar et al 2018; Backus et al 2021) – allow it to influence the way companies manage their data. Aladdin's success has largely expanded BlackRock's client base, which has increased the capital at its disposal, and enables it to invest massively in GAFA shares: BlackRock is one of the largest institutional shareholders in Google, Amazon, Facebook (Meta), and Apple.[16] This position means that its voting power and voice in corporate decisions is significant. For example, Larry Fink convinced Mark Zuckerberg to change Facebook's platform design to be more "purpose-driven," namely, to focus more on promoting posts from friends than from advertisers (Serafeim 2018). This was a costly move for Facebook, whose main revenue relies on its advertising model.

10.3.2 *Caveats*

The considerations in the previous section provide insights into the technical, legal, and managerial rules-in-use that underpin BlackRock's unparalleled data collection capabilities. The difficulty in collecting evidence is compounded by the fact that the precise data management procedures employed by BlackRock and GAFA are kept under seal, thanks to intellectual property law, trade secrets, out of court settlements, not to mention the considerable complexity of the software (Pasquale 2015, 67,

[14] "BlackRock's Black Box: The Technology Hub of Modern Finance," *Financial Times*, February 24, 2020.

[15] "Blackrock Is Making Big Data Bigger." *Institutional Investor*, November 1, 2016.

[16] See www.nasdaq.com/market-activity/stocks/goog/institutional-holdings; www.nasdaq.com/market-activity/stocks/amzn/institutional-holdings; www.nasdaq.com/market-activity/stocks/meta/institutional-holdings; www.nasdaq.com/market-activity/stocks/aapl/institutional-holdings.

103).[17] The public cannot investigate the contractual terms of joint ventures, nor can they criticize how the companies' algorithm collect and analyze data, even if companies provide public disclosure in "plain language" to comply with consumer protection law (Pasquale 2015, 7–8, 51, 103). Even internal stakeholders, who may be aware of BlackRock's business practices, and thus are great sources of information, are unable to share their observations with the public due to their contractual obligations to BlackRock. For example, BlackRock required departing employees to sign separation agreements to receive severance payments that included provisions waiving rights to whistleblower compensation for disclosing wrongdoings. This discourages whistleblowers, as it waives any right to recovery of incentives for reporting of misconduct.[18] Even though the Securities and Exchange Commission successfully removed this particular clause in a 2017 lawsuit against BlackRock, the terms of the agreement suggested that BlackRock may have been conducting acts that it wanted to stay behind closed doors, and there certainly is no guarantee that it will stop trying to prevent whistleblowers from speaking out in the future. Hence, the opacity surrounding the operations of powerful companies such as BlackRock, and its attempts to maintain a black box, makes it almost impossible to gather empirical evidence to prove BlackRock's strategy of creating a data monopoly. Aladdin's lack of transparency highlights the need for public accountability and raises concerns about potential risks and harmful impacts on stakeholders, including financial consumers.

10.4 BLACKROCK'S ALADDIN AND FINANCIAL CONSUMERS

Financial data oligopolies like BlackRock's Aladdin have emerged as dominant players in the financial market infrastructure, controlling critical data flows and analytical tools used by a vast number of investors. These platforms offer powerful solutions for risk management and investment decision-making, but their centralized nature also creates significant risks. These include the concentration of financial data and analytics in a few hands and the spread and reinforcement of similar data management models, potentially exacerbating herd behavior and amplifying market volatility in times of stress. Aladdin's global adoption across major financial institutions thus poses a systemic risk, as the investors who rely on the same financial risk management system can make and propagate the same mistakes (Zook and Spangler 2023, 119). Similarly, the dominance of these platforms raises concerns about overreliance on centralized models, the potential for overlooking idiosyncratic risks, and the creation of feedback loops that could destabilize markets. For creditors, the concentration of risk assessment tools in a few platforms may lead to

[17] "CNPD vs. Amazon, the largest GDPR fine on record – what do we know so far?" August 13, 2021. www.passwordprotectedlaw.com/2021/08/amazon-largest-gdpr-fine/.

[18] "BlackRock Charged with Removing Whistleblower Incentives in Separation Agreements." US Securities and Exchange Commission, Press Release, January 17, 2017. www.sec.gov/news/pressrelease/2017-14.html.

blind spots in credit evaluation and coordinated tightening of lending conditions. Additionally, the role of data oligopolies in complex financial instruments like securitized assets echoes concerns from past financial crises. While these platforms offer undeniable benefits, their growing influence necessitates careful consideration of the potential risks to market stability, diversity of investment strategies, and overall financial system resilience.

10.4.1 *Potential Harms to Financial Consumers*

One of the most important concerns with financial data oligopolies like BlackRock's Aladdin is their potential impact on financial consumers – ordinary individuals who use financial services, invest their savings, or rely on credit. These retail consumers often have little awareness of the extent to which their financial well-being is affected by the operations of powerful data platforms behind the scenes. The first obvious concern relates to data privacy and surveillance. Aladdin appears to collect vast amounts of data about consumer activity to identify patterns and trends in consumer consumption.[19] Aladdin must continue to scale not just the amount of data but also the types of data it collects and analyzes to maintain its competitive advantage (Zetzsche et al. 2020).[20] The more BlackRock collects nonfinancial data, such as GPS locations and online behavior, the greater the risk to consumers that their information is being misused, for commercial purposes or other harmful objectives. The massive centralization of data within a small number of platforms also makes them lucrative targets for cyberattacks or any other form of data breach, potentially exposing consumers to identity theft or financial fraud. Any failures of Aladdin can cause severe harm to consumers (Fraser 2022).

Furthermore, pervasive data surveillance enabled by financial platforms could lead to discriminatory practices. For instance, financial companies may use insights from these platforms to engage in "digital redlining," where certain consumers or even smaller companies are excluded from financial services based on data-driven risk assessments (Friedline and Chen 2021). Digital redlining occurs when lenders use algorithmic models based on data analytics to exclude specific groups of consumers from financial products, often based on factors like zip codes, income levels, race, or even social media activity. While such practices may not be explicitly illegal, they can result in discriminatory outcomes that disproportionately affect minority or low-income communities. Platforms like Aladdin, which consolidate vast amounts of consumer data and apply sophisticated algorithms, could inadvertently reinforce these biases if not carefully monitored. If data models incorporate biased assumptions or historical data that reflects past discriminatory practices, they may perpetuate exclusionary patterns in lending. This can lead to financial

[19] "When Aladdin Meets Ambani: What JV with BlackRock means for Jio Financial Services," *Economic Times*, July 28, 2023.

[20] "Blackrock Is Making Big Data Bigger," *Institutional Investor*, November 1, 2016.

exclusion and exploitation, as marginalized groups are either denied access to fair financial products or steered toward higher-cost, riskier alternatives. Over time, this exacerbates the wealth gap and deepens systemic financial inequalities.

Moreover, there is the risk that financial data oligopolies may facilitate financial exploitation of consumers (Das 2016, 27; Reynolds 2017, 18–21), including predatory lending (US Senate 2018, 51; US Congress 2019, 2). Abusive loan terms can be imposed on borrowers, often targeting vulnerable individuals such as low-income consumers, those with poor credit histories, or minority communities. Financial data platforms like BlackRock's Aladdin, which aggregate vast amounts of consumer financial data, may indirectly contribute to such exploitative practices, if their insights are misused or if the centralization of data leads to greater disparities in how consumers are treated by financial institutions. Financial data oligopolies may enable the exploitation of consumer data by identifying financially vulnerable individuals (US Congress 2019, 16–17). With access to granular data on consumers' spending patterns, credit history, income, and even social behaviors, financial companies using platforms like Aladdin can build detailed profiles of potential borrowers. While this data can be used to assess creditworthiness and manage risk, it can also be used to target consumers with exploitative loan products. For example, lenders might use data insights to offer high-interest payday loans or subprime mortgages to individuals who are unlikely to qualify for traditional credit and can least afford such predatory products, but must accept them due to lack of alternatives.

Companies using platforms like Aladdin may develop highly optimized pricing strategies based on consumer data, allowing them to extract maximum profit from specific segments of the population. This can lead to the proliferation of high-fee financial products such as payday loans, subprime credit cards, or predatory auto loans, which impose significant costs on consumers, including hidden costs. Financial companies may employ data-driven marketing strategies that specifically target low-income consumers with unfavorable terms, taking advantage of their limited access to competitive loan products. The use of sophisticated data analytics makes it easier for lenders to prey on financially vulnerable individuals, further exacerbating financial inequalities. Financial companies may leverage data insights to identify consumers who are less financially literate or more likely to overlook the fine print in loan agreements. These consumers may be saddled with loans that come with hidden fees, balloon payments, or punitive interest rates, making it difficult for them to repay their debts and trapping them in cycles of debt. In this way, financial data oligopolies may enable the use of data to exploit the most financially vulnerable consumers (US Congress 2019, 9, 16–17; Bartlett et al. 2022), undermining their financial well-being.

Additionally, financial data oligopolies may facilitate reduced competition and consumers' loss of autonomy and choice in the financial market (US Congress 2019, 8). Aladdin and similar platforms wield enormous influence over how financial companies evaluate risk and allocate capital. This concentration of power can lead to reduced competition in the financial services industry, as smaller firms struggle to compete with the data analytics capabilities of larger companies using Aladdin. Consumers may have fewer choices when it comes to where they invest or borrow, as market concentration reduces the number of available financial products tailored to their needs.

The centralization of financial data also risks creating pricing and access disparities for financial consumers (US Senate 2018, 51; Bartlett et al. 2022). Large financial companies using Aladdin's platform benefit from economies of scale and superior data analytics, allowing them to optimize their operations and pricing strategies. Smaller financial companies without access to such powerful tools may struggle to compete, leading to higher costs for consumers in certain sectors. This can create a financial landscape where large, well-capitalized companies offer better rates or products, while smaller players may charge more for less competitive services. Wealthier consumers who are more likely to engage with larger companies may enjoy better financial products, while low-income consumers or those in underserved markets may be forced to pay higher prices, leading to worsen financial inequalities (Bartlett et al. 2022, 55–56).

To illustrate how financial data platforms like BlackRock's Aladdin can undermine the position of financial consumers as a community member, erode the community governance of financial data commons, and hinder the attainment of outcomes that community members may value, consider Jio BlackRock, a 50:50 joint venture that combines BlackRock's expertise with data provided by Jio Financial Services (JFS). While this partnership aims to deliver tech-enabled access to investment solutions for millions of investors in India (BlackRock 2023), it will also harness vast amounts of data to assist JFS in expanding its lending business to consumers.[21] Yet, this effort to democratize financial services may pose risks. Reliance Jio, India's telecom giant and the parent company of JFS, has an extensive digital footprint in India, managing data from telecom, retail, and digital services. Integrating this data with financial data and insights from BlackRock's Aladdin creates immense potential for personalized services, but also raises significant concerns about privacy, data sharing, and profiling. As JFS plans to use advanced data analytics as a basis for consumer lending, leveraging information from credit bureaus, account aggregators, and consumer patterns,[22] this comprehensive data ecosystem may help develop detailed consumer profiling and surveillance, which can lead to concerns about targeted advertising, overreach, and misuse. These partnerships could exploit combined consumer data to push high-risk financial products, create opaque credit-scoring mechanisms, implement price discrimination, or engage in other unfair practices that can harm consumers' interests (Pandit

[21] "BlackRock and Jio Financial Services Agree to Form Joint Venture to Enter India's Asset Management Industry." BlackRock, Press release, July 26, 2023; "The BlackRock and Jio Financial Services Mutual Fund Joint Venture: All You Need to Know." *Economic Times*, October 18, 2024.

[22] When Aladdin Meets Ambani: What JV with BlackRock means for Jio Financial Services." *Economic Times*, July 28, 2023.

and Javed 2021, 215–216). Moreover, the reliance on technology and data-driven models may unintentionally exclude populations with limited digital literacy or access to reliable internet.

For example, in rural areas where smartphone penetration remains low, the digital-first approach of the joint venture could marginalize less tech-savvy consumers. Furthermore, data-driven credit scoring could lead to biased assessments. For instance, individuals lacking substantial digital footprints or with limited formal financial histories might face higher interest rates or outright rejection of financial products. This perpetuates existing inequities rather than addressing them. The BlackRock-JFS venture combines extensive consumer data with AI for decision-making. If not carefully designed, these systems may encode biases, leading to discriminatory practices. Algorithms might prioritize customers in urban centers or specific socioeconomic brackets, creating systemic inequalities. There is also the risk of unfair terms and predatory practices. The competitive advantages of BlackRock's financial expertise and Jio's expansive consumer base could pressure smaller financial institutions, potentially reducing competition. A monopolistic or oligopolistic environment might allow JFS to dictate unfavorable terms to consumers, such as high fees or restrictive product conditions. The partnership's promise of "low-cost" financial products could also obscure hidden costs or cross-selling practices that burden consumers.

The history of numerous consumer complaints against the Reliance Jio group suggests that concerns about potential unfair practices facilitated by BlackRock's Aladdin platform in partnership with JFS may have merit. For instance, there have been documented cases of service deficiencies, such as slow internet speeds and connectivity issues, excessive charges, price hikes, delayed refunding, and poor service to rural consumers, which have led to consumer dissatisfaction and legal complaints against Reliance group.[23] These instances highlight a possible pattern of unfair practices harming consumers' interests that could extend into the financial services domain if not addressed. While the regulatory framework in Western countries is stronger than in India, the likelihood of unfair practices that harm financial consumers is nonetheless real.

10.4.2 *Consumer Data Trusts and the Building of Data Commons*

As we have seen, financial consumers, as stakeholders in the governance of financial data commons, have the potential to play a pivotal role in overseeing financial data oligopolies and contributing to the development of the community governance of financial data commons. This engagement can represent a shift toward more participatory models of data governance, aligning with emerging concepts of data

[23] "Flipkart #1 in Consumer Complaints Followed by Jio, Amazon; Ecommerce #1 in Complaints!?" Trak.in, November 18, 2019; "Delay in Refunding 3,536 Costs Telecom Firm 15,000," *Times of India*, February 12, 2024.

stewardship and digital citizenship and departing from disclosure–individual consent models. Specifically, consumer associations can evolve into more formalized entities, such as consumer data trusts (Delacroix and Lawrence 2019; Blankertz 2020), which may act as intermediaries aggregating and representing consumer interests vis-à-vis data oligopolies. These trusts can leverage technical and legal expertise, as well as enhanced bargaining power, to oversee financial data oligopolies, including negotiating more favorable terms of data use on behalf of consumers. This approach addresses the power imbalance between individual consumers and financial companies.

The potential of consumer data trusts in *commonizing* and governing financial data, and holding financial data oligopolies to account, is exemplified by a recent court decision that underscores the growing recognition of collective consumer rights and the legal standing of entities representing these collective interests. The decision in *Meta v Federation of German Consumer Associations* (2024)[24] illustrates the role that consumer associations can play in overseeing companies, including data oligopolies and their financial technologies. The ruling clarified the legal standing of entities that may bring a complaint for data privacy breaches, and established that authorized entities, such as consumer associations, can bring representative actions on behalf of data subjects when their rights are infringed during data processing. In reaching this conclusion, the court interpreted Article 80(2) of the GDPR and broadened the scope of representative actions.

The ruling enabled consumer associations to challenge not only data breaches but also the inadequate provision of information, expanding the oversight that such entities can exercise. This gives consumer associations the ability to play a proactive role in shaping data practices, rather than merely reacting to data breaches. Moreover, by establishing clearer standards for transparency in data processing, this case sets a benchmark for the quality and accessibility of information that companies must provide to consumers. The decision reaffirmed Meta's obligation to provide clear, concise, and easily accessible information about the purposes of data processing and the recipients of the data. The case also carries significant cross-border implications. Although it involves a German consumer association challenging a global company like Meta, the case highlights how consumer associations or similar entities can operate across borders to protect consumer rights in a globalized digital economy. By lowering barriers for individuals, the ruling makes it easier for consumers to have their rights protected through consumer associations' representative action without needing to bring complex legal challenges themselves.

This decision of the European court provides some basis to suggest that representation may allow for the gradual creation of data trusts (Ruhaak 2020, 17). Consumer associations such as the German one can potentially act similarly to a consumer data

24 Meta Platforms Ireland Ltd v Bundesverband der Verbraucherzentralen und Verbraucherverbände – Verbraucherzentrale Bundesverband eV (Case C-757/22).

trust by aggregating the interests of individual consumers to bring a representative action against giant tech companies, such as Meta. While the existing legal framework, including Article 80 of the GDPR and this court decision, needs to be expanded to clearly permit data trusts (Ruhaak 2020, 17; Blankertz 2020, 26; Iwan-Sojka 2024; Ruhaak 2020, 17), these formal rules may provide some initial legal basis for empowering consumer associations to act as data trusts with a view to holding tech giants accountable. Collective action by consumer associations to oversee financial companies, including data oligopolies, may help address the information and power asymmetries between consumers and tech companies. The court's decision does not go far enough in detailing or legalizing consumer associations' powers and oversight role, but it may enable such associations to develop strategies or practices, or informal rules, aiming at supervising financial companies and their financial technologies, including eventually BlackRock's Aladdin.

Formal rules grounded in the court's decision empower consumer associations acting like consumer data trusts to contribute to building a community governance of financial data, overcoming barriers to data commons created by data oligopolies. Consumer associations or consumer data trusts can, for instance, help curb data oligopolies' self-serving rules, such as partnerships with tech companies and data-related liability exclusion agreements. Ultimately, consumer associations can rebalance power dynamics, enhance transparency, and protect consumers' interests. These associations or trusts can go far in promoting the development of formal and informal rules that favor the attainment of important social goods – such as preventing financial exclusion, exploitation, surveillance and privacy invasion – that the governing community values. Recent developments in open banking laws and policies, which grant financial consumers greater legal powers (rights to access, transparency, data portability, switching, and protection against the misuse of their data), expand the formal rules governing financial data. These advancements reinforce consumers' potential to engage in the community governance of financial data commons and further empower consumer associations or consumer data trusts to hold data oligopolies accountable.

It will be important to explore the feasibility and effectiveness of this potential of consumer associations acting as data trusts. It will be critical to think about internal governance structures and trustees' duties, and other facilitative formal and informal rules-in-use. Addressing questions pertaining to the use of technology to manage shared consumer data and implement their oversight practices (e.g., enforcement technologies) will be crucial, especially in the fact of data oligopolies' opposing strategies and control over data infrastructures.

10.5 CONCLUSION

This research has examined the growing trend of financial companies leveraging fintech to monopolize financial data, and its implications for the concept of financial data as a shared resource. Relying on the lens of the GKC framework, the chapter explored how this trend prevents the community governance of financial data, excludes important stakeholders, and disproportionately benefits a select few. The case study of BlackRock's Aladdin platform illustrated the potential for massive financial data collection that leads to the formation of data oligopolies. This example underscores the risks of financial exclusion, exploitation, and worsening wealth concentration that can result from such concentrated control over financial data.

The analysis also revealed a promising counterforce to this trend: consumer associations acting as data trusts. These entities have the potential to play a crucial role in overseeing financial data oligopolies while fostering the development of community-governed data commons. The recent European court decision allowing a German consumer association to bring a representative action against Meta-Facebook demonstrates the growing legal recognition of this potential. Furthermore, the emergence of open banking laws and policies provides additional tools for consumer empowerment, reinforcing the capacity for consumer-led activism in shaping financial data governance. The transformative potential of consumer-led activism suggests a paradigm shift away from individual consent models toward a more collective, community-oriented approach to data governance. Looking forward, further research is needed to explore the practical implementation of consumer associations as data trusts, including the development of appropriate legal frameworks, technological infrastructures, and governance models. Additionally, investigating the potential synergies between open banking initiatives and consumer data trusts could yield valuable insights for policymakers and practitioners alike.

REFERENCES

Anidjar, Leon Y., and Inbar Mizrahi-Borohovich. 2019. "Reinventing Credit Data Sharing Regulation." *Southern California Interdisciplinary Law Journal* 29(2): 177–225.

Armour, John, and Horst Eidenmuller. 2020. "Self-Driving Corporations?" *Harvard Business Law Review* 10(1): 87–116.

Azar, José, Martin C. Schmalz, and Isabel Tecu. 2018. "Anti-Competitive Effects of Common Ownership." *Journal of Finance* 73(4): 1513–1565.

Backus, Matthew, Christopher Conlon, and Michael Sinkinson. "Common Ownership in America: 1980–2017." *American Economic Journal: Microeconomics* 13(3): 273–308.

Bartlett, Robert, Adair Morse, Richard Stanton, and Nancy Wallace. 2022. "Consumer-Lending Discrimination in the FinTech Era." *Journal of Financial Economics* 143(1): 30–56.

Baxter, David, Paul Trott, and Paul Ellwood. 2023. "Reconceptualising Innovation Failure." *Research Policy* 52(7): 104811.

Blankertz, Aline. 2020. *Designing Data Trusts: Why We Need to Test Consumer Data Trusts Now.* Stiftung Neue Verantwortung. www.interface-eu.org/storage/archive/files/designing_data_trusts_e.pdf.

Chakravortl, Bhaskar. 2021. "Big Tech's Stranglehold on Artificial Intelligence Must Be Regulated." *Foreign Policy*, August 11, 2021. https://foreignpolicy.com/2021/08/11/artificial-intelligence-big-tech-regulation-monopoly-antitrust-google-apple-amazon-facebook/

Crawford, Sue E., and Elinor Ostrom. 1995. "A Grammar of Institutions." *American Political Science Review* 89(3): 582–600.

Das, Sanjiv Ranjan. 2016. "Big Data's Big Muscle." *Finance & Development* 53(3): 26–28.

Delacroix, Sylvie, and Neil D. Lawrence. 2019. "Bottom-Up Data Trusts: Disturbing the 'One Size Fits All' Approach to Data Governance." *International Data Privacy Law* 9(4): 236–252.

Fan, Mary D. 2021. "The Right to Benefit from Big Data as a Public Resource." *New York University Law Review* 96(5): 1438–1444.

Fischer, Benjamin. 2021. "The Rise of the Data-Opoly: Consumer Harm in the Digital Economy." *Washington University Law Review* 99(2): 729–750.

Fisher, Angelina, and Thomas Streinz. 2022. "Confronting Data Inequality." *Columbia Journal of Transnational Law* 60(3): 829–956.

Fracassi, Cesare, and William J. Magnuson. 2021. "Data Autonomy." *Vanderbilt Law Review* 74(2): 327–383.

Fraser, Max. 2022. "Biden and BlackRock." *New Labor Forum* 31(2): 105–108.

Friedline, Terry, and Zibei Chen. 2021. "Digital Redlining and the Fintech Marketplace: Evidence from US Zip Codes." *Journal of Consumer Affairs* 55(2): 366–388.

Frischmann, Brett M., Michael J. Madison, and Katherine J. Strandburg. 2014. "Governing Knowledge Commons." In *Governing Knowledge Commons*, ed. Brett M. Frischmann, Michael J. Madison, and Katherine J. Strandburg, 1–43. New York: Oxford University Press.

Houser, Kimberly A., and John W. Bagby. 2023. "The Data Trust Solution to Data Sharing Problems." *Vanderbilt Journal of Entertainment & Technology Law* 25(1): 113–180.

Iwan-Sojka, Dominika. 2024. "The Inclusive Data Governance Models for Algorithms – A Dream of the Already Convinced or a Realistic Way of Action?" *Information & Communications Technology Law* 34(1): 1–14.

Johnson, Garrett A., Scott K. Shriver, and Samuel G. Goldberg. 2023. "Privacy and Market Concentration: Intended and Unintended Consequences of the GDPR." *Management Science* 69(10): 5695–5721.

Jones, Charles I., and Christopher Tonetti. 2020. "Nonrivalry and Economics of Data." *American Economic Review* 110(9): 2819–2858.

Jurcys, Paulius, Christopher Donewald, Mark Fenwick, et al. 2021. "Ownership of User-Held Data: Why Property Law Is the Right Approach." *Harvard Journal of Law & Technology Digest*, September 21, 2021. https://jolt.law.harvard.edu/digest/ownership-of-user-held-data-why-property-law-is-the-right-approach

Khan, Lina M. 2017. "Amazon's Antitrust Paradox." *Yale Law Journal* 126(3): 710–805.

Lancieri, Filippo. 2022. "Narrowing Data Protection's Enforcement Gap." *Maine Law Review* 74(1): 15–72.

MacCarthy, Mark. 2011. "New Directions in Privacy: Disclosure, Unfairness, and Externalities." *I/S: A Journal of Law and Policy for the Information Society* 6: 425–456.

Madison, Michael J. 2019. "Biobanks as Knowledge Institutions." In *Global Genes, Local Concerns*, ed. Timo Minssen, Janne Rothmar Herrman, and Jens Schovsbo, 22–40. Cheltenham: Edward Elgar.

Madison, Michael J. 2014. "Commons at the Intersection of Peer Production, Citizen Science, and Big Data: Galaxy Zoo." In *Governing Knowledge Commons*, ed. Brett M. Frischmann, Michael J. Madison, and Katherine J. Strandburg, 209–254. New York: Oxford University Press.

Madison, Michael J. 2024. "Knowledge Commons Past, Present, and Future." *Lewis & Clark Law Review* 28(2): 303–331.
Martens, Bertin. 2018. "The Importance of Data Access Regimes for Artificial Intelligence and Machine Learning." JRC Digital Economy Working Paper 2018–09. https://ssrn.com/abstract=3357652.
McIntosh, Daniel. 2019. "We Need to Talk About Data: How Digital Monopolies Arise and Why They Have Power and Influence." *Journal of Technology Law and Policy* 23(2): 185–213.
Mulgan, Geoff, and Vincent Straub. 2019. "The New Ecosystem of Data Trusts." Medium, February 26, 2019. https://medium.com/@vincejstraub/the-new-ecosystem-of-data-trusts-36901fc59010.
Pandit, Urshila, and Sanah Javed. 2021. "Antitrust and Privacy Concerns: A Dilemma across Jurisdictions." *RGNUL Financial and Mercantile Law Review* 8(2): 203–246.
Pasquale, Frank. 2015. *The Black Box Society: The Secret Algorithms That Control Money and Information*. Cambridge, MA: Harvard University Press.
Purtova, Nadya, and Gijs van Maanen. 2024. "Data as an Economic Good, Data as a Commons, and Data Governance." *Law, Innovation and Technology* 16(1): 1–42.
Reynolds, Faith. 2017. *Open Banking: A Consumer Perspective*. London: Barclays.
Ruhaak, Anouk. 2020. "Data Trusts in Germany and Under the GDPR." *Algorithm Watch*, December 6, 2020. https://algorithmwatch.org/en/wp-content/uploads/2020/12/Data-trusts-in-Germany-and-under-the-GDPR-Anouk-Ruhaak-AlgorithmWatch-2020.pdf.
Ruhaak, Anouk. 2021. "How Data Trusts Can Protect Privacy." *MIT Technology Review*, February 24, 2021. www.technologyreview.com/2021/02/24/1017801/data-trust-cybersecurity-big-tech-privacy/.
Sanfilippo, Madelyn R., Brett M. Frischmann, and Katherine J. Strandburg, eds. 2021. *Governing Privacy in Knowledge Commons*. Cambridge: Cambridge University Press.
Sanfilippo, Madelyn R., Brett M. Frischmann, and Katherine J. Strandburg. 2018. "Privacy as Commons: Case Evaluation through the Governing Knowledge Commons Framework." *Journal of Information Policy* 8: 116–166.
Scassa, Teresa. 2020. "Designing Data Governance for Data Sharing: Lessons from Sidewalk Toronto." *Technology and Regulation* 2020: 44–56.
Serafeim, George. 2018. "Facebook, BlackRock, and the Case for Purpose-Driven Companies." *Harvard Business Review*, January 16, 2018. https://hbr.org/2018/01/facebook-blackrock-and-the-case-for-purpose-driven-companies.
Shkabatur, Jennifer. 2019. "The Global Commons of Data." *Stanford Technology Law Review* 22(2): 354–411.
Solove, Daniel J. 2021. "The Myth of the Privacy Paradox." *George Washington Law Review* 89(1): 1–51.
Steele, Graham. 2020. *The New Money Trust: How Large Money Managers Control Our Economy and What We Can Do About It*. American Economic Liberties Project. www.economicliberties.us/wp-content/uploads/2020/11/Working-Paper-Series-on-Corporate-Power_8_FINAL.pdf.
Stucke, Maurice E. 2022. *Breaking Away: How to Regain Control Over Our Data, Privacy and Autonomy*. New York: Oxford University Press.
US Congress, House, Committee on Financial Services, *Banking on Your Data: The Role of Big Data in Financial Services: Hearing Before the House Committee on Financial Services*. 116., 1st sess., November 21, 2019, written testimony of Lauren Saunders, Associate Director of the National Consumer Law Center, https://financialservices.house.gov/uploadedfiles/hhrg-116-ba00-wstate-saundersl-20191121.pdf.

US Senate, Committee on Banking, Housing, and Urban Affairs. *Fintech: Examining Digitization, Data, and Technology*. 115th Cong., 2nd sess., September 18, 2018. Prepared Statement of Saule T. Omarova, Professor of Law at Cornell University, www.congress.gov/115/chrg/CHRG-115shrg32753/CHRG-115shrg32753.pdf.

Van Geuns, Jochai, and Ana Brandusescu. 2020. "Shifting Power through Data Governance." Mozilla Foundation, September 16, 2020. https://foundation.mozilla.org/en/data-futures-lab/data-for-empowerment/shifting-power-through-data-governance/.

Zarkadakis, George. 2020. "Data Trusts Could Be the Key to Better AI." *Harvard Business Review*, November 10, 2020. https://hbr.org/2020/11/data-trusts-could-be-the-key-to-better-ai.

Zetzsche, Dirk A., William A. Birdthisle, Douglas W. Arner, and Ross P. Buckley. 2020. "Digital Finance Platforms: Toward a New Regulatory Paradigm." *University of Pennsylvania Journal of Business Law* 23(1): 273–339.

Zetzsche, Dirk A., Douglas Arner, and Ross Buckley. 2023. "Sustainability, Financial Inclusion and Efficiency: A Trilemma or a Trifecta for the Regulation of Digital Finance?" *Banking and Finance Law Review* 39(3): 445–466.

Zook, Matthew, and Ian Spangler. 2023. "A Crisis of Data? Transparency Practices and Infrastructures of Value in Data Broker Platforms." *Annals of the American Association of Geographers* 113(1): 110–128.

11

Decentralised Autonomous Organisations as Commons

Sinclair Davidson

11.1 INTRODUCTION

Decentralised autonomous organisations (DAOs) have emerged as an apparently new organisational form following the advent of blockchain technology. Blockchain technology was invented by the pseudonymous Satoshi Nakamoto to underpin an internet native money Bitcoin. At its core, blockchain operates as a distributed ledger that records transactions, across multiple computers (known as "nodes"), so as to ensure security, transparency, and immutability. Unlike traditional centralised databases, where a single entity has control, a blockchain is maintained by a network of participants who "validate" the blockchain. This decentralised structure eliminates the need for intermediaries, reduces the risk of fraud, and enhances the integrity of the data. The cryptographic principles that govern blockchain also ensure that once a transaction is recorded, it cannot be altered.

Davidson et al. (2018) argue that blockchain technology is *not* a new general-purpose technology, but rather a new institutional technology. In particular, we argue that blockchain technology will facilitate the emergence of new institutional forms and new business practices. One possible consequence of that new institutional technology is that existing hierarchical organisational forms should become less hierarchical and that we should expect to see more markets where we now see hierarchy. That insight, however, is not new. The Electronic Markets Hypothesis, that makes similar predictions, had been posited by Malone et al. (1987, 1989) and Malone and Rockart (1991) in the late 1980s and early 1990s. I have argued elsewhere, however, that DAOs are not simply manifestations of the electronic markets hypothesis (see Davidson 2025).

In Davidson (2025), I report several common features within the various definitions of DAO that I investigate. DAOs operate without a management hierarchy, underlining their decentralised nature. Their autonomy is a fundamental attribute, emphasised by the capability of DAOs to function independently based on preset rules that are typically encoded as smart contracts. The use of blockchain technology

This research was funded by an Ethereum Foundation Grant FY23-1053. I thank Henrik Axelsen, David Gindis, and Pavel Kuchař for valuable feedback on an earlier version of this chapter.

is a universal element across all definitions, as is the significant role of tokens in DAO governance structures, granting voting rights and organisational influence to their holders, thereby democratising the decision-making process.

It is important to note, however, that DAOs are more than just "labour-controlled" firms on the internet. Their emergence raises fundamental questions about corporate governance and the nature of the firm in the digital age. Traditional debates on corporate governance have focused on issues like shareholder primacy, stakeholder theory, and the separation of ownership and control (see Shleifer and Vishny 1997). DAOs challenge these paradigms by introducing a new model where governance is embedded in code, "ownership" is often widely distributed through tokens, and decision-making is decentralised. This connects to broader discussions about whether corporations should be viewed and governed as commons (Deakin 2012). Just as Elinor Ostrom (1990) showed how communities can effectively manage shared resources without relying on markets or state control, DAOs represent an attempt to manage shared digital resources and decision-making through community governance rather than traditional corporate hierarchies and shareholder primacy.

Davidson et al. (2018, 654) define DAOs as follows:

> A [DAO] is a self-governing organisation with the coordination properties of a market, the governance properties of a commons and the constitutional, legal and monetary properties of a nation state. It is an organisation, but it is not hierarchical. It has the coordination properties of a market through the token systems that coordinate distributed action, but it is not a market because the predominant activity is production, not exchange.

Under this definition, DAOs are a combination of several existing organisational forms that are well known and used to pursue collective action in various domains. What is not clear, however, is whether DAOs as a novel organisational form are viable. The very first DAO, "The DAO," collapsed in 2016 as a result of being hacked following a coding vulnerability. Blockchain technology, at the time of writing, is less than fifteen years old and DAOs as an organisational form are (much) less than ten years old. There is a very real possibility that DAOs – as envisaged – may not be viable or may have a small number of very specific use cases. To be fair, however, similar conclusions could have been drawn about the long-term viability of the joint-stock company after it first emerged (see Baskin and Miranti 1997). Williamson himself was initially sceptical about the importance and value of hybrid forms of organisation, such as joint venture, franchising, and the like (Ménard 2022).

In this chapter, I investigate the idea that DAOs are best understood as being *commons* as opposed to being "firms," as generally understood by economists (Coase 1937; Alchian and Demsetz 1972; Williamson 1975, 1985). Ostrom, the 2009 economics Nobel laureate (joint with Oliver Williamson), has developed a body of knowledge (both theoretical and empirical) that identifies when commons (i.e. communal governance over common pool resources) will fail or succeed (see Ostrom 1990, 2003, 2005, 2010). This difference can be best explained as being the difference between "community" governance and "private" governance. Community governance is based on collective decision-making and sustainable resource management by a community, whereas private governance prioritises individual or corporate interests and profit maximisation in resource control (see Dekker and Kuchař 2023).

Building on Ostrom's Institutional Analysis and Development (IAD) framework, as modified in Frischmann et al.'s (2014) Governing Knowledge Commons (GKC) framework, the chapter explores the internal dynamics of DAOs and their interaction with external variables, aiming to understand their potential to function effectively as commons. The chapter differentiates between *on-chain* and *off-chain* governance models within DAOs, discussing the advantages and challenges of each approach in promoting decentralisation and resolving conflicts. I also assess the viability of DAOs as robust institutions using Ostrom's design principles. Specific attention is given to unique "exit" mechanisms (Hirschman 1970), including forking and "rage-quitting," understood as innovative solutions to governance challenges within DAOs. The overall finding of the analysis is that DAOs are well understood as being commons and they should be treated as such by researchers. But are DAOs are "just" commons?

11.2 ARE DAOS "JUST" COMMONS?

Ostrom (2005, 79) defined a common-pool resource as follows: "A common-pool resource, such as a lake, an ocean, an irrigation system, a fishing ground, a forest, the Internet, or the stratosphere, is a natural or man-made resource from which it is difficult to exclude or limit users once the resource is provided by nature or produced by humans."

Hess and Ostrom (2007, 3) further define a "commons" as being a "complex system" where "a resource [is] shared by a group of people that is subject to social dilemmas." These social dilemmas consist of those human behaviours that might undermine the viability of the shared resource, such as "competition for use, free riding, and overharvesting" (Hess and Ostrom 2007, 5). Social dilemmas, such as the tragedy of the commons or congestion, involve what economists would generally describe as "negative externalities." In the Pigouvian tradition, the solution to these sorts of problems is provided via government regulation and/or taxation or subsidy. Coase (1960) proposed a series of solutions to these sorts of problems that revolved around privatisation, vertical integration, government regulation, or simply doing nothing. Ostrom, by contrast, demonstrated that local institutions often emerge or evolve to solve what were (very often) local problems. Traditionally, this research framework has been applied to "subtractive resources." But its extension to "non-subtractive" resources, such as knowledge, suggests that "the unifying thread in all commons resources is that they are jointly used, managed by groups of varying sizes and interests" (Hess and Ostrom 2007, 5).

The notion that DAOs could be thought of as being a kind of a commons raises complications. Pre-existing natural resources are very likely different from digital resources. It is possible to differentiate between the existence of a naturally occurring resource pool and the governance of that naturally occurring resource pool. It is not clear, however, that the existence of a digital resource pool and the governance of that digital resource pool can be as clearly differentiated. Digital assets must be created through human action and human design. Presumably, the governance of those digital assets is simultaneously created when the digital asset is being created. Furthermore, a governance process to create the digital asset is required in addition to a governance process to manage the asset once created – there are mixed forms of governance (Dekker and Kuchař 2024) in adjacent action arenas (McGinnis 2011). While DAOs can be thought of as being "social infrastructure" (Frischmann 2012, 67–72), the nature of the resource being governed is very different to how economists usually conceptualise commons. For example, permissionless (i.e. non-excludability) is a feature for blockchains and is not a problem. Furthermore, goods are not just non-rival, they are intended to be "antirival" (Weber 2004; Olleros 2018). The resource becomes more valuable as more users make use of it. Hess and Ostrom (2007, 5) made this point about knowledge: "the more people … share useful knowledge, the greater the common good."

The idea being investigated in this section is that DAOs are a form of "software commons" or "knowledge commons," which Schweik (2007, 277) described as follows:

> I argue that the collaborative ideals and principles applied in Free/Libre and Open Source Software (FOSS) projects could be applied to any collaboration built around intellectual property (not just software) and could potentially increase the speed at which innovations and new discoveries are made. In other words, we can conceive of a future where such "knowledge commons" are built not around software, but more generally any kind of work or "content."

As Schweik argues, in open-source commons, individuals are producing a resource – in this case, software – and need to design institutions and practices that both facilitate the production of the resource and prevent the resource from being over-harvested. That is precisely the challenge facing DAOs – where the software is specifically focussed on blockchain usage and applications.

An important feature when evaluating open-source commons is to understand "the collaborative infrastructure that helps to coordinate and manage production" (Schweik 2007, 286). In the DAO context, that *collaborative infrastructure* is the series of smart contracts that underpin the DAO. Other important features include "established systems of rules, shared norms of behavior, voting systems, and monitoring and sanctioning systems" (Schweik 2007, 298).

Considering these features as a whole raises questions such as "Can DAOs scale?" Shared norms of behaviour, for example, can be enforced in small groups, but not necessarily in large groups. Then there is the question of participation rates in voting systems – if few people actually vote, that could be indicative of free-riding problems.

The management challenge, however, still remains. Schweik (2007, 297–298) discusses *commons governance structures* and categorises them into four groups: a lead developer who maintains a centralised decision-making structure; a "benevolent dictator" model; an elected leadership model; and a consensus model. Decentralised Autonomous Organisations can only adopt the consensus model (and still be categorised as a DAO). Voting on major decisions is likely to be beneficial in promoting innovation and the like, but it can become burdensome when considering routine business decisions (Markus 2007).

It is clear that DAOs are special cases of information or knowledge commons, but it is unclear whether those structures can handle management costs and agency costs better than centralised organisations can – this issue is an empirical question.

11.3 DAOS IN THE GKC FRAMEWORK

The IAD framework is a generalised tool for understanding how institutions operate and evolve in order to resolve various social dilemmas, particularly those involving common-pool resources like fisheries, forests, and water supplies. The framework breaks down the complexities of institutional arrangements into more manageable components. The framework assists in understanding how "actors" interact within an "action situation" to produce outcomes. These action situations are influenced by a variety of considerations, including the resource characteristics, attributes of the community, and the rules-in-use, which are referred to "external factors." The patterns of interaction from the action situation are then evaluated by some criteria, such as efficiency, equity, and accountability. These assessments can then feed back into the exogenous factors or the action arena, leading to adjustments or adaptations in the rules-in-use, the actors' strategies, or the community attributes.

Frischmann et al. (2014) argue that the IAD framework is more appropriate for natural and depletable resources, and needs to be modified to analyse knowledge and information commons, which include non-depletable resources. Indeed, the resources studied under the IAD framework are typically tangible, depletable resources, where overuse by one individual can diminish the availability for others. By contrast, the GKC framework analyses resources that are intangible, non-depletable, and often non-excludable. The challenge here is less about overuse per se and more about ensuring sustainable and equitable access, creation, and distribution of knowledge. The GKC framework is shown in Figure 11.1

I now apply the GKC framework (Figure 11.1) to the analysis of blockchains and DAOs. I begin with the observation that the action arenas – blockchains and DAOs – are human constructs. They are not naturally occurring resource pools and that this difference is an important part of the analysis. What becomes particularly important is the notion of "adjacent action arenas" (McGinnis 2011; Cole 2017; Cole et al. 2019;

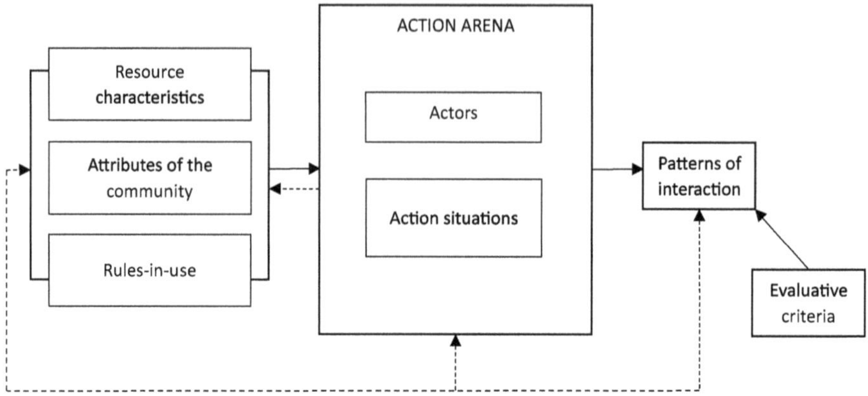

FIGURE 11.1 Stylised GKC framework. Source: Based on Frischmann et al. (2014, 19).

Dekker and Kuchař 2024). McGinnis (2011, 52–53) describes an adjacent action situation as follows: "Two action situations are adjacent to each other when outcomes generated in one action situation help determine the rules under which interactions occur within the other action situation." Indeed, "technically, an action situation X_i is *adjacent* to Y if the outcome of X_i directly influences the value of one or more of the working components of Y."

The creation of an underlying blockchain and the creation of the governance mechanism for that blockchain must occur more or less simultaneously. Dekker and Kuchař (2024) point to joint production in market governance where the rules of the exchange and the exchange itself co-evolve over time (the rules are endogenous). The argument I am proposing here is slightly different: the creation of blockchains and DAOs can be described as being private or market governance, while the operation of blockchains and DAOs constitutes community governance. The creators of the digital resource – the blockchain and the DAO – must make a series of choices. Following Ostrom (2005, 58), these rules operate at three levels: constitutional choice, collective choice, and operational rules. Where these choices and decisions are made is itself an action arena – perhaps it could be thought of as being a "meta-constitutional" action arena.

In the first instance, a series of constitutional choices must be made that define the blockchain itself (e.g. proof-of-work or proof-of-stake) and how that blockchain will be governed (e.g. which operational rules, i.e. smart contracts, are subject to collective choice rules, and which are not). Some blockchains include smart contracts that are themselves immutable, while others have smart contracts that can be updated. Then there is the question as to whether those collective choices rules are operated strictly on-chain or off-chain. It is possible to specify that some collective choice decisions can only occur on-chain, while others could occur off-chain. These constitutional choices will impact how the blockchain operates and how it is governed. Similarly, a series of constitutional choices need to be made as to how the performance of the blockchain and the DAO will be evaluated. The evaluative criteria for the blockchain itself could be technical in nature (e.g. bug-free smart contracts that perform as expected), while the evaluative criteria for the DAO could be a high level of participation, or that value accrues to the token (see the following section for more discussion). To the extent that the digital resources – the blockchain itself – and the governance of the blockchain – the DAO – can be thought of being adjacent action arenas, the first will be referred to as the *blockchain action arena* and the second the *DAO action arena*.

11.3.1 *External Variables*

The "external" variables discussed here are much the same as in a more traditional IAD analysis.

11.3.1.1 Resource Characteristics

Unlike naturally occurring commons or physical commons, the resource characteristics here consist of human capital, intangible capital, and non-specific capital. The human capital is somewhat unique in this context and is further discussed under the attributes of the community. I first discuss the characteristics of the so-called "digital economy."

Menz et al. (2021, 1698) argue that the digital economy is "enabled by four technologies – computer hardware, software applications, internet and mobile communications, and artificial intelligence." These technologies have had the effect of dramatically reducing transaction costs within the economy. The digital economy differs from the industrial economy by relying heavily on intangible capital and non-specific capital. Computer hardware, for example, is cheap and redeployable. It is human capital that is now expensive, rare, and valuable. Unlike the industrial economy, which relies heavily on (supply-side) economies of scale, the digital economy relies heavily on (demand-side) network effects. These network effects can be thought of as positive externalities, but they also often involve what Olleros (2018) describes as *antirival goods* or what Weber (2004, 154) calls *network goods*, which gain value as they are shared and used by more people. It is well known in standard economic analysis that a free market is very likely going to under-invest in activities that generate positive externalities. That standard analysis does not hold in a digital economy. Rather, the challenge for entrepreneurs in the digital economy is to create products, and business models, that generate and capture those network effects (see Lerner and Tirole 2001, 2002). In the blockchain environment, with its emphasis on open-source software, this challenge is particularly difficult.

Haskel and Westlake (2018, 58–88) argue that intangible assets have four important characteristics: scalability, sunkenness, spillovers, and synergies. Intangible assets are highly scalable, meaning they can be used or reproduced multiple times at little or no additional cost. For example, the marginal cost of redistributing software is almost zero. This scalability allows firms with valuable intangible assets to grow rapidly and dominate markets, often leading to winner-takes-all dynamics. The costs associated with intangible assets, however, are often "sunk costs," which means they are not easily recoverable. Unlike tangible assets, which can be sold or repurposed, intangible assets often have little to no resale value. This makes investments in intangibles riskier and can create barriers to entry for smaller firms.

Intangible assets frequently generate network effects and while this is beneficial for economic growth, it can also make it challenging for firms to capture the full value of their intangible assets, thereby affecting their incentives to invest in such assets in the first place. Finally, intangible assets often exhibit synergies when combined with other assets, either tangible or intangible. For example, a strong brand (an intangible asset) can enhance the value of a patented technology (another intangible asset), leading to a product that is greater than the sum of its parts. These synergies can create complex, interdependent relationships between assets, making them more valuable together than separately.

Tangible capital comprises physical assets such as machinery, buildings, and land. One of the key features of tangible assets is that they often depreciate over time, losing value due to factors like wear and tear or technological obsolescence. Additionally, these assets usually have a resale value and can be used as collateral for loans, which makes them less risky as investments. Unlike intangible assets, tangible assets are generally not scalable in the same way. For example, a factory has a production limit, and once that is reached, another factory needs to be built to increase production. The benefits of tangible assets are usually confined to the owner or the immediate environment; they do not naturally have the spillover effects commonly associated with intangible assets. Furthermore, tangible assets often have value in isolation; a machine or a piece of land has utility on its own, without the need for synergistic combinations with other assets.

Given those differences, it is (at least) plausible that very different governance mechanisms may be at work in a digital economy as compared to an industrial economy.

11.3.1.2 Attributes of the Community

Following Santana and Albareda (2022, 5), I define a DAO community as including founders, investors, developers, and miners (or validators in a proof of stake blockchain system). To that list I also add users or customers of the DAO. A DAO community could be described as being "stakeholders" in other contexts, say, in the theory of the firm.

Founders are those individuals who launch the DAO, who have the initial entrepreneurial ideas that manifest themselves in a "whitepaper" that is used to attract investors. Importantly, founders "define governance and functioning rules, but machines apply them" (Santana and Albareda 2022, 5). Developers are those individuals who code and deploy smart contracts to a blockchain protocol. The miners or validators verify and validate the transactions that occur between users of the DAO by writing them to a blockchain.

Investors are those individuals who provide finance to the founders in return for native tokens that provide voting rights and either an explicit or implicit right to earn a return from the DAOs operations. Given the relative immaturity of DAOs as an organisational form, specialised capital markets that facilitate capital raising have not (yet) fully emerged or evolved. Current exchanges where DAO tokens and other cryptocurrencies are traded tend to be secondary markets. Current investors in DAOs are likely to be cryptocurrency enthusiasts, blockchain developers and technologists, venture capitalists with an interest in blockchain and cryptocurrencies, and highly knowledgeable professional investors. These investors are all more likely to be considered "strategic partners" to the DAO than passive investors who simply own the token for portfolio investment purposes. It is less likely that many DAO investors could be considered to be "retail" investors. The common thread among existing DAO investors would be an interest in, and commitment to, the principles of decentralisation, transparency, and innovation that DAOs embody. As such, investors may also provide managerial insights or act as mentors to the founders. Importantly, for our purposes, investors would more likely be active participants than passive recipients of income.

Weber (2004, 144–145) describes the open-source community as having "strong elements of *shared* identity *and belief systems*" (emphasis original). These elements include "[a]ccess to computers should be unlimited"; "[i]nformation should be free"; "[j]udge people only on the value of what they create, not who they are or what credentials they present"; "[p]eople can create art and beauty on computers"; and "[c]omputers can change human life for the better." Most importantly for our discussion, one of the key belief systems is "[m]istrust authority and promote decentralisation." Weber (2004, 144) describes this belief system as follows: "Hierarchies are good at controlling economic markets and more importantly computing power. Control stifles creativity, which is ultimately what information-processing ought to be about."

The point to note is that individuals within open-source communities tend to be ideological. Individuals within these open-source communities exhibit a strict adherence to a specific belief system. These ideological values then manifest themselves in a series of cultural norms. These norms, in turn, support and maintain property rights (discussed in Section 11.3.1.3), along the lines outlined by Williamson (1998, 2000). Weber (2004, 161–164) sets out three sets of open-source cultural norms: how ownership is acquired, how decision-making roles are allocated, and what is described as "technical rationality" – the assumption that there are "technical solutions to technical problems" (Weber 2004, 164). Here I focus on the second set of norms that Weber identifies those that relate to hierarchy and decision-making roles.

Weber (2004, 163) poses the question: "Who has the legitimate right to make decisions about which pieces of code are included in public distributions of the software?" In small projects, Weber argues, decision-making authority follows ownership. This seems to be consistent with practices that occur in small business. In larger open-source projects, "[a]uthority follows and derives from responsibility"; in particular, "[t]he more work an individual contributes and the more she takes responsibility for a piece of the project, the more decision-making authority she gains" (Weber 2004, 163). While Weber does not use this terminology, it is clear from his description that hierarchy emerges in practice from (successful) performance. As Weber (2004, 164) suggests: "If this sounds very much like a hierarchical decision structure, that is because it is one – albeit one in which participation is strictly voluntary."

This notion of "voluntary hierarchy," however, does also give rise to additional complexity in what is already a challenging issue. The creation of software is itself a demanding task in need of high-level cooperation and coordination. As Weber (2004, 186) argues: "All complex production processes need governance mechanisms to make them work." In open-source projects there are two unique features: asynchronous communication and the lack of formal hierarchy.

> That there is no hierarchy for the division of labor – that is, assigning tasks to particular individuals – lies at the heart of the open source process. There can be a hierarchy of decision-making, for vetting and incorporating the results of distributed work, yet participation in that decision-making hierarchy is voluntary and remains voluntary for any individual developer, because it is always possible to exit and fork.

It is important to note that there is nothing inherent in open-source production or working on the internet that resolves the problem of cooperation or the division of labour. If anything, as Weber (2004, 172) concedes, these problems are increased. Operational rules, according to Ostrom (1990, 2005), relate to day-to-day decision-making. Yet the authority to make such operational rules within open-source projects appears to be informal. This forms part of what Ostrom (2005, 80) refers to as being the "commons dilemma": "Joint users of a common-pool resource often face many other problems including assignment problems, technological externality problems, provision problems, and maintenance problems."

In short, given the ideology of the community and the social norms that ideology produces, who decides what work should be done, who does the work, and to whose satisfaction? As Weber (2004, 130) asks: "How do these individuals work with each other, in a way that makes their contributions add up to a joint product?" An additional point is how do these ideological attributes and social norms contribute to the particular choices that inform which constitutional choices can be made within a blockchain–DAO ecosystem, which collective choices can be made, and which operational choices can be made? Some of these choices will be ideological, some will be technical, and some will reflect the rules-in-use.

11.3.1.3 Rules-in-Use

Rules-in-use refer to the "property rights" that govern a specific community (Ostrom 2005, 16–22). Ostrom and Hess (2007, 50) define rules-in-use as: "Rules are shared normative understandings about what a participant in a position must, must not, or may do in a particular action situation, backed by at least a minimal sanctioning ability for noncompliance."

Ostrom (2005) makes the argument that within any commons, it is important to understand the origins of the rules, what the rules are, and how predictable the rules are. In the blockchain space, it is easy to argue that bug-free smart contracts are 100 per cent predictable (which they are). Unfortunately, as I argue in Section 11.4, the actual situation is somewhat more complex. An impediment to predictability is bounded rationality (and opportunism) which remains a problem even in the blockchain space (see Davidson 2023, 2024).

Ostrom and Hess (2007, 52) identify seven different types of property rights in the case of digital knowledge commons: access, contribution, extraction, removal, management/participation, exclusion, and alienation. These in turn can be classified as *ownership* rights (access and contribution), *control* rights (management/participation and exclusion), and *disposal* rights (extraction, removal, and alienation). These categories would extend to the acquisition and use of resources; to the right to earn income from them; to exclude others from acquiring, using, or earning income them; as well as various rights to dispose of, or distribute, the resources, that is, sell it, give it away, abandon it, and so on. An important distinction between "traditional" property right regimes and open-source property right regimes is that the emphasis is not on exclusion, but rather on the distribution of property (Weber 2004, 16).

Weber (2004, 161–162) observes that property rights within open-source projects appear to follow the principles of "Anglo-American common law," that is, "Lockean property theory" (after the English philosopher John Locke). For example, ownership in open-source projects is acquired by initiating the project (the project is owned by the founder), by acquiring it from the founder, or by re-initiating an abandoned project. As Weber (2004, 162) observes: "Customs like these are relatively efficient in settings in which property is valuable, there is no authoritative allocation, and the expected returns from the resource exceed the expected costs of defending it."

Economists would recognise this argument as being associated with theories proposed by Alchian (1965) and Demsetz (1967), and Alchian and Demsetz (1973) writing together. Demsetz (1967) – the classic paper in this area – argues that property rights emerge to internalise externalities in response to changes in technology and relative prices. Although Demsetz makes no attempt to model the social and political environment in which rights arise, and consequently Eggertsson (1990) refers to this model as being "naïve," this approach is widely used and understood by economists. There is no a priori reason to suspect that it would not work well in the open-source context.

There is, however, an unanswered question, or challenge, that arises in the blockchain or DAO space. Presumably, the rules-in-use evolve into a mechanism that facilitates *self-organisation*. But as Weber (2004, 132) indicates, there are, at least, two problems with self-organisation as a concept. First, it is often used to denote ignorance of the mechanism at work. Secondly, and more importantly, "[s]elf-organization often evokes an optimistically tinged 'state of nature' narrative, a story about the good way things would 'naturally' evolve if the 'meddling' hands of corporations and lawyers and governments and bureaucracies would just stay away."

This is what Demsetz (1969) labelled the "nirvana fallacy." For our purposes, however, the problem is this: "*There is no state of nature on the Internet*" (Weber 2004, 132, emphasis original). The rules-in-use that govern the creation of a blockchain or DAO and the rules-in-use to govern the operation of that blockchain or DAO are not the same rules. One set of rules evolves and adapts to local conditions (per Demsetz), corresponding to what Dekker and Kuchař (2024) describe as private or market governance, but the rules-in-use in the DAO or on the blockchain – the blockchain action arena – must be created through human design and not human action – corresponding to what Dekker and Kuchař (2024) describe as community governance. This insight is discussed in the next section.

11.3.2 *Action Arena*

Ostrom (2005, 13) defines an action arena where participants and action situations "interact as they are affected by exogenous variables . . . and produce outcomes that in turn affect the participants and the action situation." She defines an action situation as "the social space where participants with diverse preferences interact, exchange goods and services, solve problems, dominate one another, or fight" (Ostrom 2005, 14). As I have argued, however, the rules-in-use within the blockchain action arena and those outside the blockchain action arena are not the same rules; they may not have the same origins, and certainly do not co-evolve.

11.3.2.1 Actors

The actors within the action arena are the community that created the action arena. It is very likely that users play a far more important or prominent role in the action area than they do outside the action arena.

11.3.2.2 Community Rules-in-Use

Property rights within the blockchain action arena do not emerge and evolve as per Demsetz-type explanations; rather they must be created and encoded into smart contracts. In this sense, they are chosen by the community that is creating the blockchain and DAO ecosystem. Dekker and Kuchař (2024) describe three elements of governance: "the formation and interpretation of rules, the administration of ownership claims and rules, and the enforcement of rules." They further argue that to qualify as a knowledge commons, members or users must have governance rights over all three of these elements. In this section, I adapt a model first proposed by Riker and Sened (1991) and then expanded by Sened (1997) to explain the property rights (community rules-in-use) that exist within the blockchain action arena.

Riker and Sened (1991) and Sened (1997) propose a legal-centric origin of property rights. Their argument is that property rights cannot exist without centralised law enforcement and the state having a monopoly in violence. The argument is "governments must *grant* rights before they can protect them" (Sened 1997, 6, emphasis original). In this model, property rights arise out of the interaction between political entrepreneurs who wish to internalise some opportunity and government officials. Four conditions are necessary and sufficient for rights to emerge: the right must be valuable, right holders must desire the right, rule-makers must desire to enforce the right, and some duty-bearers respect the right (Sened 1997, 78–79). It could be argued that the Demsetz model of property rights is a special case of the Riker and Sened model. In the Demsetz argument, the right is valuable and right holders desire the right. Property rights then evolve and adapt such that right holders acquire the rights to the valuable property. This can be thought of as being a demand-side model, whereas the Riker and Sened model includes supply-side factors in the emergence of property rights.

Within the blockchain and DAO space, there is no state nor violence – there is, however, a community that can choose to participate or not. It is possible, however, to adapt the Riker and Sened model to blockchain and DAO conditions. For example, interaction within the action arena must create valuable opportunities for the community, and especially for the users of the action arena. The claimants desiring the right become the founders desiring a right, and the rule makers enforcing the right are the smart contracts operating within the action arena (bug-free smart contracts will always enforce the rights). Duty bearers respecting the rights are users and investors.

In summary, the founders propose an action situation that will generate value, that action situation is governed by a series of smart contracts, and users and investors believe that they can either participate in that value creation or capture some of the value creation.

11.3.3 *Evaluative Criteria*

Ostrom (2005, 66) suggested five criteria for evaluating commons performance: economic efficiency; equity or fiscal equivalence; adaptability, resilience, and robustness; accountability; and conformance to general morality. In the context of DAOs, the question then arises as to whether that DAO is economically efficient, whether costs and benefits of participation are equitably distributed, whether the activities of the DAO are sustainable, and, importantly, whether the DAO conforms to the moral expectations of the community – this often revolves around questions of appropriate levels decentralisation and community participation. Answers to these questions can be debated and reasonable individuals can disagree. There are, however, some evaluative criteria that are easier to observe.

Is "value" being created in the action arena? For users it means that their objectives are being met – they are maximising utility, or making successful and profitable trades, and so on. For investors, it means that they are either explicitly or implicitly earning a profit on their investment. For both the founders and the investors "success" is measured by the value of the native token increasing in value (assuming that the token is not intended to be a stable coin). "Wen moon" is something of a cliché in this space – asking the question when the native token will suddenly and dramatically increase in value.

It is also worth noting that in the basic IAD framework the evaluative criteria appear to be entirely independent of external variables and the action arena. There is no obvious interaction with either the external variables or the action arena. Within the blockchain DAO ecosystem, however, to the extent that the community selects the rules-in-use within the action arena, the community must also select the evaluative criteria whereby action within the arena is evaluated.

11.3.4 *Summary of Discussion*

Based on the discussion so far, a more relevant version of the GKC framework should look something like Figure 11.2.

There are two important differences between Figure 11.1 and Figure 11.2. In the first instance, the evaluative criteria are determined by external variables – in particular, by the attributes of the community and resource characteristics. In other words, the community defines the evaluative criteria – these criteria are likely to be a mixture of economic and ideological considerations. The second important difference is that there are two sets of rules-in-use. The first set, "market rules-in-use," is an external variable and very likely follows the tradition of the Anglo-American common law. The second set, "community rules-in-use," is written into the action arena and encoded as smart contracts. These rules will not evolve through use, but rather are hard-coded into smart contracts and operate more like legislation than they do common law principles. The interesting question is to what extent these smart contracts can be modified by some sort of governance?

11.3.5 *Where Do DAOs Fit into the Analysis?*

The creation of a blockchain and the DAO that governs that ecosystem itself requires an action arena. Figure 11.3 shows what that "meta action arena" may look like.

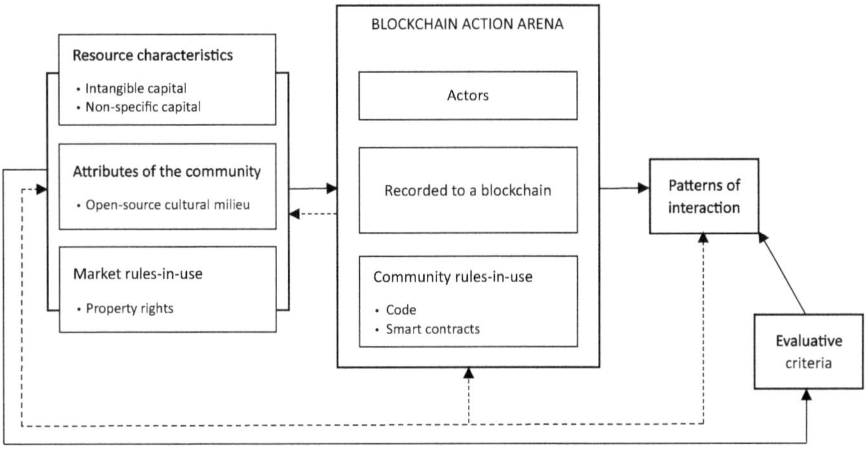

FIGURE 11.2 Blockchain as a commons.

Within this action arena, the constitutional rules, collective-choice rules, and operational rules for the blockchain–DAO system are selected and chosen. They themselves are a result of constitutional rules, collective-choice rules, and operational rules. The question is where does the DAO fit into the blockchain–DAO system that is created within this adjacent meta action arena?

The most obvious place to locate a DAO is simply to wrap it around the entire enterprise – around the external variables (i.e. the original community) and the action arena – in effect, declaring the meta action arena to be the DAO.

While this may appear to be a logical, even easy, solution, it is not practical. This DAO model, by aiming to wrap around and integrate external variables directly into its governance mechanisms, risks diluting the participatory governance model. This could lead to scenarios where the DAO's response to external pressures becomes more autocratic or less transparent, counter to the decentralised ethos. It also presupposes a level of sophistication in decision-making algorithms and governance protocols that can adaptively manage, not just internal operations but also external influences and changes.

A more "practical" approach is to differentiate DAOs in terms of "on-chain" and "off-chain" governance. These two models of governance are very distinctive, representing different approaches to how decisions are made, rules are enforced, and the overall direction of the DAO is steered.

On-chain governance is characterised by decisions and rule changes being proposed, voted on, and implemented directly on the blockchain. In this instance, the DAO is located *within* the action arena, as shown in Figure 11.4. This is not an adjacent action arena; nonetheless, a series of prior (or meta) constitutional choices will have established what level of operational control the DAO would have over the

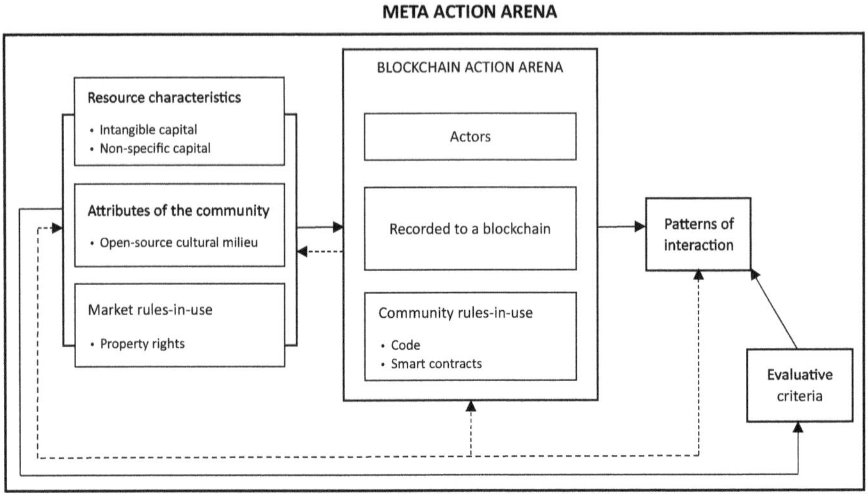

FIGURE 11.3 Meta action arena.

blockchain itself. The operational choices that the DAO can make, however, are enforced on-chain by the blockchain. This model is suggestive of a "digital democracy," where every action is transparent, verifiable, and immutable once executed. The underlying principle of on-chain governance is "decentralisation": every member of the community (i.e. stakeholder) has a say in DAO governance, with votes being cast and tallied in a manner that is transparent and immutable.

This transparency promotes trust among the community, as the rules of engagement are clear and the ledger of actions is immutable. This model, however, also introduces rigidity. Changing established protocols or smart contracts (if possible) or adapting swiftly to new circumstances can be cumbersome, requiring consensus that might be slow to achieve. Williamson (1985) refers to this problem as being "maladaptation" – in the DAO context; it is not clear whether maladaptation costs are high or low. Furthermore, there is a "technical skill" barrier to entry that could inhibit some members of the community from fully engaging in voting or decision-making, potentially limiting the DAO's accessibility. Nonetheless, if the arguments relating to the advantages of DAOs are to be believed (see Davidson 2025), then DAOs should be located within the action arena. Decentralised Autonomous Organisations with on-chain governance include MakerDAO, Compound, Aave, Uniswap, and Decred.

By contrast, Figure 11.5 shows the situation of off-chain governance. Decentralised Autonomous Organisations that fall into this category include MolochDAO, Kyber Network, and Curve Finance. Aragon is a platform that allows communities to launch DAOs, including options for off-chain governance. Snapshot offers a service that provides for off-chain voting for DAOs. In this configuration, the visualisation of an adjacent action arena that is the DAO is obvious. It could be useful to

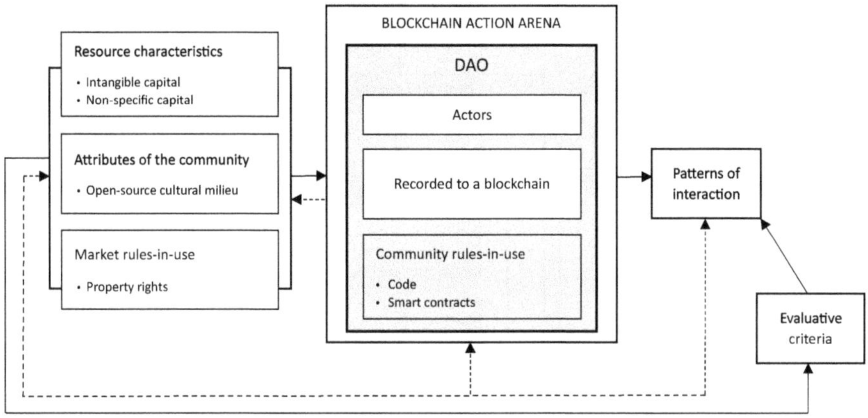

FIGURE 11.4 On-chain governance DAO.

differentiate one action arena as being the "blockchain action arena" and the other as being the "DAO action arena." A series of constitutional choices will have established which operational choices can be made by the DAO, but the collective choice will not be enforced on-chain by the blockchain. Demsetzian property rights systems, for example, could inform the operations of the DAO on an on-going basis, which in turn could inform the property rights that operate within the blockchain action arena also on an on-going basis.

Off-chain governance manages decision-making and rule-setting outside of the blockchain action arena, using more traditional methods of communication and organisation, such as forums or chats (usually Discord). This approach allows for a more flexible and adaptive governance structure. Decisions can be made rapidly, and complex discussions can occur in more traditional formats. The trade-off here is that moving decisions off the blockchain can dilute the very decentralisation that makes DAOs revolutionary. It reintroduces the potential for opacity in decision-making processes and centralises control, potentially creating disparities in influence among participants. Moreover, the reliance on traditional communication methods reintroduces the risk of manipulation or fraud, as the immutable ledger of the blockchain is bypassed.

Each model, therefore, offers a different pathway to managing DAOs as knowledge commons, and the choice between them reflects the priorities of the DAO community, whether those be the security and immutability of on-chain processes or the (greater) adaptability and human judgement facilitated by off-chain governance. On-chain governance champions the ethos of blockchain technology, promoting a high level of transparency and security. Yet, its rigidity and the technical proficiency required can stifle adaptability and broad-based participation. Off-chain governance, conversely, offers flexibility and inclusivity, facilitating dynamic

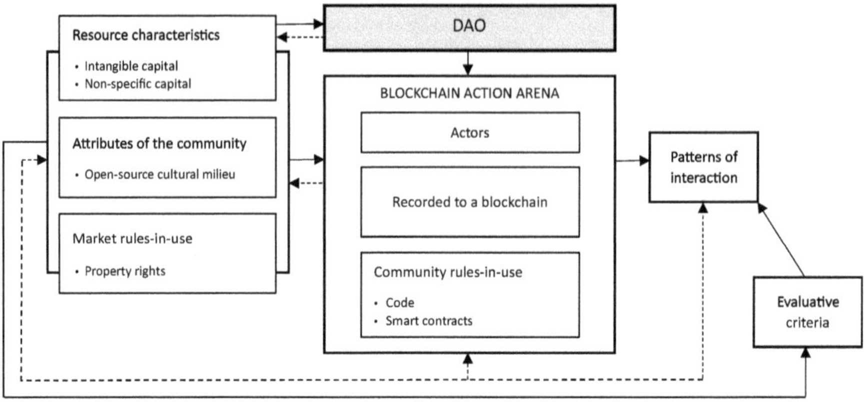

FIGURE 11.5 Off-chain governance DAO.

responses to challenges and easier engagement for those less technically inclined. These advantages, however, (may) come at the expense of trustlessness and decentralisation.

11.4 CAN DAOS ENDURE AS COMMONS?

Ostrom (2005, 256, emphasis original) suggests an impossibility theorem when she writes: "We cannot conduct full analyses of the consequences of changing *all* possible parts of a complex system interacting itself with a complex and changing environment." Here she is following the insights of Herbert Simon (1962, and generally his insights on bounded rationality) and her own experience as a researcher. She goes on: "officials and policy analysts who presume that they have the right design can be dangerous." While she does not reference Ludwig von Mises, her conclusions are very similar to those that he had made relating to the impossibility of a centrally planned economy, and the motivations that bureaucrats would have relative to entrepreneurs (see Mises 1981, 2007).

Importantly for our purposes, Ostrom (2005, 256) also argues: "We are not, however, helpless in finding ways to improve the performance of complex ... systems." To that end, she has distilled from her own research experience and that of others a set of "design principles" that describe "structural similarities" between those commons that have proven (so far) to have been robust to external disturbances and disruptions. These principles were first set out in Ostrom (1990), repeated in Ostrom (2005), and extended in Cox et al. (2010). In this section, these design principles are applied to DAOs (Table 11.1). The extended design principles are denoted as being "A" or "B" and are in italics.

As can be seen in Table 11.1, it is clear that DAOs, in theory, tend to meet the design principles, which would suggest that DAOs could be robust and

TABLE 11.1 *Ostrom's design principles applied to DAOs*[1]

	Design principle	DAO equivalent
1	Clearly defined boundaries	The smart contracts, governance tokens, and governance protocols that underpin a DAO create a well-defined structure that separates the organisation from the broader digital environment; these elements establish the "rules of the game" and provide a clear framework for collaboration, decision-making, and resource allocation
1A	*Well-defined boundaries between legitimate users and non-users*	In a world of antirival goods, can there be "illegitimate users"? One of the key features of the crypto economy is an emphasis on it being permissionless; if positive network effects are generated by users, should there be boundaries at all? This question is posed but not answered in this chapter
1B	*Well-defined boundaries define the resource system and separate it from the larger biophysical environment*	The level of technical knowledge currently needed to work in the space serves as a barrier to entry
2	Congruence between appropriation and provision rules and local conditions	Smart contracts and blockchain technology facilitate the transparent and automated enforcement of provision and appropriation rules; this ensures that the relationship between inputs and benefits is clear, auditable, and free from arbitrary manipulation
2A	*Rules are congruent with local social and environmental conditions*	In principle, DAOs can be deployed to take advantage of local conditions and knowledge (see Davidson 2023a)
2B	*The benefits obtained by CPR users, as determined by appropriation rules, are proportional to the amount of inputs required in the form of labour, material, or money, as determined by provision rules*	DAO members contribute various inputs (time, expertise, capital, or computational resources); the benefits obtained, such as voting power, revenue share, or influence, are (usually) paid in the native governance token; this alignment ensures fairness and incentivises active participation; this would correspond to notions of equity and fiscal equivalence
3	Collective-choice arrangements	DAOs are typically structured to allow members to participate in decision-making processes, including modifying operational rules; this is facilitated through (various) voting mechanisms, where members can propose changes, debate them, and vote on their adoption

[1] Adapted from Ostrom (1990, 90, 2005, 259) and Cox et al. (2010, Table 4).

TABLE 11.1 *(continued)*

	Design principle	DAO equivalent
		On-Chain Governance: voting and decision-making are automated and transparent, reducing the potential for corruption or coercion; the rigidity of on-chain governance may limit the scope for nuanced debate and consensus-building, as complex issues may be oversimplified into binary votes *Off-Chain Governance*: decision-making may be more deliberative and allow for in-depth discussion, negotiation, and compromise
4	Monitoring	Smart contracts can automate the monitoring process, enforcing rules related to contributions and benefits, and providing a transparent and immutable record
4A	*Monitors who are accountable to the users monitor the appropriation and provision levels of the users*	DAOs make use of peer-to-peer oversight where members themselves act as monitors, holding each other accountable for adhering to the agreed-upon rules
4B	*Monitors who are accountable to the users monitor the condition of the resource*	Within DAOs, the responsibility for monitoring the condition of the resource (usually an intangible asset such as intellectual property or knowledge or the DAO Treasury) falls on the members themselves, that is, the monitors are the users; it would also be possible to argue, however, that miners or validators are the monitors; if that is the case, then this would be yet another instance of adjacent action arenas being present in this space
5	Graduated sanctions	While smart contracts can be programmed to apply graduated sanctions automatically, depending on the seriousness and context of the offence, it is unclear whether many (or any) DAOs apply graduated sanctions to rules breakers (beyond slashing for validation violations)
6	Conflict-resolution mechanisms	At present, DAOs cannot access traditional dispute resolution-mechanisms, but they design and build their own internal conflict-resolution mechanisms and they can access third-party decentralised dispute-resolution services from organisations such as Kleros, Aragon, or Jur; it is not clear how many DAOs have chosen to access these services. Yet again, this is an additional instance of adjacent action arenas

TABLE 11.1 *(continued)*

	Design principle	DAO equivalent
7	Minimum recognition of rights	Generally, DAOs have not been recognised as legal entities (outside of Wyoming and Vermont in the US) by governments around the world; there is a lot of discussion and speculation that this could occur in the near future
8	Nested enterprises	DAOs can have a nested or hierarchical governance structure, and some DAOs have created sub-DAOs to manage specific projects, resources, or functions; these sub-DAOs operate within the broader framework of the main DAO but have autonomy in their specific domain
		On-Chain Governance: nested DAOs (sub-DAOs) are often governed by separate smart contracts that interface with the main DAO; this ensures a high degree of autonomy but may create challenges in coordination and integration between layers
		Off-Chain Governance: nested governance structures can be more fluid and adaptable, but this can also lead to complexities in managing different levels of authority and potential conflicts between layers

survive external disturbance and disruption. Whether DAOs in practice meet these design principles remains to be seen and would form the basis for an empirical investigation. For example, does fiscal equivalence apply in practice – are contributors equitably remunerated? Do users actively monitor the on-going performance and sustainability of the DAO? Are graduated sanctions employed to punish violations? Is the notion of a sub-DAO consistent with a lack of hierarchy? These are all questions that can and should be pursued.

There is an additional feature of DAOs that could add to their robustness. DAOs have access to an additional conflict resolution mechanism that many other institutions either do not have or can only access at a very high cost. So-called "forking" (and the associated "rage-quit option") presents innovative approaches to conflict resolution within the DAO space, offering paths to autonomy and self-determination not readily available in traditional organisations or societal governance models.

At its core, forking allows a DAO to split into two (or more) separate entities, as a result of irreconcilable differences within the DAO community. This process is akin to a digital form of secession, where part of a DAO community chooses a different path to that chosen by the rest of the DAO, while preserving the original codebase's integrity. This is made possible by the transparent, open-source nature of blockchain technology.

The "rage-quit" option, as seen in some DAOs like MolochDAO, provides an additional mechanism for conflict resolution by allowing individuals to withdraw their portion of the DAO's treasury and exit if they disagree with the direction or decisions being made. This feature ensures that members have a direct and immediate mechanism to dissociate from actions they consider misaligned with their values or expectations without resorting to complex legal or financial manoeuvres.

Comparing these mechanisms with traditional conflict resolution methods highlights several advantages. In conventional organisations, resolving disputes often involves selling shares, dissolving partnerships, or legal arbitration and even litigation, processes that can be time-consuming, costly, and emotionally taxing. These methods also typically require the intervention of external authorities or intermediaries, which can complicate the resolution process and may not always lead to satisfactory outcomes for all parties involved. At the nation-state level dispute resolution can be especially difficult – consider, for example, trade disputes at the World Trade Organization. Failure of dispute resolution at the nation-state level can result in armed conflict. Just as secession can result in the creation of new states or governance structures, forking enables the birth of new DAOs. Unlike the often violent and tumultuous processes of political upheaval or the expense of corporate break up, forking and rage-quitting provides an orderly and peaceful means for addressing irreconcilable differences within decentralised communities.

Forking and rage-quitting, however, are not costless mechanisms to facilitate exit. As argued in Section 11.3.1.1, network goods or antirival goods generate positive externalities, and a reduced community size could reduce the value of the platform. There is a literature in corporate finance that investigates the wealth effects of spin-offs (see Owers and Sergi 2021 for a recent survey). That literature suggests that spin-offs add substantial value to shareholders. The wealth effects of forking and rage-quits are yet to be empirically tested.

11.5 CONCLUSION

This chapter has examined DAOs using the IAD–GKC framework as if DAOs were "knowledge" or "software commons." Following Dekker and Kuchař (2024) there is a strong argument to be made that DAOs, being community-governed organisations, should be recognised as knowledge commons.

There are some important differences between naturally occurring resources and digital resources. At the most profound level, digital assets must be created. There is no "state of nature" in the digital economy. Everything in the digital economy is created by human design. As such, the governance of digital economies and institutions is likely to be very different from non-digital economies. Furthermore, the (market) rules-in-use that exist in the external variables of the IAD framework and (community) rules-in-use within the action arena are likely to be different from each other.

That further implies that the features of *on-chain* DAO governance are likely to be somewhat different from *off-chain* DAO governance. On-chain governance, characterised by its reliance on blockchain technology and smart contracts, offers a level of transparency and security that aligns with the core principles of decentralisation. This governance model embeds a set of predetermined rules within the DAOs technical infrastructure, ensuring that decisions and transactions are immutable and verifiable. This approach, however, introduces challenges related to the rigidity of governance structures and the technical barriers that may limit participation to those individuals with blockchain expertise.

Off-chain governance, by contrast, allows for a more flexible approach to decision-making, enabling DAOs to respond more swiftly to changes and challenges. This model facilitates governance decisions through conventional communication channels, such as online forums or meetings, potentially enhancing engagement and inclusivity. Yet, this flexibility may come at the cost of reducing transparency and increasing the potential for centralised control, thereby straying from the decentralised ethos that defines DAOs.

This distinction between the rules-in-use in on-chain and off-chain governance models is not a (minor) technical quibble but reflects broader theoretical and practical questions regarding the "optimal" structures for decentralised governance. This divergence raises important questions about the trade-off between automation and human discretion, the role of technology in facilitating democratic decision-making, and the potential for innovative governance mechanisms to address traditional organisational challenges.

The analysis undertaken in this chapter has occurred at a high level of abstraction. Understanding how DAOs actually function practice – as opposed to the theory set out here – is an important next step in better understanding how the digital economy is likely to evolve over time. Case studies of DAOs that explore the issues of joint and co-production that Dekker and Kuchař (2024) identify are necessary to examine the internal operations of DAOs. These are questions for further research.

REFERENCES

Alchian, Armen A. 1965. "Some Economics of Property Rights." *Il Politico*, 30(4): 816–829. Reproduced in Armen A. Alchian, 1977. *Economic Forces at Work*, 127–149 Indianapolis: Liberty Press.

Alchian, Armen A., and Harold Demsetz. 1972. "Production, Information Costs, and Economic Organization." *American Economic Review* 62(5): 777–795.

Alchian, Armen A., and Harold. Demsetz. 1973. "The Property Rights Paradigm." *Journal of Economic History* 33(1): 16–27.

Baskin, Jonathan B., and Paul J. Miranti. 1997. *A History of Corporate Finance*. Cambridge: Cambridge University Press.

Coase, Ronald H. 1937. "The Nature of the Firm." *Economica* 4(16): 386–405.

Coase, Ronald H. 1960. "The Problem of Social Cost." *Journal of Law and Economics* 3: 1–44.

Cole, Daniel H. 2017. "Laws, Norms, and the Institutional Analysis and Development Framework." *Journal of Institutional Economics* 13(4): 829–847.

Cole, Daniel H., Graham Epstein, and Michael D. McGinnis. 2019. "Combining the IAD and SES Frameworks." *International Journal of the Commons* 13(1): 244–275.

Cox, Michael, Gwen Arnold, and Sergio Villayor Tomás. 2010. "A Review of Design Principles for Community-Based Natural Resource Management." *Ecology and Society* 15(4): 38.

Davidson, Sinclair. 2023. "Blockchain and the Information–Calculation Problem." *Journal of Economic Behavior and Organization* 213: 142–150.

Davidson, Sinclair. 2024. "The Economic Institutions of Artificial Intelligence." *Journal of Institutional Economics* 20: e20.

Davidson, Sinclair. 2025. "The Nature of the Decentralised Autonomous Organisation." *Journal of Institutional Economics* 21: e5.

Davidson, Sinclair, Primavera De Filippi, and Jason Potts. 2018. "Blockchains and the Economic Institutions of Capitalism." *Journal of Institutional Economics* 14(4): 639–658.

Deakin, Simon. 2012. "The Corporation as Commons: Rethinking Property Rights, Governance and Sustainability in the Business Enterprise." *Queen's Law Journal* 37(2): 339–381.

Dekker, Erwin, and Pavel Kuchař. 2024. "Markets and Knowledge Commons: Is There a Difference between Private and Community Governance of Markets?" *Public Choice* 201(3–4): 533–553.

Demsetz, Harold. 1967. "Toward a Theory of Property Rights." *American Economic Review* 57(2): 347–359.

Demsetz, Harold. 1969. "Information and Efficiency: Another Viewpoint." *Journal of Law and Economics* 12(1): 1–22.

Eggertsson, Thráinn. 1990. *Economic Behavior and Institutions*. Cambridge: Cambridge University Press.

Frischmann, Brett M. 2012. *Infrastructure: The Social Value of Shared Resources*. New York: Oxford University Press.

Frischmann, Brett M., Michael J. Madison, and Katherine J. Strandburg. 2014. "Governing Knowledge Commons." In *Governing Knowledge Commons*, ed. Brett M. Frischmann, Michael J. Madison, and Katherine J. Strandburg, 1–44. New York: Oxford University Press.

Haskel, Jonathan, and Stian Westlake. 2018. *Capitalism without Capital: The Rise of the Intangible Economy*. Princeton: Princeton University Press.

Hess, Charlotte, and Elinor Ostrom. 2007. "Introduction: An Overview of the Knowledge Commons." In *Understanding Knowledge as a Commons: From Theory to Practice*, ed. Chalotte Hess and Elinor Ostrom, 1–26. Cambridge, MA: MIT Press.

Hirschman, Albert O. 1970. *Exit, Voice, and Loyalty: Responses to Decline in Firms, Organizations, and States*. Cambridge, MA: Harvard University Press.

Lerner, Josh, and Jean Tirole. 2001. "The Open Source Movement: Key Research Questions." *European Economic Review* 45(4–6): 819–826.

Lerner, Josh, and Jean Tirole. 2002. "Some Simple Economics of Open Source." *Journal of Industrial Economics* 50(2): 197–234.

Lerner, Josh, Parag A. Pathak, and Jean Tirole. 2006. "The Dynamics of Open-Source Contributors." *American Economic Review* 96(2): 114–118.
Malone, Thomas W., and John F. Rockart. 1991. "Computers, Networks and the Corporation." *Scientific American* 265(3): 128–137.
Malone, Thomas W., JoAnne Yates, and Robert I. Benjamin. 1987. "Electronic Markets and Electronic Hierarchies." *Communications of the ACM* 30(6): 484–497.
Malone, Thomas W., JoAnne Yates, and Robert I. Benjamin. 1989. "The Logic of Electronic Markets." *Harvard Business Review* 67(3): 166–172.
Markus, M. Lynne. 2007. "The Governance of Free/Open Source Software Projects: Monolithic, Multidimensional, or Configurational?" *Journal of Management and Governance* 11(2): 151–163.
McGinnis, Michael D. 2011. "Networks of Adjacent Action Situations in Polycentric Governance." *Policy Studies Journal* 39(1): 51–78.
Ménard, Claude. 2022. "Hybrids: Where Are We?" *Journal of Institutional Economics* 18(2): 297–312.
Menz, Markus, Sven Kunisch, Julian Birkinshaw, et al. 2021. "Corporate Strategy and the Theory of the Firm in the Digital Age." *Journal of Management Studies* 58(7): 1695–1720.
Mises, Ludwig von. 1981 [1922]. *Socialism: An Economic and Sociological Analysis*. Indianapolis: Liberty Fund.
Mises, L. 2007 [1944]. *Bureaucracy*. Indianapolis: Liberty Fund.
Olleros, Xavier F. 2018. "Antirival Goods, Network Effects and the Sharing Economy." *First Monday* 23(2). https://doi.org/10.5210/fm.v23i2.8161.
Ostrom, Elinor. 1990. *Governing the Commons: The Evolution of Institutions for Collective Action*. Cambridge: Cambridge University Press.
Ostrom, Elinor. 2003. "How Types of Goods and Property Rights Jointly Affect Collective Action." *Journal of Theoretical Politics* 15(3): 239–270.
Ostrom, Elinor. 2005. *Understanding Institutional Diversity*. Princeton: Princeton University Press.
Ostrom, Elinor. 2010. "Beyond Markets and States: Polycentric Governance of Complex Economic Systems." *American Economic Review* 100(3): 641–672.
Ostrom, Elinor, and Charlotte Hess. 2007. "A Framework for Analyzing the Knowledge Commons." In *Understanding Knowledge as a Commons: From Theory to Practice*, ed. Charlotte Hess, and Elinor Ostrom, 41–81. Cambridge: MIT Press.
Owers, James E., and Bruno S. Sergi. 2021. "The Ongoing Contributions of Spin-Off Research and Practice to Understanding Corporate Restructuring and Wealth Creation: $100 Billion in 1 Decade." *Humanities & Social Sciences Communications* 8: 134.
Riker, William H., and Itai Sened. 1991. "A Political Theory of the Origin of Property Rights: Airport Slots." *American Journal of Political Science* 35(4): 951–969.
Santana, Carlos, and Laura Albareda. 2022. "Blockchain and the Emergence of Decentralized Autonomous Organizations (DAOs): An Integrative Model and Research Agenda." *Technological Forecasting and Social Change* 182: 121806.
Schweik, Charles M. 2007. "Free/Open-Source Software as a Framework for Establishing Commons in Science." In *Understanding Knowledge as a Commons: From Theory to Practice*, ed. Charlotte Hess and Elinor Ostrom, 277–309. Cambridge, MA: MIT Press.
Sened, Itai. 1997. *The Political Institution of Private Property*. Cambridge: Cambridge University Press.
Shleifer, Andrei, and Robert W. Vishny. 1997. "A Survey of Corporate Governance." *Journal of Finance* 52(2): 737–783.

Simon, Herbert. 1962. "The Architecture of Complexity." *Proceedings of the American Philosophical Society* 106(6): 467–482.

Weber, Steven. 2004. *The Success of Open Source*. Cambridge, MA: Harvard University Press.

Williamson, Oliver E. 1975. *Markets and Hierarchies: Analysis and Antitrust Implications*. New York: Free Press.

Williamson, Oliver E. 1985. *The Economic Institutions of Capitalism: Firms, Markets and Relational Contracting*. New York: Free Press.

Williamson, Oliver E. 1998. Transaction Cost Economics: How It Works; Where It Is Headed. *De Economist* 146(1): 23–58.

Williamson, Oliver E. 2000. "The New Institutional Economics: Taking Stock, Looking Ahead." *Journal of Economic Literature* 38(3): 595–613.

12

The Decentralized Autonomous Corporation as Knowledge Commons

Michael J. Madison and Ilia Murtazashvili

12.1 INTRODUCTION

Corporations and governments are conventional intermediaries that record, process, and validate information in the modern economy. Blockchains reduce and in some instances eliminate reliance on these intermediaries for recording information. Like firms and states, blockchains address social dilemmas associated with resource coordination and allocation. As governance institutions, blockchains offer distinct and different approaches to power imbalances and trust concerns associated with conventional intermediaries. And blockchains offer general purpose platforms for deploying governance strategies in specific sectors of market and other cultural activities.

This chapter examines one such deployment: the decentralized autonomous organization (DAO), which combines blockchains, smart contracts, and distributed payment systems. The examination is organized under the Governing Knowledge Commons (GKC) framework to draw out features of DAOs that emphasize structured resource sharing in a collective, collaborative, or community context – the hallmark of commons governance – and to sharpen similarities and contrasts between DAOs, on the one hand, and conventional corporations, on the other hand, as specific instances of the general phenomenon of knowledge commons. In both the narrower case (the DAO) and the broader one (the corporation), we reinforce earlier arguments positing knowledge commons governance as a productive way to understand knowledge sharing within markets (Dekker and Kuchař 2022), rather than as a mode of resistance to market dynamics. We focus on the GKC framing in order to expand beyond reliance on a transactions cost perspective on DAO governance and corporate governance (Micheler et al. 2026).

Section 12.2 describes DAOs, blockchains, and corporations as related yet distinct sociotechnical governance institutions in order to facilitate the analysis of these organizations from the GKC perspective. Section 12.3 sketches the GKC framework, briefly. In Section 12.4, we examine the basic model of the DAO using the tools provided by that framework. Section 12.5 briefly considers how a knowledge commons examination of DAOs illuminates analyses of corporations and corporate governance generally and offers implications and suggestions for future research.

12.2 UNDERSTANDING DAO GOVERNANCE AS THE INTERWEAVING OF BLOCKCHAIN GOVERNANCE AND CORPORATE GOVERNANCE

12.2.1 *A Short Review of DAOs and Blockchains*

We start with a simple definition of DAOs, from Investopedia: "A decentralized autonomous organization (DAO) is an emerging form of organizational structure with no central governing body and whose members share a common goal of acting in the best interest of the entity. Popularized by blockchain enthusiasts, DAOs make decisions using a bottom-up management approach."[1]

The simplicity of that summary hints at definitional and analytic complexity. Neither researchers nor practitioners have settled on a single, standard definition of "autonomous corporation" or "decentralized autonomous organization" (Hassan and De Filippi 2023). DAOs consist of groups of people who coordinate participation in decision making via technological systems in pursuit of a shared goal (or goals) or purpose(s). As Davidson et al. (2018) have noted, blockchains are a new institutional technology, meaning a new configuration of people, practices, and resources. To blockchain promoters, these configurations offer "trustless" governance solutions to coordination dilemmas, in that decision making is irrevocably and traceably recorded on blockchains rather than subject to interpretation by managers or government regulators. They offer inclusiveness in the sense that DAO "membership" is documented by ownership of tokens that are recorded on the blockchain. Ownership enables the members to participate in governance by voting.

DAOs offer specific uses of blockchains: they consist of blockchains, executable software code operating as autonomous "smart contracts," and digital assets stored in cryptographic wallets. Wright (2021) divides DAOs into algorithmic DAOs in which software coordinates everything (examples include Bitcoin, Ethereum, and other permissionless blockchains) and participatory DAOs that raise investment capital and engage in traditional commercial endeavors, such as venture capital investing or other financing.

Wright (2021) describes blockchains as the backbone of coordination and smart contracting as the glue that holds members to other members, including through transactions. Smart contracts are rules embodied in code that structure the facilitation and operations of DAOs. For example, investment capital may be raised by humans (often, of course, acting through firms) and pooled and recorded on the

[1] "What Is a Decentralized Autonomous Organization (DAO)? www.investopedia.com/tech/what-dao/.

blockchain in the form of a named DAO, as a blockchain-based entity. The series of smart contracts that constitute the DAO in the first place are extended through investments of that pooled capital *by* the members of the DAO, investments that are likewise recorded via smart contracts on the blockchain (Reyes and Hurt, 2025). Not all DAOs are investment vehicles or businesses, however. Their technical design and purpose-driven framing mean that the DAO form may be directed to social, philanthropic, or educational uses.

A DAO is characteristically decentralized rather than centralized or hierarchical because decisions are taken and recorded via the computer code that comprises the organization rather than via the design of a legally recognized fiction such as a corporation. Membership and participation in the DAO may be pseudonymous. It is autonomous in the sense that it owes its existence and functionality to coordinated social activity that is documented in code rather than assigned by legal rule to a corporate form. It is an organization in the casual sense of "a group of people or other actors," rather than a corporation or other legally recognized entity, such as a partnership or a cooperative.

We do not suggest that DAOs are bounded definitionally by purposes or goals, as some have suggested (El Faqir et al. 2020). DAOs often operate amid ecologies of DAO-enabling platforms, peer relationships, teams, guilds, squads, and tools (Rawson 2021). Despite the intuition that DAOs operate entirely on blockchains, in practice, conversations, negotiations, and other DAO-relevant coordinating activities may take place in adjacent communications environments, such as the chat apps Discord and Telegram.

DAOs can be thought of as *autonomous* corporations in two senses. One, they do not depend on legal recognition for their existence and operation. They are, in an important sense, "autonomous" of corporate law and therefore of the state. Two, they represent distinct organizational solutions to contracting and other resource management dilemmas that have been addressed conventionally and classically by corporations. DAOs are in a sense "autonomous" of theories of corporate identity. How can law, policy, and practice determine whether actions or activities are appropriately and accurately associated with the corporation in the first place rather than with human decision makers (Gindis 2016)? How should law, policy, and practice distinguish among appropriate behaviors associated with corporate functions and purposes, on the one hand, and appropriate behaviors associated with humans who have ownership or management roles in the corporation, on the other hand (Berle and Means 1932; Jensen and Meckling 1976)? Which decisions and activities are properly undertaken within the formal boundaries of the corporation, and which engage the corporation in relationships with outside parties (Coase 1937)?

Their "autonomy" is therefore as much conceptual as technological, something that we note initially in order to create a broad potential space for our analysis and to sharpen the distinction between DAOs, conceptually, and conventional legally recognized corporations. By virtue of legal requirements of corporate organizations, in contrast to the fluid motivational impulses that may drive participation in DAOs, the formal boundaries of the corporation are defined by law. Employees, managers, and shareholders may come and go, but as a matter of identity, the corporation remains the same actor. Gindis and Cole (this volume) describe this as the "corporate mask." A given DAO remains "the" DAO as transactions are recorded on the blockchain, and members participate, or not, not by virtue of the DAOs' legally mandated identity but instead by virtue of the rules of technical recognition that permit DAO transactions to be recognized. To borrow metaphorically a slogan of early cyberlaw scholarship, in a DAO, as in a blockchain generally, code really is law (Lessig 2006). A point of alignment in these recent perspectives is that recognition is essential, whether legal and social in the case of the corporation, or technical, legal, and social in the case of DAOs.

Building conceptually on that foundation, Wright (2021) notes that the software engineer who first proposed the idea of a DAO referred to it as a "decentralized autonomous company" in which the source code serves the function of bylaws. Reyes (2021) draws attention to the idea of "autonomous corporate personhood" in the form of automated businesses operated entirely through computer code, embedded in sociotechnical architectures while acknowledging that several states have moved toward legal recognition of DAOs. Hence, technical, social, and legal recognition are in some cases converging.

12.2.2 *Studying DAOs and Blockchains as Knowledge Commons*

The role of code does not exempt DAOs from being classified as sociotechnical systems for resource governance. Despite the promise of efficient and adaptable "trustless" transacting, both DAOs and blockchains can neither fully escape social dilemmas associated with human beings interacting with one another nor fully convert social dilemmas into technical solutions. Inevitably, despite their arguably "trustless" character, DAOs and DAO members interact with humans and with other human-designed systems, including conventional corporations and legal structures. They are, therefore, participatory sociotechnical systems rather than purely "private" governance. DAOs are not governance-free. Rather, they instantiate governance in distinct ways.

In that respect, DAOs can be understood as extensions of commons-based peer production and open-source collaboration of the sort imagined by Benkler (2004, 2013). We emphasize, however, that in pointing to commons concepts we do not argue that DAOs (or blockchains) "are" commons. Nor do we equate knowledge commons with commons-based peer production. Instead, we argue that there are important insights to be gleaned from characterizing DAOs as species of knowledge commons governance, community- or collectivity-based responses to social dilemmas associated with shared knowledge and information resources, building on the definition of knowledge commons developed in the GKC literature (Frischmann et al. 2023).

Our emphasis on a GKC perspective joins analysis of blockchains as resource governance systems, with transactions "on" a blockchain providing an exhaustive and accurate record of resource ownership and transfer with respect to some relevant resource pool.

Blockchains are decentralized or distributed peer-to-peer computer networks that record information, including transactions. Human-specified rules as to what information and how it is recorded are embedded in the code of the computer networks themselves. Blockchains are "trustless" in the specific sense that they do not require trusted third parties to process or validate transactions. Permissionless or algorithmic blockchains enable essentially anyone to participate in transactions that are recorded on the blockchain. Permissioned or participatory blockchains, such as DAOs, may be more structured and involve additional rules, embedded in computer code, that determine who has the power to conduct and record transactions on the blockchain and what sorts of transactions may be included, and what cannot be.

The technical requirement that blockchains effectuate transactions by computational consensus rather than by human decision making implies that they formally involve fewer opportunities to exert human-based power or influence than organizations that rely on conventional managerial hierarchies. They are, therefore, represented by blockchain enthusiasts as both less corruptible and authoritative than conventional ledgers, or records of transactions. They can, for this reason, be thought of as comparatively free from power imbalances, thus contributing to opportunities for self-governance (Ferrari et al. 2023; Spelliscy et al. 2024). This feature can be considered a response to economic power (in that blockchains and blockchain-based organizations may be regarded as providing alternatives to corporations) or to government power (in that blockchains may provide alternatives to recording systems administered by central banks) (Cowen 2019). By design, blockchain protocols constitute governance of the resources whose ownership and identity they record, of the actors who engage in transactions on the blockchain, and *by* the actors who control the code that makes blockchain-based transactions possible. The protocols are both literally and metaphorically constitutional structures that define "citizenship" in any given blockchain network (Alston 2020).

As cryptocurrencies are well-known applications of blockchain governance, we draw on that sector for a brief illustration. According to De Filippi and Loveluck (2016), the two distinct governance mechanisms in the best-known blockchain-based currency, Bitcoin, are the technical infrastructure for cooperating in transactions and recording transactions, which governs all blockchain members (the operational layer, interpreting the underlying code), and the technical infrastructure for cooperating in managing the underlying code, which governs and is governed by a small group of core developers. Another aspect of governance involves the response to actor entry and exit in permissionless blockchains, such as forking (Berg and Berg

2020). Focusing on the infrastructural character of blockchains yields yet another governance dimension, in that they offer structural solutions to downstream resource use. Blockchains can be thought of as innovation commons: institutions that facilitate cooperative pooling of innovation resources, including capital, ideas, and talent, thereby facilitating entrepreneurial discovery (Potts 2019).

Alston et al. (2022) question the static view of blockchains as complete contracts and trustless transactions. Rather, blockchains are evolving organizations where the threat of exit by users conditions the mechanism of change in the protocol, which entails a layered and dynamic set of governance forces. Internal governance consists of protocols and collective choice rules, while external governance includes competitive pressure from public and private institutions relative to a blockchain's performance, subject matter scope, and internal governance, shaped by competitors' governance choices.

Murtazashvili et al. (2022) consider blockchains as knowledge commons. They consider (1) institutionalized community governance with sharing of resources (code developers, miners, users, founders, each with shared access to code, internet, etc.); (2) social dilemmas (social and economic systems require describing objects and assets in secure, reliable, and timely ways); (3) resource sharing (shared resources include knowledge, data, and opportunities to use outputs; general openness of blockchains to entry and exit, especially algorithmic blockchains).

12.2.3 *DAOs and Corporations as Knowledge Commons*

The conceptual affinity between DAOs and corporations as organizational forms motivates analysis of affinities between DAOs and corporations as resource governance systems. In both contexts, we offer the GKC perspective as a critical analytic tool.

Looking at corporations, our GKC focus intervenes in a well-established debate on the character of the corporation as a resource governance system, contrasting a "communitarian" or "political" framing, identified long ago by March (1962) and updated by Whitford and Zirpoli (2016), and Levinthal and Pham (2024), with a predominantly contractarian or Coasean perspective (Alchian and Demsetz 1972; Hart 1988). The scholarly debate has struggled at times to accommodate the fact of "corporate personhood," or the factual and legal identity of the corporation as a recognized legal and market actor (Gindis and Hodgson 2026). The emergence of DAOs as "autonomous" entities with sociotechnical resource governance features has sharpened the terms of that struggle and opened a new front in the existing corporate governance debate (Reyes 2021).

Scholarship, in a way, is also struggling to keep up with practice. Questions as to both governance by the corporation and governance of the corporation have been extended recently via technology developments that are stretching the notion of a corporation's boundaries even from a Coasean "nexus of contracts" perspective

(The Economist 2023). These challenges include a blurring of the conventional boundaries of firms with increasing use of AI (Petrin 2024).

The chapter examines this cluster of challenges by extending the argument initiated by Deakin (2012), who considers the corporation as commons in the Ostrom tradition, treating the corporate entity as a governance strategy for coordinating the development and distribution of many sorts of material and immaterial resources. In starting with DAOs, we focus on knowledge commons analysis rather than on Ostrom's framework and on the knowledge governance attributes of both DAOs and corporations broadly. The distinction between the GKC framework and Ostrom's approach originates in differences between social dilemmas associated with knowledge resources as opposed to those associated with biophysical or material resources (Madison et al. 2022). In practice, the two may not be sharply differentiated, and the style of analysis is similar. The choice of framework may speak less to its functional importance and more to analytic emphasis and the potential for results to be generalized beyond the corporate governance context to other knowledge commons settings. By applying the GKC framework to DAOs, we aim both to clarify the understanding of corporations as solutions to governance dilemmas and to confirm the utility of the GKC framework as part of, rather than in opposition to, governance in market contexts.

Hassan and de Filippi (2023) draw attention to the history of decentralized community governance generally and its role in adapting blockchain technologies to corporate and commercial applications. DAOs activate with specificity the instinct described by Allen and Berg (2020) that blockchain governance can be analyzed profitably with reference to corporate governance. The Coasean "nexus of contracts" framing of the corporation has a material analog in the manner in which DAOs are defined by transactions recorded via smart contracts.

Contrasts are as important as similarities. Some of the significant differences between DAOs and conventional corporate organizations include the following: (1) DAOs lack a centralized structure featuring formal managers or a managerial hierarchy in a traditional sense; (2) DAO membership is not viewed as necessarily durable or long-lasting; rather than a board of directors, distributed consensus – meaning transactions performed and executed by members of the DAO at any given time – is the basis for governance; and (3) DAOs operate with relative autonomy from external validation and regulation by traditional legal institutions. That list can be expanded as follows.

- *Source of Law:* DAOs are "rule by code," where it is hard to change rules that establish procedures for anyone interacting (De Filippi and Wright 2018). Corporations exist by virtue of and rely on law as text, as social institution, and as social practice. As Davidson (this volume) emphasizes, there exists an important distinction between "on chain" governance, or governance of the

DAO by the DAO, and "off chain" governance, that is, (possible) governance of the DAO by external authorities.

- *Nature of Interactions:* DAOs are comparatively decentralized, by virtue of the underlying peer-to-peer network structure; corporations are comparatively hierarchical (Williamson 1996).
- *Scale:* DAOs have potentially unlimited geography and participation; conventionally, corporations – though their structures can transcend geographical boundaries, and outlive their founders – are linked to specific places and people.
- *Management:* DAOs can have essentially no management (as in permissionless blockchains) or have a defined structure of core operators. Traditional legal entities are run by boards or managers. Participatory DAOs enable members to set parameters needed by the underlying smart contract and to update those parameters as needed, with governance determined through votes measured with blockchain "tokens" that represent records of transactions.
- *Membership:* For DAOs, membership is tracked with smart contracts and an underlying blockchain, with membership purchased or allocated as a reward for computing effort directed to maintaining the blockchain. "Membership" in a corporation is a legal relationship defined by role: shareholder, director, manager, or employee. For communitarian characterizations of the firm, "membership" may extend to the practical implications of long-term partnerships and supplier–customer relationship and to interdependencies associated with the firm's physical presence in a community. For contractarian characterizations, "membership" is typically an inapt perspective with which to view the firm.

12.3 THE GKC FRAMEWORK

We use "knowledge commons" as an organizing principle not because we draw a sharp distinction between commons governance and corporate governance (or network governance, platform governance, or any other genus of governance), but because it offers a useful methodological gateway to collecting and organizing critical information about the phenomenon we are interested in. "Commons," as we use the term, is not an ontologically distinct category. Instead, it is a governance practice by which members of a community or collective govern production and use of shared resources in order to address social dilemmas (Madison et al. 2010). For knowledge commons, the topic of interest here, the relevant resources are knowledge, information, data, and related immaterial resources. Even that limitation is subject to adjustment; immaterial knowledge resources are characteristically linked in complicated ways to systems of material resources.

GKC-based research searches out instances of shared knowledge, information, and data that prompt the need for, even the demand for, governance: mechanisms for people in communities or collectives to get along in creating, using, and storing it (Frischmann et al. 2014). Knowledge commons is neither a place nor a thing nor the resource or resources as such (such as a data pool, or a patent pool, or a body of knowledge or content). Knowledge commons is a governance system relative to one or more sets of shared resources. Knowledge commons may succeed, even thrive; it may fail, or produce harm rather than social benefit.

Material in a knowledge commons system is not simply or necessarily fully free and open. There are rules and guidelines indicating and sometimes determining appropriate production and contribution, appropriate extraction and use, and appropriate curation, preservation, and even destruction. Knowledge commons governance consists of systems (plural) of formal and informal rules and norms by which members of a community or collective coordinate to resolve problems, plan their affairs, and achieve their goals. Governance sometimes consists entirely of "law," sometimes entirely of "social norms," sometimes of sociotechnical devices, and often of blends of the three. Governance sometimes exists by design and intentionality. Governance sometimes emerges out of history, culture, path dependence, and accident.

The GKC research framework encourages researchers to examine a case of knowledge commons governance by breaking that brief summary into clusters of related questions that can be asked and answered in a systematic way. Is there a shared knowledge, information, or data resource? (There may be more than one.) What individual and social problems arise by virtue of the shared character of the resource? (Those problems, or social dilemmas, may operate at smaller or larger scales, may emerge at different points in time, and may both prompt the emergence of governance solutions and be caused by those solutions.) Is there a community or collective that produces or manages that knowledge, and how is that community defined and organized? (Again, there may be more than one, leading to questions about their nested or polycentric character.) What are the various rules and social norms that define the resource, define the community (including roles and responsibilities and processes for inclusion, exclusion, and participation), and determine how the resource is produced and managed, presumably to respond to the problems with governance strategies and solutions? What are the expected and unexpected outcomes, positive and negative, associated with the practice of those rules and norms? What feedback loops connect responses to those different questions? What spillover effects follow from this governance system?

The terminology of the GKC framework corresponds in part to the terminology developed by Ostrom for the Institutional Analysis and Development (IAD) framework (Ostrom 2005). The GKC framework, like Ostrom's IAD framework, encourages researchers to open their examination with questions about social dilemmas caused by or linked to resource sharing, which is to say, conflicts between self-interested behavior and other-directed or collective interests. The "classic" social dilemma in a shared resource context is the "tragedy of the commons" popularized by Hardin (1968). In the GKC environment, a "tragedy of commons" is not necessarily a starting point for researchers; openness to multiple possible social dilemmas, including dilemmas of other sorts, is key (Madison et al. 2022).

The affinities between the GKC framework and the IAD framework are important. Differences are important as well. While Ostrom's work is not always perfectly consistent or clear, three bear emphasis here.

First, "resources" in the GKC context are not "biophysical" or given as they are the IAD setting; knowledge, information, and data resources are produced, defined, and identified by human systems, including legal systems. Law is characteristically integral to knowledge commons governance but may be exogenous to natural resource commons.

Second, the IAD framework – indeed, much of the corpus of Ostrom's research on commons governance – is premised on "resources" constituting "CPRs," or "common pool resources," things that are shared but depletable. Fisheries, grazing meadows, forests, and water systems are paradigmatic cases of Ostrom's commons governance vision. These are contexts where the "tragedy of the commons" may have applied because of overconsumption (that is, opportunistic behavior) and which Ostrom wished to show could be managed successfully by prosocial collectives. The GKC framework assumes the opposite, at least initially. Knowledge and information resources are nondepletable, though they may be linked in complex ways to depletable resources. Given their (potentially) blended character, the framework recognizes social dilemmas related to abundance and associated prospects for sharing and combining knowledge resources.

Third, the IAD framework relies heavily on the assumption that "actors" are individuals operating on a rational decision making basis. Commons governance is explicitly and almost entirely linear and functional, and the individual actors play central analytic roles – even accounting for a diversity of motivations and practices among real human beings. Prosocial governance is both observed and rational, in that it sustains the resource over time for both individual and collective benefit. The GKC framework makes no such assumption. Story, myth, history, and culture, including preexisting and changing normative values, expectations, and objectives, play potentially important roles in knowledge commons governance. (That fact may disrupt the characteristic focus of IAD-motivated analysis on "action arenas," defined sociotechnical environments where actors regularly make decisions about resource generation and consumption.) The community as such may be the central analytic focus, rather than the decision making individual. The reciprocal linking of governance patterns to resource and community formation and identity is a key theme of the GKC framework and documents that possibility. One key product of the Wikipedia community, an oft-touted example of knowledge commons governance, is the Wikipedia community itself.

12.4 DAOS AS KNOWLEDGE COMMONS

The DAO form can be and has been applied to numerous sectors and forms of commercial and social collaboration. That diversity motivates the focus of this section, which uses the GKC framework primarily to organize the analysis of the concept of the DAO as a sociotechnical arrangement rather than any specific DAO. Any particular DAO is a target that is evolving more or less rapidly. The GKC framework could be applied to any specific DAO or to attributes of a specific DAO or multiple specific DAOs. Examples include the following:

- "Pleasr," found at https://pleasr.org, is a collective of artists and art collectors that invests in NFT (Non-Fungible Token) art and other digital assets.
- "ConstitutionDAO," found at https://www.constitutiondao.com, was an effort to raise capital via a crowdsourcing process for a single purpose: to bid at auction for a specific copy of the US Constitution. The fundraising succeeded; the bid ultimately failed.
- "Friends with Benefits," found at https://www.alchemy.com/dapps/friends-with-benefits, is a so-called "social DAO" in which investing in tokens grants individual members the power to meet others, especially others in their geographic location, with shared interests in Web3 development opportunities and projects. The greater the investment, the greater the powers the DAO affords for connecting.
- "Decentraland," found at https://decentraland.org, is an online virtual world governed by a DAO, in which owners of Decentraland tokens, so-called "MANA," participate in administrative and governance decision making.
- "Uniswap," found at https://uniswap.org, operates a cryptocurrency exchange on the Ethereum blockchain. It uses the "UNI" token.
- "American Cryptofed DAO," found at https://www.americancryptofed.org, bills itself as "the first Wyoming Decentralized Autonomous Organization," because its organizational standing is recognized under Wyoming state law. This DAO aims to create a cryptocurrency monetary system via tokens known as "Ducats" and "Lockes."
- "LexDAO," found at https://lexdao.org, is a collective of "legal engineering professionals" who promise to bring "the traditional legal settlement layer" to the masses, via blockchain methods.
- "Mantle," formerly known as BitDAO and found at https://www.mantle.xyz, is a vehicle for investing in Web3 and de-fi ("decentralized finance") start-ups. The original "BIT" tokens were swapped out for new "MNT" tokens as part of a governance vote in 2023.
- "The DAO," which both launched and ceased operations in 2016, is usually credited with being the "original" decentralized autonomous organization, an

exemplar of a new species of corporate governance, operating an investment fund but without a conventional management structure or governing board (Morrison, Mazey, and Wingreen 2020). The DAO's "smart contract" code, which ran on the Ethereum blockchain, was hacked, and a substantial amount of its funding (3.6 million Ether, the equivalent of roughly US$70 million) was siphoned off. In response, the Ethereum community implemented a hard fork, dividing the Ethereum blockchain between the main branch of Ethereum, on the one hand, and the original unforked blockchain, now called Ethereum Classic, on the other. The fork permitted restoration of the funds to the DAO and the original investors, but the hack caused tremendous embarrassment for Ethereum developers and exposed the idea that the blockchains are not technologically invulnerable.

We address, briefly, each of the significant clusters of GKC framing questions.

12.4.1 *Relevant Knowledge, Information, and Data Resources*

DAOs are concerned formally with digital representations of the products of computational processes: tokens, the products of proof of work and proof of stake processes on blockchains. These are outcomes of decisions to which economic and possibly cultural significance is attached by virtue of their technical and social visibility and by the computational permanence of the distributed ledger that we call "the blockchain." Tokens, as digital assets or crypto assets and sometimes denoted NFTs ("Non-Fungible Tokens"), are the first and most important layer of knowledge and information resources with which DAOs are concerned.

A token itself is not a naturally shared object, with the attributes of a public good, but the construct of a DAO operates both technologically and socially precisely because each token in itself is useless and valueless. Whatever the purpose of a particular DAO, information *about* tokens must be shared: the investment or membership value that is associated with each token, creating its status in the DAO context vis-à-vis both other members and non-members, and the governance powers associated with each token, which represent the powers of DAO members to engage with one another. Shared information about token ownership is the baseline attribute of a DAO that allows owners to engage in decision making within the DAO environment, to exercise membership rights and for token holders to engage in economic transactions. The shared character of tokens as knowledge resources is inherent with respect to their essential role in the functions of the entity.

Tokens may and often do represent other knowledge and information resources, including information about material assets (such as land or material artworks), information about immaterial assets (such as financial instruments), or information about immaterial intellectual property objects, such as copyrighted works, patented inventions, and trademarks. Tokens on blockchains may even refer to confidential information and trade secrets and to "things" that have an ambiguous status as matters of conventional intellectual property law, such as material subject to characterization as Traditional Knowledge, the growing body of law known as Geographical Indications, and matters of "know-how" that may play important roles in transactions concerning industrial innovation.

As DAOs consist of multiple layers of technological infrastructure and application – blockchain networks, smart contracts, and payment systems – the relevant code is, at each layer, a shared knowledge resource in itself, as is the technological and educational expertise that is contributed to building and maintaining the code. The Ethereum blockchain is built with open-source computer software, a well-established shared resource in its own right (Schweik and English 2012). Blockchain networks are frequently characterized as "trustless" systems, but it is now well-known that this framing is at best a rhetorical mis-direction. Collective trust in the developers and maintainers of the code is essential to the claim that blockchain networks have a technical integrity that justifies treating applications built on them as "autonomous" relative to ordinary legal frameworks (Werbach 2018).

DAOs depend on further layers of tacit knowledge and expertise, notably trust (lending weight to the characterization of blockchains as nested, polycentric governance systems proposed in Murtazashvili et al. 2022), in the sense that DAOs are initiated by human beings who share some degree of trust in one another as to the agreed-upon purpose(s) of the organization. Trust, like privacy, is a social phenomenon (Gambetta 1988); it should be characterized as a shared information resource. The hack of "The DAO" and the response that forked the Ethereum blockchain in order to restore investment capital to original investors suggest that DAO members are not always willing fully to "trust" the proposition that the "smart contract" code, and only the smart contract code, determines allocation of DAO resources. An appeal to extra-code values was made, and that appeal was successful.

The resources that shape DAO governance are analogous to but not necessarily or precisely the same as the resources that characterize the traditional firm and corporate governance. In a DAO, trust is an infrastructural immaterial knowledge resource that is integral to understanding governance practices in both contexts. Digital assets in the DAO setting *represent* works of intellectual property (in the case of NFTs) or financial interests, and in their representative forms (tokens) information *about* them is shared across the entity, even while ownership of a specific token is specific to a single actor. In a traditional corporate organization, money itself (in various forms), tangible assets, human capital and expertise, and intellectual property works themselves are related (possibly) shared assets, typically owned or controlled by the firm as an entity rather than by members of the firm (shareholders, managers, or employees) (Burk and McDonnell 2007). Information *about* those assets, including their origins, values, and uses and purposes, is shared within the firm, though in nuanced ways. Different managers and employees will access and use different information on a shared basis (at times) and on an exclusive basis (at other times), and sometimes in tacit forms and sometimes in explicit ones (Brown and Duguid 2000).

12.4.2 *Social Dilemmas*

Commons governance is often stereotyped as a response to the classic "tragedy of the commons" social dilemma, where resource users rationally overconsume a shared resource. However, with knowledge and information resources, overconsumption is typically not a primary concern. When identifying other important social dilemmas in this context, we must move beyond such stereotypical thinking. As Madison et al. (2022) note, the networked information economy sharpens some existing dilemmas relative to knowledge and information resources, particularly in identifying and promoting positive spillover effects of knowledge production and use; limiting harmful spillover effects relative to adjacent interests in privacy and security; and producing education and capacity for effective participation in (or exit from) relevant governance systems. "Knowledge commons governance" as a macro category includes different possible subsidiary categories, including innovation commons (in which knowledge pools facilitate productive coordination and combination) and infrastructure commons (in which knowledge pools offer resources to a multiplicity of different uses and users).

Social dilemmas associated with DAOs are in part species of the social dilemmas associated with any organization. Because our focus is on knowledge commons dimensions of DAOs, we focus on dilemmas associated with shared knowledge and information resources. We distinguish, where possible, between dilemmas associated with forming organizations (dilemmas for which DAOs and other organizations are meant to be governance solutions) and dilemmas associated with operating organizations (dilemmas that DAOs and other organizations may create).

Because social dilemmas are defined in the first place as conflicts between individual interest and collective interest that interfere with productive collaboration or cooperation (Dawes 1980; Kollock 1998), it is appropriate to begin by reducing all social dilemmas to problems of agency relationships (Ross 1973), meaning the risk that one party as principal, having relied on a second party as agent to act faithfully on the principal's behalf, risks betrayal or defection by the agent. One partner may rely on a second partner to act faithfully in the joint pursuit of the partnership's goals, but the second partner may fail, or defect. Those risks are compounded by the possibility that the principal cannot effectively monitor the agent's performance, by the agent's not being subject to effective accountability measures even if monitoring is present, and by the likelihood that expectations of the character of faithful performance are ambiguous or may be embodied in tacit rather than explicit understandings. It is worth noting that to a substantial extent, those elementary outlines of agency costs are matters of shared knowledge and information: The interests of principal and agent may be misaligned because they lack effective mechanisms for sharing knowledge about each other and about the conceptual and material conditions of effective cooperation.

A related set of social dilemmas arises with respect to the design and character of the organizational framework or infrastructure itself. The first-order social dilemmas described in the preceding paragraph are compounded by the second-order likelihood that both principal(s) and agent(s) will address those social dilemmas by relying on intermediaries of one sort or another – the corporate form, defined by relevant law; partnerships, nonprofit associations, or cooperatives, also defined by relevant law; material forms shaping social practice, such as cities; tradition, custom, and social norms, as in universities and faith traditions; and – in the case of open-source software, Wikipedia, and DAOs – combinations of contract and code. Each of those contexts both solves social dilemmas in part (principals need not rely directly on their knowledge of agents' behavior; they can rely on monitoring and enforcement powers of the intermediary) and creates new ones, again characterized significantly in terms of shared knowledge and information: How can both principals and agents be assured that the intermediary and its own agents and decision making are trustworthy, safe, fair, uncorrupted, and reliable?

Second-order social dilemmas may be compounded by third-order dilemmas, as second-order solutions (such as corporations) rely on additional layers of intermediaries, producing what one might refer to (depending on one's preference for spatial metaphors) as a pyramid of social dilemmas, or an ecology. Corporate partnerships may depend on relationships with lawyers, accountants, financiers, insurers, and so on, adding to the inventory of possible productive outcomes and to knowledge-based social dilemmas.

That broad description can be brought to ground in the following brief inventory of specific social dilemmas. None of these is wholly distinct from the others.

12.4.2.1 Identity

The organization may be defined and identified separately from the identities of its individual members, participants, or owners, and may have distinct rights, powers, and obligations as an entity.

12.4.2.2 Risk Allocation/Moral Hazard

Having been entrusted with certain responsibilities or decision making powers in the organizational context, the agent may act according to the agent's interests rather than the principal's.

12.4.2.3 Information Asymmetry

Principals in any part of an ecology of social dilemmas, whether individual or organizational, may have incomplete or inaccurate information about decision making by agents.

12.4.2.4 Residual Claims/Risks of Loss

The costs or harms associated with the failure of a collaborative or cooperative effort may be unfairly or unclearly distributed across the population of individual members, participants, or owners.

12.4.2.5 Efficiency and Effectiveness of Decision Making/Voice

The roles and responsibilities of principals and agents as parts of decision making in the organization may be poorly defined or inappropriately biased. Individual members, participants, or owners may be excluded or believe that they have been unfairly excluded. A social dilemma may arise by virtue of having "too many cooks" in the decision making context, not only by virtue of having too few cooks, or the wrong ones.

12.4.2.6 Entrance, Change, and Exit

Rules or practices for including new participants or members, for permitting exit by existing participants, and for enabling existing participants to modify the character or purpose of the organization, may inappropriately or unfairly bias the organization's operation in favor of the status quo; in favor of exclusion; in favor of the majority of participants, members, or owners; or in favor of destabilizing fluidity.

12.4.2.7 Allocating the Products of Spillovers, Both Positive and Negative

The word "spillovers" is in many ways simply a synonym for the proposition that a system (including an organization) has impacts and generates benefits and costs with respect to individuals, communities, and adjacent systems that are not fully internal to its operation. The "tragedy of the commons" metaphor speaks to the possibility that those spillovers will be negative, and that the external costs of the system should be internalized by its participants. An "infrastructure" metaphor speaks to the possibility that those spillovers will be positive, so that the generative potential of the system should be enhanced, even optimized (Frischmann and Lemley 2007).

12.4.2.8 Public and Private Purpose

It has become essentially an article of faith during the twentieth century that the purpose of for-profit organizations, such as corporations, is to return profits to shareholders (Lund and Pollman 2021). That framing may systematically disadvantage owners and others in the organization who wish to prioritize or simply to advance other social or public purposes.

Against that discussion, what, specifically, is distinctive about DAOs, both with respect to social dilemmas and with respect to how DAOs respond to social dilemmas and perhaps generate additional dilemmas?

In the first place, the design of the DAO offers a baseline institutional model as an alternative to the hierarchical solution provided by the corporation.

The corporation in a way "reifies" principals and agents, separating ownership (shareholders) from control (managers), structuring both internal decision making and external contacting around a hierarchy of managerial responsibility (Williamson 2000), and wrapping the entirety of the collaborative system in legal frameworks of corporate identity, corporate governance, securities law, and contract and commercial law. Law, as a shared knowledge resource, is a key element of the corporate solution to social dilemmas associated with cooperation.

The DAO collapses rather than reifies the distinction between principals and agents, and it largely substitutes the blockchain and smart contracts for law as shared information resources. The decentralized, consensus-based character of decision making on blockchain networks addresses governance dilemmas by associating participation in governance with token ownership, ostensibly open to anyone with access to the relevant public blockchain. In principle, this reduces if not fully eliminates the risk of defection, by channeling defection away from expression within the organization, subject to sanction via contract law, employment law, fiduciary duties and duties of care, and securities law, and toward expression by forking the code.

It is obviously true (to borrow a well-known phrase associated with Ostrom) that DAOs are no panaceas (Ostrom and Cox 2010), just as corporations are rife with poor decision making and harmful impacts. The code underlying the three key layers of a DAO – the blockchain, the smart contract, and the digital asset – is open and therefore stable so long as trust among developers persists to the degree that forks are avoided. The code is changeable and adaptable to the degree that DAOs can be repurposed in small and large ways to accommodate changes in the ambitions of their members. If the DAO is an investment vehicle, the investing ambitions of its members may change; the DAO may even fail if investment returns don't meet member goals.

But the technical sophistication needed to participate effectively in DAO governance is limited to a small class of experts worldwide. Because DAO assets and members inevitably touch the ground of the non-blockchain world, additional layers of institutional trustworthiness are needed to ensure their functionality. The economic value created by DAO entities (i.e., positive spillover effects) may be recognized outside of those entities only at a discount, as value encoded in tokens has to be converted to other currencies in order to be usable in other markets, or not at all. Ambitious claims that NFTs would create stable and secure markets in digital versions of copyrighted works have largely proved untrue; the NFT market is no more stable than the auction market for material artworks – which is largely a product of elite psychology rather than fixed worth (Frye 2018). In that sense, and again focusing largely on their knowledge commons dimensions, DAOs are not as fully autonomous as initially described, and as a result they are not necessarily any more successful than corporations in solving first-order social dilemmas or in avoiding second- or third-order dilemmas.

12.4.3 *Social, Cultural, Technological, and Economic Context*

Like blockchains, DAOs have been characterized both by proponents and by some researchers as examples of governance "by code" (Esener 2024). There is a kernel of accuracy in that description, in the sense that formally and technically, transactions and records of ownership on blockchain networks appear to be entirely "on-chain," that is, endogenous to those networks and to related smart contract and payment layers.

In multiple respects, however, the claim is misleading. Multiple commentators have observed how DAOs and the idea of DAOs as autonomous, self-governing communities have histories and motivating ideologies, going back not only to the idealism of the mid 1990s and late 1990s internet (Turner 2008; @keikreutler 2021) but also earlier, to a range of phenomena operating both outside the market (utopianism in communal living) and in polycentric and decentralized decision making in industrial and public sectors (Seidman 1952).

The key here, as in other knowledge commons governance cases studies, is recognizing that the virtues and drawbacks of DAO governance should not be assigned fully to the operation either of human or technological agents operating within the boundaries of the entity, coordinating their actions and then causing the entity to interact with others. Here again, the "autonomous" corporation or DAO is functionally autonomous only in part. At multiple layers of practice its human operators have histories, ideologies, and preferences that cause the entity to be constructed and operated as it is. Case studies of traditional corporations usually have little trouble distinguishing between an idealized model of the firm as an imagined "nexus of contracts" and an actually functioning corporation (Stout 2017). The study of DAOs should not be seduced by the premise that DAOs are, analytically, entirely different from the latter.

12.4.4 *Action Arenas and Rules-in-Use*

"Governance" is often reduced analytically to "the rules," both formal and informal; we take a broader view of governance as practice in context.

As Sanfilippo et al. (2018, 122–123) observe: "*Action arenas* serve as the core units of IAD and GKC analysis, functioning as policy analysis equivalents of social action and interaction settings or Goffman's frames. An action arena is simply a recurring type of situation in which community actors interact with one another." Recognizing the challenges of identifying and analyzing a single "right" action arena in a polycentric social system, McGinnis introduced the concept of "adjacent action arenas" (McGinnis 2011), which has been adapted to the GKC setting by Dekker and Kuchař (2024) and Gindis and Cole (this volume). Investigating arenas of all sorts means focusing on functional attributes and implications of patterns of interaction rather than only on definitional specificity.

We therefore do not limit the focus of GKC analysis of DAOs to "the DAO" as such as "the" or the only relevant action arena. Identifying action arenas in a polycentric context means asking whether the DAO is being characterized accurately in context, so that useful levels of details are captured relative to the DAO itself as well as relative to activity taking place off the blockchain and in ways that permit the data to be compared effectively with data generated from other cases – specific DAOs, or non-DAOs, such as the traditional corporate form. Proceeding at the right levels of generality facilitates comparison across DAOs and between DAOs and other governance systems.

Questions here include both how DAO resources are created and used, and also where and how membership is determined (to the extent to which that might be treated independently of transactions); where administration takes place; where enforcement takes place and disputes are resolved; and where and how rules are formed and interpreted. This perspective aligns with Dekker and Kuchař's (2024) framework in identifying key governance functions – resource allocation, membership, administration, enforcement, and rule-making – as structured by different actors within a system. Governance is not monolithic. Rather, governance structures vary based on who controls these functions and the degree to which these functions are integrated or stratified.

"The rules" are critical, and they are critical in part because of their definitional roles as well as their operating roles. Per Ostrom, we refer to these as "rules-in-use" to connote their significance as practices rather than only as structure or architecture. As Allen et al. (2020) observe, one of the most important contributions that Ostrom makes to the field of blockchain governance is the priority that should be given to building a "grammar" of relevant rules.

We focus on three types of rules-in-use, though in practice they reduce to a single technological construct, and we distinguish among several "action" arenas.

The three key types of rules are membership rules, decision making rules, and conflict resolution rules. In DAOs, all three are combined technically in code. In principle, anyone can become a member of a DAO by acquiring a relevant token; anyone who is a member can participate in DAO decision making; disagreements or conflicts about DAO governance are resolved on-chain, via the consensus mechanism. Unlike a classic firm, which relies on hierarchies of human responsibility, capability, and judgment, from a technical standpoint DAOs fulfill their promise of egalitarian decentralized practice. DAOs largely avoid the perils of power asymmetries and domination that are said to contaminate firms operating in market economies (DuPont 2024).

That said, there is no full avoidance of power dynamics, a fact that is exposed once we examine different action arenas as intersecting but distinct governance settings. The blockchain layer as such is a species of shared infrastructure, control of which is embedded in individual propertized objects – tokens – distinguishing it from shared physical infrastructures such as highways and bridges (Grimmelmann and Windawi 2023) and shared social infrastructures such as organizational hierarchies (Amin and Hausner 1997; Borrup 2011). In the material infrastructure setting, power dynamics are expressed as dilemmas of underproduction and possible monopoly control, leading to governance framed as government ownership, regulated industry ownership, or open access – a species of commons (Frischmann 2012). In the blockchain setting, power dynamics are expressed in terms of "standard" dilemmas of wealth accumulation rather than in terms of access to the resource (Pistor 2019).

12.4.5 *Relevant Legal Frameworks*

The typical start to a knowledge commons case study includes attention to relevant legal frameworks, as those may define relevant resources (such as patents and copyrights) or community or collective entities (such as open-source software development communities, which are defined in part by open-source software licenses). With DAOs, that approach founders: the premise of these entities is that they are self-governing, with membership, decision making, and dispute resolution processes closed off entirely from formal legal systems.

In practical terms, walling off DAOs completely from legal institutions is not feasible, even if (to some) it is desirable. Each actor with interests in DAOs at different levels – including developers, miners, users, token holders, validators, all of whom may be either organizational/institutional or individual – has a legal, economic, and social status that exists outside of the DAO environment. Just as the classic firm faces a boundary question, so do DAOs. Just as the boundary question for the classic firm leads to important interventions from a law and regulation standpoint, DAOs are increasingly exposed to the question: should they be regulated or otherwise subject to "legal" ordering, and if so, how (Reyes 2021;

Reyes and Hurt 2025)? Importantly, how do the responses to those questions affect our characterization of DAOs as knowledge commons?

The second question has a more straightforward answer than the first. We believe that the GKC framework remains useful and important for studying DAOs even as various forms of legal order intrude more deeply into DAO operations and begin to shape their boundaries. Dekker and Kuchař (2022) demonstrated that knowledge commons concepts are broadly applicable to private market settings as well as to more self-evidently "communitarian" organizations. The question to be analyzed is not whether an organization "is" a commons or not but rather whether the knowledge commons framework is useful in understanding governance of a shared resource.

The first question – what is the likely character of "legal" regulation? – has both conceptual and technical answers.

The interesting conceptual question has to do with the fact that DAOs claim not only functional self-governing powers but also a kind of right of self-determination. In that effort, DAO organizers are aligned, at least indirectly, with numerous valuable social institutions through history, all of which have achieved dramatic degrees of governance autonomy relative to both markets and states: universities, religious organizations, philanthropies, and neighborhood and volunteer organizations. That is not to say that formal law is irrelevant to these things; they are regulated in many different ways. Nor are they fully independent of the market. To own real or personal property, to hire employees, to publish and promote materials all require engagement with market firms and processes. What matters, instead, is the existence of the community or collective as a source of normative order. The university as an institution (not to mention individual universities) sets and enforces its own normative priorities. The virtue of self-governing communities has been recognized repeatedly, from De Tocqueville through Putnam (2000). In that respect, DAOs may tap into a robust tradition, and as knowledge commons governance research is useful to study those phenomena, it likewise remains useful to study new things such as DAOs.

Using the GKC framework means not only adhering to conceptual integrity but also getting the empirical details right, and here the technical aspects of law and DAOs will be fascinating to observe as they evolve. To a significant extent we expect to see regulators trying to "domesticate" DAOs, especially in the US and Europe, by attempting to assimilate DAO structures and capabilities to what has been tried and found effective with respect to corporations. DAOs and related artificial entities may be given recognized entity identities or personalities, as "things in themselves," akin to but not identical to corporations or corporate-like actors, with legal rights and powers and with legal obligations (Li, 2004).

Corporations have forms of accountability to people and entities outside the boundary of the firm, both as corporate undertakings and, under limited circumstances, in the names of their managers. Particularly in financial markets contexts, corporations have legal obligations to identify, manage, and disclose various forms of risk, to deter and refuse to participate in fraudulent practices, not to engage in money laundering, and to devise mechanisms to reasonably ensure that the entity and its people and assets are secure and stable. As interests of the state and of the broader national and global so-called "community," equivalent themes are likely to be expressed vis-à-vis DAOs, or have been expressed already (Naudts 2023). We do not think, however, that the push to wrap DAOs in certain forms of legal order compromises their essential character as decentralized decision making entities.

The possibility of wrapping DAOs in one or more legal frameworks adds an additional, important nuance to our GKC examination: Classic law and legal institutions bring into focus the relative importance of human judgment and human communities of expertise in both the internal dynamics of DAOs and in external evaluation and regulation of DAOs. Blockchain networks are famously and powerfully self-executing; decisions are made and recorded on the chain, giving rise to the belief that the "trustless" character of blockchains is part of their special power. There are no humans to corrupt, or to defect, or to make errors. By contrast, law is full of humans, often formed into expert communities: trained lawyers, judges, and (often) legislators, developing and interpreting the codes and texts of the law and using law as normative order to constrain both lay humans and also the imaginations of humans as expressed in machines. There is a sense, in short, that the very purpose of the law is called into question by the very idea of the DAO.

Notably, framing the topic in that way steps well beyond existing debates about the theory of the firm, the character of corporate governance, about the relationship between shareholders and stakeholders, between the relative importance of maximizing profits or returns, and that of the normative purposes that a firm is created to serve, whether those are to deliver valuable products or services or productively employ citizens of a community. In one respect, DAOs offer a somewhat conventional case study of a sociotechnical knowledge commons. In others, DAOs challenge researchers to think imaginatively about the ends of law and social science.

12.4.6 *Outcomes*

Assessing the outcomes of a commons governance system is notoriously difficult. Ostrom's work was largely premised on the idea the commons management of a natural resource system could be as productive as a market-based or state-managed system, with added benefits accruing via the spillover effects of community participation in governance. In the knowledge and information context, "productivity" has no accepted definition, and it is also widely acknowledged that knowledge and information often have social virtues that far exceed their value only as industrial-style "resources," inputs into production mechanisms. Sometimes characterized as cultural infrastructure, sometimes as economic asset, sometimes as a source of hedonic goods, sometimes as an attribute of a well-functioning civic sphere, knowledge and information often have to do with individual and collective well-being across multiple dimensions. It is unlikely that a single analytic framework can capture that range of purposes using a single evaluative rubric.

Given that difficulty, knowledge commons case study research has come to focus increasingly on the idea that successful knowledge commons governance systems do not necessarily only produce and sustain "more" or "better" knowledge. Instead, the resolution of social dilemmas involving shared knowledge often resolves via commons governance in sustainable, resilient, and equitable communities. Focusing on the interdependence of knowledge and community enables us to suggest that the future of research on DAOs and analogous "autonomous" entities lies not in a focus on their productivity but in the ways in which the DAO structure sustains and is sustained by some wholly or partly exogenous value or sets of values. Similarly, in suggesting that focus for DAOs, we draw on a diverse array of existing knowledge commons case studies, where the knowledge implications of knowledge commons governance are functionally indistinguishable from the community implications. That diverse array includes early citizen science collectives (Madison 2014), research universities (Madison et al. 2009), and contemporary "smart" urbanism (Frischmann et al. 2023), as well as blockchain networks themselves (Bodon et al. 2022).

In short, there are multiple possible "outcomes" of knowledge commons, some more clearly described using perspectives external to the system and to commons analysis itself, and some more clearly described using commons-specific and internal perspectives.

"External" perspectives on DAOs are chronicled well by Micheler, Werbach, and Kremer in their overview of DAOs and corporate law (Micheler et al. 2026). Analogizing DAOs to original joint stock corporations during the Industrial Revolution, DAOs arguably offer flexible, efficient, and equitable coordination of financial and human resources, aiming, as the corporate form does in principle, at productive social and economic uses. At the same time, and again reflecting patterns of corporate practice, DAOs have experienced internal conflicts and governance failures. Their decentralized premise means that it is far from certain that DAOs represent a viable long-term complement to the corporate form.

Similarly, looking at DAOs as systems that may or may not meet social needs successfully, Reyes (2021) and Reyes and Hurt (2025) have investigated the comparative strengths and weaknesses of DAOs relative to various business organizations, including not only corporations but also partnerships and joint ventures. Those analyses detail comparisons with the DAO form with respect to ways in which law traditionally domesticates and disciplines organizational forms: centrally imposed, state-mandated fiduciary duties, securities law, accounting standards, transparency regulation, compliance with security obligations and money laundering rules, and so on. The persistence and viability of any particular organization is linked closely to centralized state regulation – or to its absence. Indeed, to a significant extent investors in DAOs tend to be entities themselves that operate largely outside the purview of securities regulation, so long as they do not seek public investment (venture capital funds, for example). It is fair to consider whether DAOs are, from this perspective, a form of regulatory avoidance.

The GKC framing brings to this question an explicit focus on two dimensions of DAOs. The first is its stress on DAOs as overlapping layers of shared resources rather than as simple objects for law or other governance. The second is the GKC framework's interest in examining the details of DAO communities. DAOs, like many knowledge commons, are concerned not only with producing knowledge or information "outputs" and supplying those to the broader world beyond but also with the producing and sustaining DAO communities themselves. The distinction between the two phenomena is not sharp but is worth considering in several respects relative to the question of assessing outcomes. How do DAOs perform not only as knowledge producers, relative to criteria used for other business organizations, but also as dynamic self-governing communities?

It is evident from the discussion that the idealized aims of DAOs may not be realized in practice. DAO governance conversations taking place on Discord or Telegram channels suggest that members signal their participation and preferences not simply via their behavior in transactions recorded on the blockchain but also via private chat. That fact creates the possibility of power imbalances and an absence of transparency. As in any community governance setting, some voices may be louder or more persuasive than others, and some voices may add little value to governance processes.

Moreover, DAOs have yet to demonstrate that their self-governing sociotechnical character can sustain specific DAOs over time, as members come and go and as the purposes of the DAO may evolve. GKC research increasingly draws attention to questions of voice and exit in commons governance as measures of the durability and legitimacy of a commons system (Sanfilippo et al. 2021). A corporate shareholder who wishes to "exit" can do so, usually, by selling their shares but without necessarily involving more than a moment's reflection about the shareholder's participation in governing the firm or jeopardizing the continued existence of the firm or its business. Even the transfer of all of the shares will not necessarily lead to the demise of the entity.

By contrast, a DAO member does not own marketable "shares" in the same respect; a wholesale liquidation of the interests of a DAO member (sometimes known as "rage-quitting") will lead, at scale, to the end of the DAO, which will either go out of existence in its entirety or be reconstituted via forking. A sizeable amount of investment in DAOs comes from venture capital funds, whose decisions to remain or exit any investment are rarely unconsidered (Alon et al. 2025). (The practice of "rage-quitting" also highlights the fact that assessing outcomes from a GKC perspective may require examining DAOs at different points in time, that is, when the DAO is in formation, when it is operating, and when it is resolving conflicts or ending.) Subgroups within a DAO may "exit" in part by forming sub-DAOs, which either enhance the functionality of decentralized DAO governance or recreate a governance hierarchy that makes DAOs less "communal" or distinguishable from corporations. It is possible that durable DAOs look more like classic corporations on the inside as well as being at least partly assimilated to classic legal regulation on the outside.

12.5 THE CORPORATION, THE FIRM, AND THE GKC FRAMEWORK

Studying DAOs as knowledge commons teaches lessons about DAOs themselves, and it also teaches lessons about how to analyze business organizations. This section summarizes how work on DAOs builds toward broader uses of the GKC framework relative to general business corporations and corporate governance.

Broadening the scope of the research begins with a reversal. The chapter began by drawing attention to research on the character of corporations as the context for the discussion of DAOs. Focusing on distinctions between DAOs and corporations sharpens the GKC attributes of DAOs. Collapsing those distinctions, at least in part, offers different advantages. How might GKC analysis bring out different, useful perspectives on corporations and corporate governance? The core instinct animating GKC research remains intact. Social dilemmas associated with shared knowledge and information resources may be addressed by institutions that are neither creatures of the state nor entirely derived from private law. Commons institutions may comfortably coexist with market capitalism rather than operating in opposition to it. Could a global pharmaceutical company be characterized usefully as a knowledge commons? If so, how? And how would that characterization offer an accurate understanding of the organization and performance of actors within and in partnership with that company?

Deakin (2012), with which the chapter began its review of DAOs, steers analysis of the corporation toward institutional analysis because Deakin recognizes the pragmatic limitations of the shareholder primacy model of the corporation. The model fails to recognize the practical significance of the multiple, overlapping claims of different corporate stakeholders: not only shareholders but also managers, employees, key suppliers, customers, business partners, and possibly adjacent communities. His approach, like that of the GKC framework, is to try to describe the corporation as it actually works. Deakin uses commons concepts to assemble those stakeholders in a dynamic governance model, accepting but not demanding that corporations as they actually operate face multiple dilemmas and adopt multiple governance strategies. The corporation is an institutional solution to multiple collective action problems directed to decision making as to resource production and distribution. In a way, Deakin's view is far from novel; Knight (1921) described business organizations as complex structural responses to the imperatives of decision making in environments characterized by uncertainty and risk.

Even in the absence of the additional layers of analysis prompted by the GKC framework, Deakin's model suggests that the pharmaceutical company may govern some of its functions or resources as commons, that is, as shared resources governed so as to allow contribution, access, and use by multiple stakeholders. Research and development resources offer an obvious candidate. The GKC framework and its attention to knowledge and information resources add layers and nuances to that approach, both sharpening it and extending it.

In short, taking DAOs as case studies of knowledge commons suggests that the corporation itself, both as a conceptual form and as an actual entity, may be characterized as knowledge commons, with the implication that the social dilemmas which the corporate form addresses are principally those associated with shared knowledge and information resources. As with other knowledge commons, the corporation need not be viewed exclusively as a state-created subject and object. Not only may corporations in markets govern resources as commons but also the resources that constitute the corporation in the first place may be viewed in knowledge commons terms. In both senses, governance consists of the practices and techniques by which stakeholders in the entity make decisions that produce and reproduce its form as well as its products or services.

Scholars have often viewed the corporation as a collection of largely fixed legal rules intended to facilitate cooperative activity (Simon 1991). Because a GKC-based starting point instead takes the corporate entity as the product of structured knowledge sharing, research should look for ways in which the corporation, generally and in any specific case, is capable of being modified (from the outside) and learning (from the inside) by private management and collaboration as well as by change to public law that respond to new and changing social dilemmas. Governance is adaptable and changeable from top to bottom, not only with respect to specific corporate decisions.

This is ultimately what the study of DAOs teaches the study of the corporation. DAOs make explicit the knowledge commons character of the rules and practices and techniques that define them. For corporations, the socially produced character of the rules that give a corporation its identity and capacity, that is, of law itself and of governance, is often only implicit, or even hidden. GKC-based examination of the general business corporation makes that socially produced character explicit and can track the sources and impacts of changes, in any particular corporation, over time.

In that spirit, looking at the role of privately produced governance within the corporation, Gindis and Cole (this volume) identify the knowledge commons dimensions of what they refer to as “the corporate mask”: the stable identity of the corporation as a legally recognized entity and actor, simultaneously empowered to deal with its own employees, with customers, with securities markets and financial institutions, and with third parties. That mask is validated by public law and market recognition, but its power lies in the capacity that it delivers to corporate managers and employees, and to company suppliers and customers, in determining the actual character of the entity's business. The IBM Corporation today is in legal respects the same entity as the company given that name in 1924 and its predecessor, the Computing-Tabulating-Recording Company, established in 1911, although it is obvious that the business of IBM today bears only the dimmest relationship to its business a century ago. The syntax of that sentence is evidence of the significance of the corporate mask and how it enables private decision making within and on behalf of the corporation.

The corporate mask thus does what masks always do. It creates an artificial identity that shields from public view whatever the wearer wishes to shield. The research question is where the mask comes from and what gives it salience and credibility. The corporate mask draws on both the mechanics of corporate law itself, with techniques for recognizing registration and share issues, and the diverse array of additional legal forms, including employment law and trademark law, each of which brings a range of experts and other institutions (courts and agencies in the public sector; suppliers, customers, and clients in the private sector) into governance practices that sustain the mask on a consistent basis across markets and across time. The significance of the mask and its character as collective governance rather than static "thing" is highlighted when its presence is challenged, as in so-called "veil piercing" or "corporate disregard" litigation that seeks to hold shareholders liable for corporate obligations (Dignam and Oh 2020). Though veil piercing often reaffirms a corporate entity rather than discarding it, such consideration evinces its socially constructed features.

The instinct to study knowledge commons began with the search for more accurate descriptions of innovation processes in practice (Madison et al. 2010). Along these lines, Deakin (2012) draws together corporate law (sometimes known as company law) with related bodies of law that bear on the design and function of the corporation (property law, employment law, tax law, the law of secured credit, and insolvency law, among others) to illustrate how these constitute systems of shared knowledge that together "code" the corporation as a market instrument, operating as an agent in its own right and collaborating with other similar entities in partnerships and joint ventures. The argument goes beyond the well-known idea that law itself is a public good. The corporation is constructed via processes and products of public resources (law) and private ones (assets of the corporation). It is that blend which is treated by market actors and others as an entity with capacity and agency, that is, the entity as a person. Pistor (2019) relatedly writes of the "code" of capital, describing legal systems as providing the foundations for financialized markets, implicating governance in the politics of wealth creation and distribution as well as in the technical details that produce market actors. Deakin's argument suggests an extension to Pistor, namely, the possibility that corporation law may be described as an instance of the "code" of commons.

12.6 CONCLUSION

This chapter has applied the knowledge commons research framework to the novel form of entity known as the Decentralized Autonomous Organization, or DAO. DAOs are purpose-built computer code-based membership organizations that encode transactions electronically, as smart contracts on blockchains. The result, to DAO proponents, is a so-called "trustless" entity that offers efficient (decentralized) self-enforcing decision making akin to what (centralized) corporations promise, but without the uncertainty and risks associated with human managers, and without relying on enforcement of obligations via public legal institutions. A GKC-based review of DAOs demonstrates that governance of DAOs and governance by DAOs is anchored not solely in "trustless" computer code but instead in complex, polycentric sociotechnical systems of shared knowledge and information. Much of this, but not all of it, is produced by DAO members themselves as self-governing communities.

Studying DAOs as knowledge commons illustrates an important broader point about corporations and market economies. The institutionalists in economics were largely successful in articulating the ways in which a capitalist economy depends on rules. Implicitly or explicitly, the state is seen as a source of those rules. DAOs call that premise into question. Though corporations depend on rules, they need not all come from the state.

The next step is to see this pattern not as purely the product of private law or purely private activity. Rather, conceptually and empirically, the DAO deals in knowledge commons, a concept that gives empirical life to self-governing communities. We provide a framework for analyzing these commons. Since the work has been using examples to illustrate ideas, what is next is to embrace the empirical research agenda, with case studies describing the variation of DAOs – how they work, why they emerged, what is unique about some, and what they share in common. This agenda seems especially critical for understanding the autonomous corporation of the twenty-first century.

REFERENCES

Alchian, Armen A., and Harold Demsetz. 1972. "Production, Information Costs, and Economic Organization." *American Economic Review* 62(5): 777–795.

Allen, Darcy W. E., and Chris Berg. 2020. "Blockchain Governance: What We Can Learn from the Economics of Corporate Governance." *Journal of the British Blockchain Association* 3(1): 1–10.

Alon, Ilan, Andreas Sauge Berthelsen, Espen Bjellerås, and Bernardo Silva-Rêgo. 2025. "Decentralized Autonomous Organizations: The New Global Digital Venture Capital." *Research in International Business and Finance* 74: 102671.

Alston, Eric. 2020. "Constitutions and Blockchains: Competitive Governance of Fundamental Rule Sets." *Case Western Journal of Law, Technology and the Internet* 11(5): 133–171.

Alston, Eric, Wilson Law, Ilia Murtazashvili, and Martin Weiss. 2022. "Blockchain Networks as Constitutional and Competitive Polycentric Orders." *Journal of Institutional Economics* 18(5): 707–723.

Amin, Ash, and Jerzy Hausner, eds. 1997. *Beyond Market and Hierarchy: Interactive Governance and Social Complexity*. Cheltenham: Edward Elgar.

Benkler, Yochai. 2004. "Sharing Nicely: On Shareable Goods and the Emergence of Sharing as a Modality of Economic Production." *Yale Law Journal* 114(2): 273–358.

Benkler, Yochai. 2013. "Commons and Growth: The Essential Role of Open Commons in Market Economies." *University of Chicago Law Review* 80(3): 1499–1555.

Berg, Alastair, and Chris Berg. 2020. "Exit, Voice, and Forking." *Cosmos + Taxis* 8(8–9): 76–89.

Berle, Adolph A., and Gardiner C. Means. 1932. *The Modern Corporation and Private Property*. New York: Harcourt, Brace & World.

Bodon, Herminio, Pedro Bustamante, Marcela Gomez, et al. 2022. "Ostrom amongst the Machines: Blockchain as a Knowledge Commons." *Cosmos + Taxis* 10(3+4): 1–15.

Borrup, Tom. 2011. "The Emergence of a New Cultural Infrastructure: Lessons from Silicon Valley." *Journal of Urban Culture Research* 2(1): 16–29.

Brown, John S., and Paul Duguid. 2000. *The Social Life of Information*. Boston: Harvard Business School Press.

Burk, Dan L., and Brett McDonnell. 2007. "The Goldilocks Hypothesis: Balancing Intellectual Property Rights at the Boundary of the Firm." *University of Illinois Law Review* 2007(2): 575–636.

Coase, R. H. 1937. "The Nature of the Firm." *Economica* 4(16): 386–405.

Cowen, Nick. 2019. "Markets for Rules: The Promise and Peril of Blockchain Distributed Governance." *Journal of Entrepreneurship and Public Policy* 9(2): 213–226.

Davidson, Sinclair, Primavera De Filippi, and Jason Potts. 2018. "Blockchains and the Economic Institutions of Capitalism." *Journal of Institutional Economics* 14(4): 639–658.

Davidson, Sinclair. 2025. "Decentralised Autonomous Organisations as Commons." In *Governing Corporate Knowledge Commons*, ed. David Gindis. Cambridge: Cambridge University Press.

Dawes, Robyn M. 1980. "Social Dilemmas." *Annual Review of Psychology* 31: 169–193.

De Filippi, Primavera, and Benjamin Loveluck. 2016. "The Invisible Politics of Bitcoin: Governance Crisis of a Decentralized Infrastructure." *Internet Policy Review* 5(4): 1–28.

De Filippi, Primavera, and Aaron Wright. 2018. *Blockchain and the Law: The Rule of Code*. Cambridge, MA: Harvard University Press.

Deakin, Simon. 2012. "The Corporation as Commons: Rethinking Property Rights, Governance and Sustainability in the Business Enterprise." *Queen's Law Journal* 37(2): 339–381.

Dekker, Erwin, and Pavel Kuchař, eds. 2022. *Governing Markets as Knowledge Commons*. Cambridge: Cambridge University Press.

Dekker, Erwin and Pavel Kuchař. 2024. "Markets and Knowledge Commons: Is There a Difference between Private and Community Governance of Markets?" *Public Choice* 201(3–4): 533–553.

Dignam, Alan, and Peter Oh. 2020. "Rationalising Corporate Disregard." *Legal Studies* 40(2): 187–208.

DuPont, Quinn. 2024. "A Progressive Web3: From Social Coproduction to Digital Polycentric Governance." In *Defining Web3: A Guide to the New Cultural Economy*, ed. Quinn DuPont, Donncha Kavanagh, and Paul Dlan-Ennis, 57–74. Leeds: Emerald.

El Faqir, Youssef, Javier Arroyo, and Samer Hassan. 2020. "An Overview of Decentralized Autonomous Organizations on the Blockchain." In *Proceedings of the 16th International Symposium on Open Collaboration*, 1–8. https://doi.org/10.1145/3412569.3412579.

Esener, Esen. 2024. "Adaptive Governance for Blockchain Networks." *Stanford Journal of Blockchain Law and Policy*. https://stanford-jblp.pubpub.org/pub/adaptive-governance-blockchain-networks/release/1.

Ferrari, Valeria, Andrea Leiter, and Morshed Mannan, eds. 2023. *Log Out: A Glossary of Technological Resistance and Decentralization*. Amsterdam: Institute of Network Cultures.

Frischmann, Brett M. 2012. *Infrastructure: The Social Value of Shared Resources*. New York: Oxford University Press.

Frischmann, Brett M., and Mark A. Lemley. 2007. "Spillovers." *Columbia Law Review* 107(1): 257–301.

Frischmann, Brett M., Michael J. Madison, and Madelyn Rose Sanfilippo, eds. 2023. *Governing Smart Cities as Knowledge Commons*. Cambridge: Cambridge University Press.

Frischmann, Brett M., Michael J. Madison, and Katherine J. Strandburg, eds. 2014. "Governing Knowledge Commons." In *Governing Knowledge Commons*, ed. Brett M. Frischmann, Michael J. Madison, and Katherine J. Strandburg 1–43. New York: Oxford University Press.

Frye, Brian L. 2018. "New Art for the People: Art Funds & Financial Technology." *Chicago-Kent Law Review* 93(1): 113–139.

Gambetta, Diego, ed. 1988. *Trust: Making and Breaking Cooperative Relations*. Oxford: Basil Blackwell.

Gindis, David. 2016. "Legal Personhood and the Firm: Avoiding Anthropomorphism and Equivocation." *Journal of Institutional Economics* 12(3): 499–513.

Gindis, David and Dan Cole. 2025. "Toward a Knowledge Commons Perspective on the Corporate Form." In *Governing Corporate Knowledge Commons*, ed. David Gindis. Cambridge: Cambridge University Press.

Gindis, David, and Geoffrey M. Hodgson. 2026. "The Legal Nature of the Firm." In *Research Handbook on the Theory of the Firm*, ed. Josef Windsperger and Aveed Raha. Cheltenham: Edward Elgar.

Grimmelmann, James, and A. Jason Windawi. 2023. "Blockchains as Infrastructure and Semicommons." *William and Mary Law Review* 64(4): 1097–1130.

Hardin, Garrett. 1968. "The Tragedy of the Commons." *Science* 162(3859): 1243–1248.

Hart, Oliver D. 1988. "Incomplete Contracts and the Theory of the Firm." *Journal of Law, Economics and Organization* 4(1): 119–139.

Hassan, Samer, and Primavera De Filippi. 2023. "DAO (Decentralized Autonomous Organization)." In *Log Out: A Glossary of Technological Resistance and Decentralization*, ed. Valeria Ferrari, Florian Idelberger, Andrea Leiter, Morshed Mannan, María-Cruz Valiente, and Balázs Bodó, 109–119. Amsterdam: Institute of Network Cultures.

Jensen, Michael C., and William H. Meckling. 1976. "Theory of the Firm: Managerial Behavior, Agency Costs and Ownership Structure." *Journal of Financial Economics* 3(4): 305–360.

@keikreutler. 2021. "A Prehistory of DAOs: Cooperatives, Gaming Guilds, and the Networks to Come." Gnosis Guild. https://gnosisguild.mirror.xyz/t4F5rItMw4-mlpLZf5JQhElbDfQ2JRVKAzEpanyxW1Q.

Knight, Frank H. 1921. *Risk, Uncertainty, and Profit*. New York: Houghton Mifflin Company.

Kollock, Peter. 1998. "Social Dilemmas: The Anatomy of Cooperation." *Annual Review of Sociology* 24: 183–214.

Levinthal, Daniel A., and Dong Nghi Pham. 2024. "Bringing Politics Back In: The Role of Power and Coalitions in Organizational Adaptation." *Organization Science* 35(5): 1704–1720.

Lessig, Lawrence. 2006. *Code: Version 2.0*. New York: Basic Books.

Li, Zhaoyi. 2024. "Artificial Fiduciaries." *Washington and Lee Law Review* 81(4): 1299–1378.

Lund, Dorothy S., and Elizabeth Pollman. 2021. "The Corporate Governance Machine." *Columbia Law Review* 121(8): 2563–2634.

Madison, Michael J. 2014. "Commons at the Intersection of Peer Production, Citizen Science, and Big Data: Galaxy Zoo." In *Governing Knowledge Commons*, ed. Brett M. Frischmann, Michael J. Madison, and Katherine J. Strandburg, 209–254. New York: Oxford University Press.

Madison, Michael J., Brett M. Frischmann, and Katherine J. Strandburg. 2009. "The University as Constructed Cultural Commons." *Washington University Journal of Law and Policy* 30(1): 365–403.

Madison, Michael J., Brett M. Frischmann, and Katherine J. Strandburg. 2010. "Constructing Commons in the Cultural Environment." *Cornell Law Review* 95(4): 657–709.

Madison, Michael J., Brett M. Frischmann, Madelyn R. Sanfilippo, and Katherine J. Strandburg. 2022. "Too Much of a Good Thing? A Governing Knowledge Commons Review of Abundance in Context." *Frontiers in Research Metrics and Analytics* 7 (July): 959505.

March, James. 1962. "The Business Firm as a Political Coalition." *Journal of Politics* 24(4): 662–678.

McGinnis, Michael D. 2011. "Networks of Adjacent Action Situations in Polycentric Governance." *Policy Studies Journal* 39(1): 51–78.

Micheler, Eve, Kevin Werbach, and Bianca Krenner, eds. 2026. *Foundations of Decentralized Organizations: Blockchain and the Future of Corporate Law*. New York: Oxford University Press.

Morrison, Robbie, Natasha C. H. L. Mazey, and Stephen C. Wingreen. 2020. "The DAO Controversy: The Case for a New Species of Corporate Governance?" *Frontiers in Blockchain* 3: 25. https://doi.org/10.3389/fbloc.2020.00025.

Murtazashvili, Ilia, Jennifer Brick Murtazashvili, Martin BH Weiss, and Michael J. Madison. 2022. "Blockchain Networks as Knowledge Commons." *International Journal of the Commons* 16(1): 108–119.

Naudts, Ellen. 2023. "The Future of DAOs in Finance: In Need of Legal Status." European Central Bank. Occasional Paper Series. White Paper No. 331.

Ostrom, Elinor. 2005. *Understanding Institutional Diversity*. Princeton: Princeton University Press.

Ostrom, Elinor, and Michael Cox. 2010. "Moving beyond Panaceas: A Multi-Tiered Diagnostic Approach for Social-Ecological Analysis." *Environmental Conservation* 37(4): 451–463.

Petrin, Martin. 2024. "AI, New Technologies, and Corporate Governance: Three Phenomena." *Seattle University Law Review* 47(5): 1369–1393.

Pistor, Katharina. 2019. *The Code of Capital: How the Law Creates Wealth and Inequality*. Princeton: Princeton University Press.

Potts, Jason. 2019. *Innovation Commons: The Origins of Economic Growth*. New York: Oxford University Press.

Putnam, Robert D. 2000. *Bowling Alone: The Collapse and Revival of American Community*. New York: Simon & Schuster.

Rawson, Pat. 2021. "Ownership in Cryptonetworks." *Curve Labs* (blog). March 9, 2021. https://blog.curvelabs.eu/ownership-in-cryptonetworks-96f13f4a113e.

Reyes, Carla. 2021. "Autonomous Corporate Personhood." *Washington Law Review* 96(4): 1453–1510.

Reyes, Carla L., and Christine Hurt. 2025. "The Contractarian Joint Venture." *Alabama Law Review* 76(4):741–797.

Ross, Steven A. 1973. "The Economic Theory of Agency: The Principal's Problem." *American Economic Review* 63(2): 134–139.

Sanfilippo, Madelyn R., Brett M. Frischmann, and Katherine J. Strandburg. 2018. "Privacy as Commons: Case Evaluation through the Governing Knowledge Commons Framework." *Journal of Information Policy* 8: 116.

Sanfilippo, Madelyn R., Katherine J. Strandburg, and Brett M. Frischmann. 2021. "Privacy as Knowledge Commons Governance: An Appraisal." In *Governing Privacy in Knowledge Commons*, ed. Madelyn R. Sanfilippo, Brett M. Frischmann, and Katherine J. Strandburg, 268–290. Cambridge: Cambridge University Press.

Schweik, Charles M., and Robert C. English. 2012. *Internet Success: A Study of Open-Source Software Commons*. Cambridge, MA: MIT Press.

Seidman, Harold. 1952. "The Theory of the Autonomous Government Corporation: A Critical Appraisal." *Public Administration Review* 12(2): 89–96.

Simon, Herbert A. 1991. "Organizations and Markets." *Journal of Economic Perspectives* 5(2): 25–44.

Spelliscy, Connor, Sarah Hubbard, Nathan Schneider, and Samuel Vance-Law. 2024. "Toward Equitable Ownership and Governance in the Digital Public Sphere." *Stanford Journal of Blockchain Law and Policy* 7(1): 110–135.

Stout, Lynn. 2017. "The Economic Nature of the Corporation." In *The Oxford Handbook of Law and Economics, Vol. 2: Private and Commercial Law*, ed. Francesco Parisi, 336-357. Oxford: Oxford University Press.

The Economist. 2023. "The Fuzzy Corporation." *The Economist*, January 8, 2023. www.economist.com/business/2023/01/08/how-technology-is-redrawing-the-boundaries-of-the-firm.

Turner, Fred. 2008. *From Counterculture to Cyberculture: Stewart Brand, the Whole Earth Network, and the Rise of Digital Utopianism*. Chicago: University of Chicago Press.

Werbach, Kevin. 2018. *The Blockchain and the New Architecture of Trust*. Cambridge, MA: MIT Press.

Williamson, Oliver E. 1996. *The Mechanisms of Governance*. New York: Oxford University Press.

Williamson, Oliver E. 2000. "The New Institutional Economics: Taking Stock, Looking Ahead." *Journal of Economic Literature* 38(3): 595–613.

Whitford, Josh, and Zirpoli, Francesco. 2016. "The Network Firm as a Political Coalition." *Organization Studies* 37(9): 1227–1248.

Wright, Aaron. 2021. "The Rise of Decentralized Autonomous Organizations: Opportunities and Challenges." *Stanford Journal of Blockchain Law and Policy* 4(2): 152–176.

13

The Human Genome as Knowledge Commons

Governance through Mutual-Benefit Participatory Democracy

Benjamin Gregg

13.1 INTRODUCTION

Any resource system requires governance. Effective governance is well-tailored to target the unique characteristics and challenges of the relevant resource. I address the kind of tailoring needed for the effective governance of a resource both natural and social, one shared by all members of our species: the human genome. It is a resource for science and medicine as a valuable source of information about our species, as individuals and as various kinds of groups.

I identify and develop the governance potential of the human genome as a knowledge commons (Hess and Ostrom 2007) in five steps. First, I identify human genetic information as a social resource. Second, I detail a notable empirical example of a knowledge commons using that resource. Third, I analyze human genetic information as a resource that is non-rivalrous and non-excludable, traits that lend themselves to commons governance in analytic distinction to – although in some degree likely mixed with – market or state governance. Fourth, to illustrate how the harvesting of human genetic information confronts various social dilemmas, I focus on one – the competing imperatives of sharing and of privacy – and show how commons governance might cope with it. Fifth, I conclude with a proposal for a politically heightened form of knowledge commons governance: a proceduralist, participatory politics of democratic governance.

Like me, Evans (2017) and Contreras (2014) argue that the human genome constitutes a common-pool resource for public health research (as well as for advancements in technology and economic benefits), and that this resource can only be realized through individuals sharing their personal genetic data. Clinical validity requires comparisons across populations by means of large datasets, hence the significance of sharing. But whereas Evans seeks to overcome legal obstacles to the development of such datasets, I focus on the popular political dimension of encouraging genetic data sharing by individuals as members of commons. I show that the realization of the human genome as a knowledge commons is a distinctly *political project*. It is the project of reconciling competing imperatives: on the one hand, the public interest in collecting individuals' genetic data; on the other hand, the individual's interest in maintaining her data privacy. I show how commons governance can be designed to cope with this challenge. I propose a politically heightened form of knowledge commons governance: a proceduralist, participatory politics of democratic governance.[1] While Contreras advocates a polycentric governance institution to manage a species-wide shared resource, I attempt to flesh out in practical political terms what he suggests in general terms.

The genome is important to humankind along multiple dimensions. Along one of those dimensions, the scientific and clinical value of any person's genetic information lies in understanding it together with her genealogy, genetic profile, and health history. Perhaps the single greatest goal of this effort is to cure, if not prevent, genetic disease. Three areas of science are relevant here. First, toward understanding the causes of genetic disease, *population genomics* applies genetic techniques to entire populations. Second, by exploring gene function, the regulation of gene expression, and protein function, *functional genomics* studies how diseased genes influence the disease process.[2] Third, *genomic health therapeutics* determines how gene-based diagnostic tests can aid disease diagnosis and management, enhance risk identification and monitoring, and complement clinical tests. Knowledge of the patient's disease predisposition allows the patient to make relevant lifestyle adjustments or to use preventive medication. Genomics aids therapeutic development also by identifying precise diseased-gene targets for specific drug development and more effective treatment.[3] Differences among persons in genetically based drug response can lead to personalized treatment, toward optimizing efficacy and reducing side effects.

13.2 HUMAN GENETIC INFORMATION AS RESOURCE

I frame genetic information as a resource unit in a resource system, and then as a potential knowledge commons. I then explain some of the merits of a commons so understood.

13.2.1 *Genetic Information Is a Resource Unit in a Resource System*

Information refers to raw data, statistics, and factual statements, among other phenomena. Information is necessary for the creation of knowledge. But knowledge goes beyond mere information by incorporating understanding and insight, gained through the processing, organizing, and structuring of information to make sense of

[1] Political proceduralism supplements Nissenbaum's notion of transmission principles and context-relative informational norms with "politically and procedurally grounded rules" (Sanfilippo et al. 2021, 6).

[2] To identify disease-causing molecular pathways, research compares gene expression patterns in diseased and healthy tissues or across species.

[3] By analyzing genes involved in drug response, genomics can improve drug response through pharmacogenomics.

it and to divine patterns or implications so that the information now encompasses understanding, awareness, and skills.

Furthermore, information is not inherently meaningful; it becomes meaningful only through its manipulation and integration into a framework of understanding. Thus, a database of human genetic sequences has no inherent meaning as such. It acquires meaning when deployed in research to identify mutations that cause diseases or predispose individuals to certain health conditions; to study genetic variations and their associations with diseases, traits, and drug responses; to select the most effective medications and dosages with minimal side effects; or to trace human ancestry and study evolutionary relationships among populations, toward insights into migration patterns and historical connections among different groups (Gregg 2021b, 2022c).

Knowledge in general is transferable, encoded information involving personal or collective experience and interpretation. As the stuff of knowledge, information is a resource. A person's genetic data has social value precisely as a knowledge resource, above all for science and medicine. It has value as a resource unit within a resource system that is the aggregate value of many such units. A resource system based on human genetic information comprises the actors and infrastructures (Contreras 2014; Evans 2017) responsible for producing resource units, such as valid statistical inferences of gene variants for health conditions. Each statistically valid inference that identifies a new association between a specific gene variant and a specific health condition constitutes one resource unit. The validity of the inference is determined scientifically. And – to anticipate my discussion of the social imperatives of individuals sharing their genetic information with researchers and clinicians – the value of the inference increases as the number of users with access to it increases.

Here a resource system extracts information specific to individual cases leading, for example, to knowledge of variants never before observed or variants observed in other individuals but with unknown clinical significance or impact (Evans 2017). Some extracted information establishes the clinical validity of specific gene variants and enables clinically useful, individual diagnoses based on those discoveries. The system also extracts broadly generalizable knowledge, that is, information and understandings with wide applicability. The more generalizable a discovery about the clinical impact of a human gene variant, the more robust or analytically significant the knowledge generated. Because the genome is universally shared within the species, knowledge about it is inherently sharable.

These two types of extraction are linked. The scientist or clinician conducts individual genomic tests to detect an individual's genetic variants and then links the genomic data to detailed phenotypic information, including the patient's health records, lifestyle data, and other information about his or her environments. The researcher may identify statistically significant associations between specific gene variants and specific health conditions. And at low additional cost, the researcher may share, copy, reuse, or repurpose the data generated by the genomic testing process. He or she can also pool these linked genomic and health records for large populations. For the information contained in the human genome is harvested not only through its extraction (through genomic testing instruments, laboratories, databases, and computer algorithms) but also through its aggregation, manipulation, and interpretation, to become knowledge.

Forms of information extraction are human artifacts, cultural acts performed on a natural phenomenon, namely, the sequence of DNA that contains the instructions for building and maintaining a human being. Cultural acts include scientific practices, technologies, and methodologies by which we humans interact with the natural world. Cultural acts also reflect cultural values, goals, and priorities, as well as culturally driven objectives such as understanding the natural history of our species and improving human health, as well as medical treatments and biotechnological advancements. Here we observe the inflection of a natural phenomenon – the human genome – with a human artifact: culture. This inflection describes the governance system of the human genome as a knowledge commons. First, a resource unit is an element in a resource system that encompasses communities, their beliefs, and operational rules, as well as property rights, including rights of data access and data contribution. Second, without proper configuration, a resource system cannot generate the desired type or quantity of resource units consistently and in a sustainable manner. Hence the focus of this chapter.

13.2.2 *Merits of a Commons*

I frame the human genome as a knowledge commons, and genetic information as its resource system, for practical reasons. First, without a commons framework, authority regarding this resource may be divided among multiple stakeholders, including government regulatory bodies, private organizations, research institutions, and possibly independent ethical boards. Each stakeholder may have different criteria and standards, leading to potential conflicts and inconsistencies in defining normative appropriateness. By contrast, a commons allows members to establish a multi-stakeholder governing body, including scientists, medical professionals, ethicists, patient representatives, policymakers, and public advocates; develop a clear code of conduct and ethical guidelines that all members can agree to follow; and create a transparent and fair dispute resolution mechanism, possibly including mediation and arbitration panels.

Second, without a commons, disagreements among stakeholders may need to be handled through established legal and regulatory mechanisms, possibly involving courts, arbitration, or mediation, and possibly leading to prolonged disputes and a lack of coherent policy direction. A commons, by contrast, allows members to utilize deliberative democratic processes to address disagreements, allowing all voices to be heard and considered; aim for consensus but allow for majority voting when consensus is not achievable; and provide an appeals process for decisions that participants believe do not adequately address their concerns.

Third, absent a commons, membership criteria would be set by individual organizations or regulatory bodies, leading to fragmentation, where participants might be recognized through licensing, accreditation, or certification processes specific to each entity, rather than through a unified commons framework. By contrast, a commons allows members to define clear and inclusive criteria for membership, such as contribution to the commons, expertise, or stakeholder representation; maintain transparent records of membership and ensure accountability in the recognition process; and regularly review and update membership criteria to adapt to changing circumstances and to ensure inclusivity.

Fourth, without a commons, monitoring and enforcement likely would fall to individual entities, such as regulatory bodies, private companies, or research institutions, resulting in varied levels of enforcement and compliance, perhaps with some entities prioritizing profit over maintenance of the resource system. But a commons allows members to implement systems to track contributions to the commons, whether through data sharing, research, or other means; create incentives for contributions and penalties for noncompliance, ensuring fair and equitable enforcement; and establish community oversight committees to monitor contributions and address issues of noncompliance.

Fifth, absent a commons, relationships among participants could only be governed by contracts, agreements, and regulations specific to each context, leading to complex and sometimes conflicting relationships, with different rules and expectations depending on the specific context of interaction. By contrast, a commons allows members to develop collaborative frameworks that define roles, responsibilities, and expectations of participants; facilitate regular communication and meetings to foster relationships and address issues collaboratively; and encourage the formation of interdisciplinary teams to tackle complex issues from multiple perspectives.

Sixth, without a commons, preserving personal autonomy would depend on the policies of individual entities, with some organizations prioritizing privacy and autonomy, and with no overarching framework ensuring consistent protection of personal autonomy across different contexts. By contrast, a commons allows members to ensure the informed consent from individuals whose genetic information is included in the commons, implement robust privacy protections to safeguard personal data, and provide mechanisms for individuals to opt out or withdraw their data from the commons.

Seventh, absent a commons, each stakeholder would have different priorities and standards: scientific research might prioritize open access to data while clinical practice might prioritize patient privacy, and private corporations might prioritize proprietary control over information, thus making compatibility and regulation difficult. A commons, by contrast, allows members to develop ethical guidelines that balance the interests of scientific research, clinical practice, and private corporations with community values and democratic principles; it allows members to ensure continuous engagement with all stakeholders to understand their needs and address their concerns; and it allows members to maintain transparent decision-making processes to build trust and accountability.

Finally, without a commons, balancing information production and fair access would depend on the policies of individual entities, with some entities emphasizing open access and equitable distribution and other entities restricting access to maximize profit or to protect proprietary interests, leading to inequities and disparities in access to genetic information and the benefits derived from it.

13.3 THE HUMAN GENOME AS A KNOWLEDGE COMMONS: AN EXAMPLE

Several biotech companies seek to innovate products or therapies based on genetic information. They are constrained to observe regulatory frameworks to bring advancements to market. The story begins in 2001 when Celera Genomics and the Human Genome Project released an initial sequencing and analysis of the human genome (Sigurjonsson et al. 2023; see also Securities and Exchange Commission 2000). Since then, research and clinical practice have worked to turn information into knowledge by transforming raw sequence data into a heightened understanding of human disease and healthcare. In this effort, the Icelandic company deCODE Genetics (Islensk erfdagreining), a subsidiary of US biopharmaceutical company Amgen, is a notable example. Founded in 1966 "on the assumption that the scarce resource in human genetics is one that can yield the genetics of common diseases" (deCODE 1997), deCODE deploys modern informatics technology to gain insights into health and disease through data mining and analysis. In the following, I identify its use of genetic information in ways that constitute a knowledge commons.

deCODE initially studied variant genes linked to common diseases in Iceland's population.[4] Instead of the selectively chosen patient lists used in most current approaches, the company applied extensive bioinformatics to population genomics focused on almost the entire Icelandic population. It integrated three types of anonymous population data: data from the healthcare system, data on relationships among individuals within the system, and data about molecular genetics.

Among the world's populations, Iceland's is unusual for several reasons. The political community has maintained detailed genealogical records (parish records as well as census data) extending back thirty-five generations to the original Norwegian and British settlers of the ninth and tenth centuries. Iceland since 1915 has had a centralized national healthcare system that ensures data centralization and accessibility for scientific research. With little immigration over many

[4] Belgium, Denmark, Estonia, Finland, Germany, Iceland, Qatar, Saudi Arabia, Taiwan, the United Kingdom, and the United States also pursue national genomics initiatives of one kind or another.

centuries, a majority of Iceland's 380,000 inhabitants are descendants of the original settlers. Limited immigration ensures Icelanders' genome variability is lower than that of larger, historically less isolated nations. And while genetically homogeneous, the population is large enough to mitigate increased recessive genetic conditions from intermarriage.

Members often have similar genotypes, a similarity that helps researchers pinpoint the location of disease genes. Iceland's relative genetic homogeneity allows researchers to narrow the region containing the disease gene to as few as 250,000 base pairs. Researchers can then identify disease-causing genes by comparing family members, over generations, with and without the condition. Diseases such as cancer and heart disease, prevalent in developed nations, involve numerous genetic factors. Relatively isolated populations, such as Iceland's, display fewer genetic causes than do populations more diverse. Greater genetic homogeneity in a population simplifies the identification and analysis of genes and mutations.

On the one hand, the fact that contemporary Icelanders may carry disease-related gene mutations from the founding settlers aids in the identification of disease genes. Because specific genes correlate with certain diseases (e.g., the BRCA2 gene mutation, which can cause breast cancer), disease genes identified in Iceland's population often overlap with those identified in other populations. Discovering disease genes in Iceland can therefore reveal crucial molecular pathways implicated in the medical condition. In this way, discoveries in one national population may benefit populations far beyond Iceland. On the other hand, a population genomics approach is limited by the fact that disease genes found in Iceland may not be relevant to other populations, despite global overlaps in the presence of disease genes. The small size of Iceland's population provides a certain utility in studying rare diseases. But it may also limit the study of rare diseases. deCODE therefore focuses on diseases in Iceland that are also prevalent worldwide, including cancer, heart disease, diabetes, and Alzheimer's.

The emergence of the human genome as a knowledge commons in Iceland was contingent on a number of factors. The population's size was small enough to facilitate the necessary cooperation within the nation yet large enough to yield meaningful results. deCODE sought support from the Icelandic government and from the general population to mine genetic information. The country has a high level of public education; higher levels of education generally correspond to scientific literacy and willingness to vaccinate.[5] Finally, deCODE collects genotype data only from consenting Icelanders.

In 1998, after a bill was introduced, Iceland's parliament discussed the issue of providing public health records to a private company. Some physicians worried that

[5] deCODE Genetics emerged as an accidental and temporary knowledge commons confronting COVID-19. In March of 2020, the World Health Organization declared the respiratory Coronavirus disease COVID-19 a pandemic. deCODE secured Amgen's support for free testing and, by March 13, 2020, had repurposed its facility and intensified testing efforts, as follows. It established a website for

patients might decline to discuss their health if their information ended up in a private database. The bill was then changed to provide for encrypted personal information options, whereby deCODE would not have access to the decryption key, so that deCODE could enter only encrypted data into the database (Sigurjonsson et al. 2023). The bill also allowed individuals to opt out.

A December 1998 parliamentary debate highlighted that such a database could benefit information gathering and scientific activities in Iceland. It also emphasized the importance of handling personal information carefully, for ethical reasons, among others. It gave citizens the opportunity to opt-out of the database until June 1999. Of a population then of 275,000, approximately 11,000 decided to opt-out.

An extensive genealogy database and associated bioinformatics allowed deCODE to identify human disease genes and associated drug targets, and to discover and develop new diagnostic and therapeutic products more quickly than would otherwise have been possible. Having developed faster and cheaper gene sequencing, deCODE approached pharmaceutical companies to engage in genetic validation for drug development targets. Before studying disease-related genes, deCODE obtained approvals from the Icelandic Bioethics Committee as well as from the Data Protection Authority. When giving blood samples, patients signed consent forms approved by the Bioethics Committee. deCODE uses advanced encryption to safeguard the privacy of all participants. The encrypted patient list was processed through an encrypted genealogy database.

Not all human genome commons would look like deCODE.[6] Rather, deCODE's story constitutes empirical proof of the possibility of such a commons, even as other instances would differ from deCODE in various ways.

residents to register for testing. To facilitate sample labeling, residents received a barcode generated by an app. deCODE's lab processed 5,000 samples daily, delivering results, via text, within four to twenty-four hours. Persons testing positive quarantined for fourteen days and were logged into the hospital's database for monitoring. deCODE sequenced positive samples to identify strains as well as geographical connections. In the first half of 2020, deCODE partnered with the Icelandic government to screen and test individuals, minimizing strain on healthcare system. By April 2020, deCODE had sequenced 409 virus variants, which contributed 291 variants (70 percent of all variants) to the Global Initiative on Sharing All Influenza Database. Within six weeks, deCODE and the University Hospital had tested 50,000 people, that is, approximately 15 percent of Iceland's population (one of the world's highest testing rates).

6 Evans (2017), for example, imagines (in the United States) a consumer-driven data commons in which individuals would use their rights under laws such as the Health Insurance Portability and Accountability Act to collect and share their health data in a collaborative environment. These groups would self-govern and collectively decide how their data is used. They would generate revenue through data access fees to fund necessary services and infrastructure. For his part, Contreras (2014) examines the genome commons in terms of the roles and influence of a range of stakeholder groups: funders such as the National Institutes of Health and the Department of Energy in the United States, and the Wellcome Trust in the United Kingdom; a close-knit group of scientists specialized in generating extensive datasets; a diverse global community of data users; prominent scientists whose leadership confers credibility and a strong sense of public responsibility; data intermediaries, both commercial and nonprofit, involved in disseminating information while balancing accessibility with

13.4 GOVERNING A HUMAN GENOME KNOWLEDGE COMMONS

Governance of human genetic information involves a resource that is non-rivalrous and non-excludable, whereby commons governance may be distinguished analytically from private or public governance.

13.4.1 *The Nature of the Resource*

The nature of human genetic information lends itself to commons governance in part because the knowledge derived from it constitutes a public good: The health benefits for the donor as well as for many other persons can be shared without diminishing its availability.

Indeed, the knowledge derived from human genetic information is more beneficial precisely when used widely (in scientific research and clinical medicine) and when other donors share their genetic information (for research and clinical purposes). In other words, the resource unit is more valuable, because more beneficial, when more rather than fewer people use, share, and contribute to it. Part of the explanation lies in the fact that the extraction of information from human genetic material requires large datasets; the larger the better. Technological advances make possible the aggregation of scientific and clinical research data in collaborative repositories. Furthermore, "access to data produced through analysis" may encourage collaboration among researchers to their mutual benefit (Sanfilippo et al. 2021, 32).

The clinical harvesting of genetic variants includes statistical analysis to identify correlations between health conditions and specific genetic variants. Useful information about the clinical significance of genetic variants derives from pooling genetic data for large samples. Very large samples are needed to ascertain the impact of variants. For a sense of what the word *large* might mean in this context, consider that, by 2014, "only about 228,000 human genomes had been fully or partially sequenced worldwide" (Evans 2017, 78). Even a test of one million individuals would represent a tiny fraction of the global human population. The state does not offer a work-around. Publicly funded initiatives to develop national genomic data infrastructure are costly and not scalable for the ambitious task of creating several-hundred-million-person genomic data infrastructures. The reality is that genomic data resources assembled using incentivized consent alignment remain relatively small and may include data for only a fraction of the genetic variants possessed by persons within a community and across the globe (Larson and Chon 2017). Only a data infrastructure much larger and more comprehensive than current

financial viability; data sharers who, given the technical capacity for reidentifying anonymized data, depend on institutionalized means of data privacy protection; and the general public, in part because much genomic research is taxpayer-funded, and in part given increasing participation of patient advocacy groups and concerned citizens in shaping research practices and policies.

ones will enable scientists to identify the clinical significance of gene variants not yet understood.

13.4.2 *Community Governance Is Analytically Distinct from Private or Public Governance*

To say that not all human genome commons would look like deCODE Genetics is merely to say that there is no single model or paradigm for knowledge commons governance. Models will differ in part because they will involve the state and the market in different ways and to different extents. Ostrom raises this observation to an analytic principle along three dimensions. First, analysis should avoid dichotomies in social scientific analysis because social reality is not dichotomous. That reality is not, for example, entirely public or entirely private, entirely market or completely state; rather, reality is some mixture of market and nonmarket structures. For example, "not all forms of public enterprise are, or need to be, state owned and operated. Various forms of communal or public ownership may exist apart from state ownership" (Ostrom and Ostrom 2009, 142). Second, governance and other ordered social relationships tend to be some combination of command and consensual agreement. Analysis needs to reflect as much. Third, cases of market failure do not necessarily entail that the state should seek to compensate or correct for those failures, on the one hand. On the other hand, if "over-centralized governmental units fail to perform," privatization is not necessarily the best response (ibid, 150). Analysis should seek to identify possible incentives for improvement within the market and within the state.

Hence, the analytic distinction among commons governance, market governance, and state governance is artificial in the sense that well-functioning markets rely critically on community governance. Furthermore, markets are not independent of, or incompatible with, certain kinds of commons. Correspondingly, the commons can be part of a mixed regime of governance types, where commons-like aspects of resource governance might be combined with state or market forms of governance, if not with both. As a matter of experience, they tend to be combined. Thus, knowledge commons governance is "not necessarily opposed to integration with government-supplied resources of various sorts" (Madison et al. 2022, 9). Markets are entangled with the communities and cultures in which they are always embedded (Dekker and Kuchař 2022), just as governance types are likely to be combined. When so, then knowledge commons governance is "not necessarily opposed to integration with government-supplied resources of various sorts" (Madison et al. 2022; Dekker and Kuchař 2024).

13.5 A SOCIAL DILEMMA OF INFORMATION AS RESOURCE: COMPETING IMPERATIVES OF SHARING AND PRIVACY

An important social dilemma confronting the human genome knowledge commons arises because of the competing imperatives of sharing and privacy. The dilemma can be reformulated as a matter of information flow, regulated in the spirit of the public dimension of personal health, where the community and the individual must share information under a norm of common purpose, toward mutual benefit. The conditions and level of privacy can then be determined in terms of the normative appropriateness of any given information flow, where sharing becomes a dimension of privacy rather than its negation.

13.5.1 *The Social Dilemma: Information Flow*

Governance is inherently problematic and no form of governance escapes all social dilemmas. Many of the dilemmas that confront the harvesting of human genetic information as a resource involve the sharing of that information.[7] With regard to consent, individuals should have a veto right over how their genetic information is used, yet scientific and medical progress depends on individuals sharing their genetic information. With regard to equity, sharing genetic information advances our understanding of genetic diseases, thereby benefiting development of treatments and of improved healthcare outcomes, yet this goal is undermined by a non-equitable management of genetic information, especially for marginalized communities that might be disproportionately impacted.

I focus on a third social dilemma: one posed by privacy. Note that human genetic information is not inherently sensitive in the sense that it inevitably involves privacy issues. But in the many contexts where it is sensitive, harvesting its benefits involves a trade-off: Sharing the data with researchers might have adverse consequences for the individual sharer's privacy, yet not sharing it could have adverse *social* consequences, above all – the information's potential to contribute to social goods such as science and the clinical treatment of patients. In short, governance that privileges individual privacy over communal welfare (a *communal* welfare achieved through *individuals* sharing their data) may have adverse consequences for the common good of public health, while privileging communal welfare over individual welfare may have adverse consequences for the individual's justified interest in the privacy of her genetic information.

[7] To be sure, governance of the genetic information commons confronts additional challenges. (a) Individual patients and consumers may decline to share their data, or block the sharing of it, by using privacy and human subject protection regulations that often require individual consent for data access. (b) The sharing of health data among various stakeholders easily faces coordination difficulties. For example, the patient's health data is likely distributed among multiple data holders, including physicians, hospitals, laboratories, and insurers. Correspondingly, genomic and health data resources are likely fragmented because they likely are spread among several entities, including hospitals, laboratories, and research institutions. Data fragmentation complicates efforts to aggregate data and to share it effectively among various stakeholders. (c) The extraction of information from the human genome involves institutions and biotechnologies that are embedded in the social systems and political communities of the commons' producers and users. Within these systems and communities, various forces may hinder information extraction, forces such as poverty, discrimination, and certain cultural and religious traditions.

Not sharing would be socially harmful because the scientific and clinical value of any particular genetic information lies in its connection to genetic information from other persons. First, on their own, genomic data have "limited scientific utility" (Evans 2017: 84). Second, extraction of their informational potential requires detailed *phenotypic* data available for the same individuals to establish verifiable associations between gene variants and health conditions. To establish such associations requires not just sharing the research outcomes. It requires providing the supporting data for closer examination and analysis, that is, it requires detailed phenotypic data, such as the "patient's longitudinal health record or information about lifestyle and environmental factors" (ibid.) that help contextualize genomic findings. To access their phenotypic data, "patients would need to consent to share their complete health histories" from birth to the present (ibid.). The patient has a privacy interest here precisely because sharing such sensitive information renders her vulnerable in various ways. For example, it renders her vulnerable to potential employers who might decline employment to insurance companies that might use such information to deny the individual the purchase of health insurance.

Thus, the governance challenge posed by the social resource of human genetic information is *how* information is shared. The challenge concerns the regulation of the *flow of information*. Regulation of information flow casts the individual's genome not as something always and only personal and private but as something that, in the context of medical research and clinical practice, contributes to what might be called the *public dimension of private health*. On the one hand, the personal health interests of the individual are unattainable without the research benefits of large data bases of genetic information. On the other hand, the social goods produced by scientific research and clinical medicine are unattainable without many persons sharing their genetic information.

This notion of a public dimension of private health resonates with the idea of a *norm of common purpose*. It acknowledges the entwinement of the individual's health interests with those of her community. The entwinement provides practical and normative motivation for the individual's sharing of her personal genetic information as well as the community's motivation to treat that information in ways that secure the health-relevant benefit of the sharers. A *norm of common purpose* formulates what might be seen – even from a utilitarian perspective of mutual benefit – to be the individual's *moral obligation*[8] to participate in the collaborative generation of scientific knowledge through genetic data sharing.

With regard to *mutual benefit*, mutual benefit is possible in part because information is an inherently sharable resource; benefit from that information follows only from sharing it. Commons governance offers a viable complement to market and

[8] Moral but not legal, and flexible, depending on the level of risk and burden involved for the participant. For example, individuals have no moral obligation to participate in clinical trials that have physical risks, although they might still be morally obligated to contribute their data to studies that promise useful scientific advancements. Data sharing would require consent alignment whereby

state governance in providing for the mutual benefit of participants. If the extraction of human genetic information can yield a flow of valuable resource units only through data sharing, then extraction is sustainable only if configured in ways that are both collaborative and responsible. *Collaboration* means that users of a genome database are expected to contribute data to it. *Responsible* means the contributors are not harmed in their privacy interests.[9] With regard to *common purpose*, a norm is *common* if it is relevant in readily understandable, practical ways to the health of many other persons, and potentially to all persons in the community but also far beyond any one community. Mutual benefit and common purpose come together in a knowledge commons that collectively governs the human genome, including the participation of persons whose genetic data is circulated within the commons. In the next section, I develop this idea toward knowledge commons governance as participatory democracy.

13.5.2 *Sharing as a Dimension of Privacy*

Sharing then becomes a type or dimension of privacy rather than the negation of privacy. That is, privacy is not the opposite of information sharing; it is not only a matter of constraint; it is itself a kind or mode of sharing. If privacy is a factor in the generation of knowledge, then it is best governed in terms of the normative appropriateness of the conditions and level of privacy, or the normatively justified disposition over a person's genetic data. As Nissenbaum (2009, 127) argues, a "right to privacy is neither a right to secrecy nor a right to control but a right to appropriate flow of personal information," that is, a "right to contextual integrity" that identifies threats to the individual's privacy posed by new information technologies and systems. A right to privacy, so understood, "formulates an approach to evaluating these systems and prescribing legitimate responses to them" (ibid, 2), allowing the transmission of the individual's genetic information in some cases, and to some extent, yet constraining that transmission in others,

Normative appropriateness in privacy regulation has three components: setting boundaries that community members control may motivate individuals to participate in the knowledge commons by sharing their genetic information; "privacy constraints on personal information flow enable knowledge production by encouraging trust" (Sanfilippo et al. 2021, 16); and the sensitivity of information depends on the context of sharing. The same information can be sensitive in one context, where

both the individual and the data holder (e.g., a healthcare provider) are willing to share data. The creation of multi-million-person genomic data resources is challenged by a data-sharing requirement.

9 The market is driven above all by self-seeking profit maximization, but for the market to operate well, certain elements must be shared among participants, creating a foundation for collaboration and mutual benefit (even as the market need not always and necessarily exclude other-directed foci). By contrast, a knowledge commons approach is distinctly other-directed: participants seek their mutual benefit, recognizing that sharing knowledge and resources is essential for the effective functioning and sustainability of the market.

freely sharing it would be normatively inappropriate and constriction would be recommended, but not sensitive in another context, where sharing would be appropriate.

The preservation of contextual integrity is a matter of observing principles to govern the flow of the individual's genetic data.[10] Transmission should be tailored to fit the specific context, toward meeting ethical, legal, and security standards. These standards include context-specific principles (e.g., the principles governing the sharing of genetic data for medical research may differ from those for clinical diagnosis or personal ancestry testing); ethical and legal compliance (transmission principles should align with ethical guidelines and legal requirements relevant to the specific context); informed consent (patients should be fully aware of how their data will be used, who will have access to it, and any potential risks); data security (such as encryption and secure communication channels); minimization principle (only the necessary amount of data should be transmitted, and it should be used only for the specified purpose); and transparency and accountability (clear policies and procedures regarding the transmission of genetic data).

Different stakeholders in the knowledge commons may emphasize different privacy concerns or different kinds of privacy concerns about what information is collected, analyzed, or shared, for example: reidentification risks (even if genetic data is anonymized, it can sometimes be reidentified by combining it with other data sources); discrimination (e.g., a person might be denied health insurance or a job based on their predisposition to certain diseases); data security (highly sensitive and valuable data is vulnerable to hacking and unauthorized access); consent and control (donors might consent to one type of research but find their data being used for other purposes they did not agree to); family privacy (data about one person can reveal information about their relatives, who may not have consented to the data being shared); possible psychological impact (such as anxiety or stress about potential health issues, or unexpected information about their ancestry or biological relationships); and commercial exploitation (for instance, companies might use genetic information for developing new products or services and profit from it without sharing any benefits with the donors).

A normatively appropriate information flow involves several requirements. In addition to clear agreement on how data can be accessed and used (ensuring that stakeholders understand their rights and obligations), ethical guidelines must be in place to ensure that data usage respects privacy (with oversight bodies to monitor compliance). Transparent governance structures to oversee the data sharing process are needed. This means that there must be accessible information about data governance policies and practices (including who is responsible for data stewardship

10 Preserving contextual integrity is challenging where information privacy governance must accommodate overlapping contexts, as well as contested contexts, in addition to conflicting social values.

and how decisions are made), as well as some way of involving stakeholders in decision-making processes. Informed consent (plus an adequate understanding of how the data will be used) for individuals whose data is being shared is imperative. Individual autonomy (including the patient's right to access or delete her data as she sees fit, and the right to full information about what data is being collected, how it will be used, and who will have access to it, with revokable consent) must be safeguarded. It is equally important to ensure equitable access to the data and the fair distribution of the benefits and burdens of genetic data use, including by those persons who contribute it, and with no group disproportionately advantaged or disadvantaged by governance practices, and no group allowed to monopolize its benefits. Finally, accountability mechanisms to hold data stewards (designated bodies responsible for managing and protecting genetic data) accountable for their actions are vital. These include regular audits and sanctions for misconduct, but also ethical review by an independent board that would consider the potential benefits and harms of data use and ensure that it aligns with ethical principles and community values. Still, flow control of genetic information is likely always to "involve overlapping ethical contexts or contested values" (Sanfilippo et al. 2021, 7).

13.6 KNOWLEDGE COMMONS AND GOOD GOVERNANCE

In Section 13.2.1 I characterized the harvesting of the information contained in the human genome as a cultural act performed on a natural phenomenon. This act becomes inflected with politics at the point of solving the main social dilemma it confronts in a knowledge commons: reconciling the competing political imperatives of sharing the individual's genetic information with the individual's interest in maintaining data privacy. These imperatives are political in the narrow sense that they are matters for deliberation (and deliberation holds the possibility of agreement).[11] Hence participation in a knowledge community is political, a matter of members overseeing and harvesting aspects of a shared resource – in this case the scientific and clinical value of human genetic information. Governance by communal participation is a form of self-determination.[12] It is possible in a participatory, democratic form oriented on participants' mutual benefit. I now develop this idea with respect to privacy and democracy and proceduralism. Then I will discuss means to realizing such governance.

[11] I develop and deploy this notion of politics in Gregg (2012), Gregg (2016), and Gregg (2022a).

[12] Expanding on my attempt to tap corporate potential to advance social justice (Gregg 2021a); to uncover the distinctly political, moral, and public policy-related issues raised by rapid developments in biological research and technology as well as the use and abuse of genetic information and its interpretations for our identity as humans (Gregg 2018); and mindful that the collection, analysis, and harvesting of human genetic data does not require a democratic order – and is unlikely to encourage the liberalization of illiberal political communities when practiced there (Gregg 2024).

13.6.1 *Privacy*

Privacy concerns about the sharing of personal human genetic information involves questions such as: Do the rules governing information flow make sense for how the individual's genetic information is to be used in a specific context? Are the processes of governance constructed in ways that they endow with legitimacy the rules they generate? Inasmuch as the rules may affect some commons participants more than others, or differently from the way it affects others, how can participants be confident that the rules were designed and established fairly?

To evaluate these concerns, a knowledge commons could employ a standard of procedural legitimacy.[13] A proceduralist determination of personal information flows asks: Do the flows reflect the interest of commons members? A proceduralist determination of the appropriateness of genetic information flows does not itself assume any position on the goals of flow governance, or how they might be ranked. Rather, in each context, it evaluates context-specific governance goals with regard to how well they reflect legitimate interests of different stakeholders within the commons.

Given such concerns, legitimacy might be secured through procedural determination along three dimensions: through governing rules on privacy constructed in ways that give, to different members of the commons, good reasons to regard them as legitimate; through the legitimacy of governance practices concerning privacy that consider the legitimate concerns of all persons affected by the commons; and by means of governing privacy by rules that respect the legitimate interests of commons members.

A proceduralist determination of the legitimacy of personal information flows emphasizes inclusive and participatory rule-making processes, continuous evaluation and revision of rules, and robust mechanisms for accountability and conflict resolution. For example, individuals can report grievances and challenge rules that they find unfair or harmful; regulatory bodies can act as neutral arbitrators to resolve disputes and ensure compliance with established rules; and civil society organizations can monitor and publicize compliance and noncompliance, advocating for individuals' rights.

Principles of transmission contribute to governance of personal information flows being fair, adaptive, and responsive to the needs of all stakeholders. They do so along two dimensions, among others. First, with regard to the normative validity of rules, any rule governing personal information flows can be questioned or contested, and no rule is absolute or beyond scrutiny. Furthermore, rules are acceptable only if justified in terms of fairness, transparency, and inclusivity. Second, the legitimacy of rules governing personal information flows is derived from the processes through which they are created, evaluated, and revised: inclusive and participatory processes where stakeholders have a voice. The validity of rules is therefore always

13 On procedural legitimacy, see Gregg (2002).

challengeable and always requires defense, and is subject to continuous evaluation and potential revision. While all stakeholders can regularly review and assess the effectiveness and fairness of existing rules, regulatory bodies can lead the process of revising rules based on stakeholder feedback and emerging issues while researchers can conduct studies to inform evidence-based policy adjustments.

These principles of information transmission draw on Ostrom's (1990) work on commons governance with respect to collective decision-making (similar to how commons are managed through collective action, proceduralist determination involves the collective participation of stakeholders in setting and revising rules); clearly defined boundaries (just as commons require clear boundaries to define who has access, the governance of personal information flows requires clear definitions of what constitutes personal information and under what contexts it can be shared); and mechanisms for conflict resolution (Ostrom's emphasis on conflict resolution mechanisms aligns with the proceduralist approach's need for systems to challenge and defend rules).

13.6.2 *Democracy and Proceduralism*

Governance of such a knowledge commons can be democratic. Knowledge commons governance can be member-driven as an arrangement in which members vote and otherwise participate in commons decision-making, such that decision-making is democratic. *Democratic* means members of the commons jointly define and address issues of governance in the political sphere. To the extent that a commons displays democratic aspects, democratic self-rule by a commons is nonetheless different from the democratic self-rule of a political community. Above all, governance of a knowledge commons does not undertake tasks of the state, or tasks of the economy, whereas a democratic political community does precisely that. To be sure, a knowledge commons could constitute itself as public-driven if it embraced public participation in some of the affairs of the commons, perhaps in recognition of the likelihood of wide, public consumption of the information generated by the commons.[14] It could so constitute itself by soliciting interest in the knowledge commons by diverse members of the public and their involvement in it.

Simultaneously, governance of such a commons can be procedural. A procedural form that copes with abiding normative disagreements within the commons might secure procedural legitimacy through a process of participants deciding together the proper goals of the commons and of its data harvesting, including the normative appropriateness of information flows and of information constraints – and, in that process, by including potentially everyone who might be affected.[15]

[14] On the political challenges of achieving such public participation, see Gregg (2022b) and Gregg (2023).

[15] On the imperative for a community to include, in its social and political deliberation, persons impacted by that deliberation, compare Habermas (1991).

- Individuals Are the Primary Stakeholders: Those individuals whose personal information is being governed. Such governance would provide informed consent and allow participation in decision-making processes, the raising of concerns, and the right to challenge existing rules.
- Healthcare Providers Are Also Stakeholders: Physicians, hospitals, and clinics that collect and use genetic information for medical purposes. The proposed governance would ensure the ethical collection and use of data, adherence to privacy regulations, and engagement in discussions about appropriate information flows. These stakeholders contribute expertise on the implications of data use in medical and scientific contexts.
- Researchers Are Another Group of Stakeholders: Individuals and institutions conducting scientific research using genetic data. The proposed governance would allow for their advocacy for data access for research purposes, ensure their compliance with ethical standards, and allow their participation in setting norms for data use.
- Regulatory Bodies Can Be Stakeholders: Governmental agencies and oversight organizations responsible for privacy and data protection that create and enforce regulations, mediate disputes, and strive to ensure that data governance aligns with public interests and ethical standards. They can facilitate discussions, draft regulations, and influence the formulation of public policy.
- Private Companies Can Be Stakeholders: Some biotech firms and pharmaceutical companies, among other enterprises, utilize genetic information for commercial purposes and develop and implement privacy policies, ensure data security, and engage in transparent practices that build trust with data providers.
- Civil Society Organizations Can Be Stakeholders: Nonprofits and advocacy groups focused on privacy, ethics, and human rights that represent the interests of the public advocate for robust privacy protections, and hold other stakeholders accountable. They can participate in public consultations, provide feedback on proposed rules, and ensure that diverse perspectives are considered.

As an example of a stakeholder role, *consider individuals*: A patient participating in a genetic study provides consent; she later questions the use of her data for a new research purpose. She has a right to challenge this use and to request a revision of the consent terms. *Consider healthcare providers*: A hospital implements strict protocols for data sharing based on patient consent and participates in broader policy discussions about data privacy in healthcare. *Consider researchers*: A university research team proposes new guidelines for genetic data sharing that balances research needs with privacy concerns. The team works with other stakeholders to refine these guidelines. *Consider regulatory bodies*: A governmental agency develops new regulations for genetic data protection and holds public forums to gather input from all stakeholders before finalizing the rules. *Consider private companies*: A biotech firm creates transparent data privacy policies and engages with patient advocacy groups to ensure their practices meet ethical standards. *Consider civil society organizations*: A privacy advocacy group conducts audits of genetic data usage and publishes reports to inform the public and policymakers about potential privacy risks.

These and other stakeholder roles and interactions reflect Ostrom's (1990) principles, such as collective choice arrangements (ensuring that those affected by the rules can participate in modifying the rules); monitoring (of both the resource – genetic data – and the behavior of users – stakeholders – to ensure compliance with established norms); conflict-resolution mechanisms (providing accessible and low-cost methods for resolving disputes among stakeholders); and graduated sanctions (applying sanctions in a way that escalates, based on the severity and context of the violation, toward fairness and proportionality).

13.6.3 *Realizing the Commons*

For nonspecialist stakeholders, comprehensive understanding of the usage of their human genetic information in research and clinical practice is possible within the knowledge commons. This possibility is a matter of balancing the imperative to share genetic information with the need to protect informational privacy, such that the sharing of one's genetic information constitutes a dimension of privacy rather than the negation of privacy.

The means to this goal are several. First, clear and transparent communication requires comprehensive educational resources, including brochures, videos, and interactive websites, explaining how genetic data will be used as well as the benefits, risks, and protective measures in place. Clear and transparent communication requires simplified or plain language that avoids technical jargon to ensure that participants of varying educational backgrounds can understand the information. And it requires consent forms that are detailed yet clear, and that outline the specific uses of data, data sharing policies, and the participant's rights.

Second, an interactive consent process requires informed consent discussions, one-on-one discussions or group discussions with participants, to walk them through the consent process and to answer any questions. An interactive consent process requires interactive tools, including digital tools and apps that can guide participants through the consent process, supplying explanations and visual aids to enhance understanding. And it requires feedback mechanisms that provide options for participants to ask questions and give feedback during the consent process.

Finally, an independent ethical review board might oversee the consent process and ensure transparency and fairness. Or a participant advocacy group could help ensure that participants' interests are represented and that participants fully understand the consent process.

The validity of the assertion might be determined by various means. Surveys administered before and after the consent process can help assess participants' understanding of how their data will be used. Comprehension questions in consent forms can gauge participants' understanding of key points. Focus groups with participants can provide detailed feedback on their understanding and the effectiveness of the consent process. Feedback from focus groups can then iteratively improve educational materials and consent processes, and follow-up assessments over time can help evaluate if participants retain their understanding of data use and if their perception of privacy and trust in the system remains positive. Studying participants' behavior and willingness to share data over time will shed light on whether a comprehensive understanding influences their continued participation. Regular audits by independent bodies can review the consent process, educational materials, and participants' understanding, ensuring that the consent process complies with legal and ethical standards, and that participants are truly informed. Publishing regular transparency reports detailing how data is used, who accesses it, and the outcomes of its use, and then sharing these reports with participants, is likewise important, as is collecting feedback on these reports to see if participants feel informed and satisfied with the information provided.

In these ways, the political design principle of procedural legitimacy promotes, within the knowledge commons, normatively appropriate flows of human genetic information. And it helps resolve disputes concerning matters and norms of privacy.[16] It would deal with the trade-off between the imperative to encourage the individual to share her genetic information, and the imperative to protect the sharer's informational privacy, by establishing clear rules for participation in the commons, by controlling access to the human genetic information collected, by removing identifying information before sharing that information, and by making data storage secure. It would not simply obtain the participant's informed consent when collecting her genetic information. It would also help her fully understand how her data will be used in the commons, in this way to provide her some control over the future use of that data. Finally, the political design principle of procedural legitimacy would link genotypes and phenotypes in normatively appropriate ways, with a view to research using genome-wide association studies, and with a view to state regulation of genome databases, including those in knowledge commons, to prohibit the identification of donors from their data and to enforce strict standards of donor confidentiality.

16 Political proceduralism supplements Nissenbaum's notion of transmission principles and context-relative informational norms with "politically and procedurally grounded rules" (Sanfilippo et al. 2021, 6).

13.7 CONCLUSIONS

Human genetic information should be managed within a commons governance framework that balances sharing and privacy, involves collaborative and inclusive governance, and ensures the information's ethical and effective use for research and medical advancements through participatory and transparent processes. I developed five arguments in support of this proposition. First, the commons framework treats human genetic information as a resource for scientific and medical progress, for individual members of a commons and for the entire commons and beyond. Second, deCODE Genetics not only offers empirical evidence for the very possibility of the human genome as a knowledge commons; it demonstrates the importance of public cooperation, ethical safeguards, state support, and consent and privacy in utilizing genome data for realizing a commons that identifies disease genes and develops medical products. Third, human genetic information is a non-rivalrous, non-excludable public good that can be governed collaboratively by some mixture of commons, state, and market. Fourth, balancing the benefits possible only from large genetic datasets – hence the imperative of individuals to share their own genetic information – with every person's interest in the privacy of sensitive information vulnerable to misuse involves recognizing that sharing and privacy are intertwined aspects of a commons governance that supports the ethical flow of genetic information for individual and social benefit. Fifth, effective governance of the human genome as a resource includes participatory and transparent rule-making, addressing privacy concerns, and providing mechanisms for grievances, rule challenges, arbitration, and monitoring in ways democratic and proceduralist.

Two internally complex conclusions follow from knowledge commons governance that balances individual sharing of genetic information with the individual's privacy interest. They relate (a) to advances in understanding human biology and addressing genetic diseases and (b) to the promise of knowledge commons governance of the human genome.

With regard to the former, several points should be emphasized. First, enabling scientific and clinical research on genetic mutations and variations that cause or contribute to diseases leads to more accurate diagnoses and targeted treatments. Second, providing researchers with large genomic datasets to explore genetic targets accelerates the development of new drugs and therapies. Third, tailoring medical treatment to an individual's genetic profile increases healthcare's effectiveness. Fourth, predicting an individual's likelihood of developing certain diseases allows for early intervention and preventive measures.

Several points also deserve emphasis concerning the latter. First, treating the genome as a knowledge commons lends itself to making this critical information accessible to all researchers, regardless of their financial or institutional resources, and also to the equitable distribution of a shared resource (thus preventing monopolization of a public good by private entities). Second, knowledge commons governance fosters a collaborative environment that accelerates scientific progress and innovation in part because researchers share data, tools, and findings. Further, it encourages contributions from a wide range of researchers, including those from underrepresented and resource-limited regions, leading to a more comprehensive understanding of human genetics. Third, knowledge commons governance can protect individual privacy and ensure that genetic information is used ethically, with informed consent, and that it can include mechanisms for regulatory oversight and public accountability, toward ensuring that genomic data is used responsibly and ethically. Finally, framing the human genome as a commons strengthens the possibility of its long-term preservation and stewardship, protecting an invaluable resource for future generations, and allowing for the sustainable allocation of resources toward the maintenance, updating, and expansion of genomic databases.

REFERENCES

Contreras, Jorge. 2014. "Constructing the Genome Common." In *Governing Knowledge Commons*, ed. Brett M. Frischmann, Machael J. Madison, and Katherine J. Strandburg, 99–135. New York: Oxford University Press.

deCODE Genetics. 1997. "Icelandic Genomics Company Identifies Location of Gene for Essential Tremor." August 25, 1997. www.decode.com/icelandic-genomics-company-identifies-location-of-gene-for-essential-tremor/.

Dekker, Erwin and Pavel Kuchař, eds. 2022. *Governing Markets as Knowledge Commons*. Cambridge: Cambridge University Press.

Dekker, Erwin and Pavel Kuchař. 2023. "Markets and Knowledge Commons: Is There a Difference between Private and Community Governance of Markets?" *Public Choice* 201(3–4): 533–553.

Evans, Barbara. 2017. "Genomic Data Commons." In *Governing Medical Knowledge Commons*, ed. Brett M. Frischmann, Katherine J. Strandburg, and Michael J. Madison, 74–101. Cambridge: Cambridge University Press.

Gregg, Benjamin. 2002. "Proceduralism Reconceived: Political Conflict Resolution under Conditions of Moral Pluralism." *Theory and Society* 31(6): 741–776.

Gregg, Benjamin. 2012. *Human Rights as Social Construction*. New York: Cambridge University Press.

Gregg, Benjamin. 2016. *The Human Rights State: Justice Within and Beyond Sovereign Nations*. Philadelphia: University of Pennsylvania Press.

Gregg, Benjamin. 2018. "How to Read for Current Developments in Human Genetics Relevant to Justice." *Politics and the Life Sciences* 37(2): 262–277.

Gregg, Benjamin. 2021a. "Beyond Due Diligence: The Human Rights Corporation. *Human Rights Review* 22(1): 65–89.

Gregg, Benjamin. 2021b. "Il contenimento di Covid-19: diritto alla privacy contro diritto alla salute pubblica" (trans. P. Monti and C. Rebuffo). *Lessico di etica* 2021(1): 125–163.

Gregg, Benjamin. 2021c. "Against Essentialism in Conceptions of Human Rights and Human Nature." *Human Rights Quarterly* 43(2): 313–328.

Gregg, Benjamin. 2022a. *Creating Human Nature: The Political Challenges of Genetic Engineering*. New York: Cambridge University Press.

Gregg, Benjamin. 2022b. "Political Bioethics." *Journal of Medicine and Philosophy* 47(4): 516–529.

Gregg, Benjamin. 2022c. "Regulating Genetic Engineering Guided by Human Dignity, Not Genetic Essentialism." *Politics and the Life Sciences* 41(1): 60–75.

Gregg, Benjamin. 2023. "Imperfect Methods for Imperfect Democracies: Toward Increasing Public Participation in Gene Editing Debates." *American Journal of Bioethics* 23(7): 77–79.

Gregg, Benjamin. 2024. "Might the Bioethical Principle of Individual Decisional Autonomy Have a Politically Liberalizing Effect on Soft Authoritarian Communities?" *Politics and the Life Sciences* 43(1): 132–151.

Habermas, Jürgen. 1991 [1962]. *The Structural Transformation of the Public Sphere*. Cambridge, MA: MIT Press.

Hess, Charlotte, and Elinor Ostrom, eds. 2007. *Understanding Knowledge as a Commons: From Theory to Practice*. Cambridge, MA: MIT Press.

Larson, Maja, and Margaret Chon. 2017. "The Greatest Generational Impact: Open Neuroscience as an Energizing Knowledge Commons," in *Governing Medical Knowledge Commons*, ed. Brett M. Frischmann, Katherine J. Strandburg, and Michael J. Madison, 166–191. Cambridge: Cambridge University Press.

Madison, Michael J., Brett M. Frischmann, Madelyn R. Sanfilippo, and Katherine J. Strandburg. 2022. "Too Much of a Good Thing? A Governing Knowledge Commons Review of Abundance in Context." *Frontiers in Research Metrics and Analytics* 7: 959505.

Nissenbaum, Helen. 2009. *Privacy in Context: Technology, Policy, and the Integrity of Social Life*. Stanford: Stanford University Press.

Ostrom, Elinor. 1990. *Governing the Commons: The Evolution of Institutions for Collective Action*. Cambridge: Cambridge University Press.

Ostrom, Vincent, and Elinor Ostrom. 2009. "Postscript: Rethinking Institutional Analysis and Development. Dialogues with Vincent and Elinor Ostrom." In *Challenging Institutional Analysis and Development: The Bloomington School*, ed. Paul Dragos Aligica, and Peter Boettke, 142–159. London: Routledge.

Sanfilippo, Madelyn R., Brett M. Frischmann, and Katherine J. Strandburg. 2021. "Privacy and Knowledge Commons." In *Governing Privacy in Knowledge Commons*, ed. Madelyn R. Sanfilippo, Brett M. Frischmann, Katherine J. Strandburg, 5–49. Cambridge: Cambridge University Press.

Securities and Exchange Commission. 2000. "deCODE Genetics Inc. Annual Report 2000, December 31, 2000. www.sec.gov/Archives/edgar/data/0001022974/000089322001000311/w45228e10-k.txt.

Sigurjonsson, Trostur Olaf, Robert H. Haraldsson, and Jordan Mitchell. 2023. "deCODE Genetics," in *Corporate Governance and Business Ethics in Iceland: Studies on Contemporary Governance and Ethical Dilemmas*, ed. Trostur Olaf Sigurjonsson, Robert H. Haraldsson, and Jordan Mitchell, 199–220. Leeds: Emerald Publishing.

Strandburg, Katherine J., Brett M. Frischmann, and Michael J. Madison eds. 2017. *Governing Medical Knowledge Commons*. Cambridge: Cambridge University Press.

14

Commoning through Interactions

Governing Offline and Online Communities in the German Video Game Influencer Industry

Deike Schulz

14.1 INTRODUCTION

In 2022, the online magazine *Vice* discussed the impact of influencers on business and society by highlighting the problematic practices of influencers on social media platforms like Instagram, YouTube, and other social media channels.[1] Examples of problematic practices included damaging public property for photo opportunities, trivializing serious historical issues, exploiting personal relationships for content, and buying followers and likes to expand their social media channels and presences. In 2024, the BBC reported for the fifth time about Andrew Tate, the "self-proclaimed misogynist influencer" whose content, which often includes disparaging remarks about women, influences young men and boys, many of whom view him as a role model, despite his controversial statements and actions even after his arrest in 2022.[2] Given the current sentiment in the media, influencers and their online and offline activities (are perceived to) have a negative impact on business and society.

Yet, the global influencer marketing market is growing rapidly. The global market tripled since 2020 and is expected to achieve a valuation of US$32.5 billion in 2025.[3] Considering the fast growth of this *influencer economy* and the negative impacts of social media content creation, if a set of best practices is to emerge, studies of current practices in influencer content production and sharing are essential. This chapter relies on in-depth interviews to propose a case study of INSTINCT3, an influencer management agency in the German video game industry, a vibrant and rapidly growing sector within the broader gaming ecosystem of online and offline video gaming. The Governing Knowledge Commons (GKC) framework (Frischmann

The author thanks all participating employees and the two founders of INSTINCT3 for facilitating this research. Special thanks go to Lea Stöter and Lara Hoffman for their contribution in transcribing and co-analyzing the interviews at various stages of the study.

1 "Insiders Tell Us about All the Terrible Things Influencers Get Away With," *Vice*, May 5, 2022. www.vice.com/en/article/insiders-influencers-instagram-social-media-toxic/.

2 "Who Is Andrew Tate? The Self-Proclaimed Misogynist Influencer," *BBC News*, February 27, 2024. www.bbc.com/news/uk-64125045.

3 www.statista.com/statistics/1092819/global-influencer-market-size/.

et al. 2014; Sanfilippo et al. 2018) is mobilized to understand how INSTINCT3 governs two action arenas – its online influencer communities and its offline employee community.

14.2 THE INFLUENCER INDUSTRY

Influencers can be identified as internet users who reach significant followings on social media platforms by sharing written and visual narratives of their personal lives and lifestyles (Schulz 2020). Through active interaction with their audience in both online and offline settings, influencers monetize their platforms primarily by integrating "advertorials" within their posts or social media content. In recent years, many studies have addressed the "dark side" of the social media industry, where influencers and their practices have been linked with the promotion of online gaming (Haenlein et al. 2020), parasocial (or one-sided) interactions with human and virtual influencers (Stein et al. 2022), and addiction (Bhargava and Velasquez, 2021). Moreover, a growing number of studies also addresses the well-being of influencers as content creators, including for example the anxiety of influencers as both a negative side-effect of content production and an unethical tactic to gain attention from followers on social media (Hund 2023; Lehto 2022).

Overall, influencers are often portrayed by both media and academic sources as inconsiderate, unethical, and self-centered digital entrepreneurs. They are characterized as exploiting their online communities irresponsibly, prioritizing personal profit over ethical considerations. This raises the question of how organizations operating in this industry are developing ethical or value-based community practices and how they might translate these values to their large followings online.

14.2.1 *Influencer Management Agencies*

Influencers are increasingly managed by or integrated into larger organizations known as *influencer management agencies* (IMA). IMAs represent a new development in the institutionalization of online content creation and online community interaction. An IMA recruits, manages, and supports influencers in creating, sharing, and promoting content on specific topics (e.g., video gaming, traveling, lifestyle); handles contract negotiations, campaign planning, and reputation management; and assists in building and maintaining their online and offline communities. INSTINCT3 is a German IMA specialized in video gaming, a term that here refers to both online and offline games that may offer online interactions with other players. As most games now provide online interactions, the distinction between video games and online games is no longer used.

Influencers play a crucial role in the industry, shaping the video gaming landscape, connecting with audiences, and driving engagement with video gaming content (using, for example, YouTube reviews or live gaming streams platforms such as

Twitch). Video game influencers engage with their followers (users interested in online or offline video gaming) through online communities on platforms such as YouTube, Twitch, TikTok, or X (Twitter). IMAs support the development of influencers, and help them create and share special interest content with these communities and its members, including in collaboration with different organizational actors, such as artists and project managers, creative designers, content developers, editors, and other influencers. IMAs are involved in the management of their influencers' online communities by monitoring comments and engaging with community members. They respond to participants who comment on content shared by influencers, and interact with readers and viewers who reach out via direct messages or emails. Overall, IMAs are key actors that craft an organizational community of practice that develops and operates influencer channels, aiming to produce high-quality, engaging content while safeguarding the reputation of the influencers involved.

14.2.2 *IMAs and Communityship*

The activities of IMAs align with Mintzberg's (2009) concept of *communityship*, which emphasizes the importance of cultivating a sense of community within organizations. For Mintzberg (2009, 2–3), the combination of individual leadership and collective citizenship is essential for the creation of communityship, which requires what he calls "engaged and distributed management" (wherein a community leader is personally engaged in order to engage others) and "just enough leadership" (which involves intervening when appropriate) so that anyone and everyone can exercise initiative and collaborate toward the achievement of a shared purpose. These principles have proven valuable in creating resilient and adaptive organizations, such as Wikipedia, which thrive on collective effort and shared values.

Given that they coexist in close relation with the online communities they operate and govern, IMAs deploy communityship beyond the boundaries of a single organization. Online communities are computer-mediated online forums where individuals exchange text or audiovisual content to discuss, share information, or learn about topics of interest (Schulz 2020). These communities facilitate public and private communication among participants. They can be organization-driven (e.g., about a public or commercial organization) or citizen-driven (e.g., forming around certain societal topics or goals). Influencer communities can be defined as organization-driven online groups or forums where influencers are the primary content producers and channel owners – sharing organizational, industry, and personal content pertaining to their chosen topic of interest, according to a well-specified business model – and citizens, viewing or commenting on the content produced by the influencers and other participants. Both influencers and citizens can individually or jointly promote ideas, seek answers, offer critiques, or provide improvement tips within these communities (Schulz 2021).

14.3 GOVERNING KNOWLEDGE COMMONS IN THE INFLUENCER INDUSTRY

The study of a specific case in the German video game influencer industry proposed in this chapter draws on the GKC framework (Hess and Ostrom 2007; Frischmann et al. 2014; Cole 2014; Standburg et al. 2017; Sanfilippo et al. 2018), which is an extension of the Ostromian Institutional Analysis and Development (IAD) framework (Ostrom 2005, 2010) to knowledge commons – namely, to the community-led governance of creating and sharing of information, data, ideas, and various other forms of intellectual and cultural resources. Specifically, the study examines how actors in the German video game industry are producing and sharing information, innovations, and creative works to cultivate communityship, and based on the rule-in-use of communityship govern their offline and online community(ies).

14.3.1 *The GKC Framework*

The study focuses on the flow of information and knowledge both within the IMA and within its online communities, and considers its impact on the continuity, mutual trust, and safety of these two communities. To connect these two worlds, I rely to earlier work (Schulz et al. 2018; Schulz 2021) using the inside–out (organization-driven) perspective in online community communication and the evaluation of specific community practices. This perspective reveals how organizations engage with citizens in cocreating community processes and resources, but aim to control these as providers of resources, which is to say online content.

All the relevant actors engage in various action situations within specified action arenas. In this case, there are two organization-driven action arenas: (1) the organizational community, which is mostly offline and consists of the IMA's employees; and (2) the online community, which includes IMA employees and a range of online community members. Specifically, in both action arenas, actors "engage with the particular narratives of the community, which may be grounded in storytelling, metaphor, history and analog" (Frischmann et al. 2014, 25) and "interact with rules, resources, and each other" in a manner that is "inextricably linked with and determinative of the form and content of the knowledge or informational output of the commons" (Frischmann et al. 2014, 27). The multiple resources pooled in both action arenas include communication practices and their outcomes, such as personal values, ideas, concepts, processes, feedback, and agreements, all of which are related to the development and sharing of audiovisual and written content. These resources and their characteristics, along with community attributes (including members and their roles) and a set of governing rules-in-use, serve as "inputs to an action arena" (Sanfilippo et al. 2018, 123), where various actors "interact with resources, rules, and one another" (Strandburg et al. 2017, 16). This analytical setup is captured in Figure 14.1.

The GKC framework was recently applied by Gradoz and Raux (2021) to study within a French online video game community the rules-in-use of troll forums,

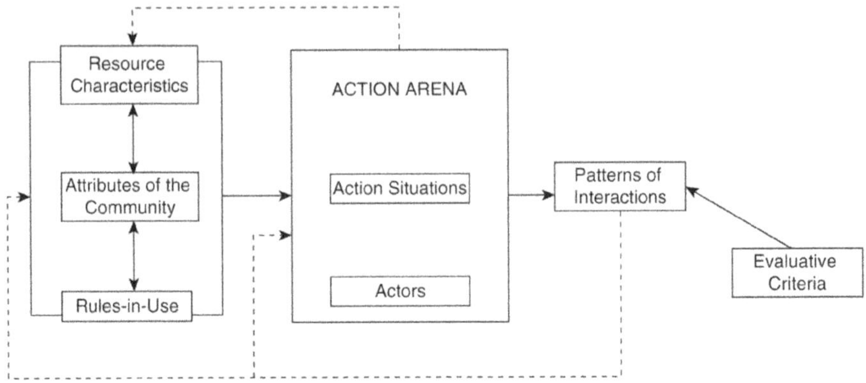

FIGURE 14.1 The GKC framework. Source: Frischmann et al. (2014, 19).

where abusive and provocative content about societal topics is shared. This online forum and its community – the local commons – is valued by its members, while society calls for the closure of these transgressive spaces. This chapter extends this type of research by investigating the rules-in-use of a specific IMA, with a special focus on how its communities are maintained and governed by a specific set of value-based practices. These practices capture the rules-in-use, which can be understood as "what is considered acceptable to do within the community" (Gradoz and Raux 2021, 219). They are reflected in the communication and interactions between the actors in both action arenas, and because their goal is to mediate among "communities with different default norms" (Frischmann et al. 2014, 33), they are central to the knowledge commons under consideration.

14.3.2 *Research Questions*

To help researchers study knowledge commons, and more specifically to help researchers evaluate case studies using the GKC framework, Sanfilippo et al. (2018) have provided a useful set of representative research questions (Table 14.1).

To understand how INSTINCT3 governs its online influencer communities and its offline employee community, the GKC framework and these representative research questions informed the research. Two general questions served as central themes for the case study:

1. What rules, routines, roles, and mindsets are essential for a value-driven and responsible employee community?
2. How are these elements introduced, practiced, and evaluated by different actors? Based on these questions an interview guide was developed. The following paragraph outlines how the GKC framework and the representative research questions were integrated in the research methodology.

TABLE 14.1 *Representative research questions*

Background environment

- What is the background context (legal, cultural, etc.) of this particular commons?
- What normative values are relevant for this community?
- What is the "default" status of the resources involved in the commons (patented, copyrighted, open, or other)?
- How does this community fit into a larger context?
- What relevant domains overlap in this context?

Attributes

- What resources are pooled and how are they created or obtained?
- What are the characteristics of the resources?
- Are they rival or nonrival, tangible or intangible?
- Is there shared infrastructure?
- What is personal information relative to resources in this action arena?
- What technologies and skills are needed to create, obtain, maintain, and use the resources?
- What are considered to be appropriate resource flows?
- How is appropriateness of resource use structured or protected?
- Who are the community members and what are their roles?
- What are the degree and nature of openness with respect to each type of community member and the general public?
- Which noncommunity members are impacted?
- What are the goals and objectives of the commons and its members, including obstacles or dilemmas to overcome?
- Who determines goals and objectives?
- What values are reflected in goals and objectives?
- What are the history and narrative of the commons?
- What is the value of knowledge production in this context?

Governance

- What are the relevant action arenas and how do they relate to the goals and objective of the commons and the relationships among various types of participants and with the general public?
- Are action arenas perceived to be legitimate?
- What legal structures (e.g., intellectual property, subsidies, contract, licensing, tax, and antitrust) apply?
- What are the governance mechanisms (e.g., membership rules, resource contribution or extraction standards and requirements, conflict resolution mechanisms, and sanctions for rule violation)?
- What are the institutions and technological infrastructures that structure and govern decision-making?
- What informal norms govern the commons?
- What institutions are perceived to be legitimate or illegitimate?
- How are institutional illegitimacies addressed?
- Who are the decision-makers and how are they selected?

TABLE 14.1 *(continued)*

- Are decision-makers perceived to be legitimate?
- How do nonmembers interact with the commons?
- What institutions govern those interactions?
- Are there impacted groups that have no say in governance?

Patterns and outcomes

- What benefits are delivered to members and to others (e.g., innovations and creative output, production, sharing, and dissemination to a broader audience, and social interactions that emerge from the commons)?
- What costs and risks are associated with the commons, including any negative externalities?
- Are outcomes perceived to be legitimate by members?
- By decision-makers?
- By impacted outsiders?

14.4 METHODS

To understand an IMA's action arenas, their rules-in-use, and their governing mechanisms from an inside-out perspective, a single case study looking into community practices of INSTINCT3 was developed. My qualitative inquiry is based on semi-structured interviews and additional desk research. The GKC framework serves as a reference for data collection, while the research questions outlined in Table 14.1 help structure the analysis.

A case study can have three important uses: (1) motivation, showing why a phenomenon is important, or using a real-life situation as appealing example, (2) inspiration for new ideas, and (3) illustration to make a conceptual contribution (Siggelkow 2007). In this context, the primary goal is to provide insights into the emerging influencer economy, focusing on the self-governing mechanisms of influencer management agencies and online special interest communities led by influencers. In this sense, I apply the GKC framework to a novel and significant domain of research and industry that has not been previously explored in the existing literature on knowledge commons, in order to make a conceptual contribution and further research about knowledge commons in digital spaces.

14.4.1 *Introducing the INSTINCT3 Case*

INSTINCT3 was chosen because this agency recently entered the market (in 2018) and grew into a full-service agency in influencer management and creative content production, employing eighty professionals with various backgrounds, including creative concepting, artist management, influencer marketing, production, editing,

HRM, finance, and project management.[4] Additionally, this company has developed a novel approach in building interdisciplinary teams that work together in a community-like setting to develop online concepts and content (e.g., text, images, live or prerecorded videos) and manage and support influencers who share this content addressing online and offline gaming with their communities on social media platforms such as YouTube, Twitch, TikTok, Instagram, and X/Twitter. INSTINCT3 combines artist management and creative agency services and externally recruits or trains influencers in-house, with the aim of providing a permanent contract for internal influencers or to collaborate with external influencers based on a project fee. Influencers employed by the company are also supported by various teams in the areas of creative concepting, video editing, project management, event management, innovation, merchandising, and so on. Essentially, they are provided with relationship-, reputation, and legal management services to help them deal with everything from brand partnerships to crisis management.

All the employees, including artists and project managers, creative designers, content developers, editors, and influencers, form an organizational community of practice. Together, they develop and implement rules, roles, and agreements for content creation, production, distribution, and online community interaction. As such, they are both users of and contributors to the shared knowledge and information developed within this community of practice. For example, they engage in collaborative research for content production, jointly develop creative ideas and outputs, and share content through online communities. Knowledge commons research distinguishes specific actors, such as *users* "appropriating digital information at any point in time," *providers* who "make content available," and *information managers* who may be "a voluntary and self-governing community of insiders" contributing to, using, and managing a knowledge commons (Hess and Ostrom 2007, 48) – digital information and creative works/content in our case. These actors can be identified at INSTINCT3, where creative content is developed, produced, shared, and governed by members of this organizational community (in close relation) with members of their online communities.

14.4.2 *Selection of Interviewees, Interview Guide, and Planning*

Interviewees were selected with the support of the company, with the aim of meeting employees from various departments, roles, work experiences, and backgrounds. Prior to the interview, interviewees were provided with an interview guide outlining details of the study, such as its aim and the topics to discuss. Additionally, at the outset each interviewee was informed about the secure handling of data and the steps taken to ensure respondents' anonymity. The interview guide covered a range of topics, starting with familiar and overarching subjects, such as the

[4] See https://instinct3.de/.

individual's position within the company and their professional as well as personal use of social media platforms. Subsequent questions delved into specifics regarding responsibilities, policies, core beliefs, and engagements within the organization, including interactions with online community members.

The interview guide, which was developed in close relation with the GKC framework, included two central topics, with additional sub-questions. In essence, this study addresses two types of communities (the action arenas), specifically from an inside-out viewpoint. The first action arena revolves around the interaction and communication within INSTINCT3's *offline* community of employees, including its CEO, artists and project managers, creative designers, content developers, editors, and influencers. The second action arena exists in communication and interaction with the *online* influencers' communities operated by INSTINCT3, and consists of influencers and their supporting team of artists and project managers, creative designers, content developers, editors, and active community members, including moderators and followers who comment on content or engage with others within the social media channel of the influencer.

The offline community within INSTINCT3 was studied in terms of *organizational communityship*, which has been used in the literature on healthcare management to study staffing (Kerfoot and Douglas 2010) and the literature on higher education to foster collective creative practice (Nerantzi et al. 2024). As explained in Section 14.2.2, the general question raised by this concept is whether people working for a company see themselves as responsible citizens of the broader community. In this chapter, I explore how organizational community members of INSTINCT3 translate individual values into community values for the organization, and vice versa. Interview questions sought to capture the interviewees' views about the rules-in-use that are essential for the development of a value-oriented and responsible employee communityship. Interviewees were furthermore invited to reflect on how these elements are introduced, practiced, and/or evaluated.

The online community was examined through the concept of *influencer-driven communityship*, which I suggest can emerge through circular communication between influencers, their supporting team, and their online community members. Thus, interview questions also sought to capture the interviewees' views about whether and how rules-in-use of organizational members (influencers) were transferred through interaction and communication in their online communities. Interviewees were also asked about whether and how online community members provided feedback, and how this feedback influenced the way in which the company shaped the communication between the organizational offline and influencer online community.

The semi-structured interviews with the employees were conducted between December 2022 and June 2023. After analysis of this data, further interviews and evaluations of the findings with the founders took place in March 2024. Each interview lasted approximately sixty to ninety minutes. A total of sixteen interviews were conducted: fourteen with employees, and two specifically dedicated to

TABLE 14.2 *Interviewees*

Participant	Role	Gender	Age	Pseudonym
1	Artist management	Female	25–34	P1
2	Project and campaign manager	Male	25–34	P2
3	Production manager	Male	18–24	P3
4	Producer	Female	25–34	P4
5	Junior artist manager	Female	25–34	P5
6	Artist management	Female	25–34	P6
7	Creative concept developer	Female	25–34	P7
8	Merchandise joint venture	Male	25–34	P8
9	Senior concept developer	Male	25–34	P9
10	Production services lead	Male	18–24	P10
11	Content creator/influencer	Male	25–34	P11
12	Influencer	Male	25–34	P12
13	Project manager influencer-marketing	Male	25–34	P13
14	Influencer	Male	25–34	P14
Additional interviews to evaluate findings				
15	(Former) CEO and founder	Male	35–44	P15
16	Content creator/influencer	Male	35–44	P16

evaluating findings with the company founders. Interviews were conducted at locations convenient for the interviewees, such as their workplaces or home offices (two interviews were held via Microsoft teams).

Table 14.2 presents an overview of the interviewees' roles (as described by the interviewees), gender, age, and reporting pseudonym.

14.4.3 *Transcription and Analysis*

The interviews were transcribed by two student assistants who had entered into a confidentiality agreement prior to the beginning of their work. This agreement was established to guarantee confidentiality and secure deletion of all data once the students had completed their tasks. Upon transcription and anonymization, the data was transferred to ATLAS.ti[5] for thematic analysis, exploring the dataset to uncover patterns or themes for new insights (Braun and Clarke 2013). Initially, two overarching themes were deduced based on the German interview guide topics – organizational communityship and influencer-driven communityship – and their related sub-questions. The translated interview guide can be found in Appendix A. The process involved two rounds of inductive coding, where four interviews were independently coded by two coders. The codes were reviewed, refined, and merged. A final codebook was then developed for the fourteen interviews, consisting of three top-level codes

[5] https://atlasti.com/

TABLE 14.3 *Data analysis process*

Steps		Interviews	Who
1	Deducing two overarching themes (organizational communityship and influencer-driven communityship) from the interview guide to start the inductive coding process		Coder 1
2	Two rounds of inductive coding	4 interviews	Coder 1, 2
3	Reviewing and refining the codes, adding sublevel codes		Coder 1, 2
4	Developing final codebook and applying top-level and sublevel codes		Coder 1, 2
5	Coding all interviews	14 interview	Coder 1, 2
6	Additional desk research		Coder 1
7	Developing four central themes (role-modeling, feedback culture, work–life balance, and innovative topics and education) from analysis and desk research		
8	Integrate themes into interview guide for additional interviews/evaluation with two CEOs of the company	2 interviews	Coder 1
	Refine and finalize themes based on all interviews	16 interviews	Coder 1, 2

(demographics/community characteristics, organizational communityship, and influencer-driven communityship) and twenty sublevel codes to identify rules-in-use within and across the action arenas. Tables B.1 and C.1 provide an overview of the codes, their assigned definitions, and their connection with the representative research questions listed by Sanfilippo et al. (2018) and reproduced in Table 14.1.

Table 14.3 provides an overview of the various steps taken during coding to ensure validity and reliability. The interview data was analyzed, including multiple evaluation sessions. To prepare both coders independently wrote additional memos to summarize their findings using specific quotes from interviewees to illustrate these findings. These memos and quotes were compared to identify matching and additional themes in line with the research.

Further desk research was conducted to collect information from German-based websites and YouTube channels that shared industry insights, information, or interviews with employees of the company. Four central themes were deduced from the analysis (see Section 14.5) and integrated into a revised interview guide to conduct two additional interviews with the founders. The received feedback and insights from additional desk research were used to evaluate the findings.

14.4.4 *Data Storage and Use of AI*

The data collected in this study was stored in a safe password-protected university environment, accessible only to the research team. I used a corporate version of

Microsoft Copilot[6] to translate the quotes from German to English, using the following prompt: "Produce a concise translation into English while retaining the context." Moreover, to shorten and check certain sentences, I applied another prompt: "Refine for clarity, shorten and check grammar." Additionally, experimental evaluation memos were produced using the ATLAS.ti AI-summary function,[7] without using prompts, to summarize the interviews and uncover potential insights that may have been missed during coding. No new themes were identified based on this approach. Both ATLAS.ti and Microsoft Copilot safeguard research by ensuring that the data is encrypted and not used to train OpenAI and Microsoft language models.

14.5 FINDINGS

Four central themes were identified during the analysis of the interviews: *role-modeling, feedback culture, work–life balance,*and *innovation and education*. These integrate organically into the GKC framework as presented in Figure 14.1 and are supported by the research questions outlined in Table 14.1. I begin with a general characterization of the resources and outputs developed and shared by INSTINCT3, highlighting the two action arenas as described by employees during the interviews, before considering community attributes and rules-in-use that govern interactions and communication within and across these arenas. I then discuss some of the governance mechanisms that are part of the employees' resource management and engagement with online communities. Finally, I briefly address important outcomes and patterns, including the benefits and risks arising in interactions in offline and online settings.

14.5.1 *Resource Characteristics and Action Arenas*

The IMA's main output produced, thanks to these (communication) practices, are various types of online content, including, for example, the conceptual development, creation, production, editing, and sharing of online videos. These videos primarily consist of video game (industry or event) reviews and announcements, and gameplay or interaction with other video game influencers. With their teams, influencers create (daily or weekly) video content, which is recorded either at the company studio or in their home office, in collaboration with the offline organizational community. The content is then shared across various social media platforms with the online influencer communities. YouTube is used as the main outlet to share videos via a main channel (to test and review video games) and a more informal sub-channel (for special announcements and meetups with other internal or external influencers) at a fixed

6 https://copilot.microsoft.com/.

7 This function guarantees safeguarding the interview data through various protection approaches. See, e.g., https://atlasti.com/ai-data-security-and-privacy.

time and day. Another approach is to share live stream videos on Twitch. Community members who follow these platforms and channels can engage by commenting, either after a video is published or during a live stream.

Thus, the main resources created by the online community members are comments, direct messages, e-mails, and textual content moderations via live chats in live streams, which represent and store their ideas and feedback on the content. Communication practices and their outcomes are thus the key intangible and non-rival resources that IMAs strive to develop and rely on to develop and share new audiovisual and written content. These resources are pooled in both action arenas. According to Matzat (2009), online communities function effectively only when members' interests align with those of the broader group. The same principle applies to IMAs, which operate successfully only when such alignment ensures that enough people are attracted to the community and remain actively engaged. Because online influencer communities therefore thrive on active participants who are passionate about the influencer and the shared content, IMAs are confronted with a perennial collection action problem. The most active members invest time in commenting, sharing their thoughts, answering questions, monitoring discussions, and providing feedback, while others choose to follow a channel and solely view the content created by the influencer and the active participants. The system only works if there is a sufficient number of truly active members.

14.5.2 *Community Practices and Their Community Attributes*

Interviewees – both at INSTINCT3 and in online influencer communities – singled out openness, transparency, and the principle of treating each other as equals as essential values. The team is often referred to as a "family." As P13 put it: "It's a very familial atmosphere, which I find beautiful. However, we don't lose sight of the professional aspect. We maintain our goals, strive for excellence, and ensure that our quality remains high. I think it's a well-balanced approach."

To develop and create content, influencers work via various approaches and in different configurations with other experts. In a *large community approach*, an influencer operates at a senior level, creating content for an online community with hundreds of, thousands of, or even millions of followers who watch and contribute on a regular basis. These influencers collaborate with a diverse team of creatives, producers, and editors, who support the influencer, in close contact with a team of senior and junior artist managers at the IMA. In a *small community approach*, an influencer operates at a junior level, creating content for a smaller but growing community, supported by an artist manager and some creative staff. Often these influencers operate independently in different roles to create, edit, and publish content, with the support of an artist manager, and with the option to engage with a more experienced influencer to share ideas and evaluations or to ask questions. As the community grows, an influencer will earn additional income, which can be used to outsource additional tasks, such as editing, to members of a growing team.

14.5.2.1 The Role(s) of Online Community Members

Online community members can have various roles, such as viewers (passive, without liking or commenting), participants (actively liking and commenting), or moderators (supporting the influencer by moderating comments, making announcements in chat, etc.). Influencers and artist managers work together with moderator teams consisting of community participants, who either volunteer or are recruited by the influencer or his/her artist management team. In channels such as YouTube or Twitch, it is possible to grant selected participants administration rights to moderate or flag comments as part of a specific channel, but also to ban other users from the channel if they misbehave. Moderators often work in teams, creating channel guidelines in close alignment with artist managers and/or influencers. These guidelines may address what is (un)acceptable and can cover various topics, such as hate speech, violence, copyrighted material, or "backseat gaming" (offering unsolicited advice, tips, or instructions to an influencer currently playing a video game by a participant). As P5 explained, these roles are taken up on a voluntary basis and moderators mostly connect via digital media with the influencers and their team:

> these are mostly people from the community who have distinguished themselves on platforms like Twitch. They were present in every stream, very active in the chat, and even without being moderators themselves, they often reminded other viewers of the rules. We have a moderator now for P14, who is relatively new to the role, but even before becoming a moderator, she used to say, "Hey folks, please no backseat gaming." These are moments where either established moderators or our team approach people and ask, "Wouldn't you like to join us?"

Influencers and their team may also meet offline with their moderators and community members at industry-specific events such as the Gamescom – "the biggest games event in the world"[8] and Europe's most comprehensive business platform for the gaming industry. As moderators are offering unpaid support, they often receive gifts, such as tickets for events, merchandise, and other game-related items. According to P15, in general moderating teams work on a voluntary basis and view this as an honorary external contributor role.

14.5.2.2 Interdisciplinary Background of the Organizational Community

As Table 14.2 shows, in addition to the four influencers in different stages of their career (two with large and two with small communities), most interviews were conducted with individuals in organizational and management or creative roles. A significant portion of the IMA's employees are so-called "career changers," as are

[8] www.gamescom.global/en. Since 2009, Gamescom has been held annually in Cologne.

most of the influencers. They started their careers in other industries or graduated from nonindustry-related studies (e.g., sociology, history, management science or law, political science, public relations, tourism, insurance). But several interviewees had a degree in industry-related areas, such as film-editing, event management, marketing, video journalism, or multimedia design. Notably, a significant number of interviewees participate in (online) gaming as a recreational activity. Frequently, this engagement began during early childhood or was influenced by family or friends. P13, for example, said:

> My father used to play computer games in the past. Not social media, but more like LAN gaming at home with friends – before widespread internet access. I practically grew up in that environment, playing games with friends. It was a lot of fun. While my family encouraged physical activity and social media use, they also emphasized balancing it with school and friendships.

14.5.2.3 Main Roles and Supporting Roles in Line with Education and Innovation

Often employees have a supporting role, next to their main role in the company. Supporting roles can involve responsibilities such as project management, supporting an artist manager, and educating others about specific topics, based on specific expertise, including editing content, learning about Twitch user groups, discussing innovations like AI-produced content and virtual influencers, or addressing societal issues aligned with company values. Employees receive additional time to work on such topics, practice new skills, and share insight, for example, by organizing a forum discussion. As P7 observed:

> We've just initiated this … and we're currently organizing the first forum. It's essentially an after-work forum for anyone interested. Each forum will focus on a specific topic. The first topic will be the basics of gender identities. The second forum will likely discuss why it's crucial for us to be aware, in our client pitches, that our influencer constellations need to be as diverse as possible. This way, we can represent diversity outwardly. It's essential to acknowledge that it's not just the same six gamers who have been around for ten years.

However, often employees learn on the job to operate certain work processes. New employees sometimes find it challenging to learn specific skills due to time constraints, as P4 explained:

> Definitely, and overall, there was a lot of self-improvement. I've developed significantly, but formal training opportunities were limited. It was mostly learning by doing. Attending a seminar specifically for production skills was always planned but never materialized. Having a team lead who ensures such opportunities would be crucial, I believe.

Additionally, as P4 added, taking initiative is crucial but also rewarding:

> specially the continuous learning process – almost with every production, there's something new to learn. But in terms of significant experiences, for me, it was primarily about a high degree of independence. In this job, self-reliance and initiative are crucial. Waiting for others to solve problems leads to disaster. Everyone needs to stay vigilant every day, ensuring everything functions smoothly and solving challenges as effectively as possible. It's a significant level of personal responsibility and initiative, but it's also rewarding.

14.5.2.4 Professional and Private Use of Social Media

For many respondents, private and professional aspects come together, especially on social media platforms such as YouTube, Twitch, and Discord. TikTok and Instagram are used for relaxation and unwinding. X (Twitter) is used for networking and staying up to date, but is also being questioned as the tone has become harsher (e.g., polarizing content, shitstorms). Notably, most of the interviewed influencers use social media only sparingly for personal use, as noted by P14: I primarily use social media for professional purposes, but I still have a few moments or hours each day when I use it briefly for personal reasons.

All respondents demonstrate a critical understanding of social media platforms and have developed strategies for navigating content on these sites. They emphasize the importance of prioritizing their role in (co)producing and engaging with social media, both personally and professionally. P8 explained:

> Personally, I consider the sources I look at. For instance, if I come across a YouTube video from an account with only a hundred subscribers and around 500 views, I assume that this might be not legit. However, I do pay attention to accounts with a certain reputation or a substantial following to narrow down my choices. Still, I don't go as far as researching citations and references immediately. So, I can't exempt myself from the need to prioritize this issue, which likely applies to many topics and individuals.

Additionally, employees often stress that everyone has to decide on his/her own how they would practice digital literacy, such as fact-checking, and persuading others to do so as well. P5 observed:

> when I hear about scandals or incidents – like TikTok users getting hacked and their addresses exposed (which happened in the USA with several journalists) – I take note. It's an alarm signal for me. However, since we work only with adult creators, and all my colleagues are adults, it's ultimately a decision each responsible adult must make for themselves. I don't want to interfere with anyone's choices. After all, anyone with an Android phone has given their data to Google, and iPhone users have done the same with Apple. So, it's always a personal decision.

14.5.3 *Rules-in-Use in the Organizational Community*

Interviewees at INSTINCT3 provided more detailed insights into how their organizational community operates. Various value-based approaches, closely tied to daily practices, emerged during the interviews. These included feedback culture, mentoring, and both professional and mental support. A close connection between personal and organizational values was identified, particularly in terms of how these values are shown and passed on – both within the organization and in online communities – through role-modeling and communication practices. Additionally, work–life balance was a recurring theme, highlighting both the appreciation for supportive practices and the challenges of producing content and engaging in online communities.

14.5.3.1 Feedback Culture

The interviewees frequently discussed the importance of feedback culture and mentoring as part of their organizational community – whether within the team, one-on-one, or at eye level with the CEO. Providing open feedback across various levels of the company is actively promoted and practiced as P6 stressed:

> always love to share this because I'm currently involved in many job interviews, and I adore the feedback culture here. You can give feedback to anyone, regardless of their role or whether they're above you in the organizational hierarchy. You have the freedom to provide honest feedback and express your own thoughts. Additionally, there are weekly meetings with the supervisor where you can pour out your heart, share everything you want, and express how you feel. I've never experienced this level of openness and zero tolerance for gossip in any other company.

Or to further develop teamwork, according to P4:

> Especially within a team, it's not only desired but also expected that everyone contributes – not just for personal fulfillment, but also to continually shape the team. It's crucial that anyone who identifies room for improvement or sees ways to enhance performance shares their ideas.

Often the interviewees positively discussed that both founders stimulate this open feedback culture. P15 also noted that this information is conveyed as part of the onboarding process for new employees. However, some employees faced challenges during their initial period, as P8 pointed out:

> Difficult. One had to admit a lot, and it was sometimes painful. I had 1-2 conversations with P15. . . . It was truly an experience at the beginning – speaking openly with a CEO and even criticizing them, and the CEO actively asking for criticism . . . and that's when I discovered a new approach for myself.

Additionally, this feedback culture is also incorporated in interactions with members in online communities, at various levels. For example, after posting, comments are monitored by an interdisciplinary team consisting of artist managers and the influencer involved. When participants provide constructive feedback, it is taken seriously and integrated into strategies or new content, with the team oftentimes discussing the feedback to implement improvements and passing them on to the influencers. As P4 put it:

> what many viewers don't know is that we genuinely read almost everything. Nearly every comment under every video has been read by someone on the team. We're aware of everything that comes in, and if there's something genuinely constructive, we even discuss it within the team. We ask ourselves, "Okay, was that feedback? Should we really do it that way in the future?" Or sometimes we admit, "Okay, that didn't go so well with the project or the video. It wasn't cool, and they're right."

Employees point out that the dialogue between influencers and the community, including constructive criticism, is important. Creating a positive and safe community is crucial for influencers and strengthens the connection among influencers and community members. Influencers also request feedback from their communities, as P4 explained:

> It's quite diverse. We have projects where we actively seek feedback, and others where we ask for tips. For example, an influencer completed Game X, essentially some of the most challenging games on the market. Especially with such projects, the influencer often asks, "Do you have feedback? What could be improved?" We do inquire about it, but sometimes feedback also comes spontaneously, perhaps even a bit too much. If there's constructive feedback, we take it to heart.

14.5.3.2 Being a Role Model

In the interviews, there was frequent discussion about a personal/professional values compass (e.g., social media behavior in private settings, brand checks, as well as specific topics such as vegetarianism, sexism, gendering, gambling racism, trans, and homophobia). It was also emphasized that personal values must align with organizational values, and that the founders of the company must exemplify these values. Moreover, often employees underlined the important role of influencers as role models in business and society. As P9 emphasized:

> It's about the conscious use of social media and how people perceive it. Unfortunately, many young individuals view it as a given, and they allow it to influence them significantly. Whether it's about appearance or other aspects, there's a pressure to conform with. However, social media presents a curated version of people's lives – it's not the full reality. As a young person bombarded by this content, you might start believing it represents the entire truth. It's crucial to consume this

> image consciously and critically. We need extensive education on this, and content creators can play a role in shaping awareness because they have a voice on these platforms. For me, this is the most critical issue.

Additionally, interviewees also articulated the view that INSTINCT3 operates a "value-based compass" in line with the values of staff, influencers, and founders, and that they strive to connect these while developing and sharing content. This concerns various topics, such as vegetarian lifestyle, animal welfare, anti-racism, and misogyny toward female gamers or female game influencers or advocates for LGBTQ+ rights. P03 observed:

> Our company's general value compass aligns strongly with social aspects. . . . This is often beautiful because it precisely reflects the interests that P16 holds, which also align with the company's values. We can delve into topics such as vegetarianism, vegan living, the environment, animals, and social assistance in our content. These are all themes we can seamlessly incorporate and gladly explore.

Influencers also strive to share these values with their communities, for example by sharing their thoughts via video content or during a live stream. Often this is supported by the community, but it can also be criticized by community participants. Influencers or other team members do not actively participate when these views or values are discussed in response to a video or live stream, as long as debaters are respectful toward each other. P14 pointed out that he is not persistently pushing one's viewpoint onto others, but leads by example:

> For me, it would be a bit out of context if I were to say, "You all should gender now because I think it's cool." Personally, I just do it naturally. On the internet, there are always people who say, "Why are you bothering with gendering? It's annoying." That's just an old mindset. Some sad souls at home find it bothersome because it doesn't sound as nice anymore. But for me, it doesn't make a difference. I know my community very well, and many people genuinely appreciate it. That's where the focus should be.

14.5.3.3 Work–Life Balance

To support a healthy work–life balance, INSTINCT3 has integrated various rules-in-use. One example that came up during the interviews was an unlimited number of vacation days. Most of the employees appreciate such approaches. However, for influencers, not all of the implemented rules are workable, as they are expected to continually create content. Pre-producing content is a fair solution for influencers with a larger team, but for junior influencers additional workload and stress can develop, which makes it more difficult for them to apply these rules. Another issue that impacts the work–life balance of influencers and their teams is handling parasocial relationships between influencers and followers, and dealing with the decline of channel visits and views. Since there are no formal rules addressing these issues, mentoring plays a crucial role. For instance, the informal rule is that more experienced influencers guide new influencers. This collaborative approach helps them cope more effectively with the challenges they face. In general, the influencer's community members embrace and even share their values, as P10 stated:

> I don't get recognized on the street very often – occasionally, but it's super rare. However, the Gamescom event was truly intense. Many people recognized me there, and it's nice to have the opportunity to briefly interact with them. Even though many of them may not want to engage beyond taking a photo, which I find a bit sad, I understand that it's what they're used to. You see, if a major influencer, someone like P16, were in my shoes, they couldn't move freely because within seconds, a huge crowd would form around them – people wanting photos or something else. It's a reality we're aware of. While events like Gamescom are intense, P16 is already frequently approached on the street. But I don't think it's bothersome; of course, there are situations where interruptions during meals can be annoying. In those moments, it's our responsibility to communicate that it's not cool to interrupt someone while they're eating. As creators, we're accountable for our content, and that extends to shaping our community. We can say, "This is my community, and this is how I want it."' Of course, if we create objectionable content – like gambling, for example – I know my viewers wouldn't watch it because we share the same values. It's about that shared feeling, even at events like Gamescom, where there are so many gaming enthusiasts.

14.5.4 *Governance of Offline and Online Communities*

At INSTINCT3, the managing content is an essential part of the governance of their offline and online communities, as well as a means of transferring individual and company values. This takes place before, during production, and after the publication of content in their online communities.

14.5.4.1 Content Governance Before or During Production

Advertorials are a component of INSTINCT3's content. Employees emphasize the importance of clearly labeling advertisements, whether through visual markers or by having influencers utilize "talking points" – scripted reviews of products or services – while always disclosing them as advertisements. However, all employees are free to decide the kind of advertorials they might include in their content. "Brand checks" are carried out by the artist managers and project members when other organizations approach the company with the aim to include their products or services as part of live streams or prerecorded videos. The background of the brand is investigated via desk research and certain keywords. If an organization has a questionable background, a team member but also an influencer can decide to reject the assignment. P6 explained this process:

> we discuss the campaigns that express interest in you. We ask for your thoughts and opinions. Personally, I share my own opinion. Before that, we always conduct a brand check. We assess whether the brand has a positive or negative reputation, including any dark history. For instance, consider Beauty-brand X, where antisemitism is prevalent. They've never been held accountable, but we refuse to collaborate with them due to our ethical values. We don't make exceptions just because someone hasn't faced consequences. Similarly, we avoid working with Food-brand X. However, we give our influencers the freedom to decide if they want to collaborate. We provide them with our research – both positive and negative aspects – so they can make an informed choice.

This can be decided on the individual as well as company level. For example, an employee who experiences that a certain brand is not in line with her/his personal values, he/she may decide not to work on a specific project involving this brand. As P6 added:

> we can say that it's ethically unacceptable for me to work on the campaign. Another Artist Manager should handle it on my behalf, please, because it's personally intolerable for my ethics. We definitely make that distinction.

14.5.4.2 Content Governance after Distribution

After distribution, participants may also provide feedback on the content in relation to certain advertisers with whom INSTINCT3 collaborates. If an issue was overlooked at the brand-check stage and is broadly addressed by community participants after publication, the team will discuss this issue with the advertiser, as P2 clarified:

> We directly approach the client and say, "We've recently received the following feedback from the community, and we'd like to reiterate this or address it." We take a determined approach when communicating with the customer because, as representatives of our artists, we don't want to limit their opinions. It's essential for us to be honest with the community, not blindly promoting any products, but rather presenting them in the light they are meant to be seen.

Employees often discussed if and how influencers respond to feedback, especially negative feedback, and how they use constructive criticism to evolve. As mentioned in the previous section, interviewees underlined the appropriate responses to criticism and considered constructive feedback as essential for continuous content improvement. Handling hate comments and filtering feedback were crucial aspects of the process, as was creating a safe environment for creators and their community. As P4 put it:

> Everyone [from the team] has access to the channel. … For instance, I can moderate comments. Generally, if we read a comment and think, "Okay, this one is really bad" or "This one is genuinely discriminatory toward a group," we always ban or delete such comments. But things like subjective rambling about influencers or disliking a video – well, that's just how it is.

While extreme or harmful comments are deleted, haters are more closely monitored. After upload, team members monitor the comments section within an hour, especially when the influencer also engages with other influencers (specifically female influencers, to make sure that they are not harmed) and the community feels safe and comfortable. P4 added:

> They also watch the comments live, and if something hurtful comes up or offends them, or if someone targets the rest of the community just because there was a black sheep involved, that's why we still moderate a bit more strictly. It's simply to ensure, as I mentioned, that others in the comment section feel comfortable as well.

More generally, YouTube provides features to block unwanted words in comments using "blocked word lists." Harmful or extreme comments can be automatically deleted via the platform organizations or manually deleted, hidden or flagged by the team. These mechanisms are also used to govern the amount of hate comments or troll accounts that add negative comments. In some cases, influencers also "pin" negative comments to the top of their comments feed or try to reach out via direct messaging with the comment contributor. Community participants who repeatedly add harmful or disrespectful comments via YouTube, TikTok, or live stream sessions are also warned by influencers and/or their (moderating) team, and eventually are blocked from the channel (temporarily) if the behavior does not change. As noted, moderator teams also play a crucial role in governing other community members, although other participants also may support "their influencer" by commenting on harmful, unjustifiable or superficial comments by others. P14 explained:

> the community almost acts a bit protective or defensive toward me. They collectively respond to the comment – since you can also reply to YouTube comments – and they write things like I would: "Well, then just leave"' or "It's unpleasant how you're being offensive here."' … Of course, not everyone does this, but if everyone did, it would be overwhelming. Personally, I'm not much of a commenter; I usually just watch without leaving comments. But it's nice to see the community taking a protective stance in such situations.

14.5.5 *Mapping INSTINCT3's Knowledge Commons*

Figure 14.2 visualizes INSTINCT3's knowledge commons as derived from the interviews.

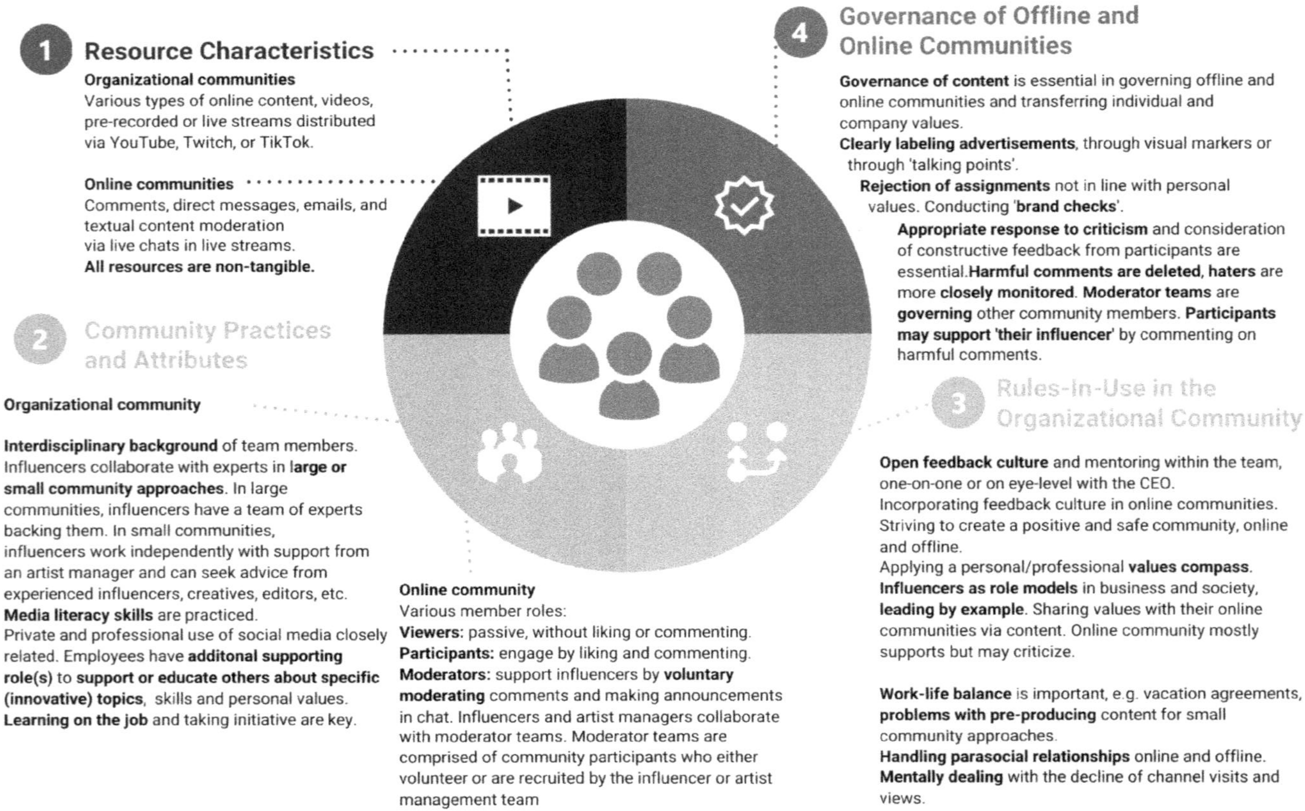

FIGURE 14.2 INSTINCT3's knowledge commons.

The findings of the study can also be represented in a community map (Figure 14.3) that illustrates how INSTINCT3 employees (managers, producers, creatives, content creators, hereafter influencers) and the followers of the influencer channels managed by INSTINCT3 operate as polycentric communities in offline as well as online action arenas. Specifically, the (circular) transfer of organizational as well as online community rules, routines, roles, and mindsets of both communities are visualized. As noted in Section 14.5.2, two main approaches in fostering communityship were identified: a small-scale and a large-scale community approach. Both coexist in the same organizational action arena but relate to a second action arena – the online communities operated by the influencers and their teams and supported by online community participants. The rules-in-use and values practiced in the offline arena are also transferred into the online action arena, as outlined in Figure 14.2.

14.6 CONCLUSION

This chapter explored how employees of a Germany-based influencer management agency, INSTINCT3, operate through polycentric communities in two action arenas: an offline or organizational action arena, where the primary actors are the company's employees, and an online action arena, where influencers–followers interactions are mediated by the influence channels managed by the IMA. The chapter adopted an inside-out perspective, which is to say that it focused on the organization-driven governance of online communities. Reliance on the GKC framework helped disentangle how organizational community values, from the perspective of employees and founders, are transferred from offline to online communities.

The case study provides new theoretical as well as practical insights about online communities developed by organizations and governed by influencers, their supporting teams, and active and passionate community members, such as voluntary moderators. Theoretically, this research shows how various layers of offline and online communication and knowledge sharing may safeguard communities and their members through nonhierarchical, self-organization, mutual adjustment, and communityship approaches. It also aligns with earlier research into online communities relying on the GKC framework: "the commons at hand is considered as a good (as opposed to a bad), in the sense that it is universally understood that this resource has value, and that infrastructures should be built around it in order for the community to enjoy it to the fullest while protecting it" (Gradoz and Raux 2021, 235).

This study shows that the IMAs employees are striving to build and protect a joint infrastructure that serves their offline as well online communities by employing distributed leadership in both action arenas. This involves the promotion of a feedback culture among employees, experienced and new influencers, their support teams, and online community members; role modeling by influencers who convey personal and organizational values without imposing them on their community; and educational activities organized by employees to discuss personal values. These practices were identified both as important attributes of the communities and a means for establishing and implementing rules-in-use. My research demonstrates how in both action arenas community attributes, rules-in-use, and value-based communication practices are interconnected and exchanged among the participants. The role of online moderators and their connection with online as well as organizational communities warrants further investigation because in combining voluntary roles with organizational roles, their activities are interesting examples of polycentric and distributed leadership.

The study further uncovered valuable insights into the implementation of organizational communityship and the challenges associated with its integration within the influencer industry. Considering frequent criticism regarding the "commercialization of influence" within the industry (Hund 2023, 170), INSTINCT3's strategy of cultivating an open workplace atmosphere, prioritizing values within the organization, and nurturing a safe and friendly online community culture could serve as a source of inspiration for other small and medium-sized enterprises operating in this sector. INSTINCT3's foundation is built upon a diverse and interdisciplinary team of employees. The demographic shows career changers with an interest in gaming who apply digital/media literacy skills in professional and private circumstances. All team members work on developing and fostering a safe and open community environment, both offline and online. Employees experience support in different areas and from different actors within their organizational community but, first and foremost, enjoy the prospect of working autonomously, contributing their own ideas, providing and receiving feedback, and having the possibility to opt-out of working on specific projects that do not align with their values. Finally, they can share these values with others through workshops and forum discussions, or even transfer these into the content produced by INSTINCT3. Importantly, influencers and their supporting team members set standards in advertising production based on shared values, and by developing rules-in-use to carry out brand checks. Influencers may struggle with some of the rules-in-use, for example, because their content production schedule prevents them from making use of flexible vacation agreements that INSTINCT3 employees enjoy. This shows that implementing "just enough leadership" (Mintzberg 2009) is challenging in situations where influencers cannot exert full control due to external obligations.

With regard to the transfer of values, influencers strive to lead by example and ask for feedback from online community members. Parasocial relationships play a significant role in their engagement with community members, especially for influencers with large communities. However, clear communication about boundaries is essential for influencers with large or small(er) communities. Influencers receive support from moderating teams that operate rules-in-use that cut across the two action arenas to ensure a safe and friendly online environment. Essentially, influencers are aware that they must live with negative comments and even hateful

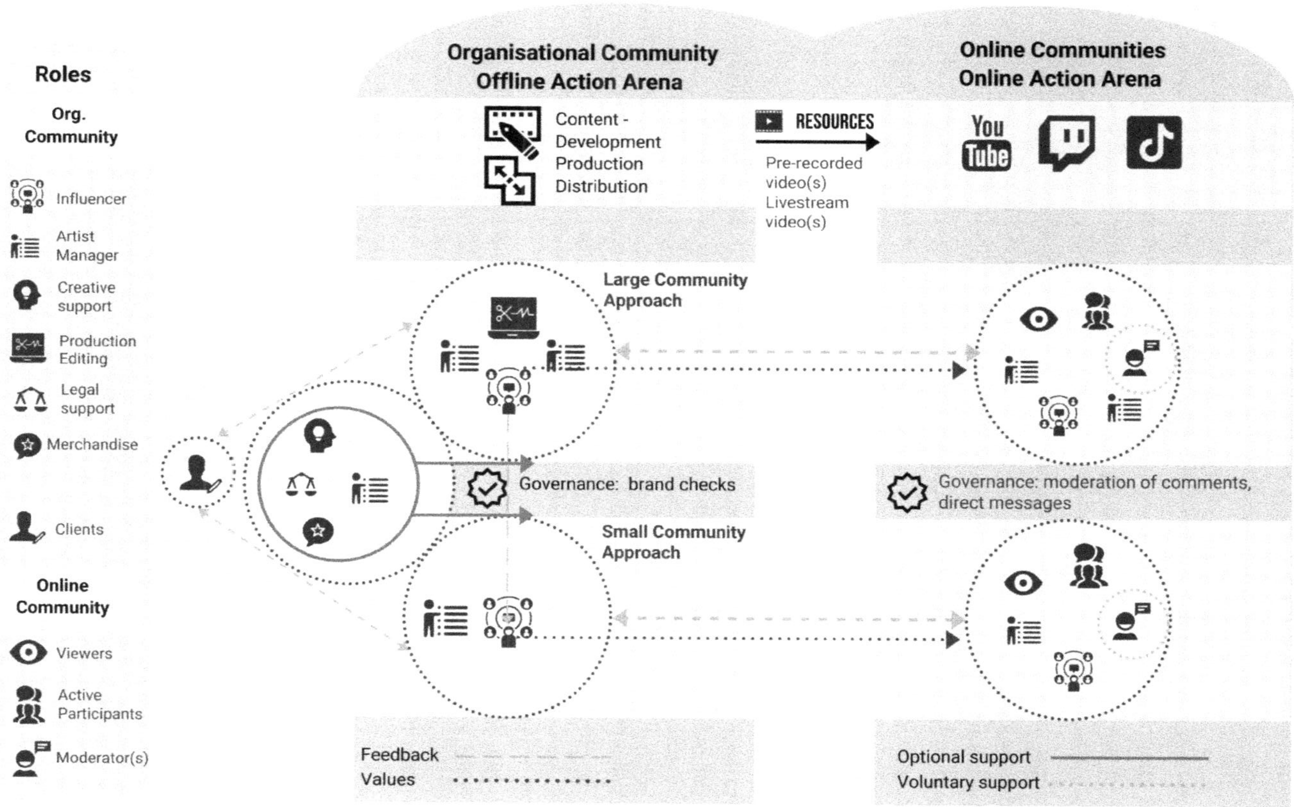

FIGURE 14.3 Patterns and interactions community map.

responses, but they also have backing and support from their organizational and online communities when these appear. But influencers often find that their values align with those of most community members.

Because this chapter focused on understanding organizational and online community practices from an inside-out perspective, the data collected solely concerns interviews with employees from INSTINCT3. This means that an essential perspective – the perspective of online community members – is missing. My next study will focus on examining the transfer of offline values to online communities from the perspective of online community members who follow, engage with influencers, or support them as moderators. This will enable a richer analysis of whether and how these communicative community practices, their values, and their rules-in-use are shared by online community members. Whatever the methodology, more research along these lines is needed. The case study developed in this chapter may serve as an example of how to research the interconnections between organizational and online communities in the influencer economy.

REFERENCES

Bhargava, Vikram R., and Manuel Velasquez. 2021. "Ethics of the Attention Economy: The Problem of Social Media Addiction." *Business Ethics Quarterly* 31(3): 321–359.

Braun, Virginia, and Victoria Clarke. 2013. *Successful Qualitative Research: A Practical Guide for Beginners*. London: SAGE.

Cole, Daniel H. 2014. "Learning from Lin: Lessons and Cautions from the Natural Commons for the Knowledge Commons." In *Governing Knowledge Commons*, ed. Brett M. Frischmann, Michael J. Madison, and Katherine J. Strandburg, 45–68. New York: Oxford University Press.

Frischmann, Brett M., Michael J. Madison, and Katherine J. Strandburg, eds. 2014. *Governing Knowledge Commons*. New York: Oxford University Press.

Gradoz, Julien, and Raphaël Raux. 2021. "Trolling in the Deep: Managing Transgressive Content on Online Platforms as a Commons." In *Governing Markets as Knowledge Commons*, ed. Erwin Dekker, and Pavel Kuchař, 217–237. Cambridge: Cambridge University Press.

Haenlein, Michael, Ertan Anadol, Tyler Farnsworth, et al. 2020. "Navigating the New Era of Influencer Marketing: How to be Successful on Instagram, TikTok, & Co." *California Management Review* 63(1): 5–25.

Hess, Charlotte, and Elinor Ostrom. 2007. "Introduction: An Overview of the Knowledge Commons." In *Understanding Knowledge as a Commons: From Theory to Practice*, ed. Charlotte Hess, and Elinor Ostrom, 3–26. Cambridge, MA: MIT Press.

Hund, Emily. 2023. *The Influencer Industry: The Quest for Authenticity on Social Media*. Princeton: Princeton University Press.

Kerfoot, Karlene, and Kathy Douglas. 2010. "Evidence-Based Staffing and 'Communityship' as the Key to Success." *Nursing Clinics of North America* 45(1): 81–87.

Lehto, Mari. 2022. "Ambivalent Influencers: Feeling Rules and the Affective Practice of Anxiety in Social Media Influencer Work." *European Journal of Cultural Studies* 25(1): 201–216.

Matzat, Uwe. 2009. "A Theory of Relational Signals in Online Groups." *New Media & Society* 11(3): 375–394.

Mintzberg, Henry. 2009. “Rebuilding Companies as Communities.” *Harvard Business Review* 87(7-8): 140–143.
Nerantzi, Chrissi, Emma Gillaspy, Sandra Sinfield, et al. 2024. “Like the Sea: Living Communityship as a Form of Participatory Leadership within the Creativity for Learning in HE (#creativeHE) Community.” *Innovations in Education and Teaching International* 61(5): 1058–1074.
Ostrom, Elinor. 2005. *Understanding Institutional Diversity*. Princeton: Princeton University Press.
Ostrom, Elinor. 2010. “Beyond Markets and States: Polycentric Governance of Complex Economic Systems.” *American Economic Review* 100(3): 641–672.
Sanfilippo, Madelyn R., Brett M. Frischmann, and Katherine J. Standburg. 2018. “Privacy as Commons: Case Evaluation through the Governing Knowledge Commons Framework.” *Journal of Information Policy*, 8: 116–166.
Schulz, Deike. 2020. “Online Communities.” In *Encyclopedia of Sustainable Management*, ed. Samuel O. Idowu, and René Schmidpeter, 2508–2512. Cham: Springer.
Schulz, Deike. 2021. *Evaluating the Evaluators: Investigating the Multilevel Dimensions of Outside-in Constructions of Organizational Legitimacy*. Doctoral Dissertation, Radboud University, Nijmegen School of Management. https://hdl.handle.net/2066/231163.
Schulz, Deike, Jan Jonker, and Niels Faber. 2018. “Outside-In Constructions of Organizational Legitimacy: Sensitizing the Influence of Evaluative Judgments through Mass Self-Communication in Online Communities.” *International Journal of Communication* 12: 290–312.
Siggelkow, Nicolaj. 2007. “Persuasion with Case Studies.” *Academy of Management Journal* 50(1): 20–24.
Stein, Jan-Philipp, Priska L. Breves, and Nora Anders. 2022. “Parasocial Interactions with Real and Virtual Influencers: The Role of Perceived Similarity and Human-Likeness.” *New Media & Society* 26(6): 3433–3453.
Strandburg, Katherine J., Brett M. Frischmann, and Michael J. Madison. 2017. “The Knowledge Commons Framework.” In *Governing Medical Knowledge Commons*, ed. Katherine J. Strandburg, Brett M. Frischmann, and Michael J. Madison, 9–18. Cambridge: Cambridge University Press.

Appendix A

PURPOSE OF THE STUDY

In this case study, we aim to examine both organization-driven and influencer-driven communities to compare which elements support value-oriented and responsible communities among the different described actors. Two main topics guide this research: *organizational communityship* and *influencer-driven communityship*.

TOPIC 1: ORGANIZATIONAL COMMUNITYSHIP

The topic of organizational communityship addresses how INSTINCT3 translates the individual value-oriented leadership of its employees into collective values for the company. What rules, routines, roles, and mindsets are essential for developing a value-oriented and responsible employee community? How are these elements introduced, practiced, and/or evaluated?

QUESTIONS

- Can you briefly introduce yourself? (Also, media usage, socials, how long active on socials?)
- How long have you been with the team?
- What is your role at INSTINCT3, and who do you work with?
- What does a typical workday look like for you?
- What important experiences have you had on the job since you started working here?
- What opportunities do you have to contribute to the team's tasks and content?
- How do you handle feedback from the team?

TOPIC 2: INFLUENCER-DRIVEN COMMUNITYSHIP

The Topic of Influencer-Driven Communityship Concerns Communication between Influencers and Their Community

How is the organizational community approach (and its rules, routines, roles, and mindsets) translated by influencers through interaction and communication in their online communities? How do community participants evaluate this interaction and communication from influencers? How do these evaluations/feedback influence the way INSTINCT3 cocreates communication with both communities (organizational and influencer-driven)?

QUESTIONS

- How does your role in the team relate to working (as/with) content creator in the team?
- What aspects are important in the collaboration between the team and content creators in the team?
- Which socials are important for the connection between content creators and followers?
- What aspects/topics related to socials are currently important to you?
- How do these topics integrate into your daily work?
- How do you handle feedback from the communities/socials?
- What is the role of participants in the communities concerning your content creators? How do they interact with each other?

Appendix B

TABLE B.1 *Codebook*

Codes (**top** and *sublevel* codes)	Definition
Demographics	General background information interviewee
○ 1. Age	Code age
○ 2. Career	Description of career path
○ 3. Gamer (private)	Does the employee play games for leisure?
○ 4. Games played privately	What types of games does the interviewee play for leisure?
○ 5. Primary role in company	What is the interviewee's primary role?
○ 6. Media literacy	What does the interviewee mention about their media literacy skills or awareness?
○ 7. Supporting role in company	Is there a supporting role? Description of that role.
○ 8. Since when using socials?	Year
○ 9. Social media platforms used	Which platforms/channels are used personally and professionally?
○ 9a. *Professionally*	
○ 9b. *Personally*	
Influencer-driven communityship	**How is influencer-driven communityship developed, applied, and governed?**
○ 10. Role of participants in online communities	What roles do participants play in relation to content creators? How do they interact?
○ 10a. *Role(s) of online communities' participants*	Roles mentioned by the interviewee that participants/ followers have in online influencer communities.
○ 10b. *Dealing with haters*	How do the team and influencers handle hate or negative interactions?
○ 10c. *Dealing with participants in general*	How does the team, the influencer, deal with participants within the online influencer communities? Are there ground rules?
○ 11. Coping with feedback from online communities	How does the team or the influencer handle feedback that comes from the online communities (from followers)?
○ 11a. Experiencing feedback	How does the interviewee perceive feedback from participants?
○ 11b. Negative feedback	How does the interviewee address feedback from participants? Are there ground rules?
○ 11c. Positive feedback and tips	How does the interviewee handle positive feedback from participants? Are there ground rules?
○ 12. Important social media topics	Which social media topics are currently important to the interviewee?
Organizational communityship	**How is organizational communityship developed, applied, and governed?**
○ 13. Organizational culture	How does the interviewee describe the company culture?
○ 14. Feedback culture	How is feedback given and received among employees?
○ 15. Learning by doing	How do employees acquire new skills or knowledge?

TABLE B.1 *(continued)*

Codes (**top** and *sublevel* codes)	Definition
○ 16. Mentoring	Who mentors whom within the organization?
○ 17. Personal values	What are the interviewee's personal values, and how do they influence their professional role?
○ 18. Shaping the team	How does the interviewee contribute to team processes and values?
○ 19. Typical day at work	What does a typical workday look like?
○ 19a. *Workflows/typical workday.*	Description of tasks, responsibilities, and assignments.
○ 19b. *Collaboration*	Who does the interviewee work with? Description of roles and relationships.
○ 19c. *Collaboration with influencers*	What aspects are important in working with content creators?
○ 20. Important job experiences	What key experiences has the interviewee had since joining the company?

Appendix C

TABLE C.1 *Connections between coding and GKC research questions*

Representative research questions (Sanfilippo et al., 2018)	Codes
Background environment	
• What is the background context (legal, cultural, etc.) of this particular commons?	1–9
• What normative values are relevant for this community?	6,17, 20
• What is the "default" status of the resources involved in the commons (patented, copyrighted, open, or other)?	19
• How does this community fit into a larger context?	6, 10
• What relevant domains overlap in this context?	6, 10, 12, 17
Attributes	
• What resources are pooled and how are they created or obtained?	19
• What are the characteristics of the resources?	19
• Are they rival or nonrival, tangible or intangible?	19
• Is there shared infrastructure?	19
• What is personal information relative to resources in this action arena?	10,11,14,16
• What technologies and skills are needed to create, obtain, maintain, and use the resources?	15,16
• What are considered to be appropriate resource flows?	13, 17, 18
• How is appropriateness of resource use structured or protected?	17, 18, 19
• Who are the community members and what are their roles?	5, 7, 10, 17, 19
• What are the degree and nature of openness with respect to each type of community member and the general public?	10, 11, 14, 17, 18
• Which noncommunity members are impacted?	10, 11, 19b
• What are the goals and objectives of the commons and its members, including obstacles or dilemmas to overcome?	10, 11, 13, 14, 15, 16, 18, 20
• Who determines goals and objectives?	19
• What values are reflected in goals and objectives?	17, 18, 20
• What are the history and narrative of the commons?	2, 3, 4, 8, 20
• What is the value of knowledge production in this context?	13, 14, 15, 16
Governance	
• What are the relevant action arenas and how do they relate to the goals and objective of the commons and the relationships among various types of participants and with the general public?	10, 11, 13, 14, 15, 16
• Are action arenas perceived to be legitimate?	na
• What legal structures (e.g., intellectual property, subsidies, contract, licensing, tax, and antitrust) apply?	5,7, 19

TABLE C.1 *(continued)*

• What are the governance mechanisms (e.g., membership rules, resource contribution or extraction standards and requirements, conflict resolution mechanisms, and sanctions for rule violation)?	10,11,14,16
• What are the institutions and technological infrastructures that structure and govern decision-making?	13
• What informal norms govern the commons?	17, 18
• What institutions are perceived to be legitimate or illegitimate?	17, 18
• How are institutional illegitimacies addressed?	13, 14, 16, 17
• Who are the decision-makers and how are they selected?	19
• Are decision-makers perceived to be legitimate?	19
• How do nonmembers interact with the commons?	na
• What institutions govern those interactions?	na
• Are there impacted groups that have no say in governance?	10a
Patterns and outcomes	
• What benefits are delivered to members and to others (e.g., innovations and creative output, production, sharing, and dissemination to a broader audience, and social interactions that emerge from the commons)?	3, 4, 6, 7, 10, 11, 14, 16
• What costs and risks are associated with the commons, including any negative externalities?	10, 11, 12
• Are outcomes perceived to be legitimate by members?	14, 16
• By decision-makers?	14, 16, 20
• By impacted outsiders?	19

15

Supply Chain Commons

Organic Waste, Climate Change, and Regenerative Farming in Peri-urban Sydney

Stephen Healy, Amy J. Cohen, and Abby Mellick Lopes

15.1 INTRODUCTION

Australia, like everywhere else, is amid a polycrisis. In the past five years, the effects of climate change have intensified: extreme drought from 2017 to 2019 (Wittwer and Waschik 2021), unprecedented bushfires in 2019–2020 (Deb et al. 2020), and widespread flooding in 2020–2022 (Climate Council 2022). During this same period, the "waste crisis" reached a tipping point precipitated by China's summary withdrawal as the world's recycler (Gregson and Crang 2019). In an important sense, both are different expressions of the same phenomenon: the Anthropocene (Crutzen 2002). Whether the Anthropocene is a new geologic era or, more hopefully, a punctuation point (Haraway 2016), one of its defining features is an accumulation of anthropogenic matter in the lithosphere, hydrosphere, atmosphere, and biosphere. In 1970, the weight of human-designed material was 3 per cent of earth's living biomass. By 2020, human-designed material outweighed living biomass (Elhacham et al. 2020).

What defines this polycrisis is interconnection. All along supply chains, the production, circulation, and consumption of designed objects generates waste that deepens our shared predicament. For example, the initial industrial production of single use plastics adds greenhouse gases to the atmosphere, while their "end-of-life" micro plastic waste floating in the ocean continues to add to the store of atmospheric carbon and, when consumed, delivers a toxic payload first to marine life and then to all life (Royer et al. 2018; International Union for Conservation of Nature 2021).

It is widely recognised that business as usual cannot go on. Policy paradigms like the circular economy promise comprehensive transformational change, while frameworks like the Sustainable Development Goals (SDGs) provide a way of tracking progress. Both paradigms (at times) emphasise the need for cooperation and intergenerational action. We argue that for these policy paradigms to *actually* achieve the transformative change they promise, people must learn continuously to build and maintain commons. As Ostrom's pioneering work has demonstrated, human communities around the world have been effectively stewarding commons-resources for centuries. The present moment requires us to translate this commoning capacity across scales and in response to multiple challenges (Gibson-Graham et al. 2016). In the decades that follow, human communities will continue to engage in activities of all sorts – from e-commerce to construction – but in parallel to this ongoing business, practices of shared stewardship of oceans, earth, atmosphere, and life itself will be absolutely necessary for survival.

We also argue that a commoning response to the polycrisis requires not only new material practices but also new ways of knowing, including new ways of knowing ourselves as commoner-subjects (Singh 2017). We need to learn to "think" and act like commoners for the long term and by extension to engage ourselves with others in an ongoing process of education and learning (Bollier 2014; Schneider 2018). Indeed, one could conclude that there will be no material commons without a corresponding knowledge commons to bring it into coherence and sustain it, as well as commoner-subjects who will do the work of caring for it.

In this chapter, we explore one such attempt to build a material and knowledge commons in tandem. We describe an engaged research project to create a circular economy for organic waste in Sydney. At the centre of this story is a material object – spent coffee grounds (SCG) and other coffee-related waste – enrolled into regenerative farming. A regenerative farmer had been collecting dehydrated food waste containing a significant portion of SCG from the university where she worked, which had installed an industrial food waste dehydrator to process campus organic waste. She was then windrow composting it on a farm where she grew heirloom garlic. Along with researchers, she convened a collaborative design workshop among inner city cafes as well as a range of other actors who could contribute to moving this material from city to country by creating links among material resources and infrastructure (SCG, trucks, roads, food dehydrators) through creating new exchange relationships and simultaneously producing and sharing new knowledge.

We describe an emergent relationship among a *material commons* (organic waste), a *knowledge commons* (the data encoded in the waste and the story this data can tell), and a *community of commoners* forging links to move waste from city to farm, that together constitutes what we call a supply chain commons. That is, we describe a *community of practice* or what we refer to as an "alliance" that is currently comprised of individual entrepreneurs, private enterprises, and public organisations that coordinate both market and gift exchanges in a decentralised manner in order to move materials and information along a supply chain. Like all moments of genesis, the shape of this innovation remains unknown to us: it is presently unclear if this alliance will assume a more durable form, perhaps by integrating into a business organisation, as recent efforts to formulate an entity (Ground to Ground) suggest. But it is precisely for this reason that we describe this incipient commons. Its potential to generate value (and values) depends first and foremost on establishing the kinds of social practices and coordination that we map here: most especially the commoning of knowledge about the value and the management of waste.

In the following sections we first distinguish the supply chain commons from more business-as-usual approaches to the circular economy. Second, we illustrate how the particular supply chain we describe functions as a commons. To that end, we recount the pivotal role a design workshop played in enabling people to explore the diverse economic relationships that could allow for a commoning of knowledge and, through it, the commoning of a supply chain. Bearing in mind that workshop participants are only at the start of a commoning process, we pay particular attention to how the disciplinary field of design and a university-supported workshop space enabled social learning, data gathering, and data sharing. We conclude by reflecting on how commoning can redraw more capacious and open-ended notions of circularity that function to create a more liveable world.

15.2 FROM CIRCULAR ECONOMIES TO WASTE AS COMMONS

We position our collective efforts to devise a supply chain commons for organic waste as both part of circular economy theory and practice and as an effort to redefine and reimagine it. In Australia, the circular economy gained currency in the late 2010s after nation-wide kerbside recycling was imperilled by China's abrupt withdrawal from international markets in recyclable materials. With China and other international recyclers out of the picture, Australia needed to assemble "in-house" approaches to circularity, while new policy frameworks like the SDGs launched in 2015 created global governance expectations for change over a fairly short time scale. For example, in 2017 the City of Sydney set a target of 70 per cent diversion of waste from landfill by 2030, which has significant implications for the organic waste comprising 50 per cent of the city's waste by volume (City of Sydney 2017; Food and Agribusiness Growth Centre 2021).[1]

As a response to this polycrisis, the "circular economy" holds varied meanings. In the late 1960s and 1970s, it grew out of theories of industrial ecology and discussions around the limits to growth. Indeed, it emerged as part of a critique of capitalist development just as globalisation was starting to take off (Gregson and Crang 2015). Over the past twenty years, the powerful advocacy organisation Ellen MacArthur Foundation has done much to make the circular economy central to European Union policy but also to make it politically palatable by recasting it as a new pathway to economic growth (Ellen MacArthur Foundation 2012, 2013, 2017). By the 2010s, the circular economy had become a promissory note, a path nations must follow to be both "rich and green" (Monbiot quoted in Hobson 2016, 5). Tellingly, in 2017, Kirchher et al. analysed 114 definitions of circular economy in a sample of academic and policy literature, concluding that circularity as a pathway to prosperity overshadowed sustainability concerns, while social justice concerns were nearly absent

[1] These goals anticipated an even higher target of 80 per cent set by the federal government a year later in the National Waste Policy Action Plan 2019 (Australian Government 2019).

(Kirchher et al. 2017, 229). Valenzuela and Bohm (2017) have therefore criticised circularity as a palliative fantasy: the persistent idea that growth without ecological consequence is possible. Corvellec and Paulsson (2023) similarly see circularity as repositioning waste as assets into a new regime for capital accumulation.

The "circular economy" has thus been shaped by two contradictory value frames: an originating idea that might be read as prefiguring postcapitalist theories and practices such as degrowth, and a more recent dominant policy understanding aligned with capitalist growth and business as usual (Savini 2023). In Australia, this dominant, and we think impoverished, understanding of circularity means that as long as it remains cheaper to landfill waste materials than divert them to other uses, Australians will remain on the well-trodden path, even as the failure to recoup the value of organic waste degrades terrestrial and atmospheric commons as this waste rots (Papodopolus et al. 2022). Indeed, it would now seem that the horizon for Australia, following Europe, is to invest in "waste-to-energy" incinerator projects so that the next iteration of a "circular" solution merely involves redirecting the rubbish and "recycling" trucks from the landfill to the incinerator.

Today, however, we also see different opportunities to revitalise a more open and transformative version of circularity away from market-based definitions of prosperity. In part, this opportunity is practical: there is growing recognition that the revalorisation of waste is more expensive than anticipated and the rewards are fewer, at least when the metric is economic growth. Indeed, the vast proportion of wasted anthropogenic material that lies in a hole in the ground is a long way from ready for marketisation. In part, this opportunity also reflects new efforts by scholars and policymakers ascribing new socioecological understandings to waste governed by values such as innovation, care, social justice, and inclusion (Kirchher et al. 2021; Savini 2023). For example, Savini (2023) argues that it is possible to reframe circularity around collective rather than individual action, emphasising bioregional transformation over technical reconfiguration, where the animating value is not "profit" but rather the intrinsic value of assuming the socioecological "burden" of waste – a paradigm shift he calls "circular degrowth". In particular, Savini's emphasis on collective action in a defined bioregional context is meant to spur us to identify who is shouldering the burden of waste *and*, as a consequence, who needs help.

To that end, we see this moment as an invitation to recast waste as a commons (though we are hardly the first to make this connection; see for example, Lane 2011; Zapata Campos and Zapata 2023). The commoning of waste material involves an inventive reuse of a material that has been discarded, that is to say, momentarily released from being the property of a particular individual and thus available for new forms of reuse by a collective.[2] Building on the vast literature spawned by Ostrom's (1990) work on resources held as collective property, we also suggest that the

[2] Drawing on our research we hasten to add that at other times the appropriate response to a waste material is to "detach" from it – that is to say, to learn how to live without it (Hawkins and Madden 2023). Australia has followed many other parts of the world in banning certain forms of single use

commoning of waste is an opportunity to reconsider both the community and the rules-in-use that surround it (Sacks and Galabo 2021). Ostrom's analysis famously testifies to how communities can effectively manage common resources like fields, forests, fisheries, and water supplies, preventing the so-called "tragedy of the commons" that can occur when resources are left open and unmanaged by either state regulation or private property rights.

But waste also brings something distinct to discussions of commons, commoners, and the process of commoning. When it comes to waste, more is needed than the rules and practices for shared governance of common materials. To think of waste as a commons in the first instance requires a break from existing habits of thoughts in how we put waste in its place, as Mary Douglas (1966) famously observed. Rather than a habituated response of managing, containing, sanitising, and disposing of waste, we must call into question what we think we know about waste and how to manage it as a quantum of material (Hird 2012; Hawkins 2005). To put this another way, we are arguing that the first step of reinventing the circular economy is a commoning of knowledge production – so that the commoning of reclaimed value of waste becomes a context for thinking with others about its potentiality.

To be sure, many scholars have articulated the concept and relevance of a "knowledge commons." For example, Madison et al. (2010) draws attention to how immaterial goods, such as open-source software systems, can be developed for common benefit. Likening to a material commons, they also draw attention to an analogous free-rider problem: rather than overuse of a material resource, people in a knowledge commons may lack incentives to produce intellectual resources, such as information, absent state subsidies/sanctions, or private property rights. Our efforts to identify a "knowledge commons" pose a related, but perhaps prior, inquiry. We submit that responding to today's polycrisis requires new ways of being and doing that spur people to revalue and redeem what was previously wasted (Marres et al. 2018). Hence, if for Madison et al. (2010), the knowledge commons is significant insofar as it successfully institutionalises the sharing of intellectual resources in ways that obviate the need for either private property endowments or state regulation to incentivise the "right" supply of information, for us, its significance lies in how it functions as a context in which commoner-subjectivities emerge (Singh 2017; Chitranshi and Healy 2022).

To consider how people may produce new forms of rules, information, and subjectivities in tandem, Healy, Mellick Lopes, and others began a three-year Australian Research Council (ARC) Discovery project titled "Investigating

plastic – and what is of course required here is a reconfiguration of commerce, adjustments to health and safety, particularly in relation to food, and shipping and logistics. In other words, making something disappear also involves us in the work of social reinvention, including changing the habits of practice that makes a particular world seem convenient. This too, in our view, is a type of commoning practice, and further benefits of "breaking up" with single use plastics have many common benefits.

Innovative Waste Economies: Redrawing the Circular Economy." The project asks if social, economic, and ecologically innovative responses to waste could provoke new shared understandings of waste management in organics, single use plastics, and bulk textile waste (Hawkins and Healy 2023; Healy and Mellick Lopes 2023; Lane 2023). In the section that follows, we describe one effort to common knowledge using a collaborative design workshop as a method to understand the various agents and value frames that might shape a reverse logistics supply chain for organic waste in Sydney.[3] What emerged in the workshop was a process of both imagining and then negotiating disparate investments in a circular waste economy in ways that highlight the enabling role that the material properties of waste plays, alongside the crucial role that data gathering and information plays, in together making this economy happen.

15.3 DESIGNING A COMMONS

Creating and sustaining new cultures and economies entails a "massive social learning process" (Manzini et al. 2008). Strategic designer Ezio Manzini once compared the challenge to changing a jet engine mid-flight. Most often, however, learning how to do and be otherwise does not happen at scale or speed. Indeed, recent splashy failures in designing new so-called "circular" approaches to waste management (e.g. the collapse of the nation-wide soft plastics recycling scheme REDcycle in Australia) tells us that bigger and faster is usually not better.

To create space for slow collective learning and practice, in December 2022 researchers of the Investigating Innovative Waste Economies project partnered with strategic designer Dom Svejkar and regenerative farmer Michelle Zeibots to convene a range of actors and institutions in a collaborative design workshop. Participants gathered at the University of Technology Sydney (UTS) to explore the transformation of urban organic waste into an input for regenerative farming that would, in turn, find its way into high value-added crops like heirloom garlic sold back to consumers in Sydney – creating the possibility for a circular system. The workshop had three key aims:

[3] Here, the work of diverse scholars on the process of commoning with others, and in the context of engaged research, is instructive. St Martin and others (cf. St Martin 2001; Papaioannou et al. 2021) have used community mapping in their work with fishers to represent their livelihoods as both the use of and the care for fisheries through time for a community benefit. Technologies, and in particular participatory geographic information systems, have played a pivotal role in allowing fishing communities to see and understand themselves as commoners (rather than utility maximising individuals) and, in doing so, directly influence fisheries policies in places throughout the world. Petrescu et al. (2021) and Dombroski (2019, 2023) have applied similar thinking to urban commons, looking at how the commoning of urban farming, composting, and community learning spaces can have a transformative effect on how people understand themselves to belong to a place, recover from disasters, or act more effectively as citizens. Closer to our efforts, Morrow and Davies (2022) describe various experiments in community-based compositing in urban areas as a basis for shared social learning on how to effect transition.

- To understand the diverse perspectives, experiences, and aspirations of participant actors.
- To create a shared vision for an organics circular supply chain.
- To explore how participants could work together going forward, and what resources might be required to do so.

Organisers structured the design space – big, open, and airy with moveable tables and chairs, props, reams of "butcher's paper," stacks of coloured pens, and traces of previous gatherings – to invite thinking and provoke imagination. For design experts, workshops provide an important space for participants to "sit with ambiguity," exploring how the affordances of material objects are open-ended and imagining different uses and destinations for them (Asquith and Soble 2023).[4] Organisers here encouraged participants – all with different vantage points and resources along the supply chain – to cultivate a sense of ambiguity and possibility as a precondition for new ways of knowing waste and new possibilities for our relationship with it (Stark 2011).[5] Coffee roasters brought networks of cafes, a social enterprise organisation brought skills in waste transport, local government representatives brought knowledge about disused council spaces that could be used to store waste, the university brought its food waste dehydration technology and formal commitment to "circular" goals as well as an appetite for engaged social learning, and Michelle brought other farmers with much larger acreages who were interested in regenerative farming. This group – which represented the whole reverse logistics supply chain from the coffee shop where SCG are "produced" to the farm (Table 15.1) – was brimming with relevant knowledge and experiences, promising a level of maturity in the conversation and investment in what it generated.

TABLE 15.1 *Reverse logistics workshop participants*

Farmers	One vermiculturist
	One small-scale farmer
	One broad acreage farmer
Social enterprise	One trucking, hauling, and logistics representative
Private enterprise	Three coffee roasters
	One cafe manager
Not for profit (large scale)	One representative from UTS operations and management
Local government	One City of Sydney representative
	One Inner West Council representative
Researchers	Four academics

4 Remarks made by Lindsay Asquith and Leanne Soble, during a Concept Note talk, "Re-Imagining Disability Care: Supporting Human Connectedness Through Design," May 16, 2023, University of Technology Sydney.

5 Stark's analysis points to the productive role of dissonance in clarifying different senses of value; this sense of the possible is in turn facilitated by design workshops that are at the centre of our research approach.

Participants also brought a will to engage as incipient *commoner-subjects*. The workshop opened with a "circular" form of participation where each person was asked to share an object that evoked the circular economy to them. In one instance, an inventory manager at a local coffee roaster introduced chaff, a by-product of the coffee roasting process, expressing dismay that this clean, dry material was going straight to landfill. Immediately, others in the room offered practical ideas for how the chaff could be recirculated. But more than offering ideas, participants offered their own pressing sense that organic waste was a socioecological burden to be borne by a particular set of somebodies – namely, them – connected by a common purpose: reducing urban landfills, contributing to living soils, and sequestering carbon through regenerative cropping practices. More broadly, and in keeping with the spirit of the Discovery project, the workshop provided a space for participants to think with one another, and with the "waste" in the room, to see what it could "tell" us about assuming collective responsibility for our common future (Healy and Mellick Lopes 2023).

The design task then became how to orchestrate diverse knowledge and common commitments to socio-environmental values around the practical challenge of inventing a supply chain commons. Organisers spread a four-metre-long map on the floor. The map illustrated a tentative circular supply chain journey through a series of loops representing the interactions and exchanges from the university and coffee shops to the farm, and then back to urban markets. Rather than a tight circle of neat flows that obscure the messy realities of reverse logistics, this enormous, open-ended temporal structure acted as a scaffold (Sanders 2006) that participants used to build out through knowledge-sharing and conversation (Figure 15.1).

To be sure, the basic contours of the reverse logistic supply chain design were already visible to many of the participants. Michelle had been at work since 2017 drawing on relationships with operations staff at UTS to take food waste across Sydney up to her Blue Mountain farm, and people came to the workshop cognizant of what regulatory agencies and measurements might be important, potential obstacles along the way, and the larger context in which this supply chain might take shape. But rather than starting with a ready-made solution, the workshop opened space for Agamben's (1993) "coming community," by continually foregrounding the question – what are we designing here? – in the presence of others who share a common concern (Wernli and Chan 2023). As relationships began to coalesce into what we came to call an "alliance" of people committed to a commons, it became clear that participants needed to understand others' valuations to coordinate common action and create common value.

In what follows, we describe how participants had different vantage points for *knowing* the value of waste, including through different ways of taking its measure. Depending on where one sits in the supply chain, waste becomes a gift to be received, desirable for its use value, a source of revenue/an employment opportunity, or a cost to manage and mitigate – different valuations that, in turn, enable commons

FIGURE 15.1 Mapping the reverse logistics supply chain.

coordination.[6] We also describe how the workshop surfaced a common interest in waste *as information* (Offenhuber 2017) that participants proposed to communicate – and futher create the value of the supply chain.

15.3.1 *Farmers*

Farmers talked about the unique qualities of SCG-rich composting piles – the way they repel vermin when they are first set in windrows, how at a certain point in their decomposition they attract earthworms that recondition the soil as they digest this material. Farmers desire this "pure" waste stream, they explained, for its use value – for how it can be windrow composted and added to soil without fear of introducing weed seed to their fields. Unlike commercially prepared soil amendments that are sterilised through heating before being sold, composted material is readily available

[6] What we describe recalls Anna Kornbluth's (2010) characterization of Marx's *Capital* as a Victorian novel in which the story of capital is re-narrated from different vantage points – the commodity itself, the perspective of the capitalist appropriator, the merchant, the landlord, and the banker. For Kornbluth, following Karatani (2005) – the "truth" of surplus capital is found in the movement among these vantage points attesting to both the power and the uncertainty of how surplus value is actualized through circulation. In contrast, what we are describing is how the value of SCG undergoes transmutation – from waste to asset to a source of livelihood, a gift gladly received, and finally to something that regenerates the vitality of soil through its reconnection with the more than human world. What emerges as it changes hands is a commonwealth that accrues to a broad community.

to microbial life. But to remain fertile, soil conditioned with compostable material needs continuous amendment – continuously adding organic matter improves soil quality, particularly its tilth, which allows it to retain moisture.

For farmers, then, the relevant unit of measure for what they value in SCG is volume. One farmer with a larger acreage stated, "I need about six and a half thousand trucks to put a five-millimetre cover of composted soil over it. So that puts into perspective [as] a small farm in the … central west how much capacity there is, but [also] how much volume needs to go over the hills."[7] Coffee roasters and cafes, we should in turn stress, produce volume: one of the larger roasters at the workshop estimated they generated 20 tonnes of SGC per week across a network of more than 600 stores – an amount sufficient to satisfy the need for composted soil for a 20-hectare regenerative farm.

15.3.2 *Social Enterprise Haulers*

The social enterprise representative explained that she valued this waste stream for how it could advance the enterprise's social and commercial mission: providing training and employment opportunities for ex-prisoners in commercial hauling and logistics. The enterprise could (and does) use regular service contracts to haul SCG and chaff away from roasters and cafes. But current Environment Protection Authority EPA regulations create an opportunity. Farmers can receive pure compostable materials like SCG and chaff as a "gift," and if the enterprise gifts waste to farmers, they are not paying a tipping fee to dispose of it. But the EPA limits a gift to 200 tonnes/200 cubic metres per year.[8] For waste haulers, then, one relevant unit of measure is weight. Weight in freighting is a practical concern connected to hauling capacity; what roads, bridges, and other infrastructure will allow for transport as well as the costs associated with this movement? But weight here also determines the possibility of a mutually advantageous gifting relationship.

The social enterprise representative had a second interest in this waste stream. While workshop participants initially focused on the "biophysical" dimensions of the supply chain, they very quickly identified both the necessities and possibilities

7 The reference here is not to a dump truck but a "ute" (utility vehicle, or in the US parlance a pick-up truck), where the truck bed capacity is about one to three cubic metres or roughly half to three-fifth of a metric tonne of compostable material.

8 Current New South Wales EPA guidelines encourage on-farm composting but balance this commitment against concerns about odour, vermin, disease, the presence of weed seed, or groundwater contamination. Schedule 12 of the Protection of the Environmental Operations Act 1997 states that farms may receive up to 5,000 tonnes per annum of non-putrescible organic waste (e.g. wood chips, saw dust, leaf mould) but only 200 tonnes per annum of putrescible waste (which SCG and chaff is currently classified as), without needing to apply for special licencing that would reclassify the farm as a commercial waste facility. It is the putrescible waste that triggers many of these aforementioned concerns that understandably require regulatory oversight. The live question in the workshop, however, was whether SCG and chaff should rightly be considered putrescible waste or if they should, instead, be exempt from this limit.

surrounding the collection and disposition of data alongside coffee grounds. The social enterprise representative put the point bluntly: "We do not collect waste without collecting data" (Social Enterprise representative, in post-workshop follow-up conversation, 2023). This valuation of data, in turn, reflects new measures created by private global governance regimes such as the Environmental, Social, and Governance (ESG) system. Indeed, just as farmers had used the word "pure" to describe the qualities of SCG as a waste stream free from contaminants, the social enterprise representative adopted the adjective "pure" to describe the information this waste contains and why this data is valuable – it directly satisfies metrics for landfill diversion and social procurement set forth by relevant ESG criteria. In her words: "because it's a pure stream we can get [an ESG] rating on it" (Social Enterprise representative, in workshop 2022). The rating, in turn, communicates to relevant audiences the amount of organic waste the enterprise has successfully diverted from landfill. This information was similarly valued by the local government official present at the workshop, who was eager to signal the council's contribution to responsible waste treatment. He proposed to incorporate the council into the supply chain by contributing disused council land and facilities in an inner-city adjacent suburb as a site where SCG and chaff could be stored before being hauled to the hinterland.

15.3.3 *Private Enterprise Coffee Roasters and Cafés*

Coffee roasters and café owners similarly valued the waste stream for how it could enable them to improve both current waste management practices and their own ESG commitments. One of the roasters had previously experimented with requiring corporate customers to include (and pay for) sustainable waste management in their service contracts. The roaster stressed that making this arrangement visible – for example, SCG stored in bins outside cafes awaiting pickup – created value for them by signalling that they are "part of the circular economy" to an audience of urban customers (Coffee Roaster representative 1, in workshop 2022). "There is a storytelling value," he emphasised. Another roaster similarly ventured that they could create value "through PR, marketing at a bigger scale," that communicates the worthiness of a circular arrangement for organic waste that is cared for by producers and users across the chain (Coffee Roaster representative 2, in workshop 2022). A third roaster emphasised "pride" in their story and not simply publicity (Coffee Roaster representative 3, in workshop 2022). As the local government representative summarised, workshop participants were all eager to use this supply chain to "influence [others] to try and change their behaviour to do something for the better … [through] telling that story of saving the coffee grounds or food waste from landfill" (Local Council representative, in workshop 2022).

15.3.4 *Not for Profit: UTS*

A representative from UTS Operations and Management Team valued this waste stream for how it reduced recurrent operational expenses associated with waste management – their primary measure was cost savings. The representatives explained the university had purchased a second large capacity food dehydrator to minimise the cost of waste management. Rather than have a dump truck pick up "putrescible food waste twice a day," UTS hoped instead "to store the dried food output of the machine on campus and have one truck a week" (UTS representative, in workshop 2022). From the UTS representatives' perspective, it was serendipitous that Michelle offered to move a portion of this waste for free, setting into motion the workshop's aspirations to expand this relationship to include other local coffee roasters and cafes and indeed the current waste services provider. UTS also values the waste stream for its research, education, innovation, and engagement activities.[9] It has a remit, even a responsibility, to enact propositional futures ahead of the business-as-usual status quo, given its status as a signatory to the University Commitment to the UN SDGs among other commitments and aspirations.[10] Like the social enterprise and local government representatives, UTS also values information about waste – data about where a consumer's coffee grounds go – and the supply chain commons tells a story that aligns with its values and commitments.

Of course, UTS and other universities are also comprised of researchers, including the authors of this chapter, who also value this waste stream in particular ways. Higher educational institutions are all in a position of having to demonstrate leadership in environmental and social governance in ways that predispose them to innovations around waste management. We as individual researchers value data about waste for its potential to contribute to theoretical and empirical insights measured by requirements for academic performance, including generation of research funding and outputs, as well as curriculum development. We also value information about this waste stream for its potential to generate methodological insights: how to "do" action research that facilitates and creates the conditions for commoning. While these values are not dependent on the success of the supply chain commons (a possible point of tension with other participants), researchers share with other participants a *political* value: successfully producing a "knowledge commons" would make explicit the capacity of the university to take a coordinating role and custodial responsibility for commons-making as part of the research enterprise.

9 A number of learning and teaching opportunities have emerged since the installation of the food dehydration technology at UTS, including a Transdisciplinary Living Lab (TDLL) as a mechanism to link curriculum, operations, and research (Fam et al. 2021).

10 Indeed, the initial purchase of a food waste dehydrator was instigated by a researcher at the Institute for Sustainable Futures at UTS, Dr Dena Fam, with a grant from the EPA. See https://www.uts.edu.au/case-studies/circular-economy-food-waste-recycling-uts.

15.4 COMMON KNOWLEDGE TO COMMONS POSSIBILITY

The relationships that began or recommenced in the collaborative design workshop allowed for an initial identification of diverse and common interests, brokering connections and beginning to set the practices of coordination and rules (in the broadest sense) necessary to configure a circular supply chain that connects waste to those points where it might be meaningfully redeemed. People articulated different value frames for waste as they discussed their own economic activity – a freely received gift for farmers which enriches the soil and adds value to products for market, service contracts for waste haulers that can benefit from regulatory exemptions, a source of livelihood generation for haulers, reduced operational expenses and other synergistic benefits for educational organisations such as universities. The way participants valued organic waste was, in turn, indissociable from how they took its measure – as volume, weight, cost, or ESG criteria.

Moreover, as people discussed how they valued the material qualities of SCG, it became clear that they valued information about the waste stream as much as the waste stream itself: they thus repeatedly described the importance of creating a traceable and data-driven supply chain so that they could communicate (and further enhance) the value of circularity as economic activity. The sharing of information among participants thus functioned as a complementary currency of variable worth: from information about how SCG performs as a soil amendment to how this diversion of organic waste consummates ESG commitments. Participants discussed how getting this information to flow through the appropriate channels mattered as much as the flow of organic waste material from city to country. They envisioned recruiting an array of actors: other regenerative farmers who might make use of organic waste, waste haulers, cafe owners, other universities and receptive local councils, accommodating regulators, coffee roasters, and custodial staff. Each would play a role in managing the flow of organic waste in the system and each would be attuned to the data it expresses and its different measures. Or to put the point in Frischmann et al.'s (2014, 2) words, the workshop allowed for the beginning of an "institutionalised sharing of [intellectual] resources among members of a community," a "knowledge commons," as they define it.

This knowledge commons, in turn, depends upon and helps to solidify an incipient commoner-subjectivity who cares for waste and human and more-than-human life. Workshop participants hoped to use information about the supply chain to enrol more people into a capacious, caring, and felt understanding of circularity. They also wanted to build relationships of solidarity and care across the chain. For example, participants discussed ways to disburden Michelle and her family from carrying the entire system on their shoulders through redistributing the efforts required to move organic waste from the city to peri-urban farms. For those of us interested in putting the circular economy to work, the task here really does involve a practical reinvention of the social in ways that expand the capacity of those who, in

Savini's (2023) terms, are carrying the socioecological burden. The commons offers an entry point that emphasises the possibility of redistributing who (or what) shoulders the burden in ways that make it more manageable.

The workshop (and the convivial lunch that followed it) cemented the sense that something more than the sum of its parts had been created. As Michelle remarked, the workshop enabled what she had achieved thus far "to be reimagined and renewed in a really positive way." "There is scale here *and* it's clean," she said, summarising learning from the day. "You've got to get it started with something that is very doable," she advised, "but if people get used to the idea that this is what's possible within a circular economy, then I think suddenly, it's much easier to then throw [in] other parts of the putrescible waste," potentially catalysing broader-spread changes in knowledge, practices, self-understandings, and social relationships.

To carry forward this sense of possibility, solidarity, and social innovation, the strategic designer Dom Svejkar collaborated with the researchers to synthesise workshop findings into an illustrated report that included the map now populated with the ideas and comments of the participants. Since the workshop concluded, there have been several meetings of the proto-alliance, and more voices have been brought to the table, including a logistics professional and a "parent" company sustainability manager to trial a larger-scale version of what Michelle had been doing over the last six years. This supply chain commons is thus taking shape – not as a linear chain as much as a co-evolutionary trajectory of knowledge production and exchange, and quite possibly through the creation of a new organisational form whose principle objective is coordinating flows of materials and information.

We must however stress that at present this supply chain is closer to Lauren Berlant's (2021) depiction of the commons as a series of patches and improvisations than to Ostrom's (1990) conception of the commons as something with intergenerational durability. And yet we would also submit that the flow of organic waste matter from Sydney's Central Business District (CBD), over the Blue Mountains, and onto regenerative farms – and the corresponding flows of information (data/knowledge) to and from all points of the supply chain – represents a concrete instance of what Çalışkan and Callon (2009, 2010) term *economisation*. Economies are made, not given, they argue; work is required to establish the relationships and practices that enable exchange and to maintain these relationships over time. Expanding on this proposition, the supply chain we identify here is an instance of more-than-market economisation: a set of exchange relationships that are both market and nonmarket, in particular the giving and receiving of gifts. More-than-capitalist agencies are involved in the process of valuation: family farms and social enterprises operating alongside for-profit companies and large organisations like the university. In turn, the communication of these agents' diverse and common valuations – to regulatory authorities, stakeholders, boards, and investors – is a condition of common possibility for people who want to assume the socioecological burden of waste.

The future success of this endeavour depends on how actors continue to coordinate their diverse forms of measuring, tracking, exchanging, and most centrally valuing waste material (see, for example, Cohen 2020). Because success depends, in other words, on shared knowledge production, we also wish to highlight the crucial role that universities can play in enabling in vivo experimentations of the kind sparked by the workshop (see, for example, Çalışkan and Callon 2009, 2010; Fam et al. 2021). Against an array of all-too-familiar forces that pressure universities to produce proprietary research and commercialisable data for business and industry traditionally defined, universities as knowledge custodians can play a particular role in helping the commons to cohere (Erdem and Akin 2019). Our case suggests that universities can yet provide a kind of "safe-to-fail" space for experimentation in our current situation of climate and civic emergency (Fam et al. 2021).

In the months since this initial workshop, the university researchers involved in this project (Stephen and Abby) have continued to organise follow-up meetings and conversations. Very quickly the group prioritised additional research to pilot the set of relationships and logistics required to move organic waste from central city locations to farms in the central west region at a larger commercial scale. Participants also decided to form an entity that could act as a partner-investigator able to collaborate with university researchers and speak on behalf of the individuals, organisations, and sectors that comprise the commons-supply chain—an entity the group named the Ground to Ground (GtG). From a commons perspective, the GtG now acts as a custodian charged to consider and attend to the broader community located along this supply chain. These custodial duties include developing a transparent set of norms and practices to govern the coordination of activities and relationships that move SCG and other waste from the CBD to the urban periphery. They also include developing principles to ensure that all parties have the relevant data that would allow them to communicate the value of this circular supply chain and to mediate conflicts as they inevitably arise. The GtG's immediate goal is to lay the groundwork for a pilot study that will test developing the supply chain at a commercial scale, beginning by moving ten tonnes per month of SCG and other waste from city to periphery.

The stakes are high for such experiments. The state government of New South Wales has set clear targets around overall waste diversion of all types by 2030. As noted, government planners continue to propose large-scale waste-to-energy facilities as the easiest "circular" response to meet these targets. Whereas the GtG alliance aims to recover the value of organic waste by returning it to the soil, these facilities would use organic waste in place of coal to generate electricity – a proposal that has prompted community concern about public health effects. For example, in 2022, the state government proposed to build a waste-to-energy plant in Lithgow, a municipality near Michelle's regenerative farm.[11]

11 www.planning.nsw.gov.au/assess-and-regulate/state-significant-projects/energy-from-waste.

Community outcry has for the moment scuttled these plans (Hogan 2022). But what this conflict makes clear is that responding to the complex and competing uses of organic waste will require robust data collection to help demonstrate the economic, social, and ecological value of composting waste at scale. This data could include landfill diversion rates for local councils, universities, cafes and roasters, potential jobs created for social enterprises, and enhanced soil quality, including estimates for carbon capture for farmers and state government. Data of this sort would help make the value of a *supply chain commons* visible, legible, and comparable in a moment when the meaning of the circular economy is by no means settled.

Writing in what would seem a different context of Odisha, India, Neera Singh (2018) describes how commoner subjects are not given but made through their ongoing interactions with what they share and how they care for it. They come to know themselves as commoners and, precisely for this reason, there are no physical commons without corresponding knowledge commons. The context might be different, but the task is much the same; we *learn* to become commoners by continually revisiting the rules of use, ministering to the commons and taking away new insights over time. Ground to Ground offers one way of making commons, flows of organic waste and knowledge more durable. But, again, possibilities to entrench successful partnerships will depend on how people, embedded within their larger and multiple ecosystems, can coordinate their diverse forms of valuations. We can all too easily attest to the challenges university researchers face when they endeavour to integrate or translate *community engagement* into the research enterprise. As such, part of what the developing GtG alliance must deliberate about is how to generate, share, and manage information in ways that can both respond to and influence the future of universities as custodians for "the preservation, defence and expansion of knowledge commons" (Erdem and Akin 2019, 158, quoting Caffentzis).

15.5 CONCLUSION

Like others contributing to this series, our intention in describing this incipient supply chain has been to extend the conceptual purview of the commons, which involves, in the first instance, making them visible (Gibson-Graham 2006). A community of commoners managing a shared biophysical asset like a field, fishery, or forest is today easier to discern. But the commons we have traced here is more diffuse and provisional: in our example, commoners are the people convened along a supply chain, sharing knowledge, data, and valuations to make the chain function for their common benefit as well as for a larger community benefit that accrues to both human and more-than-human life, including improved soil vitality, sequestered carbon, improved farm viability, and flood risk mitigation, improved livelihoods, and regenerative peri-urban futures.

Even as it is diffuse and provisional, this commons, then, is crucial. It sits in the context of the state's commitment to achieving an 80 per cent diversion of solid waste from landfill by 2030. Given that half of all waste moving through the municipal waste stream is organic waste, readers can appreciate the power of connecting urban organic waste to a reinvigorated practice of farming in the region.

Above all we have stressed that thinking like a commoner involves people in a different way of *knowing* waste. All too often, the dominant approach to circularity founders on the difficulties of profitably economising waste. That waste materials are expensive to sort, process, or redeem, and that these practices depend on skills that are currently not widely valued, means that we are measuring these costs against the cheapness of simply abnegating our responsibility for those materials with which we share a common world. Against a dominant conception of circular economy that measures the costs of landfill against the costs of alternatives – where costs are again narrowly defined – this experiment in commoning links waste-generating organisations, those capable of hauling it away, and those who could enrol it into a regenerative farming practice. In so doing, it offers a new context for reinventing our relationship with waste, new possibilities for livelihood, and for meeting our collective responsibility. This process of commoning requires new ways of setting rules, as Ostrom insists, but also new ways of measuring and knowing waste alongside a different sense of how we connect to the world and one another.

REFERENCES

Agamben, Giorgio. 1993. *The Coming Community* (trans. M. Hardt). Minneapolis: University of Minnesota Press.

Australian Government. 2019. National Waste Policy Action Plan 2019. www.agriculture.gov.au/sites/default/files/documents/national-waste-policy-action-plan-2019.pdf.

Berlant, Lauren. 2022. *On the Inconvenience of Other People*. Durham: Duke University Press.

Bollier, David. 2014. *Think Like a Commoner: A Short Introduction to the Life of the Commons*. Gabriola Island: New Society Publishers.

Çalışkan, Koray, and Michel Callon. 2009. "Economization, Part 1: Shifting Attention from the Economy Towards Processes of Economization." *Economy and Society* 38(3): 369–398.

Çalışkan, Koray, and Michel Callon. 2010. "Economization, Part 2: A Research Programme for the Study of Markets." *Economy and Society* 39(1): 1–32.

City of Sydney. 2017. *Leave Nothing to Waste Sydney: Managing Resources in the City of Sydney Area*. www.cityofsydney.nsw.gov.au/-/media/corporate/files/2020-07-migrated/files_l/leave-nothing-to-waste-strategy-and-action-plan-20172030.pdf.

Chitranshi, Bhavya, and Stephen Healy. 2022. "Shared Survival and Cooperation in India and Australia. *Asia Pacific Viewpoint* 63(1): 151–162.

Cohen, Amy J. 2020. "Negotiating the Value Chain: A Study of Surplus and Distribution in Indian Markets for Food." *Law and Social Inquiry* 45(2): 460–492.

Cohen, Hart, Francesca Sidoti, Alison Gill, et al. 2021. "Sustainability, Living Labs and Repair: Approaches to Climate Change Mitigation." In *Right Research: Modelling Sustainable Research Practices in the Anthropocene*, ed. Chelsea Miya, Oliver Rossier, and Geoffrey Rockwell, 357–3 98. Cambridge: Open Book Publishers.

Corvellec, Hervé, and Alexander Paulsson. 2023. "Resource Shifting: Resourcification and de-Resourcification for Degrowth." *Ecological Economics* 205: 107703.

Deb, Proloy, Hamid Moradkhani, Peyman Abbaszadeh, et al. 2020. "Causes of the Widespread 2019–2020 Australian Bushfire Season." *Earth's Future* 8(11): e2020EF001671.

Dombroski, Kelly, Gradon Diprose, and Irene Boles. 2019. "Can the Commons be Temporary? The Role of Transitional Commoning in Post-Quake Christchurch." *Local Environment* 24(4): 313–328.

Dombroski, Kelly F., S. M. Waliuzzaman, David Conradson, Gradon Diprose, and Stephen Healy. 2023. "Commoning for Urban Wellbeing in Majority and Minority Worlds." In *Wellbeing: Global Policies and Perspectives: Insights from Aotearoa New Zealand and Beyond*, ed. Annelies Kamp, Cheryl Brown, Trish McMenamin, Veronica O'Toole, 225–241. Oxford: Peter Lang.

Douglas, Mary. 1966. *Purity and Danger: An Analysis of Concepts of Pollution and Taboo*. London: Routledge.

Elhacham, Emily, Liad Ben-Uri, Jonathan Grozovski, Yinon M. Bar-On, and Ron Milo. 2020. "Global Human-Made Mass Exceeds All Living Biomass." *Nature* 588: 442–444.

Ellen MacArthur Foundation. 2012. *Towards the Circular Economy, Vol 1: An Economic and Business Rationale for an Accelerated Transition*. www.ellenmacarthurfoundation.org/towards-the-circular-economy-vol-1-an-economic-and-business-rationale-for-an.

Ellen MacArthur Foundation. 2013. *Towards the Circular Economy, Vol 2: Opportunities for the Consumer Goods Sector*. www.ellenmacarthurfoundation.org/towards-the-circular-economy-vol-2-opportunities-for-the-consumer-goods.

Ellen MacArthur Foundation. 2017. "What Is the Circular Economy?" www.ellenmacarthurfoundation.org/topics/circular-economy-introduction/overview.

Erdem, Esra, and Kamuran Akin, 2019. "Emergent Repertoires of Resistance and Commoning in Higher Education: The Solidarity Academies Movement in Turkey." *South Atlantic Quarterly* 118(1): 145–163.

Fam, Dena, Abby Mellick Lopes, and Cynthia Mitchell. 2021. "Transdisciplinary Learning within Tertiary Institutions – A Space to Skin Your Knees." In *Interdisciplinary and Transdisciplinary Failures: Lessons Learned from Cautionary Tales*, ed. Dena Fam, and Michael O'Rourke, 198–216. London: Routledge.

Food and Agribusiness Growth Centre. 2021. *Annual Report 2020-2021*. www.fial.com.au/about/annual-report-2020-2021.

Gibson-Graham, Julie K. 2006. *A Postcapitalist Politics*. Minneapolis: University of Minnesota Press.

Gibson-Graham, Julie K., Jenny Cameron, and Stephen Healy. 2016. "Commoning as a Postcapitalist Politics." In *Releasing the Commons: Rethinking the Futures of the Commons*, ed. Ash A. Amin, and Philip Howell, 192–212. London: Routledge.

Gregson, Nicky, and Mike Crang. 2019. "Made in China and the New World of Secondary Resource Recovery." *Environment and Planning A: Economy and Space* 51(4): 1031–1040.

Hawkins, Gay. 2006. *The Ethics of Waste: How We Relate to Rubbish*. Lanham: Rowman & Littlefield.

Hawkins, Gay, and Anisah Madden. 2023. "Reducing Plastic Use: From Problems and Solutions to Problematisation." In *New Horizons for Innovation Studies: Doing Without, Doing With Less*, ed. Frédéric Goulet, and Dominique Vinck, 88–105. Cheltenham: Edward Elgar.

Hawkins, Gay, and Stephen Healy. 2023. "Waste/Economy/Ecology: Redrawing the Circular Economy." *Journal of Cultural Economy* 16(4): 576–578.

Hogan, Hugh. 2022. "Waste-to-Energy Plans Binned, but Door Left Open for Controversial Industry in Central Tablelands." *ABC News*, May 25, 2022. www.abc.net.au/news/2022-05-25/wallerawang-waste-to-energy-plans-scrapped-nsw/101094346.

Healy, Stephen, and Abby Mellick Lopes. 2023. "Postcapitalist Composting: Reverse Logistics and Organic Waste, Designing for Diverse Livelihoods." *Journal of Cultural Economy* 16(4): 622–630.

Hird, Myra J. 2012. "Knowing Waste: Towards an Inhuman Epistemology." *Social Epistemology* 26(3-4): 453–469.

Hobson, Kersty, and Nicholas Lynch. 2016. "Diversifying and De-growing the Circular Economy: Radical Social Transformation in a Resource-Scarce World." *Futures* 82: 15–25.

International Union for Conservation of Nature. 2021. "Marine Plastic Pollution." *Issue Brief*, November 2021. https://iucn.org/sites/default/files/2022-04/marine_plastic_pollution_issues_brief_nov21.pdf.

Karatani, Kojin. 2005. *Transcritique: On Kant and Marx*. Cambridge, MA: MIT Press.

Kirchherr, Julian, Denise Reike, and Marko Hekkert. 2017. "Conceptualizing the Circular Economy: An Analysis of 114 definitions." *Resources, Conservation and Recycling* 127 (2017): 221–232.

Kirchherr, Julian, Nan-Hua Nadja Yang, Frederik Schulze-Spüntrup, Maarten J. Heerink, and Kris Hartley. 2023. "Conceptualizing the Circular Economy (Revisited): An Analysis of 221 Definitions." *Resources, Conservation and Recycling* 194: 107001.

Kornbluh, Anna. 2010. "On Marx's Victorian Novel." *Mediations* 25(1): 15–37.

Lane, Ruth. 2011. "The Waste Commons in an Emerging Resource Recovery Waste Regime: Contesting Property and Value in Melbourne's Hard Rubbish Collections." *Geographical Research* 49(4): 395–407.

Madison, Michael J., Brett M. Frischmann, and Katherine J. Strandburg. 2010. "Constructing Commons in the Cultural Environment." *Cornell Law Review* 95(4): 657–709.

Manzini, Ezio, Stuart Walker, and Barry Wylant 2008. *Enabling Solutions for Sustainable Living: A Workshop*. Calgary: University of Calgary Press.

Marres, Noortje, Michael Guggenheim, and Alex Wilkie. 2018. "Introduction: From Performance to Inventing the Social." In *Inventing the Social*, ed. Noortje Marres, Michael Guggenheim, and Alex Wilkie, 17–37. Manchester: Mattering Press.

Morrow, Oona, and Anna Davies. 2022. "Creating Careful Circularities: Community Composting in New York City." *Transactions of the Institute of British Geographers* 47(2): 529–546.

Offenhuber, Dietmar. 2017. *Waste is Information: Infrastructure Legibility and Governance*. Cambridge, MA: MIT Press.

Ostrom, Elinor. 1990. *Governing the Commons: The Evolution of Institutions for Collective Action*. Cambridge: Cambridge University Press.

Ostrom, Elinor. 2010. "The Institutional Analysis and Development Framework and the Commons." *Cornell Law Review* 95(4): 807–815.

Papadopoulos, Dimitris, Natasha Myers, and María Puig de la Bellacasa. 2022. *Reactivating Elements: Substance, Actuality, and Practice from Chemistry to Culture*. Durham: Duke University Press.

Papaioannou, Eva A., Rebecca L. Selden, Julia Olson, et al. 2021. "Not All Those Who Wander Are Lost – Responses of Fishers' Communities to Shifts in the Distribution and Abundance of Fish." *Frontiers in Marine Science* 8: 669094.

Petrescu, Doina, Constantin Petcou, Maliha Safri, and Katherine Gibson. 2021. "Calculating the Value of the Commons: Generating Resilient Urban Futures." *Environmental Policy and Governance* 31(3): 159–174.

Royer, Sarah-Jeanne, Sara Ferrón, Samuel T. Wilson, and David M. Karl. 2018. "Production of Methane and Ethylene from Plastic in the Environment." *PloS One* 13(8): e0200574.

Sacks, Justin, and Rosendy Galabo. 2021. "A Framework for Infrastructuring Commons Creation." In *With Design: Reinventing Design Modes*, ed. Gerhard Bryuns, and Huaxin Win, 1016–1036. Singapore: Springer.

Sanders, Elizabeth B.-N. 2006. "Scaffolds for Building Everyday Creativity." In *In Design for Effective Communications: Creating Contexts for Clarity and Meaning*, ed. Jorge Frascara, 65–77. New York: Allworth Press.

Savini, Federico. 2023. "Futures of the Social Metabolism: Degrowth, Circular Economy and the Value of Waste" *Futures* 150: 103180.

Schneider, Nathan. 2018. *Everything for Everyone: The Radical Tradition That Is Shaping the Next Economy*. New York: Bold Type Books.

Singh, Neera. 2017. "Becoming a Commoner: The Commons as Sites for Affective Socio-Nature Encounters and Co-Becomings." *Ephemera* 17(4): 751–776.

Stark, David. 2009. *The Sense of Dissonance: Accounts of Worth in Economic Life*. Princeton: Princeton University Press.

St. Martin, Kevin. 2001. "Making Space for Community Resource Management in Fisheries." *Annals of the Association of American Geographers* 91(1): 122–142.

Strandburg, Katherine J., Brett M. Frischmann, and Michael J. Madison. 2017. "Knowledge Commons and the Road to Medical Commons." in *Governing Medical Knowledge Commons*, ed. Katherine J. Strandburg, Brett M. Frischmann, and Michael J. Madison, 1–8. Cambridge: Cambridge University Press.

Valenzuela, Francisco, and Steffen Böhm. 2017. "Against Wasted Politics: A Critique of the Circular Economy." *Ephemera* 17(1): 23–60.

Wernli, Markus, and Kam Fai Chan. 2024. "Are We Repairing Soils and Each Other Here? Exploring Design Cosmotechnics in the Waste Age." In *Design/Repair: Place, Practice and Community*, ed. Eleni Kalantidou, Guy Keulemans, Abby Mellick Lopes, Niklavs Rubenis, and Alison Gill, 123–148. Cham: Springer.

Wittwer, Glyn, and Robert Waschik. 2021. "Estimating the Economic Impacts of the 2017–2019 Drought and 2019–2020 Bushfires on Regional NSW and the Rest of Australia." *Australian Journal of Agricultural and Resource Economics* 65(4): 918–936.

Zapata, Campos, María José, Patrik Zapata, and Jessica Pérez Reynosa. 2023. "(Re)gaining the Urban Commons: Everyday, Collective, and Identity Resistance." *Urban Geography* 44(7): 1259–1284.